The Lodger Shakespeare

The Chemical Theatre

A Cup of News: The Life of Thomas Nashe

The Fruit Palace

Borderlines

The Reckoning: The Murder of Christopher Marlowe

The Creature in the Map

Somebody Else: Arthur Rimbaud in Africa

Leonardo da Vinci: The Flights of the Mind

Shakespeare and his Contemporaries (National Portrait Gallery)

Journeys (anthology)

William Shakespeare with undercropper (see Chapter 17)

CHARLES NICHOLL

The Lodger

His Life on Silver Street

VIKING

VIKING
Published by the Penguin Group
Penguin Group (USA) Inc., 375 Hudson Street,
New York, New York 10014, U.S.A.
Penguin Group (Canada), 90 Eglinton Avenue East, Suite 700,
Toronto, Ontario, Canada M4P 2Y3
(a division of Pearson Penguin Canada Inc.)
Penguin Books Ltd, 80 Strand, London WC2R 0RL, England
Penguin Ireland, 25 St. Stephen's Green, Dublin 2, Ireland
(a division of Penguin Books Ltd)
Penguin Books Australia Ltd, 250 Camberwell Road, Camberwell,
Victoria 3124, Australia
(a division of Pearson Australia Group Pty Ltd)
Penguin Books India Pvt Ltd, 11 Community Centre, Panchsheel Park,
New Delhi – 110 017, India
Penguin Group (NZ), 67 Apollo Drive, Rosedale, North Shore 0632,
New Zealand (a division of Pearson New Zealand Ltd)
Penguin Books (South Africa) (Pty) Ltd, 24 Sturdee Avenue,
Rosebank, Johannesburg 2196, South Africa

Penguin Books Ltd, Registered Offices:
80 Strand, London WC2R 0RL, England

First American edition
Published in 2008 by Viking Penguin,
a member of Penguin Group (USA) Inc.

1   2   3   4   5   6   7   8   9   10

Copyright © Charles Nicholl, 2007
All rights reserved

Published in Great Britain as *The Lodger: Shakespeare on Silver Street* by Allen Lane, a
division of Penguin Books Ltd.

Nicholl, Charles.
The lodger Shakespeare : his life on Silver Street / Charles Nicholl.
p. cm.
Includes bibliographical references and index.
ISBN 978-0-670-01850-5
1. Shakespeare, William, 1564–1616. 2. Dramatists, English—Early modern, 1500–1700—
Biography. 3. Shakespeare, William, 1564–1616—Homes and haunts—England—London.
4. Cripplegate (London, England)—Social life and customs. I. Title.
PR2907.N53 2008
822.3'3—dc22
[B]
2007042553
Printed in the United States of America

In memory of
Jan Farrell
and
Mary Ensor

'*Every contact leaves traces . . .*'
Edmond Locard, *Manuel de Technique Policière*, 1923

Contents

CONTENTS

List of Illustrations

End-papers. The 'Agas' map of London, *c.* 1561. Copyright © Guildhall Library, London.

Frontispiece. Engraved portrait of Shakespeare by Martin Droeshout (second state). Title-page illustration from *Mr William Shakepeares Comedies, Histories & Tragedies* [the First Folio], 1623.

1. Shakespeare's deposition at the Court of Requests, 11 May 1612 (PRO REQ 4/1/4). Copyright © The National Archives.

2. Jacobean law-court. Seventeenth-century woodcut reproduced in *The Roxburghe Ballads*, ed. William Chappell and J. W. Ebsworth (The Ballad Society, 1871–91).

3. Witness-list for the Belott–Mountjoy suit, May 1612 (PRO REQ 1/199). Copyright © The National Archives.

4. Signatures of Daniel Nicholas, William Eaton, Noel Mountjoy and Humphrey Fludd, May–June 1612 (PRO REQ 4/1/4). Copyright © The National Archives.

5. The Wallaces at the Record Office, *c.* 1909. Papers of Charles William Wallace, Huntington Library, San Marino, Calif. (Box 15 B 37).

6. Detail from the 'Agas' map, *c.* 1561. Copyright © Guildhall Library, London.

7. The Coopers' Arms, Silver Street, *c.* 1910. From *Harper's Monthly Magazine*, Vol. 120, March 1910. Photo: Huntington Library, San Marino, Calif.

8. St Giles, Cripplegate, after the bombs, 1941. Pen, ink and wash drawing by Dennis Flanders. Guildhall Library Print

Preface

This book looks into some aspects of Shakespeare's life in London over a couple of years in the early seventeenth century. Larger issues of interpretation belong to the book itself. I will confine this preface to a few procedural points and some hearty thanks.

Many Jacobean documents use the 'old style' year, which ran from 25 March ('Lady Day'). This is useful to know when reading them – it means that an event dated 1 January 1605 took place a month *after* an event dated 1 December 1605 – but is liable to cause confusion when quoting them. Where necessary I have amended to modern style (in the example cited I would give the first date as 1 January 1606).

On the matter of original spellings the demands of authenticity and readability pull in opposite directions. To modernize everything is to lose a certain richness – an orthographic brogue intrinsic to the period. On the other hand, quoting everything in archaic spelling can make things hard going for the reader. Inconsistency has seemed a lesser evil than either of these. I have tended to quote documents, letters, diaries and so on in original spelling, and literary texts in modern form.

Sums of money mentioned in the text cannot be correlated precisely with modern values. Based on the retail price index, it is estimated that £1 in 1604 had a purchasing power equivalent to about £144 in 2006. However, this is not always helpful as an overall conversion factor. In 1604 you could lease a large London town-house for £20 per annum, buy an unbound copy of *Hamlet* for sixpence, and drink a pint of beer for a halfpenny. A printer paid £2 ('forty shillings and an odd pottle of wine') for a pamphlet, and the author might get the same again for a slavish dedication to 'my Lord What-call-ye-him'. Wages were low: a labourer might earn 5 shillings a week. There are too many anomalies to make it very meaningful, but as a rough rule of thumb I use an exchange rate of 1:200. That is, an early Jacobean pound was worth about £200 today, a shilling (1s) about £10, and a penny (1d) something under £1.

My research on this book has been greatly assisted by staff at the National Archives, British Library, Guildhall Library, London Library, Victoria and Albert Museum, French Protestant Church and Ealing Local History Centre in London, the Bodleian Library in Oxford, and the Bibliothèque Municipale in Amiens. I am particularly grateful to James Travers for his help in tracking down some elusive documents; to Susan North and Jenny Tiramani for advice on early Jacobean costume; and to Matt Steggle, Colin Burrow, Christiane Gould-Krieger, Elsie Hart, Thomas Dumont and the late Eric Sams for help and expertise generously given. My thanks also to my agent David Godwin, my editor Stuart Proffitt, my picture-editor Cecilia Mackay and my copy-editor Peter James, and – as ever – to my mother, my wife and my children.

PART ONE

'One Mr Shakespeare'

Simply the thing I am
Shall make me live . . .
                    All's Well that Ends Well, 4.3.322–3

1

The deposition

On Monday 11 May 1612, William Shakespeare gave evidence in a lawsuit at the Court of Requests in Westminster. His statement, or deposition, was taken down by a clerk of the court, writing in an averagely illegible hand on a sheet of paper measuring about 12 × 16 inches (see Plate 1). At the end of the session Shakespeare signed his name at the bottom. It is one of six surviving signatures, and the earliest of them (though it can hardly be called early: he was forty-eight years old and already in semi-retirement).[1] He signs quickly and rather carelessly. The initial W is firm and clear, with the characteristic looping and dotting of the final upstroke, but the surname becomes a scrawl and is abruptly concluded with an omissive flourish: 'Willm Shaks'. These abbreviations were not dictated by space, as they were in a mortgage-deed of 1613 ('Wm Shakspe'), which he had to sign on a thin tag of parchment. They contribute a note of perfunctoriness, or perhaps impatience.

The signature draws the eye. It is, as the graphologists say, a 'frozen gesture'; it touches this otherwise unlovely piece of paper with Shakespeare's physical presence. But what makes this document special is not just – not even primarily – the signature. It is the anonymously scripted text above it, the text which the signature authenticates as Shakespeare's sworn statement. We know the thousands of lines he wrote in plays and poems, but this is the only occasion when his actual spoken words are recorded.[2]

The case in which he was testifying is listed in the court registers as Belott v Mountjoy. It was a family dispute: trivial, pecuniary,

3

faintly sordid – standard fare at the Court of Requests, whose function was broadly equivalent to the Small Claims Courts of today. The defendant, Christopher Mountjoy, is described as a 'tiremaker' – a maker of the decorative headwear for ladies known generically as 'head-tires' or 'attires'. The plaintiff, Stephen Belott, had once been Mountjoy's apprentice and was now his son-in-law. Both men were French by birth but had lived for many years in London. The Mountjoys' house was on Silver Street, in Cripplegate, close to the north-west corner of the city walls. This is the setting of the story which unfolds in the court proceedings – a story which involves William Shakespeare.

The dispute concerned a dowry: a sum of £60 which, Belott alleged, had been promised when he married Mountjoy's daughter in 1604, and which had never been paid. (This is a good but not a huge dowry: according to the rough rule-of-thumb outlined in the Preface, it would be equivalent to about £12,000 today.) Belott also claimed that Mountjoy had promised to leave the couple a legacy of £200 when he died. Mountjoy denied both claims, and now, eight years after the event, the case was before the court.

Shakespeare was one of three witnesses called on the first day of hearings (see Plate 3). What does he have to say? Not a lot would be the short answer, though this book attempts a longer one. The 'interrogatories' are put to him, five in number; he answers them briefly – one cannot say curtly, because his answers are shaped to the formulae of court depositions and cannot be reconstructed as to their particular tone, but he does not elaborate much, as some of the other witnesses do, and on some points he remains a little vaguer, a little less helpful, than one feels he might have been. His statement, like the signature beneath it, is adequate and no more. He says he has known both men, the plaintiff and the defendant, 'for the space of tenne yeres or thereaboutes' – in other words, since about 1602. He remembers young Belott as a 'very good and industrious servant', one who 'did well and honestly behave himselfe'. Yes, he was 'a very honest fellowe', and was accounted so by his employer. As to the particular matter in dispute, Shakespeare is sure Belott had been promised a dowry – a marriage 'porcion' – but he cannot remember the sum mentioned. Nor does he remember 'what kinde of houshould stuffe' had been given to the couple when they married.*

And he says – and here, amid the general blandness of his statement, there is a hint of something more – he says that he had himself been asked by the girl's mother, Marie Mountjoy, to 'perswade' the apparently reluctant apprentice to go through with the marriage. In the unwieldy language of the law-courts, 'This deponent sayethe that the said deffendantes wyeffe did sollicitt and entreat this deponent to move and perswade the said complainant to effect the said marriadge, and accordingly this deponent did move and perswade the complainant thereunto.' This presents him as a kind of counsellor or go-between, a romantic or perhaps merely practical advocate. But another witness in the case implies that Shakespeare's role went further than this. He says the couple was 'made sure by Mr Shakespeare', and speaks of them 'giving each other's hand to the hand'. These phrases have a precise significance. They suggest that Shakespeare formally betrothed the young couple, performing the simple lay ceremony known as a 'troth-plighting' or 'handfasting'. An intriguing little scene flickers up before us.

Shakespeare does not actually say why he was involved in these family affairs *chez* Mountjoy, but the answer is not far to seek. It is provided by the Mountjoys' former maidservant, Joan Johnson, when she refers in her deposition to 'one Mr Shakespeare that laye in the house'. In Elizabethan and Jacobean usage to 'lie' in a house meant to be staying there, and in this context undoubtedly means he was the Mountjoys' lodger. Shakespeare quibbles on this sense of the word in *Othello* –

DESDEMONA: Do you know, Sirrah, where the lieutenant Cassio lies?

---

* All depositions and other documents in the Belott–Mountjoy suit are fully transcribed in the Appendix. Quotations from them in the text are sometimes pruned of repetitious legalisms.

CLOWN: I dare not say he lies anywhere . . .

DESDEMONA: Go to, where lodges he? . . .

CLOWN: I know not where he lodges, and for me to devise a lodging, and say he lies here or he lies there, were to lie in mine own throat.

(3.4.1–11)

A similar pun is in Sir Henry Wotton's famous definition of an ambassador, 'An honest man sent to lie abroad for the good of his country'.[3] This is one of the primary nuggets of information which the Belott–Mountjoy case offers – it gives us an address for Shakespeare in London. How long he lodged or lay in Silver Street is something to look into: he was certainly there in 1604, when the marriage in question took place.

'One Mr Shakespeare . . .' I think it was the marvellous banality of this phrase that first sparked my interest in the case. For a moment we see him not from the viewpoint of literary greatness, but as he was seen by the maid of the house, a woman of no literary pretensions, indeed unable to sign her name except with a rather quavery little mark. 'Mr' is perhaps not quite as banal as it looks, because it was at that time a contraction of 'Master' rather than of 'Mister' – it is the term of address for a gentleman, a connotation of status. But the effect is the same. We have a fleeting sense of Shakespeare's 'other' life, the daily, ordinary (or ordinary-seeming) life which we know he must have led, but about which we know so little. He is merely the lodger, the gent in the upstairs chamber: a certain Mr Shakespeare.

Shakespeare's deposition in the Belott–Mountjoy case has been known for nearly a hundred years, but has been oddly neglected as a biographical source. It was found in 1909, along with others in the case, at the Public Record Office in London. Its discoverer was a forty-four-year-old American, Dr Charles William Wallace, Associate Professor of English at the University of Nebraska. If you have an image of the archival scholar Wallace is not it. There is a photograph of him, taken around the time of the discovery (see Plate 5). He is black-bearded, glossy-haired, elegantly dressed; his wife Hulda stands beside him, primly bonneted. They might be minor characters from an Edith Wharton novel, but instead they are standing in the fusty surrounds of the old Record Office on Chancery Lane, with a fat bundle of old parchments on the table before them.

The Wallaces – they were very much a team – had been sleuthing in the archives for some years, and had already made some Shakespeare-related finds. They had turned up some legal documents relating to the Blackfriars Gatehouse, purchased by Shakespeare in 1613, and some lawsuits involving two of his closest theatrical colleagues, Richard Burbage and John Heminges.[4] Wallace had also experienced the sniffiness of the British academic establishment, which regarded him as a brash American intruder. He has 'boomed' his discoveries 'in true Transatlantic manner', wrote one critic. His prose-style, winced a reviewer in the *Athenaeum*, 'does not always economize the reader's attention'. Wallace particularly clashed with C. C. Stopes, doyenne of Edwardian Shakespeare studies (and mother of the birth-control pioneer Marie Stopes), whom he suspected of cajoling Record Office employees to show her documents he had ordered up.[5]

Wallace's earlier discoveries touched on Shakespeare, but none of them had the sheer archival glamour of the deposition. Acting on certain clues, he tracked it down among the then uncalendared Court of Requests proceedings – 'great bundles of miscellaneous old skins and papers', some still pristine, some 'mouldered' and 'grimed', some still tied up with hempen rope 'harsh to handle'.[6] His account breathes the thrill of the chase but the reality was dogged labour. Even today the Court of Requests collection is something of a jungle, especially for the Jacobean and Caroline periods when the court was at its busiest. In some private notes, Wallace describes his paradoxical feelings when he finally came upon the sheet of paper he was hunting. He felt 'glad, but disappointed in measure'. 'We were aware of the bigness of what we had' – not only Shakespeare's signature, but 'a personal expression from him' – but it 'was so much less than we had wished!' They felt a strange anti-climactic calm: 'We exchanged a few words over the document, but no-one in the room might have guessed that we had before us anything more important or juicy than a court-docket.' Perhaps this sang-froid was in part the paranoia of the document-hunter, for whom primacy of discovery is everything. Nothing was given away, no cries of 'Eureka!' – the spies of Mrs Stopes were everywhere. And anyway there was work to do. 'We saw that we had only a part of the documents in the case: we must find the rest.'[7]

Wallace announced his discovery the following year, in an article in *Harper's Monthly* (March 1910). He had by then recovered a total of twenty-six documents relating to the Belott–Mountjoy suit, some merely administrative, and some very 'juicy' indeed. Twelve contain some kind of reference to Shakespeare. He published a complete transcript in the October 1910 issue of *Nebraska University Studies*. This choice of periodical does not now make for easy availability, but seems commendable as one in the eye for the *Athenaeum*.

Shakespeare's deposition was exhibited for a while in the Record Office Museum, mounted under glass, but is now back where it ought to be, safely and unceremoniously stored in a stout cardboard box at the National Archives' new headquarters in Kew. There, duly vetted, one may consult it. Ensconced behind two locked doors in the Safe Room, I carefully extract from the box this sheet of greyish, coarse-grained paper which Shakespeare once handled, rather less carefully, on a Monday morning nearly four centuries ago. It is hard to say quite what the page has which the photographic reproductions of it do not. The signature is clearer, of course. That dot inside the arcade of the *W* is very sharp: it stares out like a beady eye. The ill-formed *k* is perceivable as a sudden blotching of ink – a malfunction of the unfamiliar courtroom pen, perhaps. Beyond this one has to resort to vaguer sensations. This bit of paper has presence, or anyway pedigree – an unbroken lineage back to Shakespeare's writing hand.

After some moments of cargo-cultish reverence, and some futile speculation about fingerprints and DNA traces, I turn to the other papers in the box, also found by Wallace, most of which have never been reproduced. There are four sets of documents. The first set consists of four parchments – or 'skins', as Wallace liked to call them – fastened at the upper-left corner with a grubby white cord. These are the initial pleadings of the case. There is the Bill of Complaint lodged by Stephen Belott, through his solicitor Ralph Wormlaighton, dated on the verso 28 January 1612, and then the 'Answeare of Christopher Mountioy', of 3 February, signed by his solicitor George Hartopp. Some phrasings suggest these texts had been written, in the first instance, a year or more previously.[8] They are followed by a further exchange: Belott's 'Replication', dated 5 May, and Mountjoy's 'Rejoinder', undated. These largely echo the previous documents and perhaps served more to fatten the attorneys' fees than to throw further light on the dispute.

The remaining three sets of documents correspond to three separate sessions at the Court of Requests, at which witnesses testified or 'deposed' in answer to a prearranged list of questions. The court sat in the legal precinct of Westminster, in a first-floor chamber reached by stairs from Westminster Hall – thus John Stow, the great topographer of Shakespeare's London: 'By the King's Bench is a going-up to a great chamber called the White Hall, where is now kept the Court of Wards and Liveries, and adjoyning thereunto is the Court of Requests.'[9] At the first two sessions the witnesses (including Shakespeare) were called on behalf of Belott; at the third they were *ex parte* Mountjoy. All the depositions were recorded by the same clerk, on the same kind of paper, written on one side only. A courtroom scene in a seventeenth-century woodcut (see Plate 2) gives us something of the set-up – the clerk writing, the judge listening, the papers on the table.

The first set, of 11 May, contains the statements of Joan Johnson, 'wife of Thomas Johnson, of the parish of Ealing in the county of Middlesex, basketmaker'; Daniel Nicholas 'of the parish of St Olphadge [Alphage] within Cripplegate, London, gent'; and William Shakespeare 'of Stratford upon Avon in the county of Warwickshire, gent'. They were examined in that order

– the clerk's hand is visibly tired by the time Shakespeare takes the stand. The papers, four folios in all, are in good condition apart from some mouldering down the lower-right edge, with some minor loss of text.

At the second session, on 19 June 1612, there were six deponents. First up was Daniel Nicholas, again: he is the most active and involved of the witnesses. Then follow the testimonies of William Eaton or Eyton, who was Belott's apprentice; George Wilkins, 'victualler', of St Sepulchre's parish; Humphrey Fludd of St Giles, Cripplegate, who was Belott's stepfather, and who is described as 'one of His Majesty's trumpeters'; Christopher Weaver, 'mercer'; and Noel Mountjoy, 'tiremaker', who was the defendant's younger brother. These last two are both of St Olave's, Silver Street – the parish where the Mountjoys lived, where Shakespeare lodged, and where Stephen Belott married Miss Mountjoy in the parish church.

At the third session, on 23 June, witnesses called by the defence were examined. There were just three: Christopher Weaver and Noel Mountjoy, who had both testified previously; and Thomas Flower, 'merchant tailor' of the parish of St Albans, Wood Street.

Of the nine witnesses in the case, five have a specified relationship to one or other of the disputants (a brother, a stepfather, an apprentice, a lodger and a maid) and four can be summed up under the general heading of friends and neighbours. Three have artisan occupations (basketmaker, tiremaker, tiremaker's apprentice), three are tradesmen (victualler, mercer, merchant tailor), two are in the entertainment business (playwright, trumpeter), and two are gentlemen (who do not need to have an occupation, though at least one of them has). Seven of the nine live in London, either in or immediately adjacent to the Cripplegate area; and the two that do not – Joan Johnson of Ealing and Shakespeare of Stratford – had formerly lived in the area. This is a local story: its physical boundaries can be paced in half an hour.

Eight of the nine witnesses are men, and there are two women central to the story whose testimony one sorely misses – Christopher's wife, Marie Mountjoy, who had died before the case came to court; and their daughter, Mary Belott, who was not called to testify, presumably because she was the plaintiff's wife. That the mother and daughter have the same forename is a small inconvenience. The name is often written 'Marye'. To avoid the nuisance of 'senior' and 'junior', I use Marie for the mother and Mary for the daughter (which is vaguely logical, as Marie was almost certainly born in France and Mary in England). Many immigrant families Anglicized their names, as this one seems to have done – hence Christopher Mountjoy rather than Christophe Montjoi or Montjoie. This is not to deny their foreignness, an intrinsic aspect of the story, nor their sense of themselves as French. They lived the immigrant's double-life. After half a century in London Stephen Belott would sign his will, 'Par moy Etiene Belot'.[10]

In these depositions we make our first acquaintance with some of the protagonists of this book – people personally known to Shakespeare: his landlord and landlady, the apprentice Belott and others. We get an impression of them, though conscious that a lawsuit can give a distorted, or anyway narrow, view of those involved.

Our first impression of Christopher Mountjoy is that he is a mean and rather crabby sort of man. The meanness is apparent in the whole case, which hinges on his refusal to pay his daughter's dowry (his refusal is not in doubt: the matter before the court was whether he was breaching a promise to pay). That Mary was his only child compounds this impression, as does the opinion of witnesses that he was a man of 'good estate', in other words well off enough to pay up. We are also told that in the time of Belott's apprenticeship Mountjoy was 'strict unto' him – 'strict' meaning tight or stingy – and that Stephen's mother and stepfather had to find him 'sutes of apparel', and 'were fain many times . . . to pay the barber for cutting the hair of his head' (deposition of Humphrey Fludd). Later, as litigation approaches, we hear Mountjoy's blustering tone. He said that 'if he were condemned in this suit undeserved he would lye in prison before he would give the plaintiff anything' (Noel Mountjoy). And in similar vein – or perhaps the same occasion differently reported – that 'he would rather rott in prison than geve them any thinge more than he had geven them before' (Christopher Weaver).

His antagonist Stephen Belott is no less intransigent but the tone is cooler. Some of the witnesses had tried to patch up the 'unkindnes' between them before the matter came to court. They went to talk to Belott – who had left Mountjoy's house, with Mary, for the last time in about 1607 – but could get no concession from him. 'Where I have a penniworth of anything, I would I had more of his,' he told Thomas Flower, 'and if I owe him anything let him come by it as he can.' This is, unusually, given as direct speech, as if verbatim.

In contrast, one gets a gentler, more amenable note from the late Mrs Mountjoy. Her encouragement of the hesitant young couple is recalled by the maidservant Joan Johnson – 'There was a shewe of goodwill' between Stephen and Mary, 'which the defendant's wife did give countenance unto and thinke well of.' And then later, when everyone was falling out over the dowry, she tries to mollify the situation: 'Marye, the late wife of Christopher Mountjoy the defendant, did in her lifetime urge him to give something more unto Belott and his wife than he had done' (Christopher Weaver). To which Mountjoy retorted: 'He would never promise them anything, because he knew not what he should need himself.'

The depositions of Daniel Nicholas have an interesting twist, for they supply a kind of secondary recording of Shakespeare's comments on the matter. It seems Nicholas visited Shakespeare at Belott's request, presumably within the context of the impending lawsuit. As there is evidence that the litigation began some while before the case came to court, this visit might be around 1610 or so. Belott, says Nicholas,

did request him this deponent to go with his wife to Shakespeare, to understand the truth how much and what the defendant did promise to bestow on his daughter in marriage with him the plaintiff, who did so. And asking Shakespeare thereof, he answered that he [Mountjoy] promised if the plaintiff would marry with Mary his only daughter, he would by his promise, as he [Shakespeare] remembered, give the plaintiff with her in marriage about the sum of fifty pounds in money and certain household stuff.

One notes a discrepancy here. When he was asked by Daniel Nicholas what dowry Mountjoy had promised, Shakespeare said it was about £50; but when he was asked the same question in court, under oath, he said he could not remember the figure. Does this tell us something? Was his memory – that miraculously agile and sensitive instrument – beginning to fail? The vagueness of his statements in court has been interpreted this way, but it seems that his memory was, in this instance, more selective than defective. It is an anomaly, a little fault-line in Shakespeare's testimony, and I will return to it later.

Nicholas also adds to the small store of Shakespearean utterances we have gleaned from his own deposition. 'Shakespeare told this deponent', Nicholas says, 'that the defendant told him that if the plaintiff . . . did not marry with Marye and she with the plaintiff she should never coste him the defendant her father a groat.' Given the lapse of time, those last words are more likely to be Shakespeare's paraphrase than Mountjoy's exact words in 1604. So here again, among the tiresome exactitudes of legal-speak, nestles an authentic Shakespeare phrasing: 'She should never cost him a groat.' As we might say, 'She wouldn't get a penny out of him.'

We might have had another quotation, courtesy of Belott's apprentice William Eaton, but all that remains is a curtailed half-sentence: 'And Mr Shakespeare tould the plaintiff . . .'. For whatever reason, the court considered this inadmissible. The words were immediately crossed out, and replaced with the formulaic conclusion, 'And more he cannot depose.' Whatever it was that Shakespeare had said to Stephen Belott remains off the record.

Finally, on 30 June 1612, the court handed down its judgment.

Or rather, it failed to reach a judgment, but referred the 'matter of varyance' to the French Church, of which both parties were – nominally, at least – members:

It is by His Majesty's said counsel of this Court, in presence of the said parties and of counsel learned on both sides, ordered by and with the full consent of the said parties, that the same matter shall be referred to the hearing, ordering and final determination of the reverend & grave overseers and elders of the French Church in London.

The ledgers of the French Church, which was then on Thread-needle Street and is now in Soho Square, have some fragmentary records of the case.[11] On 30 July four representatives of the Church were assigned to argue the matter, two for each of the disputants. But of more interest – to the prying biographer, at least – is a disparaging note at the end of the entry: 'Tous 2 père & gendre débauchez' ('Both the father and the son-in-law are debauched'). One suspects the Calvinist elders of the French Church had a pretty inclusive idea of 'debauchery', but in the case of Mountjoy more explicit charges are found in later entries:

Montioye fut censuré d'avoir eu 2 bastardes de sa servante . . .
Montioye, ayant souvent esté exhorté d'estre pieux, de sa vie dereglée & desbordée . . . [et] ayant esté tiré au Magistrat pour ses paillardises & adultères . . . [est] suspendu publiquement pour ses scandales.

According to this, Mountjoy had been censured by the Church elders for having fathered two bastards by his serving-maid; had been often exhorted to piety because of his irregular and outlandish lifestyle; had been hauled before the magistrate for his lewd acts and adulteries; and had been publicly suspended from the Church on account of these scandals. We may not be as aghast as the elders were – Mountjoy was by this stage a widower, and cohabiting with his maid does not seem very heinous. Nonetheless, these perceived sexual irregularities – 'paillardises & adultères' – are noted as we embark on our enquiry into the Silver Street milieu.

The case was adjudicated at a meeting of the *consistoire* or Church council in December. They found in favour of Stephen

Belott, but the sum they ordered Mountjoy to pay was only 20 nobles (£6 13s 4d), scarcely a tenth of what Belott claimed was owed to him. Thus the long-awaited judgment managed to satisfy neither party. Some months later it is noted that Mountjoy has still not paid up. The case peters out; nothing much is resolved.

The events narrated in the Belott–Mountjoy suit are part of the story I want to tell, but they are not the story itself. Rather, these documents are a way into the little world of Silver Street, and to Shakespeare's living presence within it. For Charles William Wallace, they revealed Shakespeare as 'a man among men' (and indeed women). For Samuel Schoenbaum, the Belott–Mountjoy suit is unique because alone among the Shakespeare records it 'shows him living amidst the raw materials for domestic comedy'.[12] These are splendid invitations, and it is curious that no one has fully responded to them. The broader story that emerges from the case has not been told; this unexpected little window into Shakespeare's life remains to be opened.

The Mountjoys themselves are a tantalizing quarry. Since Wallace there have been some additions to our knowledge of them – important new material was published by Leslie Hotson in 1941 and by A. L. Rowse in 1973[13] – but there is more to come out. The court case itself has details about them which have been ignored, and others have lain unnoticed in parish registers, subsidy rolls, probate records and medical casebooks. The evidence remains fragmentary, but we begin to know the Mountjoys a little better – and one of them in particular, whose personality has begun faintly to glow as my researches have progressed.

Other interesting characters hover at the periphery of the story. There is Belott's stepfather, the trumpeter Humphrey Fludd: a professional entertainer, a man on the outer fringes of the royal court, and sounding in that brief synopsis not unlike Shakespeare himself. There is Henry Wood of Swan Alley, whose business as a cloth merchant brings him into professional contact with the Mountjoys, but whose relationship with Marie goes a good deal further than that.

And then there is the difficult figure of George Wilkins, another of the witnesses in the case. In his deposition he calls himself a 'victualler', which is true up to a point. He would hardly describe himself as a 'brothel-keeper', though this would convey more precisely the nature of his establishment; 'pimp' would also be correct. He was frequently in trouble with the law, some of the charges involving acts of violence against prostitutes. But there is a further twist to Wilkins: he was also a writer. Shakespeare knew this dangerous and rather unpleasant character – indeed it is almost certain Wilkins wrote most of the opening two acts of *Pericles*.[14] Written in *c.* 1607–8, *Pericles* was notably absent from the great collection of Shakespeare's plays, the 'First Folio' of 1623, probably because of Wilkins's extensive contribution; it was first included in the Third Folio of 1664. In this book I explore Shakespeare's relations with this underworld figure. Though his literary career was brief and minor, Wilkins is a writer of considerable bite, as best seen in his play *The Miseries of Enforced Marriage*, loosely based on a real-life murder case, and performed by Shakespeare's company in *c.* 1606.

The first law of forensic science, otherwise known as Locard's Exchange Principle, is that 'every contact leaves traces'.[15] I cannot call this book a 'forensic' study – the word refers to criminal investigations – but it is animated by a similar idea of proximity: of lives that touch, and the traces of evidence they leave. To find out more about the Mountjoys and their world has seemed to me worthwhile in itself, but is primarily a means to find out more about their lodger, the famous but so often obscure Mr Shakespeare, with whom they were in casual daily contact. His deposition is a beginning: a few curt sentences of reminiscence. From there the paperchase leads on, through the dark streets and alleys of Jacobean London, to arrive at a certain house where a light burns dimly in an upstairs window. After 400 years the traces are faint, but he is there.

2

Turning forty

*O*f the house where Shakespeare lived, and the people he knew there, I will give a full account in later chapters, but to begin with it is important to know when he was there – to place this slice of his life in a precise chronological context.

Though the deposition dates from 1612, the testimony it gives takes us back to the early years of the century. On his own evidence Shakespeare first knew Christopher Mountjoy in about 1602. There may be some imprecision in the recollection, but without evidence to the contrary this is the earliest possible date – the *terminus post quem* – for his presence in the Mountjoys' house. He may have moved in to the house in that year, or in 1603. The latter was a disrupted year: the death of Queen Elizabeth, a savage outbreak of plague, the closure of the theatres. The last two are reasons – and there are others – for thinking Shakespeare was not in London at all during the summer of 1603, so we are more likely to find him on Silver Street in the later months of the year. One should not, anyway, think of his presence in the house as continuous. This was rented accommodation; he came and went as he wished.

We can be sure, at least, that he was lodging there in mid-1604. The wedding of Stephen and Mary took place in November that year. It was some time before that, obviously, that Shakespeare 'persuaded' them to marry. Probably, as I will show, it was not very long before, a few weeks or a couple of months at the most. At that point – as Joan Johnson tells us – Mr Shakespeare 'laye in the house', and indeed his status as the lodger, in a sort of provisional intimacy with the family, seems intrinsic to the part he plays.

How long after this he remained with the Mountjoys is difficult to say. The court case offers no hint, and we know little of Shakespeare's whereabouts in the later stages of his London career. The death of Marie Mountjoy in the autumn of 1606 may have made the arrangement less congenial to him. His collaboration with George Wilkins in 1607 may be the fruit of an earlier connection within the Mountjoy ambit, but does not presuppose he was then still living on Silver Street. There is one bit of evidence which suggests Shakespeare was *not* there in the later years of the decade. It is a document dated 6 April 1609, which lists him among the 'inhabitants' of Southwark being assessed for 'weekly paiment towards the relief of the poore'.[16] This seems to show that Shakespeare was living in Southwark by 1609, though it is possible he features on the list as a representative of the Globe theatre, which was located there.

The exact termini of Shakespeare's tenancy must remain vague, but within that vagueness there is a point of chronological certainty centred on the year 1604, when he is identifiably present in the house. And while the ups and downs of the Belott–Mountjoy marriage may be 'raw materials for domestic comedy', one does not require Mr Shakespeare to hurry in immediately prior to the marriage negotiations, and rush out again as soon as the church bells chime at St Olave's, so it seems legitimate to express the known period of his tenancy as *c.* 1603–5. It is this period which is the focus of my book – the years when Shakespeare approached, and passed, the age of forty.[17]

Shakespeare in 1603 was a man at the peak of his profession. He had written many of the plays by which he is known today – *Romeo and Juliet* and *Richard III*, *A Midsummer Night's Dream* and *The Merchant of Venice*, *As You Like It* and *Twelfth Night*, the Falstaff comedies, *Julius Caesar*, *Hamlet*. The latter, staged in about 1601, had plumbed its hero's psyche with a subtlety and complexity never before seen on the Elizabethan stage. It was a watershed, and he was now in that ambivalent stage after the production of a masterpiece – his reputation assured by it, but the way forward from it unmapped. The period which follows *Hamlet* is characterized by those awkward, paradoxical, *noir*ish works often called the 'problem plays', two of which – *Measure for Measure* and *All's Well that Ends Well* – belong to the Silver Street years.

Uncertainty was anyway the keynote of his profession – his profession, that is, as a man of the theatre: not just a writer of plays, but an actor and company 'sharer' or shareholder. The theatre companies operated in a crowded, competitive market; some prospered but many went to the wall. They were prey to the hostility of officialdom, which saw the playhouses as a civic nuisance – a potential for riotous assembly, for prostitution and pickpocketing, for the transmission of infectious diseases and (no less dangerous) of dissident ideas. Shakespeare's company was the Lord Chamberlain's Men, founded in 1594, under the patronage of the Queen's Chamberlain and first cousin, Henry Carey, Lord Hunsdon. By the end of the decade they were established as London's leading troupe, performing at the newly built Globe theatre. But the road was never smooth – patrons died, theatres were summarily closed, irate grandees protested at impertinences real or imagined. A performance of *Richard II* at the Globe in February 1601 earned the ire of the Queen herself. The play was already controversial – its deposition scene ('deposition' in the other sense of toppling a ruler) does not appear in early editions – and it was even more so when requested by followers of the Earl of Essex, and played on the eve of Essex's futile uprising; Shakespeare's colleague Augustine Phillips was summoned before the Privy Council to explain matters.[18] Two years later Ben Jonson was up before the Council after his *Sejanus* – in which Shakespeare acted – was accused of 'popery and treason'. Jonson was twice imprisoned for overstepping the mark of political comment. On the second occasion, in 1605, 'the report was' that he and his fellow-authors 'would have their ears cut, and noses'.[19] Controversy was the element they lived in, and the shadow of punishment hung unpredictably over the playhouse.

For the company's chief playwright – 'our bending author', as he styles himself in the epilogue to *Henry V* – professional worries become also a literary pressure. The tides of theatrical fashion changed quickly. There were younger authors coming up: Jonson, John Marston, Thomas Middleton and others, bringing a new brash mood, satirical and salacious. And there was competition from the boys' companies – the Children of St Paul's, the Children of the Chapel Royal, and so on – those 'little eyasses', as Hamlet calls them, who 'so berattle the common stage'. (An 'eyass' is a fledgling hawk, but there is doubtless an indecorous pun about young boys' orifices.) Rivalry between the play-companies spilt over into a fad of abusive mud-slinging between authors (the 'War of the Theatres') in which it seems Shakespeare participated. In the gossipy Cambridge comedy *The Return from Parnassus* (Part 2, c. 1602), actors playing the real-life actors Kemp and Burbage discuss this. 'O that Ben Jonson is a pestilent fellow,' says Kemp, 'but our fellow Shakespeare hath given him a purge that made him bewray his credit.' From the context, this literary laxative would be a caricature of Jonson onstage. Perhaps it is big, morose Ajax in *Troilus and Cressida* (c. 1602) – 'churlish as the bear, slow as the elephant, a man in whom nature hath so crowded humours that his valour is crushed into folly' (1.2.21–3) – though there are other candidates.[20] These were the rough imperatives of theatrical fashion: to be aloof from it all (as he is sometimes said to have been) was not really an option.

In this context of professional uncertainty and cut-throat rivalry, the year 1603 brought Shakespeare a new promise of stability. On 19 May, just twelve days after King James's arrival in London from Scotland, letters patent were issued licensing the Chamberlain's Men as 'His Majesty's Players'. Nine actors are named, including Shakespeare, Burbage, John Heminges, Henry Condell, Augustine Phillips, William Sly and the comic actor Robert Armin. They are authorized 'to use and exercise the art and faculty of playing comedies, tragedies, histories, enterludes, morals, pastorals, stage-plays and such others like . . . as well for the recreating of our loving subjects as for our solace and pleasure when we shall think good to see them for our pleasure'.[21] Henceforth Shakespeare's company was called the King's Men. This translation was timely, for just a few days earlier the company's current patron – George Carey, 2nd Lord Hunsdon – had been forced to resign as Lord Chamberlain due to ill-health; by September he was dead, according to the rumours from syphilis.[22]

The company's new status assured them of prestige and a measure of royal protection – indeed it made them, nominally at least, members of the royal household. In James's coronation procession Shakespeare and his fellows are ranked as Grooms of the Chamber, though the listing of them under the subsection 'Fawkeners [falconers] &c' indicates their not very grand status.[23] They also had the promise of court performances ('when we shall think good to see them'). These they would need, for on the same day their letters patent were issued the theatres were closed down due to the plague. The court decamped hurriedly from London, and the King's Men went on the road. Their first known performance under their new royal name was at Bath; they received 30 shillings. The beginning is anti-climactic but the company's new solidity is real, and it will last.

We see in this brief résumé something of what Shakespeare would mean to the Mountjoys – a man pre-eminent in the theatrical world, with which they were themselves probably connected; a man with a minor foothold in the new court of King James, to which they doubtless aspired. It is possible that the appearance of 'Marie Mountjoy, tyrewoman' in the royal accounts of 1604–5 (see Plate 23) is a direct result of her contact with Shakespeare. She supplied the new Queen – James's Danish-born wife, Anne or Anna – with head-tires, and perhaps other items, for which she received payments totalling £59.[24] One of the payments is dated 17 November 1604, just two days before the wedding of Mary and Stephen which Shakespeare had helped to bring about.

Shakespeare at forty was, by the expectancies of the day, a man well advanced into middle age. 'Youth's a stuff will not endure.'

He might feel himself slipping towards the fifth of Jaques's 'seven ages' – the portly justice,

> With eyes severe and beard of formal cut,
> Full of wise saws and modern instances . . .
>
> (*As You Like It*, 2.7.155–6)

– and one might think this an appropriate mien for the Silver Street marriage-counsellor. There is a theatrical tradition that Shakespeare played old men – the ghost in *Hamlet*, Adam in *As You Like It*.[25] He was perhaps already balding, as he is in all the known portraits, a condition humorously associated with tonsured friars and sufferers from syphilis – thus prostitutes, in *Timon of Athens*, 'make curl'd-pate ruffians bald' (4.3.162).

Of the portraits only three have any real claim to authenticity – the engraving by Martin Droeshout in the front of the First Folio; the 'Chandos' portrait at the National Portrait Gallery, attributed to John Taylor; and the funeral effigy at Holy Trinity, Stratford, attributed to Gheerart Janssen. The first and the last are true likenesses by virtue of their context – they are definitely *of* Shakespeare – but as portraits they are maddeningly bland and uncommunicative. The funeral bust has been famously described as looking like a 'self-satisfied pork-butcher', a judgment laden with Edwardian snobbery but unfortunately apposite. The 'Chandos' portrait is not certainly of Shakespeare, but it has a convincing provenance, and a degree of similarity to the other two portraits, and its compellingly saturnine portrayal answers needs which the others leave untouched. In terms of execution, the 'Chandos' is the earliest (*c.* 1610) – the other two are post-humous – but the Droeshout engraving is based on an earlier portrait, now lost, which for various reasons can be plausibly dated back to around 1604.[26] Somewhere behind that iconic but incompetent little cartoon which adorns the First Folio is an image of Shakespeare in his early forties – Shakespeare the lodger on Silver Street.

One saw a respectable-looking man but something shadowed that respectability. His status was dubious, tinged with the ambiguous aura of the playhouse, a place associated with moral dangers and depravities as much as with poetry, music and laughter. He was nominally a gentleman – *Mr* Shakespeare – with a fancy coat of arms which he had purchased on behalf of his father, and which was now his own since his father's death in 1601. (The motto, 'Non sanz droict', was parodied by Jonson as 'Not without mustard'.) But there were unresolved problems with the Herald's Office as to the exact nature of his gentility. The herald who had awarded the coat of arms, Sir William Dethick, was under investigation. A note written by one of his antagonists lists some questionable awards, among them 'Shakespeare ye player'.[27] The inference – that a mere player or actor could not really be a gentleman – is a commonplace attitude of the time, and one that rankled in Shakespeare deeply. He expresses bitterness at his ill-starred profession in Sonnet 111:

> O for my sake do you with Fortune chide,
> The guilty goddess of my harmful deeds,
> That did not better for my life provide
> Than public means which public manners breeds.
> Thence comes it that my name receives a brand
> And almost thence my nature is subdued
> To what it works in, like the dyer's hand.

A more genial expression of the matter is found in an epigram addressed to Shakespeare in 1611:

> Some say (good Will), which I in sport do sing,
> Hadst thou not plaid some kingly parts in sport,
> Thou hadst bin a companion for a King.[28]

To paraphrase, he had ruined his prospects of social advancement by choosing the career of an actor.

If he was a man of substance, it was the substance of money and property. Shakespeare's earnings were high – estimates vary wildly, but something around £250 a year is plausible. By 1602 he owned three houses in Stratford, and 107 acres of tenanted farmland north of the town; three years later he invested £440 acquiring a 'moiety' or half-share in the income of Stratford tithe-lands.[29] These are big sums, conjured out of the 'insubstantial pageant' of the playhouse and swiftly solidified into bricks, mortar and land. He did not neglect the small sums, either. In 1604, around the time he was betrothing Stephen and Mary on Silver Street, his lawyers were suing a Stratford neighbour for an outstanding debt of 35s 10d. He would not necessarily agree with Iago's view that 'who steals my purse steals trash' (*Othello*, 3.3.161).

In an anonymous pamphlet of 1605, *Ratsey's Ghost*, a provincial player is advised to go to London and 'play Hamlet' for a wager. 'There thou shalt learn to be frugal . . . and to feed upon all men, to let none feed upon thee; to make thy hand a stranger to thy pocket, and when thou feelest thy purse well lined, buy thee some place or lordship in the country.' Yes, says the player, 'I have heard indeed of some that have gone to London very meanly, and have come in time to be exceeding wealthy.' The author may have had the acquisitive player Mr Shakespeare in mind when he wrote this.[30]

Jonson jibed at Shakespeare's pretensions to gentility (at least that is one interpretation of some lines in his 1599 satire *Every Man out of his Humour*) but when he came to praise Shakespeare in the preface to the First Folio, the first adjective he uses of him is 'gentle'. This does not necessarily have the softness of its modern meaning – it refers to the perceived qualities of a 'gentleman': courtesy, loyalty, probity.

What else do we know of him as he takes up his tenancy on Silver Street? He was a married man, but his wife Anne *née* Hathwey or Hathaway was up in Stratford, rather too distant to impose husbandly virtues on him. He was a father scarred by the death of a child – his only son, Hamnet, had died at the age of eleven in 1596.[31] His remaining children were daughters – Susanna, who was twenty in 1603, and Hamnet's twin sister, Judith. Neither was yet married. The problem of the 'succession' which had dogged Queen Elizabeth's last years had been resolved, but Shakespeare had his own uncertainties of succession.

That he was a man of charm and geniality is attested by many eyewitnesses. In 1592, our first personal notice of him, the author Henry Chettle reported: 'Myself have seen his demeanour no less civil than he excellent in the quality he professes. Besides, divers of worship have reported his uprightness of dealing, which argues his honesty, and his facetious grace of writing, which approves his art.'[32] 'Civil' in his demeanour and 'upright' in his dealing – that was ten years ago, but there is no reason to think he was any less so now. However, one notes the circumstances of this testimonial: some gritting of the teeth may be discernible in Chettle's compliments, for they are in the nature of a public apology. Shakespeare had complained to him about that notorious passage in *Greene's Groatsworth of Wit*, which tilted furiously at 'Shakescene', the 'upstart crow beautified with our feathers' (in other words, a mere actor who was presuming to write plays). Ostensibly this was a pamphlet by Robert Greene, edited for publication by Chettle after Greene's death, though some argue that Chettle cooked up most of it himself. Either way, it was he whom Shakespeare held responsible.[33] Chettle also mentions some men 'of worship' who have come forward to vouch for Shakespeare – character witnesses, one might say. The description is precise – men 'of worship' were inferior to nobles or knights, who were men 'of honour': they were gentlemen, citizens, professionals, etc. One adds to Shakespeare's civility and uprightness a certain steely quality – a young man ready to call on powerful backers, if needed, to assert his 'honesty'.

Other contemporaries have left testimony, including two out of that mob of minor authors who are as much his literary milieu as the more famous names we remember today. Here is the calligrapher and poet John Davies, writing in praise of 'W.S.' and 'R.B.', undoubtedly Shakespeare and Burbage:

> Players, I love yee and your qualitie,
> As ye are men that pass time not abus'd . . .
> Wit, courage, good shape, good partes, and all good,
> As long as all these goods are no worse us'd;

And though the stage doth staine pure gentle bloud,
Yet generous yee are in minde and moode.[34]

And in 1604 one 'An. Sc.', sometimes identified as Anthony Scoloker, refers to him – on what precise grounds we do not know – as 'friendly Shakespeare'.[35]

John Aubrey said he was 'a handsome, well-shaped man, very good company, and of a very ready and pleasant smooth wit'. Aubrey could not have seen him – he was born in 1626, ten years after Shakespeare's death – but he had spoken to those who had. Among his named sources were the Davenant brothers, who had known Shakespeare personally, as children, when he stayed at their father's tavern, the Crown in Oxford. Sir William Davenant's testimony is complicated by his claim to be Shakespeare's illegitimate son (of this more later), but his elder brother, the Rev. Robert Davenant, born in 1603, gives us a childhood memory of uncomplicated warmth. Thus Aubrey: 'I have heard Parson Robert D say that Mr W. Shakespeare here [at the Crown] gave him a hundred kisses.'[36]

These are contemporary testimonies of Shakespeare the man – 'civil' despite provocation, 'gentle' whether or not truly a gentleman, 'friendly' to a junior author, lavishly affectionate to a little boy, 'generous in mind and mood'. They are the upbeat impressions and memories: that there was a darker side must be inferred from his writing. How else could he impersonate so acutely every shade of cruelty and falsehood, every nuance of betrayal, every murky twinge of sexuality? He is not Iago or Edmund or Thersites, but he has found them in himself.

He was, in Jorge Luis Borges's famous conundrum, 'many and no one'.[37] But that is metaphor. Biography stands by the idea – more prosaic but ultimately more mysterious – that he was someone.

3

Sugar and gall

*W*hat was Shakespeare writing during his residency with the
Mountjoys in *c.* 1603–5? There are five plays which
belong in that broad time-span. They are, in probable order of
composition: *Othello, Measure for Measure, All's Well that Ends
Well, Timon of Athens* and *King Lear.* A rate of two plays a year
is about average for Shakespeare's working life, and may even
reflect an agreed productivity rate as the company's 'playmaker'.
The cross-currents of composition, rehearsal and rewriting were
complex. He was seldom working on less than two plays at once:
ideas refract and reverberate between them.

    Othello and *Measure for Measure* can be dated quite precisely.
Both have references which suggest Shakespeare was at work on
them in 1603, and both were performed at court towards the end
of 1604 (their first recorded performances, though not necessarily
their first performances).[38] By contrast, *All's Well* and *Timon*
have no documentary dating. Neither was printed before its
appearance in the First Folio of 1623, and no early performances
are recorded. (The recording of King's Men performances is anyway very sketchy: there exists no ledger for the Globe comparable
to Philip Henslowe's diary, which lists performances and box-
office takings at the neighbouring Rose.) *All's Well* is generally
dated to *c.* 1604 because of its affinities with *Measure,* and *Timon*
to *c.* 1605 because its verbal parallels with *King Lear* seem more
likely to be anticipations than echoes.[39] *Lear* itself, that mightiest
of works, was first performed at the end of 1606, and its early

gestation can also be placed, in a purely topographical sense, on Silver Street.

It is in many ways a curious list. Bookended by two of Shakespeare's greatest tragedies are these three rather odder, less popular works. One could call them 'experimental' but Shakespeare was constantly an experimenter, so perhaps one means they are experiments which do not wholly come off.

Measure for Measure and *All's Well* are two of that group traditionally called the 'problem plays', or the 'dark comedies' – also in this group is the earlier *Troilus and Cressida* (*c.* 1602), which falls outside my defined time-period but belongs with it in mood. The term 'problem play' is old fashioned but still more or less serviceable. It was coined by F. S. Boas in 1896, taking a tinge of the chief dramatists of the day, Ibsen and Shaw. Shaw tended showily to disparage Shakespeare, but liked these particular plays, where he found Shakespeare 'ready and willing to start at the twentieth century if the seventeenth would only let him'[40] – as perverse a statement of Shakespeare's intentions as one could hope to find.

They are 'problem' plays because they are hard to categorize. Their tone is elusive, blurred, faintly unwholesome. 'The air is cheerless,' in Dover Wilson's aphoristic summary, and 'the wit mirthless'. The admirable characters are not entirely likeable, and the likeable characters not at all admirable. The humour is bitter; it has 'a grating quality which excludes geniality and ensures disturbing after-thoughts'.[41] They are also 'problem plays' in a more direct sense: plays which deliberately pose problems – ethical conundrums, tangled motives, characters 'at war 'twixt will and will not'. They continue, in a different register, the mood ushered in by *Hamlet* at the beginning of the new century – nervy, questioning, 'sicklied o'er with the pale cast of thought'; and sickly also in the perception of malaise and corruption beneath the veneer of society: something 'rotten in the state'. This is a particular theme of *Measure for Measure*, where the city's ills lie less in the visible squalor of its prisons and brothels than in the concealed corruption of those in government:

Authority, though it err like others,
Hath yet a kind of medicine in itself
That skins the vice o' th' top . . . (2.2.135–7)

The overall quality of these plays is summed up by A. P. Rossiter – one of the most eloquent of the mid-twentieth-century analysts – as 'shiftingness':

All the firm points of view or *points d'appui* fail one, or are felt to be fallible . . . Like Donne's love-poems, these plays throw opposed and contradictory views into the mind, only to leave the resulting equations without any settled or soothing solutions. They are all about '*Xs*' that do not work out.

Or as it is sinuously expressed by the sceptical Lafeu in *All's Well*: 'Hence it is that we make trifles of our terrors, ensconcing ourselves into seeming knowledge when we should submit ourselves to an unknown fear' (2.3.3–6).

In formal terms – indeed in terms of theatrical fashion and therefore partly market-driven – these plays are Shakespeare's experiments in tragicomedy. The term originates with Plautus, the Roman comic dramatist much admired by Shakespeare, who called his play *Amphitryon* a 'tragicomoedia' because it improperly mingled gods and ordinary middle-class Romans. In Shakespeare's day the new models were Italian writers like Giovanbattista Giraldi Cintio (known in England as Cinthio) and Giovanbattista Guarini, both products of the sophisticated court of Ferrara. The poet and diplomat Guarini, whose pastoral tragicomedy *Il Pastor Fido* ('The Faithful Shepherd') was translated into English in 1602, offers some interesting precepts. 'True' tragicomedy, he writes, avoids the 'great themes' of tragedy. It is realistic rather than fantastic, it blends 'contrary qualities', and it brings the characters through dangers and perplexities – through what he calls the 'feigned knot' (*il nodo finto*) of the story – to happiness.[42] These elegant definitions, from an essay published with the English *Pastor Fido* in 1602, could well have been in Shakespeare's mind when he was writing *All's Well that Ends*

Well a year or two later. The very title of the play is a somewhat ironic definition of tragicomedy, though at the end of it the best the King can muster is 'All seems to be well.'

Hamlet has a humorous comment on these fashionable hybrids, as Polonius struggles to itemize the repertoire of the players newly arrived in Elsinore – they are, he assures us, 'the best . . . either for tragedy, comedy, history, pastoral, pastoral–comical, historical–pastoral, tragical–historical, tragical–comical–historical–pastoral . . .' (2.2.397–400).

The keynote of this new kind of tragicomedy is its mingling of disparate tones and emotions – what Guarini calls 'contrary qualities'. Again *Hamlet* is a prototype, with its intrusions of sharp and sometimes seamy banter into the traditionally relentless format of Senecan revenge-tragedy. This is precisely the quality praised in what is probably the earliest surviving critical comment on the play. In his preface to *Daiphantus* (1604), the mysterious 'An. Sc.' hopes his own poem will be popular with the 'vulgar' (he means ordinary people; the phrase is not here pejorative), like 'Shakespeare's tragedies, where the Comedian rides when the Tragedian stands on tip-toe: faith, it should please all, like Prince Hamlet'.[43]

In *All's Well*, the mingling of tones is particularly elusive. Its central narrative is based on old folk-motifs ('Healing the King', 'The Clever Wench'), and there is a jarring between this fairy-tale tendency and the more modern timbre of scepticism and paradox. We are lulled by the sweet autumnal melancholy of the verse, and then we are laughed at for giving in so easily. With their intrinsic ambiguities, and their testing of credibilities, the problem plays have been called 'Mannerist'[44] – in other words, they share something with the distorted figures and perplexing perspectives of mid-sixteenth-century Italian painters like Parmigianino and Bronzino.

The heyday of Jacobean tragicomedy comes later – Beaumont and Fletcher, Webster's *The Devil's Law Case*, Massinger – but already in 1603 John Marston had produced a very idiosyncratic, urban type of tragicomedy, *The Malcontent*, which showed how the form could be adapted to the concurrent taste for satire and topicality. This play has analogies with *Measure* and was probably another spur – a competitive one – to Shakespeare.[45]

A simple and beautiful synopsis of these plays' appeal is found in a couplet from *Othello* –

> These sentences to sugar or to gall,
> Being strong on both sides, are equivocal. (1.3.216–17)

To paraphrase prosaically – these sentences tend equally to sweetness or to bitterness, both of these qualities being powerfully present in them. The lines are spoken by Desdemona's father, Brabantio, and have their own business within the dramatic moment, but extracted they serve as a kind of emblem or motto for Shakespeare's tragicomedies.

If the tragicomedies balance, more or less measure for measure, their helpings of sugar and gall, *Timon of Athens* is pure gall. It is the bleakest of all Shakespeare's plays, and vies with *Cymbeline* (though for different reasons) as the least staged work of Shakespeare's mature years. It dramatizes a story he found in Plutarch's *Lives*, of a rich Athenian whose followers and flatterers deserted him when the money ran out, and who turned his back on the world and lived wild in the woods: 'Timon *misanthropos*'. The play has some magnificent patches of poetry, but the overall tone is harsh.

As it comes down to us – in the only contemporary text available, that of the 1623 Folio – *Timon* seems still in parts rough, unpolished, with loose ends ungathered. One reason for this irregularity is that the play was a collaboration. Shakespeare's co-author was Thomas Middleton, a Londoner in his early twenties: a rising young star.[46] He had begun as a poet in the satirical vein of Marston. His *Microcynicon* (1599), with its 'six Snarling Satyres', had been among the 'unseemly' works called in by the Archbishop's censors in 1599. In the new century he began to work in the theatre, initially for the Admiral's Men, chief rivals of Shakespeare's company. Henslowe records payment to him in

May 1602 for his contribution to a lost historical drama ('Caesar's Fall', also called 'Two Shapes'), a patchwork collaboration that also involved Dekker, Michael Drayton, Anthony Munday and the young John Webster. Then comes the wonderful series of brash, smutty 'city comedies' that made his name – *The Phoenix* was performed at court at Christmas 1603, followed over the next few years by *The Family of Love, A Trick to Catch the Old One, A Mad World, my Masters, The Puritan* (also called *The Widow of Watling Street*), *Your Five Gallants* and others, mostly written for the children's companies. Jonson called Middleton a 'base fellow', but the list of authors he disliked was a long one. Versatile, prolific and full of promise, Middleton was a prize catch for the King's Men.

Shakespeare was no stranger to collaboration, but he did not, one suspects, take naturally to it, and as far as the evidence remains his partnership with Middleton was the first for about a decade. Early in his career he had tacked and botched with other writers: the hand of Nashe has been discerned in the *Henry VI* plays, and that of Peele in *Titus Andronicus*. In around 1593–4 he contributed to 'Sir Thomas More', a play which survives only in manuscript and was perhaps never performed.[47] But once his career gets going he is remarkably solo. Over at the Rose – on the evidence of Henslowe's accounts and diaries – it was the norm for a play to be written by anything from two to five writers. Few of the collaborations listed by Henslowe made it into print – we have lost such plays as Ben Jonson's *Hot Anger Soon Cooled*, his first known work, writtten with Henry Chettle – but among the younger writers in the new century collaborations were frequently printed as such – *Eastward Ho!* by Chapman, Jonson and Marston; *Westward Ho!* and *Northward Ho!* by Dekker and Webster; *The Honest Whore* and *The Roaring Girl* by Dekker and Middleton; and many works by Beaumont and Fletcher. It seems to have become a selling point – two or three talents (often very different kinds of talent) for the price of one.

Though *Timon* cannot be called an unqualified success, the passages now assigned to Middleton – which include almost all of Act 3 – are powerfully written, and it seems his connection with the King's Men prospered. In about 1606 he turned out two fine tragedies for them: *The Revenger's Tragedy* (published anonymously in 1607) and the short, topical *A Yorkshire Tragedy* (published in 1608). The title-page of the latter credits the play to 'W. Shakspeare'.[48] Similarly the first edition of Middleton's comedy *The Puritan* (1607) is attributed to 'W.S.'. These are opportunistic title-pages, marketing ploys, but they express accurately a new literary twinning. It is possible Shakespeare contributed some passages to the *Yorkshire Tragedy*.

Shakespeare may have been edged into this collaboration by professional pressure. He may have felt (or others in the company may have felt) that he needed the input of younger, sharper-edged writers like Middleton and, a little later, George Wilkins, who was sharp-edged in an altogether more dangerous way.

These are, in broad outline, the literary aspects of Shakespeare on Silver Street – the 'bitter and complex music' of the tragicomedies; the flawed collaboration with Middleton; the impending mental tempest of *King Lear*. It is a period of transition, of experiment, of paradox and contradiction: 'a mingled yarn, good and ill together' (*All's Well*, 4.3.67).

How far this can be related to Shakespeare's frame of mind during this period is, of course, a matter of debate. It was once fashionable to speak of Shakespeare's output in the early seventeenth century as the product of a period of depression or illness, or what we might now call a mid-life crisis. This was energetically challenged in a famous lecture by C. J. Sisson, 'The Mythical Sorrows of Shakespeare' (1934). Sisson attacked the idea that Shakespeare wrote the tragicomedies as 'a sufferer from pessimism and disillusionment, a victim of seventeenth century blues'. It simply does not follow, he thought, any more than 'the proposition that tragic writing in a great creative writer is evidence of a tragic mood or personal unhappiness'. On the contrary, as Coleridge observed, 'When a man is unhappy he writes damned bad poetry.' This is a corrective view, and the critical pendulum has continued to swing away from such personal interpretation of the plays (though the great modern maverick of Shakespeare studies, John Berryman, had a point when he said he was looking forward to 'Professor Sisson's studies of the mythical sorrows of St Paul, Villon, Dostoevsky, Father [Gerard Manley] Hopkins and Hart Crane' – a point drastically underscored by Berryman's own later suicide).[49]

It is true that biographical readings of the plays are dangerous, unregulated, prone to sentimentalization. It is absurd to cherry-pick passages of poetry, written over more than two decades, and infer from them a consistent personal attitude. Lines belong in a dramatic context, and in the psychological context of the character who utters them, and cannot be taken to reflect Shakespeare's views. But perhaps the scepticism has swung too far in the direction of a bloodless text. Biography and literature do not fit together like Lego bricks, but they are not totally divorced either. Even E. M. W. Tillyard, a fine-toothed textual analyst who thought biographical interpretation 'superfluous', concludes an examination of the poetic unevenness of *All's Well* by saying, 'Some of these couplets are doing much what his couplets usually do; others in their strangeness point to an unusual mood in him when he wrote the play.'[50]

I am interested in recreating the physical and cultural circumstances of a period of Shakespeare's life. The plays he was writing at the time are part of those circumstances. They are on his desk; they are on his mind; and it is permissible, within precise chronological boundaries, to draw links between them and the milieu in which he was living when he wrote them.

If Shakespeare had written – say – a play about a young Frenchman being pressed reluctantly into marriage, and if it could be shown that he wrote the play at a time when he was himself pressing a young Frenchman into marriage, then one might think it worth asking whether there was a connection between the fictional nuptials on stage and the actual ones he was involved in. That is in fact the case – the play is *All's Well* – and it would be perverse to ignore these connections in the name of academic correctness. I would not call Stephen Belott a 'model' for Bertram, Count Roussillon, and I would not want to suggest that Shakespeare was 'inspired' by the small dramas of the Mountjoy household when he was writing of the troubled betrothal of Bertram and Helena. But the analogies are there. The 'unconsidered trifles' of domestic life are snapped up by the dramatist. They go into the mix, enriching it with secret flavours of particularity which are, for the most part, unknown to us.

4

Shakespeare in London

The story of Shakespeare and the Mountjoys is a small chapter in the larger and longer story of Shakespeare in London. He was not actually a Londoner, of course. He was born, married and buried in Stratford-upon-Avon, and this provincial market-town remained, in most senses of the word, his home. His parents, wife, children and most of his siblings and cousins lived there. He inherited, as an adult, the house where he had spent his childhood. In 1598 he bought his own rather grand house on the edge of town, New Place, where he spent more and more time in his later years, and where he died, at the age of fifty-two, in 1616. In these fundamental ways Shakespeare was – precisely as he says in his deposition – 'of Stratford-upon-Avon in the countie of Warwickshire'.

But, for all this, the fact remains that the 'sweet swan of Avon'[51] spent a lot more of his adult life in London than he did in Stratford. It was his place of business, the theatrical and literary capital to which he was drawn and in which he struggled to success and eminence. He was there out of professional necessity, though this need not imply he was there unwillingly. He was, like so many other Londoners, an incomer: part of a demographic rip-tide which saw the city double its population during the sixteenth century, reaching about 200,000 at the beginning of James's reign. Many of his literary contemporaries were also of provincial stock – Christopher Marlowe and John Lyly from Canterbury, Thomas Nashe from Lowestoft, Robert Greene from Norwich, George Chapman from Hitchin, Francis Beaumont from Leicestershire, and so on. Even Sir Walter Ralegh, the acme of courtly sophistication, 'spake broad Devonshire to his dying day'.[52]

'London, thou art the floure of cities all,' ran the old ditty, though the pamphleteer Thomas Nashe had a different angle: 'London, thou art the seeded garden of sinne, the sea that sucks in all the scummy chanels of the realme.'[53] Perhaps both views are true – by the end of the sixteenth century London was one of the largest, liveliest and most sophisticated cities in Europe, but it was also overcrowded, squalid, corrupt, crime-ridden and plague-infested. A rich whiff of danger and pleasure blows through those narrow wood-built streets, a human profusion which for the provincial newcomer must have been intoxicating. A sense of the city's sheer verve plays into the wonderful 'low-life' strata of Shakespeare's drama – Falstaff and his cronies drinking at East Cheap, the brothel-world of Nan Quickly and Doll Tearsheet, Pompey Bum and Mistress Overdone.

It is not known when Shakespeare first came to the city. The last record of him as a young man in Stratford is the baptism of his twins, Hamnet and Judith, on 2 February 1585 (it is not *per se* a record of him, but one assumes he was there). He was then twenty years old. The first records of him in London date from mid-1592 – the appearance of 'harey the vi' (almost certainly the play we now call *Henry VI Part 1*) at the Rose theatre; the attack on him in Greene's *Groatsworth of Wit*.[54] Between these sightings lie the legendary 'Lost Years', a documentary desert seven years wide in which the early biographers placed unsubstantiated oases of activity – he had been a 'schoolmaster in the country' (John Aubrey) or a 'lawyer's clerk' (Edmund Malone) – and which more recent commentators have interpreted in terms of the clandestine movements of a young Catholic.[55] Any or all of these might be true, but a good part of the so-called lost years must be located in London. The whole tenor of Greene's attack on him in 1592 shows he had by then acquired some success both as an actor and as a writer of plays, and was thus, in Greene's view, an 'upstart crow beautified with our feathers'. ('Our' refers to the clique of university-educated writers which also included Marlowe, Nashe, George Peele and Thomas Watson: the 'University Wits', as they are called.) The only place Shakespeare could have achieved this success, or notoriety, was in London, and it is generally agreed he was living there at least by the end of the 1580s.

At the close of his career he retired back to Stratford, but again the dates are vague. *The Tempest*, performed in 1611, has a valedictory note – 'Our revels now are ended' – but he continued to contribute work for the stage. *Henry VIII*, premiered at the Globe in the early summer of 1613, was a collaboration with John Fletcher, but the editors of the First Folio considered it (unlike *Pericles*) to have enough Shakespeare in it to merit inclusion in the canon. But two later ventures with Fletcher – *The Two Noble Kinsmen* and the lost *Cardenio* – had slighter contributions and were not included. It was during an early performance of *Henry VIII* that the Globe was burnt down, after a spark from a cannonade ignited the thatched roof. The razing of the great playhouse he had built and nurtured makes the day of the fire, 25 July 1613, a symbolic date for Shakespeare's retirement from the city – though only a symbolic one, for he is spotted briefly in London in November 1614, when a Stratford acquaintance writes: 'My cosen Shakspeare commyng yesterday to towne I went to see him howe he did.'[56]

If these dates are broadly accurate, Shakespeare spent about twenty-five years living and working in London, and it is with Shakespeare in – if not quite of – London that this book is concerned.

We know something of Shakespeare's residences in London before he took up his lodgings on Silver Street. According to John Aubrey, Shakespeare had 'lived in Shoreditch'. Aubrey is not always reliable, but he was an expert sniffer-out of information, and his informant was in this case a good one – an aged actor-manager, William Beeston, whose father Christopher had acted alongside Shakespeare in the 1590s. In a manuscript note Aubrey writes, 'W. Shakespeare – Q [*quaere*, ask] Mr Beeston, who knows most of him'. He interviewed him in the summer of 1681, a year before Beeston's death. Perhaps he came too late, for he got just a few scraps of reminiscence about Shakespeare, one of which was that he had lived in Shoreditch.[57]

The likelihood is that Shoreditch was an early Shakespeare residence in London, since it was here that the first purpose-built playhouses were located – the Theatre, built in 1576 by James Burbage, father of the actor Richard Burbage; and the Curtain. These predated the Bankside playhouses south of the river.

In the late 1580s, when Shakespeare was establishing himself in the theatre world, Shoreditch was little more than a shanty-town, a rampant overspill of 'poor cottages' and 'alleys backward' spreading through the fields and marshes and dissolved-monastery gardens outside the city walls. But it was also, because of that connection with the theatres, the Bohemian haunt of Elizabethan London. Along its dirt roads lived some of the greatest literary and theatrical talents of the day. Thomas Watson and Christopher Marlowe had lodgings in Norton Folgate just south of Shoreditch, and in 1589 they are glimpsed with weapons drawn in an 'affray' on nearby Hog Lane. The comedian Richard Tarlton lived his last days on Holywell Street (now Shoreditch High Street) with a prostitute named Em Ball. The red-bearded pamphleteer Robert Greene, author of that bitter sortie against Shakespeare, was another habitué. His mistress, whom Gabriel Harvey describes as a 'sorry ragged quean', was also named Ball – her brother was a cutpurse known on the street as 'Cutting' Ball. She was probably related to Tarlton's mistress Em Ball, and may have been the same woman. Their illegitimate son Fortunatus – little Lucky Greene – died in infancy and was buried in the parish church of St Leonard's. Shakespeare's future collaborator George Wilkins may also have spent his early years in the area: his father was buried at St Leonard's in 1603. Actors and their families abound in the church register – Burbages, Brownes and indeed Beestons.[58] Aubrey's interview with William Beeston actually took place in Shoreditch, at Beeston's house 'on Hog Lane, six doores down'.

By the mid-1590s Shakespeare had moved to the parish of

St Helen's, Bishopsgate. He is still close to the northern theatres but now inside the city gates, within the pale. We find him there in the lay subsidy rolls, which record tax assessments and payments, parish by parish, throughout the country. The subsidies were levies by the Crown, usually collected in three annual instalments. The rate of taxation was controlled by Parliament. Property-owners were taxed on the value of their 'lands'; others, at a lower rate, on their 'goods'. The partially surviving London rolls, preserved in the National Archives, are an invaluable resource – the nearest we have to an Elizabethan telephone directory – and I will refer to them often in the course of this book.

The earliest record of Shakespeare in Bishopsgate is in October 1596. He was assessed on goods valued at £5, on which he owed tax of 5 shillings.[59] This immediately tells us something about his circumstances. First, his appearance in the subsidy rolls indicates that he is a 'householder' in the parish. This does not mean he owned a house there, which is unlikely, but suggests he had a long-term lease or tenancy agreement on a property. The assess-ment of £5 is a middling one. Among his fellow-parishioners, Sir John Spenser was assessed on lands worth £300, and another on £150, but the majority were assessed at £10, £5 or £3. The latter is the lowest assessment, though 'strangers' – in other words, immigrants – who fell below this threshold had to pay a poll tax of 4d per head. Comments in the literature of the day suggest that assessments of goods were as much an impression as a docu-mentation of wealth. A character in John Lyly's *Mother Bomby* (1585) says, 'He that had a cup of red wine to his oysters was hoisted in the Queen's subsidy books' (2.5); and in the anony-mous collection *Jack of Dover*, a man is rated at 'five pound more than he was before' because of his wife's fondness for wearing expensive stockings.[60] These exaggerate the matter, but we can infer that Mr Shakespeare was doing reasonably well for himself by the mid-1590s.

Payment of the tax owed on the 1596 assessment fell due the following February. But Shakespeare did not pay it. He is listed as a defaulter in a certificate dated 15 November 1597. In the default notices the 'petty collectors' of the parish affirm that the persons listed were 'ether dead, [or] departed and gone out of the sayde ward, or their goodes so eloigned or conveyed out of the same, or in such a pryvate and coverte manner kept' that the money owed could not 'be levyed of them'. Of these possible reasons for non-payment we can discount the first: Shakespeare was not dead. Nor, it seems, had he moved out of the parish, for on 1 October 1598 he is again listed at St Helen's, with the same assessment of £5.[61] The conclusion seems to be that he was evading payment. This is not remarkable – the system was chaotic, and evasion was common – but it is piquant to find that the first actual documentation of Shakespeare in London is as a tax-dodger.

The interest of Shakespeare's tax affairs lies more in the company we find him in. The St Helen's roll of 1598 shows him as one of nearly fifty names. Biographers have noted one of these, Thomas Morley – almost certainly the musician of that name, whose *First Book of Airs* (1600) has a setting of Shakespeare's song, 'It was a lover and his lass', from *As You Like It*.[62] But there are others of interest. One who catches my eye is Henry Mawnder. It is not a particularly common name, so it seems likely he is the same Henry Maunder who was serving a few years earlier as a 'Messenger of the Chamber'. This rather bland job-description covered a multitude of activities, some of them shading into politically sensitive areas. It was Maunder who was despatched from court in May 1593 with a warrant for the arrest of Christopher Marlowe; he found his man down in Chislehurst, Kent, and delivered him to the Privy Council on 20 May. Marlowe died in suspicious circumstances ten days later. This may not have endeared Mr Maunder to Shakespeare, who had known and admired Marlowe, but perhaps he was able to elicit from Maunder some details of the Marlowe affair, which was still shrouded in rumour.[63]

Here is another name that swims out of St Helen's in the 1590s: Anthony Elbow. He is among the 'straungers' of the parish assessed in the subsidy rolls. He was probably the Anthony

Helbow listed a few years earlier in a census of foreigners in London – a French silk-weaver from 'Leley' (Lille), with a wife named Margit, and an English servant. Like Shakespeare he failed to pay up, but in his case he was exempted by 'the fell sergeant, death', for the St Helen's parish register records that Anthony Elbowe 'out of Staveley's Alley' was buried on 13 October 1596.[64] It is a wonderful name, and it lodged in the capacious memory of Shakespeare, emerging some years later as Constable Elbow in *Measure for Measure*, a comic turn in that mood-shifting play, and perhaps one whose malapropisms – 'cardinally' for 'carnally', 'Hannibal' for 'cannibal', 'respected' for 'suspected' – elaborate a memory of the real Elbow's broken English.

Shakespeare also failed to pay the tax due on that second assessment of October 1598, but in this instance his non-payment was because he had moved. The wheels of the Elizabethan bureaucracy turned slowly, but in time his arrears showed up in the Exchequer's Pipe Rolls. There are two references to him. The first indicates that in 1599 he was resident in the county of Surrey; the second has the words 'episcopo Wintonensi' beside his name.[65] From this it appears that some time after October 1598 (when he was still listed in Bishopsgate), Shakespeare moved across to the southern, Surrey side of the Thames, and more specifically to the Liberty of the Clink in Southwark, which was under the jurisdiction of the Bishop of Winchester ('Episcopus Wintonensis'). This move can be related to the opening of the new Globe theatre, built in the early months of 1599 on a leased site in Southwark, a few hundred yards away from the Rose theatre, where the Admiral's Men played, and the baiting-pits of Paris Gardens, where bears were chained to a stake and harried by packs of mastiffs.

These are records of Shakespeare's lodgings or tenancies prior to his move to Cripplegate in about 1603. He is plausibly glimpsed in Shoreditch, and he is definitely recorded in Bishopsgate and Southwark. These earlier addresses place him physically close to the playhouses which are his life and livelihood, but this is not at all the case with his new lodgings *chez* Mountjoy. To reach the Globe theatre from Cripplegate he had to walk southwards right across town, and then take a wherry or water-taxi over the river to Southwark. It seems inconvenient – interestingly so.

At this time, as I have noted, Shakespeare was at the peak of his profession. With that success come stresses and pressures. He is something of a celebrity – a subject for poets ('Honey-tongued Shakespeare . . .') and topical comedies ('O sweet Master Shakespeare, I'll have his picture in my study at court!') and Inns of Court anecdotes (as recorded in the diary of John Manningham: see Chapter 27 below).[66] His face is known: he is an actor in his own and others' plays. But celebrity – 'the bubble reputation', as Jaques calls it – is always double-edged, a burdensome illusion as much as an achievement. Is there a note of escape in his removal to Silver Street? Is this rather quieter, more respectable, more anonymous neighbourhood something of a bolt-hole from the boisterous and very public world of players and playgoers?

Aubrey's source William Beeston gives us a hint of this, for another thing he remembered, or had heard from his father, was that Shakespeare 'was the more to be admired q [*quia*, because] he was not a company keeper'. He 'wouldnt be debauched, & if invited to, writt he was in paine'. This is unverifiable but has the backing of common sense. It refers us to the reclusiveness of authorship, the staking out of mental space. Instead of partying – those tempting debaucheries – he will settle down to write, by candlelight, in the silence of the city at night. How else could his output – at least thirty-seven plays, two book-length narrative poems and 154 sonnets, not to mention his involvement in acting, directing and general theatre management – have been achieved? An avoidance of 'company', for this more pressing purpose of composition, may be a factor in his move across town to Cripplegate.

There survives among the Cecil papers at Hatfield House a rather huffy letter from a court official, Sir Walter Cope. He writes to Robert Cecil, Lord Cranborne:

I have sent and bene all this morning hunting for players, juglers & such kind of creaturs, but find them harde to finde, wherefore leavinge notes for them to seeke me, Burbage ys come, & sayes ther ys no new playe that the Quene hath not seene, but they have revyved an old one cawled Loves Labore Lost, which for wytt & myrthe he sayes will please her excedingly.

Cope does not date the letter, but it is endorsed '1604' by one of Cecil's secretaries, and this date is confirmed by a performance of *Love's Labours* at court in January 1605.[67] Shakespeare would doubtless have been one of the players so fruitlessly 'hunted' by Cope. Was he out that morning, when Sir Walter or one of his minions called by at the Mountjoys' house? Or was he so 'harde to finde' because his whereabouts were uncertain, his private address not generally available? Let others in the company deal with snobbish courtly fixers like Cope, who considers actors on a par with 'juglers & such kind of creaturs'. Perhaps the quibbling Clown in *Othello* gives the correct answer to such enquiries: 'I know not where he lodges, and for me . . . to say he lies here or there were to lie in my own throat.'

Thanks to the Belott–Mountjoy suit we do know where the famous but elusive Mr Shakespeare lodges, and we now head for Silver Street in search of him – a metaphorical visit, of course, but with a faint lingering sense that we too come uninvited.

PART TWO

Silver Street

In the street I met him,
And in his company that gentleman.
The Comedy of Errors, 5.1.226–7

5

The house on the corner

The house where the Mountjoys lived is long gone, but its location can be gauged quite exactly. We learn from the deposition of William Eaton – Stephen Belott's apprentice – that it stood on the corner of Silver Street and 'Muggle Street'. The latter, more generally called Monkwell Street, ran northwards out of Silver Street, towards the city walls. Mountjoy's house, therefore, was on the north side of Silver Street, just about opposite the little churchyard of St Olave's on the south side. Muggle or Monkwell Street was also the boundary between two of the city's administrative 'wards': the west side of the street was in Farringdon Ward and the east side in Cripplegate Ward. Christopher Mountjoy, as we know from taxation records, was an inhabitant of Cripplegate Ward. Thus the Mountjoy dwelling – the house where Shakespeare lodged in and around 1604 – stood precisely on the eastern corner of Silver Street and Monkwell Street.

You can see the house quite clearly in the woodcut map of Elizabethan London, formerly attributed to the engraver Ralph Agas and still known for convenience as the 'Agas map' (see Plate 6). It has steeply pitched gables, and a projection suggestive of a 'pentice' or penthouse above a shop-front, and then those four tantalizing windows upstairs – but here the map fails us, for the windows are only little blocks of printer's ink which the magnifying-glass cannot pry into. Of course, what one sees in the map is not actually an image of the Mountjoys' house, only a stereotypical indication of its existence. It looks much the same as all the others around it: Agas's London, seen from a hypothetical bird's-eye viewpoint, tends to the neat uniformity of a modern housing estate, far from the higgledy-piggledy, in-filled, architecturally opportunist reality: 'the muddled truth of building use'.[1] It is also not the Mountjoys' house *per se* because the map dates from the early 1560s, some thirty years before they are first heard of on Silver Street. But this is, nonetheless, a visual record of the house, specific in location if not in detail: a limited record, but the best we have.

Importantly we see the street in its context. Not far to the south is the great commercial thoroughfare of Cheapside, and beyond that St Paul's cathedral (still shown with its wooden steeple, destroyed by lightning in 1561). Closer in, to the north and west, lie the city walls; the neighbourhood nestles comfortably in the angle. To the east is Wood Street, leading out through the walls at the Cripple (or Creple) Gate which gives the area its name. Legends of healing the lame attach to the gate, but the name merely refers to its lack of headroom – literally, a gate which one has to creep through. Beyond the gate, and across the unsavoury city ditch, you were soon out into the greenery of Moorfields. The map shows market-gardens, hedgerows, archery butts, tenter-yards, and a pleasant prospect north to the windmills of Finsbury Fields. Some of this would already have been lost to development by the time Shakespeare was here, but London remained a city hemmed in by countryside. Nuts were gathered on Notting Hill, sheep grazed at Shepherd's Bush, hogs were kept at Hoxton, and one went for a day out to Islington to shoot duck and 'eat a messe of creame'.[2]

The house Shakespeare knew may have survived for half a century or so after his lifetime, but it cannot have survived the cataclysm of 1666. Cripplegate was near the northern edge of the area destroyed by the Great Fire, which began at Pudding Lane in Billingsgate, and was fanned generally westwards through the tinder-dry city. It was probably on the third day of the fire, 4 September 1666, that Silver Street went up in flames. The former Mountjoy house was one of an estimated 13,000 properties razed in the conflagration.

A Restoration house arose in its place. A survey of the period shows this property having a frontage of 63 feet along Silver Street and the same going up Monkwell Street – this may or may not give us the dimensions of the original house.[3] In the mid-nineteenth century there was a public house on the site, the Coopers' Arms. By the end of the century almost all the houses of Silver Street had been replaced by Victorian warehouses and 'manufactories', but the pub remained. There is a photograph of it in around 1910, taken by or for Charles William Wallace: a tall, grimy-looking building on four floors (see Plate 7). A sign-board on the corner offers Meux Original London Stout, draught and bottled; handwritten signs at the doorway promise Teas and Dinners. A fire hydrant stands at the kerb. The scene has the dingy look of Eliot's 'Preludes' (1917) –

> The showers beat
> On broken blinds and chimney-pots.

The address of the pub was No. 13 Silver Street – though there were no street-numbers in Shakespeare's day.[4]

That the house does not survive is unremarkable. Because of the Fire, the centre of London is almost devoid of Elizabethan and Jacobean houses. But we are still further from the physical reality of the house because Silver Street itself no longer exists. It disappeared in the second great cataclysm to hit the area – the London Blitz. A German raid on the night of 29 December 1940 reduced the entire area to rubble. During three hours the bombers dropped an estimated 130 tons of high explosives and 600 incendiary bombs on the city: a whole tract between Aldersgate and Moorgate stations to the north and Cheapside to the south was burnt out. An atmospheric pencil-and-wash drawing by Dennis Flanders shows the devastation, looking north to St Giles, Cripplegate, with the debris of Silver Street in the foreground (see Plate 8).

Many streets rose again from the ashes of the Blitz, but Silver Street did not. It was dealt a final death-blow by redevelopment and traffic-planning – we are at the outer edge of the giant

Barbican estate, opened in the early 1960s. All that survives visibly of the previous lay-out of the area are the old churchyards, which have been left as public open spaces. You can find the churchyard of St Olave's, watched over by gleaming high-rise offices. No foundations of the church are visible, as they are in some others in the vicinity, but on a low brick wall among the municipal shrubs is a small faded inscription on a block of whitish stone (see Plate 9) – it looks like part of an old gravestone, and indeed it has a skull and crossbones incised on it. It reads: 'THIS WAS THE PARISH CHURCH / OF ST OLAVE SILVER STREET / DESTROYED BY THE DREADFVLL / FIRE IN THE YEAR 1666'. Opposite is another inscribed stone, most of it now illegible. The bottom lines read, 'BY THE / COMMISSIONERS OF SEWERS / AT THE REQUEST OF THE VESTRY'. Below is a date, 18-something, perhaps 1865. The vestry would have been that of St Alban's, Wood Street, with which the parish was twinned. It is likely both tablets date from the nineteenth century, though the skull was probably on the stone before the commemorative words were added. If so it would be a fragmentary pre-Fire relic of the original churchyard.

The churchyard of St Olave's stood almost directly opposite the Mountjoys' house on Silver Street. The site of it now lies on the edge of the busy traffic-road called London Wall (part of the A1211). The name London Wall is misleading at this point, where the road runs south of, and at an angle to, the true line of the old walls, whose fragmentary bastions can be seen to the north. The line of Silver Street lies partly under and partly alongside this road. Pacing it out I would say that the closest one can now get to the Mountjoys' house is underneath the road, in London Wall car-park. We are physically near, for the pre-Fire stratum is indeed some feet below the current surface, but this is on the whole a depressing proximity. An underground car-park is unmistakably an underground car-park whether or not Shakespeare once lived on the site of it.

Climbing back up to present-day levels I take some comfort in the thought that the opposite scenario – the house's survival –

might have been even grimmer: the postcard rack, the polished oak panelling, the lute musak following you from room to room.

We must find other ways to specify the house and the street as they were in Shakespeare's day. The obvious place to turn is John Stow's *Survay of London*, published in 1598 and updated in 1603. But this corner of Cripplegate did not spark the roaming antiquary's enthusiasm. Voluble with history and curiosities elsewhere, of Silver Street he has only this to say: 'Down lower in Wood streete is Silver streete (I think of silversmithes dwelling there) in which bee divers fayre houses.'[5] His conjecture about the name is correct, but the association is medieval: there is no particular evidence of silversmiths here in Shakespeare's time, though there were some goldsmiths. Other than this Stow gives just one crumb of information – that the street had 'fair' houses. 'Fair' is a favourite word when he has nothing much else to say: a bland term of approval. He means that the buildings are of a good size, the street well kept, the area respectable. It continued to be so in its post-Fire manifestation. In Maitland's *London* of 1756, Silver Street is described as a 'handsome broad street with well-built houses'.[6] Jacobean London had few broad streets, however, and to our eyes Silver Street would be narrow.

The Mountjoy establishment was probably quite a large house. It served the family as both work-place and dwelling-place. The ground floor would have contained a workshop, where the Mountjoy 'tires' were made, and probably also a shop in the retailing sense, where customers came for viewings and fittings. (In theory immigrant craftsmen were forbidden to retail directly to the public, but this was not strictly enforced.) Upstairs were the family's living quarters, and doubtless the room or rooms let out to lodgers, and then the higher, smaller rooms which accommodated apprentices and servants. A 'snapshot' of the Mountjoy household in the late 1590s shows half a dozen workers in their tiremaking business – Christopher and Marie, their daughter Mary (whom Christopher had trained 'to a good perfection in his sayd trade of Tyermakeinge'), and three apprentices – plus at least two other live-in servants. Then, a little later, there is the lodger, Mr Shake-speare. There had probably been a lodger there before him, and there was certainly one there after him, for in court in 1612 Christopher Weaver says Mountjoy 'hath a sojourner in the house with him'. On this evidence the house had at least nine adult residents in it. By 1612 there were considerably fewer, and Mountjoy was letting out half the property to tenants. 'The house wherein he dwelleth', says Noel, is 'divided into two tenements.' These tenants are distinct from the lodger or sojourner, who is 'in the house with him'.

These roomy tradesmen's houses were a popular choice for writers' lodgings. We hear of Robert Greene living, and dying, in the house of a 'cordwainer' (leather-worker) in Dowgate; of Ben Jonson lodged 'at a comb-maker's shop about the Elephant and Castle'; of Matthew Roydon 'making his abode' at a shoemaker's house in the Blackfriars; of Nashe billeted with the catchpenny printer John Danter in Hosier Lane.[7] Shakespeare was typical, then – except that none of those hard-up writers owned houses elsewhere. They were lodgers by necessity, not for professional convenience. Shakespeare has an apartment in town, which is a different matter.

We have a broad guideline to the value of the house. Mountjoy was not the owner of the property: he leased it. In 1612, according to Noel, he had recently renewed the lease: 'He hath a time in his lease of the house wherein he dwelleth of some thirty years to come, which he renewed but lately.' He also had the leasehold of another house, out in 'Brainforde' – Brentford in Middlesex – which he sub-let to tenants. (This second Mountjoy property will be of interest to us later: see Chapter 25.) We have a figure for the two leaseholds combined. Mountjoy 'payeth yearly rent for those leases some seventeen pounds per annum' (Christopher Weaver).[8] We cannot know the proportioning of this figure, but might guess that the London house was worth more than the Brentford house (though, as I will show, Brentford could be an expensive area). Perhaps something between £10 and £12 per annum is a reasonable estimate for the house in Silver Street.

This suggests a good-sized house but not a grand one. Speaking of Dutch immigrants in Billingsgate John Stow says, 'In the chief and principall houses, they give twentie pound the yeare for a house latelie letten for foure marks [£2 13s 4d].' The discrepancy sounds exaggerated but we gather that around the beginning of the seventeenth century the lease on a large London house could be as much as £20 a year.[9] Stow's comment reminds us that immigrants were often charged extortionate rents, so our estimated £10 to £12 rent for the Silver Street house may exaggerate its market value.

The house was probably a timber-framed building. Freestone houses were a rarity in the city: in medieval times, says Stow, 'the houses in London were builded in stone for defence of fire ... but of later time for the winning of ground taken downe, and houses of timber set up in place'. Ground was won – in other words, space saved – because it was easier to build timber houses tall: five storeys were not uncommon. We see these houses in contemporary paintings and engravings, and we know them from many fine examples scattered around the country, in a style we generically call 'Tudor', though the black and white look they often have today is not authentic. The colours of a typical London street were softer – the silvery grey of untreated oak, the beiges and umbers of unpainted loam. Resting on a shallow foundation of brick and stone, the framework consisted of horizontal, load-bearing beams – the 'sill beams' at the base and the 'bessamers' above – into which upright and diagonal timbers were slotted. The bessamers had to be particularly strong to bear the weight of the overhanging jetties (or 'jutties') which projected out from the front of the house, giving it that stacked, teetering look. These were often a source of dispute: they cut out light from the narrow streets, they invaded others' privacy, and they altered the ground-area on which house values were partly based. A larger upper-floor protrusion was the pentice or penthouse, a storage space with a sloping roof, as possibly seen on the house in the Agas map. Shops like Mountjoy's often had one: in the Dekker–

Webster comedy *Westward Ho!* (1607) we hear of 'penthouses which commonly make the shop of a mercer or a linen-draper as dark as a room in Bedlam' (1.1).

The fabric of such a house can be broadly gauged from the tenancy conventions of the time. The tenant (or lessee, like Mountjoy) was responsible for repairing 'stone, brick and tiling where need is'; for the upkeep of timbers, floorboards, glass windows and gutters; for providing planks for stable doors and 'quarters for pentices'; and for 'daubing of the walls with lathe, nail, loam and quarters whereas the walls be broken'. The tenant was also responsible for 'cleansing of the sieges and withdraughts' (cesspits and drains).[10] The days of the flushing lavatory were far in the future, though a prototype was discussed in Sir John Harington's half-serious, half-scurrilous *Metamorphosis of Ajax*, published in 1596 (Ajax = 'a jakes' = a privy). He exaggerates – but not by much – the particular stench of shared urban drains:

What with the fish-water coming from the kitchens, blood & garbage of fowl, washing of dishes, and the excrements of the other houses, and all these in moist weather stirred a little with some small stream of water . . . these thus meeting together make such a quintessence of a stink that if Paracelsus were alive, his art could not devise to extract a stronger.[11]

An account survives of the emptying of a cesspit in Elizabethan London. The owner of the house paid 32 shillings for two 'night-men' and their crew; sixteen barrels of night-soil were carted away. Other costs were bread, cheese and beer for the workers; bricks and mortar to make good the 'funnels' or downpipes from the privy; and threepence for 'juniper to refresh the pit'.[12]

By good fortune we have a more detailed insight into the structure and measurements of one of those 'fair' houses on Silver Street. It was called Dudley Court. It stood on the north side of the street a couple of doors down from the Mountjoys' place. It had once belonged to the priory of Holy Trinity in Aldgate, but in the mid-sixteenth century it was owned by John Dudley of Hackney, who held the tasty-sounding post of Sergeant of the Pastry to Queen Elizabeth. In 1599 Dudley Court was purchased by Christ's Hospital – considerable landowners in London – and a few years later it was surveyed for them by Ralph Treswell. His precise and elegant plan of it survives, along with many others he did, in the Hospital's 'Evidence Books'.[13]

The house was by then split into three tenements – one large and two small – but is still recognizably a single house. It is set back from the street, with entry via a courtyard. The house is on three floors, with an irregular frontage of about 60 feet; part of the frontage is 'jettied', with projections of 2 feet on the first floor and a few inches on the second. In the main part of the house there are four rooms on the ground floor, including a kitchen and a 'parlour'. The two largest rooms, at the back of the house, are about 15 feet by 15; they have windows looking on to a narrow garden, 44 by 30 feet. There is a well in a corner of the yard.

The dimensions may be similar to those of the Mountjoys' house along the street, though the lay-out would be different, as Dudley Court was purely residential. Many of the houses surveyed by Treswell have a front room or rooms designated 'shoppe', opening straight on to the street, and this would probably be the case at the Mountjoys'.

This being a ground-plan there is no view of the upper floors, but they are described in an accompanying note. Across the whole property there are eight upstairs rooms. Two are designated as 'garrets' – low-ceilinged rooms up under the eaves of the house. Garrets are often associated with poverty-stricken poets, but we are unlikely to find Mr Shakespeare accommodated in one at the Mountjoys'. He could afford better. The biggest upstairs room in Dudley Court, 'a chamber over the parlour with a chimney', measures about 20 by 17 feet. This is not a bad-sized room but in general the Treswell surveys confirm what one knows from surviving Jacobean houses – that rooms were on the whole small, and ceilings low, and window-light not overly generous due to the expense of glass, not to mention the extra heating incurred.

Upstairs also, not far from the main bedroom, is the privy or 'house of office'. They are often found upstairs in the houses surveyed by Treswell: the fall was better. They were narrow closets, seldom more than 5 by 7 feet. If the literary jokes are to be believed, old pamphlets and manuscripts met an ignominious end here.[14] It was unusual for a household to have more than one privy, so it is likely Shakespeare shared this facility with the family.

6

The neighbourhood

What would you have seen, and who might you have met, if you were walking in and around Silver Street on a day in 1604?

Standing at the front door of the Mountjoys' house there were three directions in which you might go (that is one of the desirable things about corner-houses). To your right, across the other side of Muggle or Monkwell Street, was the last western stretch of Silver Street, before it veered off southwards into Noble Street. Here stood the grandest house in the immediate neighbourhood, Windsor House, formerly known as Neville's Inn. Stow calls it a 'great house builded of stone and timber'. The Neville family, Earls of Westmorland, had owned it in medieval times, before it passed to the Windsor family by marriage. Henry, 5th Lord Windsor was the incumbent in Shakespeare's day – he features as Lord 'Windser' or 'Windzer' in the parish register. His wife Ann was a Wiltshire squire's daughter. Baptisms of some of their children are recorded, but it is noted they were 'baptized in his house', rather than at the church: there was probably a small chapel there. In June 1600 an infant daughter, Grizzel – the contemporary form of Griselda – was buried at the church. Lord Windsor does not seem to have done anything very memorable. In 1600 an amorous clergyman's wife, Alice Blague, had hopes of becoming his mistress. In 1601 he was one of the peers who sat at the arraignment of the Earl of Essex. On his death in 1605, aged about forty-three, Parliament ordered the sale of some of his lands to pay his debts. Windsor House was probably sold, for it seems it was later owned by Sir David Fowles.[15]

To the south of Windsor House was a large walled garden. At the top of Noble Street, says Stow, 'ye come to the stone wall which incloseth a garden plot before the wall of the city'. He gives its length as '95 elles' – an ell (an old English word for the arm, still discernible in 'elbow') was about 45 inches, so Lord Windsor's garden was over a hundred yards long. This stone wall is shown in the Agas map. Looking west down Silver Street from the Mountjoys' front door it would seem you were in a cul-de-sac. You were not, because you could turn south down Noble Street, but that is how it would seem, as your eye met His Lordship's garden wall built across the line of the street.

We touch here an older part of the street's story, for this wall was only the latest of the obstructions blocking the western end of the street. Excavations have shown that in Saxon and early medieval times Silver Street led out through the city walls: a minor gateway between the proper city gates of Cripplegate and Aldersgate. Around the twelfth century this exit was progressively blocked off. It was first made impassable to wagons, then later to pedestrians.[16] The street became quieter, no longer a thorough-fare. It was after this closure, probably, that it became known as Silver Street – the earliest record of the name, 'Selvernstrate', dates from 1279. Before that it was merely the western continuation of Addle Street, the derivation of which is from Anglo-Saxon *adel*, 'cow dung'. It was a drover's road, a short-cut leading west to the great cattle-market of Smithfield. With the blocking of the exit through the walls this usage desisted, making the street more desirable to residents and craftsmen, among them the metal-workers who give the street its new name, and whose presence in the medieval period is evident from archaeological remains. This is the first rise in the respectability of the street that was once just a stretch of Dung Street.

Across the street from the Mountjoys' house stood the small churchyard of St Olave's.[17] Its area was about 330 square yards, considerably less than Lord Windsor's garden across the way. The combination of the two makes the immediate prospect from the Mountjoys' front door a pleasantly leafy one. The church itself stood at the western end of the churchyard, abutting on to Noble Street. The dedication, sometimes miswritten 'Olive's', is to the Norwegian king Olaf II, or Olaf Haraldsson, who fought in England against the Danes in the early eleventh century, and was canonized for converting Norway to Christianity. This suggests a Viking origin for the church, though the earliest record of it is twelfth century. There were other St Olaves in the city (on Hart Street and Bread Street, and in the Jewry) and another across the river in Southwark.

Stow passes the church with scarcely a glance – 'the parish church of St Olave in Silver Streete, a small thing and without any noteworthy monuments'. This insignificance tends to be confirmed by the Agas map, which does not specify the church at all (most of the city churches are represented with a tower, and some are identified by a keyed numeral). The church was perhaps in poor repair when Shakespeare knew it, for in 1609 it was demolished and rebuilt.[18] But though it was small and scruffy, St Olave's possessed a peal of bells: there are records of payments for ringing the bells on Queen Elizabeth's birthday.

Shakespeare would have worshipped there – a statement which says nothing about his religious feelings or lack of them: regular attendance at church was compulsory, and shirkers were fined. The minister was John Flint, a Cambridge graduate a few years younger than Shakespeare. His college, Christ's, had a strong tinge of Puritanism, and his reputation there as a 'great preacher' suggests he was of that tendency. It was Flint who officiated at the wedding of Mary Mountjoy, and at the burial of her mother, and it is his fluent hand which records these events in the parish register, on the cover of which he wrote shortly after his arrival:

> St Olave in Sillver streete
> The Register of this Parishe, truely
> transcripte, or copied out by me John
> fflinte minister and Parson thereof
> in the yeare of our L. God 1593[19]

*

Opposite the churchyard the narrower Monkwell Street ran northwards towards Cripplegate. You might turn this way if you were in search of fresh air and leisure activities beyond the walls, or indeed if you were headed for the playhouses and pleasure-dens of Shoreditch, north-east across Moorfields (though Shakespeare's own connection with the northern playhouses was now past).

On the left-hand side, Monkwell Street was dominated by the hall and gardens of the Barber-Surgeons' Company. In medieval times the barber and the surgeon (or 'chirurgeon') were one and the same – a man skilled with a razor and other cutting accessories. Gradually the occupations separated, as surgery became more ambitious in the wake of Renaissance anatomical study, but barbers continued to perform minor surgical and dental operations, particularly 'blood-letting' or phlebotomy. The red and white barber's pole, still seen outside old-fashioned hair-dressers, refers to the blood and tourniquet of phlebotomy. Actual surgery, with little in the way of antiseptic or anaesthetic, was alarmingly hit-or-miss. Here is the procedure for removing a kidney-stone, as described by the diarist John Manningham in 1601:

There is a seame in the passage of the yard [penis] neere the fundament, which the surgeons searche with a crooked instrument concaved at one end (called a catheter), whereinto they make incision and then grope for the stone with another toole which they call a duckes bill. Yf the stone be greater than may be drawne forth at the hole made by the seame, the partie dyes for it.[20]

In Shakespeare's day the Barbers' Hall, as it was generally called, lay further east than its later manifestations (post-Fire and post-Blitz), and more or less fronted on to Monkwell Street. It consisted of a large single room, or hall, with a kitchen and other domestic offices for the serving of dinners. In 1605 the company bought up land behind the Hall, formerly let to Lord Windsor, and added a courtroom. The famous circular anatomy theatre next to the city walls, designed by Inigo Jones on the model of the *teatro* at Padua, was not built until the 1630s, but dissections were performed at the Hall long before that.[21] A painting of about 1580 (see Plate 10) shows the Elizabethan surgeon John Banister delivering the 'Visceral Lecture' – one of four lectures held at the Hall every year, open to freemen of the Company and their guests. He points to a skeleton, beside which there is an open medical text; in front of him there is a body undergoing dissection. Banister himself lived on Silver Street, as he tells us in the preface of his *Antidotarie Chyrurgicall* (1589), but as he died in 1599 he was not co-resident with Shakespeare.[22] The burials of bodies used for dissection – traditionally the cadavers of executed criminals – are recorded in the St Olave's register: Henry Stanley, 'anatomized by the chirurgeons'; Katherine Whackter, 'anatomised by Dr Pallmer', and so on. One thinks of *King Lear*:

Let them anatomize Regan, see what breeds about her heart... (3.6.34–5)

> Let me have surgeons!
> I am cut to th' brains ... (4.5.188–9)

The Dr Pallmer who dissected the body of Katherine Whackter on 17 June 1600 is Richard Palmer, a leading physician of the day. A former Fellow of Peterhouse, Cambridge, he was licensed by the Royal College of Physicians in 1593, elected a Fellow in 1597, and Censor in 1599 (and several times thereafter). In a Treswell survey of 1612 he is shown as the owner of a property on Monkwell Street adjoining the Barber-Surgeons' lands; it was perhaps here that these anatomies were performed. In that year Dr Palmer was one of the physicians attending the dying Prince Henry, along with his neighbour Dr John Giffard, of whom more below. He died in 1625, his will describing him as a resident of St Olave's parish.[23]

There was another fine garden at Barbers' Hall. It is first mentioned in the Company annals in 1555, when the clerk was given an allowance for maintaining it. A later entry refers to purchases of a hundred sweet briars for a hedge, together with strawberries, rosemary, violets and vines. The latter were probably for producing verjuice (juice from unripe grapes for pickling and cooking) rather than wine.

The Barber-Surgeons' garden is of special interest because of its connection with the great horticulturalist John Gerard. He was a surgeon by training, and held a number of official positions in the Company, culminating in the Mastership in 1607, but he was better known for his green fingers than for his dexterity with catheter and duck-bill. He had designed gardens for the great Lord Burghley, and his own garden in Holborn, off Chancery Lane, was a lush acreage of 'trees, fruits and plants both indigenous and exotic'. In 1597 he published his famous *Herball*, which remains a landmark in botanical description and classification. It is illustrated with over 1,800 woodcuts, though many of them were plagiarized from an earlier continental work.[24] Gerard was also curator of the 'physic garden' of medicinal plants at the Royal College of Physicians (similar to the Apothecaries' Garden still extant in Chelsea), and in the late 1590s he was urging the Barber-Surgeons to plant a similar garden at the Hall. On 2 November 1602 a 'committee for Mr Gerrard's garden' had a meeting. It is not clear what was planted, or where, but it is likely that when Shakespeare lived here there was a physic garden designed by Gerard round the corner from him. Again it is *Lear* that springs to mind.

> LEAR: Give the word.
> EDGAR: Sweet marjoram.
> LEAR: Pass. (4.5.92–4)

> > Our foster-nurse of nature is repose
> > The which he lacks. That to provoke in him
> > Are many simples [herbs] operative, whose power
> > Will close the eye of anguish. (4.3.12–15)

Shakespeare's own knowledge of herbs is acute: a countryman's knowledge. It has been shown that Iago's herbicultural metaphor in *Othello* – 'our bodies are our gardens', in which we may 'plant nettles or sow lettuce, set hyssop and weed up thyme, supply it with one gender of herbs or distract it with many' (1.3.320–26) – makes perfectly good sense in terms of contemporary gardening practice.[25]

Many other livery companies had their headquarters round here – this is one of the features of the neighbourhood which contributes to an idea of its respectability. Just off Monkwell Street by the walls was Bowyers' Hall. Nearby were Curriers' Hall (they 'curried' or drubbed leather), and Plasterers' Hall (formerly the site of Pinners' Hall), and Brewers' Hall on Addle Street. Further south, towards Cheapside, stood Haberdashers' Hall, Embroiderers' Hall and the most opulent of all, Goldsmiths' Hall.

Goldsmiths – the epitome of flashy Jacobean success – were plentiful in the area. There was at least one, William Pierson, living on Silver Street itself. He leased his house from Thomas Savage of Addle Street, also a goldsmith – and a man known to Shakespeare, as he was one of the sureties of the land-lease for the Globe theatre.[26] Another goldsmith on or near Silver Street was Henry Bannister, probably a relative of John Banister the surgeon. This Bannister was also a 'broker' or moneylender, as was John Wolfall, a skinner by trade, whose extortionate dealings resulted in a Star Chamber suit in 1593, in which he is described as 'of Silver Street'. Both of them employed a shady character called Nicholas Skeres as a tout to wind in 'young gents' in need of cash. Conman, spy and sometime employee of the Earl of Essex, Skeres has a dubious place in literary history – he was one of the companions of Christopher Marlowe on the night he was killed.[27]

Continuing up Monkwell Street, you passed on your right a neat row of alms-houses. Thus Stow: 'On the said east side of Monkeswell street be proper Almeshouses, 12 in number, founded by Sir Ambrose Nicholas.' Accommodated there, rent-free, were a dozen 'poore and aged' people, 'having each of them seven pence the week, and once the year each of them five sackes of charcoales, and one quarter of a hundreth of faggots, of his gift forever'. Occupants are designated 'almsman', 'almswidow', etc, in the St Olave's registers. The charitable founder, Sir

Ambrose Nicholas, a salter by trade, served as Lord Mayor in
1575–6. He died a couple of years later, so Shakespeare would
not have known him, but he certainly knew his son, Daniel
Nicholas (born about 1560).[28] This was the friend of Stephen
Belott, who testified in 1612 that he had visited Shakespeare 'to
understand the truth' about the disputed dowry.

At the top of the street, close to the city gate, was a former
chapel or 'hermitage', St James-by-the-Wall. It was now converted
into tenements, one of which housed a private school run by one
Thomas Speght. Near by was an old well, formerly belonging to
the hermitage. Stow suggests this as the origin of the name
Monkwell or Monkswell Street but it seems he is wrong. The
earliest records of the street, from the twelfth century, call it
'Mukewelle' or 'Mogwelle' Street. The first syllable is probably a
family or clan name. Thus the rougher-sounding Muggle Street –
as used by the apprentice William Eaton in his deposition, and
also found on the Agas map – is more correct.

Immediately outside the gate was the extramural parish of
St Giles, Cripplegate – the tall-towered church still stands, despite
the efforts of fire and bombs, and can be seen clearly from the
site of Silver Street. In this parish there were writers living at one
time or another – Ben Jonson, Thomas Dekker and Shakespeare's
future collaborator George Wilkins. Here too lived an actor who
appears in the St Giles registers as 'Edward Shakespeere, player',
but who is more probably the dramatist's younger brother,
Edmund. This was in 1607, the occasion the burial of an illegitimate child. Sixteen years younger than Shakespeare, it seems he
had followed his big brother into the glamorous but uncertain
world of the London theatres.[29] Also near by, in the parish of
St Mary Aldermanbury east of Wood Street, lived two of Shakespeare's closest colleagues in the King's Men – John Heminges
and Henry Condell, the future editors of the First Folio. A monument in the former churchyard notes that Heminges lived in the
parish 'for upward of 42 years', and Condell for over thirty;
between them they had twenty-one children baptized and ten
buried at the church, where both served as churchwardens.[30]

Thus there were fellow-writers and actors living in the vicinity, though none, it seems, living in St Olave's itself. Other than Shakespeare, Silver Street's only literary resident was a publisher, Thomas Nelson, who is described on a title-page of 1592 as 'dwelling in Silver streete, neere to the signe of the Red Crosse'. Nelson also turned his hand to writing, mostly ballads and other topical verse, and so is a minor harbinger of Shakespeare's presence. That book of 1592, a pamphlet by Shakespeare's rival Robert Greene, is his last known venture as a publisher, and he was probably one of the two Thomas Nelsons buried at St Olave's in 1594.[31] It seems the street was free of writers – a fractious trade – when Shakespeare took his lodgings here.

Turning eastwards up Silver Street towards the busy thoroughfare of Wood Street you would pass the house of Dr Giffard – he was either the Mountjoys' neighbour, or possibly next door but one. He is referred to respectfully in the registers as 'Master John Giffard, doctor of physic'. He was a Wiltshire man of about the same age as Shakespeare; his relationship to the troublesome Giffords of late Elizabethan politics – the spy Gilbert Gifford, the Catholic exile Dr William Gifford, the courtier and adventurer George Gifford – is not proven. He studied at New College, Oxford, and was licensed by the Royal College of Physicians in 1596. Like his neighbour Richard Palmer, Dr Giffard was a respected practitioner, and on 5 November 1612 we find the pair of them in august consultation at the bedside of Henry, Prince of Wales. The cordial they administered to him had no effect, for the Prince died the following day.[32]

Next door to Dr Giffard's house was Dudley Court, of which I have already given some account from Ralph Treswell's survey of it. The date of that survey is c. 1612, thus around the time of the Belott–Mountjoy litigation, but the tenant in the main part of the house, John Cowndley or Cownley, was living there at least ten years earlier and may have been known to Shakespeare. His first wife, Joan, died in the plague summer of 1603, but the following spring he was at the altar again. His wedding to

Elizabeth Greenham was on 19 April 1604; their daughter Elizabeth was baptized exactly nine months later, on 20 January 1605. These are the rhythms of parish life within a radius of yards around Shakespeare's rooms on Silver Street.

Behind Dudley Court, entered via a passageway from Wood Street, was a tavern and wine-shop called the Talbot.[33] As far as the evidence remains this was the nearest watering-hole to the Mountjoys' house. It is Shakespeare's local. He is more famously associated with the Mermaid on Bread Street – the evidence is anecdotal, but it is plausible he was among the 'sireniacall fraternitie' of wits and poets who met there, among them Ben Jonson, Francis Beaumont and Thomas Coryate; and plausible also that the William Johnson who was one of Shakespeare's sureties when he purchased the Blackfriars Gatehouse in 1613 was the man of that name who ran the Mermaid. The Talbot was not a literary club, just a run-of-the-mill tavern, which may at times be a considerable advantage. The host there was one Francis Wright. He rented the building from the Clothworkers' Company. It had formerly been a 'callendring house' – a 'calender' was a weighted box placed on top of rollers, used to press finished cloth. This mechanism was powered by horses, so the building had stables, convenient for its new use as a tavern.

Also close by was the Castle on Wood Street, but this was an inn rather than a tavern, and chiefly offered bed, board and stabling for travellers. There were many such in this neighbourhood at the edge of the city – the Axe in Aldermanbury, the Cock in Philip Lane, and most famously the Swan with Two Necks, which rambled almost the entire length of Lad Lane (now Gresham Street), an alley running east off Wood Street to the top of Milk Street. (The inn's curious name is still found in English pubs. 'Necks' was originally 'nicks': it was a privilege of vintners to keep swans, which were otherwise the preserve of the sovereign, and to distinguish them their swans had their beaks marked with two nicks.) This Swan was in business by 1556 when the diarist Henry Machyn noted that a woman had drowned herself in a well near 'the Swane with the ii Nekes at Mylke Street end'.

Around the turn of the century the innkeeper was Richard Bolton. In 1598 he delivered a quarter load of hay to 'the Muze' (the Royal Mews): these were the 'hay dues' levied from inns. The Swan survived into the nineteenth century. An engraving of 1831 shows the enormous inn-yard, with entrances on three sides, and galleried accommodation on two upper floors.[34]

These were carriers' inns – they would later be called coaching inns, but there were as yet no regular stage-coach services. Coaches were essentially covered carts, unsprung, and were not much used for longer journeys (though increasingly fashionable as an urban vehicle). The common mode of travel was on horseback, preferably in the company of the carriers, who travelled the country delivering goods and letters. In *1 Henry IV* there is a scene with two carriers, set in an inn-yard in Rochester (2.1). One has 'a gammon of bacon and two razes [roots] of ginger to be delivered as far as Charing Cross'; the other carries live turkeys in his 'pannier'. They are saddling up their horses, and waiting for certain gentlemen who 'will along with company for they have great charge' – in other words, travellers carrying valuables who will accompany the carriers for safety.

These nearby inns suggest another aspect in favour of the area in Shakespeare's mind – they are a boarding-point for travel and postage upcountry. Aubrey says, sensibly enough, that Shakespeare 'was wont to goe into his native country once a yeare', and here at Cripplegate he was well placed for the journey. The wherryman and rimester John Taylor, known as the 'Water Poet', tells us in his *Carriers Cosmographie* (1637) that the Castle Inn on Wood Street was the place to find carriers for (among other places) Worcester and Evesham.[35] This run would also serve Stratford, branching off north after Oxford (where Shakespeare was reputed to stay at the Davenants' tavern, the Crown).

The well-known Stratford carrier was William Greenaway. It is likely Shakespeare had accompanied him on journeys to and from London, but he did so no longer, for Greenaway retired or died around 1601. On one occasion he carried up to Stratford a letter referring to Shakespeare. Its recipient replied, 'Yr letter of the 25 October [1598] came to mi handes the laste of the same att night, per Grenwai, which imported that our countryman Mr Wm. Shak. would procure us money.' In that case the letter took up to six days to reach its destination, but perhaps there were particular delays. The customary journey-time from London to Stratford (just under a hundred miles) was three days. For a horse for the journey Greenaway charged 5 shillings.[36]

At Wood Street one met the noise and bustle of a large London street. I have referred to the modern London Wall as a 'traffic-road', and that is exactly what Jacobean Wood Street was. And together with the travellers' inns and their transitory population were other associated amenities. The first turning left off Wood Street as you walked south was an alley called Love Lane – 'so called of wantons', Stow says, which presumably means sex was on sale there. (Another Love Lane, in Billingsgate, had a 'stuehous' or stew-house in it: though technically a steam-room, this invariably means a brothel.)[37] It is a discreet presence, perhaps – this was not a red-light district like the notorious Clerkenwell, to the north of the city walls, or indeed Southwark across the river, where the theatres stood cheek by jowl with 'bawdy houses'.

Further down Wood Street, nearing the great commercial hub of Cheapside, stood another monument to the seamier side of Jacobean life – the Wood Street Counter, one of various prisons in the city known as Counters or Compters. Others were in Bread Street, Poultry, and Southwark. These were primarily (but not exclusively) debtors' prisons; chronic insolvents could live there for years. A charitable bequest of 1592 provides for the relief of 'poore Prisoners in the Hole or Twopenny Wardes' of the Counters. These were the two lowest, darkest 'wards' or quarters of the prison. Posher prisoners were accommodated in relative comfort in the Master's Ward and the Knights' Ward.[38] It was not as dire in underworld lore as the 'Limboes' in Newgate, or the 'Pit' and the 'Little Ease' at the Tower, but life in the Hole cannot have been pleasant. The one at the Poultry Counter was less than 20 feet square, and sometimes held more than forty inmates. The prisons were notorious for their smell – 'To walk by the Counter gate', says Falstaff in the *Merry Wives*, 'is as hateful to me as the reek of a lime-kill' (3.3.71–3). This stench contrasts in Shakespeare's mind with the finest of London smells, mentioned by Falstaff a few lines earlier – 'Bucklersbury in simple time', Bucklersbury being a street full of grocers and apothecaries, and 'simple time' being spring and early summer when medicinal herbs ('simples') were on sale there.

This was Shakespeare's London habitat – or one of them – in the first years of King James. We find it a leafy neighbourhood, with secretive walled gardens. Birdsong mingles with the noises of trade, the aroma of medicinal herbs vies with chimney-smoke, cooking-smells and cesspits. We note the area's association with doctors and surgeons and the macabre arts of anatomy. We scent prosperity – goldsmiths and usurers and grave-looking guildsmen on their way to the livery hall. Shakespeare lodges in a quiet, well-to-do street, an urban backwater, though as always in London you were not far from the more pungent life of the city: the taverns and inn-yards of Wood Street, the girls down Love Lane, the penury of the Hole at the Counter.

And between the upper and lower echelons of the neighbourhood there is the middle rank of tradesmen, artisans and servants who perhaps give more acurately the tone of this rather middling London parish. We get a blueprint of trades carried on in the parish from the burial register. In the plague year of 1603 – whether by coincidence, or because of the sudden spate of mortalities – the vicar John Flint decided to add the extra information of a trade to the names of adult males being buried. Living (or at any rate dying) in the parish during the ten years 1603–12 were: Henry Sandon, minstrel; John Smith, porter at Barbers' Hall; William Linby, painter; John Hely, weaver; Richard Lardinge, tailor; Anthony Spenser, cook; William Burton, needlemaker; William Lightwoode, scrivener; John Browne, scrivener; Nicholas Sharpe, porter; John Dodson, scrivener; Nicholas Cooke, pewterer; William Tailer, embroiderer; William Allen, jeweller;

William Smith, salter; William Rieve, salter; Roger Turner, saddler; Richard Roberts, clothworker; and John Walker, porter.

Of these forgotten people who lived in Shakespeare's vicinity there is one who might be shown to have had some kind of interaction with him – the embroiderer William Tailer or Tailor. He may have known the Mountjoys in a professional context: their tire-business required a supply of embroidered work. On 1 December 1605 a daughter of Tailor's was baptized at St Olave's. She was christened Cordelia.[39] The name – spelt thus in the register – was still unusual, and was more often found in the Celtic form, Cordula (or Cordell). The most famous Cordelia, of course, is the fictional one – the daughter of King Lear. The Tailors could not yet have seen or read the play: it was first performed in 1606, and first printed in 1608. Just possibly they got the name from the author himself, lodged around the corner and then at work on the play – asked him, sensibly enough, for a nice name for their new daughter, and received from him the beautiful gift of Cordelia.

7

'Houshould stuffe'

O ne of the few compensations for the obliteration of Silver Street and its environs is that the area has been thoroughly studied by archaeologists. Most of the excavation took place in the 1950s, under the aegis of W. F. Grimes, Keeper of the London Museum. His work, done before the wholesale redevelopment of the area, has been supplemented by more recent, small-scale digs under Elizabeth Howe and David Lakin.[40] Finds relating to the sixteenth and seventeenth centuries are sparse, because this stratum was disturbed during the Victorian era, when cellars and basements were dug beneath existing properties. The sparseness of evidence may also relate to the social status of the area, for it suggests that most household rubbish was hauled away, rather than dumped in the yards behind properties – a desirable state of affairs for the Jacobean resident but disappointing to the later archaeologist.

Two sites have been excavated just to the south of Silver Street, one between St Olave's churchyard and Oat Lane, and the other near the churchyard of St Mary Staining.[41] Most of the finds that belong at least broadly to our period are the usual relics – shards of pottery, including bowls, jugs, cups, cauldrons and cooking-pots. The pottery is of various kinds popular in the city – 'post mediaeval redware' (fired from clay with a high presence of iron, giving it a reddish-brown tinge), 'Tudor green ware', 'Cheam whiteware' and 'coarse border ware' originating from the Surrey–Hampshire border. But among these fragments were found some objects which offer a more intimate glimpse of

71

daily life in this corner of Cripplegate – a knife with a spirally decorated bone handle; a tobacco pipe; a porringer; and, in the back-fill of a brick-lined pit, a complete seventeenth-century chamber-pot.

There was also found some imported ware – two stoneware drinking jugs, one from the famous kilns of Raeren in eastern Belgium; and, more unusually, a small bowl in Valencian lustre-ware, decorated in blue and copper lustre with motifs suggestive of Arab calligraphy – a flicker of exotic colour in a sombre Cripplegate interior.

Another interesting discovery was part of an alembic, or, as Shakespeare spells it in *Macbeth*, a 'limbeck'. This was a vessel used in distillation: a domed container with a long spout near the rim. Its presence could be connected with metal-working in the area, or possibly with the medical profession. The use of distillation and sublimation in preparing medicines was part of the controversial new 'chymicall physick' proposed by the followers of the German mystic and healer Paracelsus – mercury preparations for syphilis were especially popular.[42] An alembic was also an essential part of the alchemist's laboratory.

Also suggestive is the skeleton of a female peregrine falcon, found in a stone-lined cesspit off Oat Lane. The peregrine – 'the most spectacular and prestigious bird used in falconry' – is an indicator of high status. Elsewhere were found remains of a goshawk and three sparrowhawks. These were birds kept for hunting and sport – the open land beyond the city walls was used for falconry. Shakespeare was knowledgeable about hawking (as about so much else), and deploys his knowledge in over forty separate images in his plays, as in the marvellous lines from *Othello* likening an unfaithful wife to a 'haggard' or untrained falcon –

> If I do prove her haggard,
> Though that her jesses were my dear heart-strings,
> I'd whistle her off and let her down the wind
> To prey at fortune. (3.3.264–7)

*

These random relics come from the kitchens, bedrooms, work-shops and bird-roosts of houses close to Silver Street, at a time close to Shakespeare's residence there. We could guess at hundreds of other objects that might have been there, but these things were actually there. There are not very many of them, and most are only fragments, but they are authentic in the way that a guessed object – the costume-drama prop – is not.

They belong to the community of which Shakespeare was briefly a part, but they do not take us into the Mountjoy house. To cross that threshold we have to turn not to the preserved contents of the parish's tips and middens, but back once more to the papers and parchments of the Belott–Mountjoy suit. Shake-speare could not remember 'what implementes and necessaries of houshould stuffe the defendant gave the plaintiff in marriadge', but the plaintiff himself remembered well enough, and they are listed in the first set of interrogatories. We are thus privileged with a brief inventory of some of the furnishings – though by no means the best or smartest of them – in the Mountjoy house in 1604:

One old featherbed
One old feather bolster
A flock bolster
A thin green rug
Two ordinary blankets woven
Two pair sheets
A dozen of napkins of coarse diaper
Two short tablecloths
Six short towels & one long one
An old drawing table
Two old joined stools
One wainscot cupboard
One twisting wheel of wood
Two pair of little scissors
One old trunk and a like old trunk
One bobbin box

The list is precise – the furnishings go from the bedroom to the dining room to the workroom – and somewhat bitter in its phrasing: things are 'old' or 'little' or 'thin' or 'coarse', when they might have been new, large, plush and soft. Belott refers to them at one point as 'some few trifles' (deposition of Thomas Flower). The list has an agenda – how stingy the provisions of the father-in-law for the new couple setting up together – though it also offers a broader sociological point. These meagre furnishings – these few 'parcells of goodes' – convey the bareness, the unaccoutredness, of the great majority of rooms in Jacobean London.

This is lumber from the house on Silver Street – not the actual stuff in Shakespeare's rooms, but something very similar: the featherbed, the green rug, the wainscot cupboard.

8

The chamber

We are almost at the door of Mr Shakespeare's 'chamber' – the habitual word of the day for a person's private room or rooms – but for what lies the other side we must resort once more to guesswork and generalization. I do not want to mock up a room full of early-Jacobean furnishings (and anyway early-Jacobean rooms were not exclusively filled with early-Jacobean furniture) but it may be instructive to look into some furnished rooms through the eyes of contemporary writers and artists.

We have a vivid description of a professional writer's lodgings, published in 1604. The lodgings are unlike Shakespeare's in that the writer described is a down-and-out pamphleteer, 'Pierce Pennyless' (a fictionalized version of the late Thomas Nashe, author of *Pierce Penniless*), and the passage is a vignette of squalor in a rented room in London's Pickt-hatch. But the author of the passage is Thomas Middleton, soon to embark on his collaboration with Shakespeare, and on the principle of proximity it seems a good place to start. Pruned of its foliage of extended comic similes it gives the following account of visiting Pierce's chamber –

I stumbled up two pairs of stairs in the dark, but at last caught in mine eyes the sullen blaze of a melancholy lamp that burnt very tragically upon the narrow desk of a half bedstead . . . The bare privities of the stone walls were hid with two pieces of painted cloth, but so ragged and tottered that one might have seen all nevertheless . . . The testern or shadow over the bed was made of four ells of cobwebs, and a number of small spinners' ropes hung down for curtains . . . The coverlet was made of pieces a' black cloth clapt together . . . On this miserable bed's head lay the old copy of his Supplication [*Pierce Penniless*] in foul-written hand.[43]

In this exaggerated but essentially realistic interior shot of a writer's chamber we see a bed, a fold-down desk, a wick-lamp, and some 'painted cloth' hanging over an unplastered wall. One notes that even in these forsaken circumstances the bed is expected to be a four-poster, with a canopy ('testern') and curtains, though in Pierce's case these are formed entirely of cobwebs. Another writer who dodged in and out of debtors' prison was Thomas Dekker, and we have an actual picture of him in bed – a woodcut of 1620 illustrating his pamphlet, *Dekker his Dreame* (see Plate 11). It shows a bearded man in a nightcap with an upturned brim; the bed is again a four-poster, with a simple wood-framed canopy, heavy-looking curtains, and sturdy rather than elaborate posts. This is not, of course, Dekker's bed, but it is the type of bed which a contemporary artist envisaged him as having.

The four-poster nowadays is given a rather rakish, aristocratic air, and one can forget how very practical it was. It offered warmth in winter and protection from flying insects in summer, and its enclosure made it a kind of compartment, a moveable bedroom within a larger multi-use room: the Jacobean bed-sit. On such a bed Othello suffocates Desdemona – 'Soft, by and by, let me the curtains draw' – and in such a bed lie the lovers importuned by daylight in Donne's 'The Sun Rising':

> Busie old foole, unruly sunne,
>   why dost thou thus
> Through windowes and through curtaines call on us?[44]

Shakespeare no doubt slept in one in his room at Silver Street, 'cribbed' and 'confined' but not unpleasantly so, though we do not know if his nights in this musty cocoon were always peaceful – 'I could be bound in a nutshell and count myself a king of infinite space, were it not that I have bad dreams' (*Hamlet*, 2.2.255–7)

– or if sleep always came easily to him: 'My thoughts . . . keep my drooping eyelids open wide, Looking on darkness' (Sonnet 27). Nor do we know if he always slept there alone. That he was entirely faithful – in other words, celibate – during his long absences in London seems improbable, and some contemporary anecdotes suggest he was not.

Here are two 'chambers' visualized by Shakespeare. The first is brief – Sir John Falstaff's room at the Garter Inn in Windsor, as described by the innkeeper: 'There's his chamber, his house, his castle, his standing-bed and truckle-bed. 'Tis painted about with the story of the Prodigal, fresh and new' (*Merry Wives*, 4.5.5–7). Again the four-poster, together with a smaller camp-bed ('truckle' means on wheels) for a servant. The paintings featuring the story of the Prodigal Son could be wall-hangings or bed-curtains. In Middleton's *Mad World* (*c.* 1605), the same story is embroidered on the bed-curtains in Sir Bounteous Progress's guest-bedroom, where the bed has 'cambric sheets', a 'cloth o' tissue canopy' and curtains 'wrought in Venice with the story of the Prodigal Child in silk and gold' (2.2.4–6).

There is more detail in Imogen's well-appointed 'bed-chamber', viewed furtively by the flame of a taper by the wicked Iachimo in *Cymbeline* (*c.* 1609). It is a woman's chamber, but Shakespeare's visualizing is itself interesting:

To note the chamber – I will write all down:
Such and such pictures, there the window, such
The adornment of her bed, the arras, figures,
Why, such and such, and the contents o' th' story . . . (2.2.24–7)

The scene is nominally set in Roman Britain, but the room is in all aspects Jacobean. The 'adornment' of the bed is once again the canopy and curtains of the four-poster. The 'arras' is a wall-hanging, named after the northern French weaving town of Arras. This particular one is later specified as a 'tapestry of silk and silver', and the 'story' represented in it is 'proud Cleopatra when she met her Roman' (i.e. Antony, thus discreetly plugging a recent Shakespeare production). An arras is distinct from the 'painted cloths' that hang in Pierce's dingy chamber – its design is woven rather than painted – but serves the same basic need to cover the 'bare privities' of untreated interior walls. In *Merry Wives* an arras hangs in the Fords' parlour, and serves as a hiding-place for Falstaff – 'I will ensconce me behind the arras.' Characters hide behind one in *Much Ado* ('I whipt me behind the arras'), and fall asleep behind one in *1 Henry IV*. Most famously, Hamlet hears 'something stir' behind the arras, and stabs at it crying, 'A rat! A rat!', thus killing the eavesdropping Polonius. That to fit unseen behind an arras is considered credible, even for the corpulent Falstaff, confirms what common sense suggests, that these tapestries were hung from the ceiling or from brackets, rather than attached to the wall, leaving air-space – and a hiding-place for rats or snoops – behind.

Iachimo also notes the fireplace in Imogen's chamber, with its 'figures' carved on the chimney-piece, and a pair of silver andirons or firedogs sculpted in the form of 'two winking Cupids'. It is a key feature of his description – it orientates the room ('the chimney is south the chamber'); its accoutrements are more noticeable than the pictures on the wall, which are mentioned but not described. The fireplace was the heart (or 'hearth', originally synonymous) of a room: the defence against the enemies of cold and damp. Damp – on the walls, in the air, in the bed – was one of the elements Englishmen lived in; colds, catarrhs and 'rheums' were chronic.

To the bed, the wall-hangings and the fireplace we must add two further items of furniture necessary to the writer – a desk or table, and a chair. A woodcut of the pamphleteer Robert Greene shows him writing at a table covered with a cloth, on which rest an ink-well (or 'standish'), a paper-knife and a mysterious object which could either be a dust-box (for sprinkling powder over wet ink) or a fat book with a clasped binding. The woodcut is fanciful – it shows the 'ghost' of Greene, complete with shroud – but is useful for its casual enumeration of the tools of the writer's trade. He sits on a straight-backed wooden chair with curved arms, not very comfortable looking. According to Aubrey, Ben

Jonson favoured something with more give in it – 'I have seen his studyeing chaire, which was of strawe, such as olde woemen used.'[45]

If commodious by the standards of the day, the room was doubtless low ceilinged and ill lit, so I mentally place the writing-desk close to a window, and then immediately start wondering what the window looks out on to. Do we look down into the Mountjoys' backyard, or out across the roofs and chimneys of Silver Street? Do we see pleasant suburban treetops? From a high window there might be a view down to the garden of Dudley Court, shown in the Treswell survey, or to Lord Windsor's walled garden to the west. Perhaps one of these gave him the features of Angelo's garden in *Measure for Measure* – 'A garden circummur'd with brick, / Whose western side is with a vineyard back'd'. There is a 'planched gate' into the vineyard, and then a more secretive 'little door / Which from the vineyard to the garden leads' (4.1.28–33). In the dramatic context this is certainly a town-garden he is describing, and it is plausible that the lines were written in his room on Silver Street in 1604.

On Shakespeare's desk, and round about it, there are books, manuscripts and notebooks, 'foul papers' and 'fair copies': the comfortable loam of literature. There is a traditional view of Shakespeare as a thoroughly unbookish sort of writer: intuitive, flowing, 'natural', drawing his material from life rather than books – 'Sweetest Shakespeare, Fancy's child' who 'warble[s] his native wood-notes wild' (John Milton, 'L'Allegro'). This view was contemporary with him and must to some extent be based on truth. 'His mind and hand went together,' wrote the editors of the First Folio, Heminges and Condell, who knew as much about his working methods as any, 'and what he thought he uttered with that easinesse that we have scarce received from him a blot in his papers.' This is the famous comment, but an earlier version of the same idea is found in a verse-letter by Francis Beaumont, written in about 1615 – thus during Shakespeare's lifetime:

> Here I would let slip
> (If I had any in me) scholarship,
> And from all learning keep these lines as clear
> As Shakespeare's best are, which our heirs shall hear
> Preachers apt to their auditors to show
> How far sometimes a mortal man may go
> By the dim light of Nature.[46]

The idea of Shakespeare's 'natural' style was enshrined early in the mythos, but in a contrary movement scholars have, at least since the eighteenth century, been patiently unpicking this fabric of native wit to disclose the many threads of 'learning', or at any rate reading, that went into it. Shakespeare was a voracious, though probably – like most creative writers – an opportunist, reader. He read for what he needed as often as for pleasure.

In 1604 Shakespeare's bookshelf – a metaphorical item of furniture, which in the convention of the time would more likely be one or more book-chests – contained the customary mix of old favourites and new purchases or borrowings. Among the former were the works of the Roman poet Ovid, who might be claimed as Shakespeare's favourite author, and especially the sleek, evocative legends of the *Metamorphoses*. From this Shakespeare took the story of Venus and Adonis, the subject of his first published poem, and Pyramis and Thisbe in *A Midsummer Night's Dream*, and much else. In his early tragedy, *Titus Andronicus*, the book is named as a young boy's reading, the title perfectly forming the back half of an iambic pentameter –

> TITUS: What book is that . . . ?
> LUCIUS: Grandsire, 'tis Ovid's *Metamorphoses*:
>   My mother gave it me . . . (4.1.41–3)

And in *Cymbeline* it is the book Iachimo finds by Imogen's bedside:

> She hath been reading late:
> The tale of Tereus – here the leaf's turn'd down . . . (2.2.44–5).

Shakespeare was still turning the leaves of the *Metamorphoses* at the end of his career. Writing Prospero's valediction to the spirits in *The Tempest* (c. 1610) he had before him the incantations of the sorceress Medea. In the standard 1567 translation by Arthur Golding the passage begins:

> Ye airs and winds, ye elves of hills, of brooks, of woods alone,
> Of standing lakes, and of the night, approach ye everychone,
> Through help of whom (the crooked banks much wondering at the
>   thing)
> I have compelled streams to run clean backward to their spring.
>
> (*Metamorphoses* 7.197–200)

Shakespeare writes:

> Ye elves of hills, brooks, standing lakes and groves,
> And ye that on the sands with printless foot
> Do chase the ebbing Neptune, and do fly him
> When he comes back . . . (5.1.33–6)

Comparisons like this are a master-class. His first line is almost straight plagiarism, but then comes the airy elaboration of the next lines, transforming the archaic 'fourteeners' of Golding's Ovid to the litheness and fluency of Shakespeare's late blank verse. Some details of the speech show that he also used the original text of the poem, employing his skills in Latin, which Jonson perhaps under-estimated, or deliberately undervalued, when he spoke of Shakespeare's 'small Latin and less Greek'.[47]

Also much thumbed is his copy of Plutarch's *Lives*, in Sir Thomas North's vigorous English version: the first edition was 1579, but perhaps the edition in Shakespeare's chest was that of 1595, published by his old Stratford friend Richard Field. He first used North's Plutarch extensively for *Julius Caesar*, which opened the new Globe theatre in 1599. The Life of Mark Antony was of particular interest, and as he read it for *Caesar* other stories were lit on the back burner – not just Antony and Cleopatra but also Timon, whose life is sketched there *en passant*. Another trusty was Raphael Holinshed's *Chronicles* (1587), the mother-lode of

Shakespeare's history plays, not much consulted of late but soon to be of use again in its account of the reign of an eleventh-century Scottish king, Macbeth.

Two books published in 1603 are soon to be found on his desk. One is an exposé of supposed exorcisms performed by Catholic priests, unsnappily titled *A Declaration of Egregious Popish Impostures . . . under the pretence of casting out devils, practised by Edmunds alias Weston a Jesuit, and divers Romish priests his wicked associates*. Its author, Samuel Harsnett, was rector of St Margaret's on New Fish Street Hill, and chaplain to the Bishop of London (and thereby involved in the licensing of books for the press). Some think Shakespeare's interest in it relates to his own involvement in the clandestine Catholic world of the Midlands, but I would relate it more to authorial opportunism. He found in Harsnett's tract an arcane and archaic language of religious mania, which proved decisive in one of his strangest and greatest stage-creations, the possessed beggar 'Poor Tom' in *King Lear*. Many of the demons and familiars invoked by Tom – Flibberti-gibbet, Smulkin, Modo, Mahu, Hoppedance, Obidicut and the rest – come straight from the pages of Harsnett.[48]

Also published in 1603 was an influential book which reflects and perhaps partly inspires the questioning temper of the problem plays or tragicomedies. This was the handsome folio edition of the *Essays* of Michel de Montaigne, translated from the French by John Florio. The Montaigne motto, 'Que scays-je' – 'What do I know?', as distinct, perhaps, from 'What do I erroneously assume that I know?' – echoes through these plays, which interrogate and indeed 'assay' (the original sense of the Montaignian 'essai') the philosophical and ethical assumptions of the age. Isabella's words in *Measure* are an attenuated echo of this motto – 'Go to your bosom, / Knock there, and ask thy heart what it doth know' (2.2.137–8).

Shakespeare doubtless knew the translator Florio, twelve years his senior, Italian by blood but English born – a brilliant linguist, a prickly and proud figure. They may have met in the circle of the young Earl of Southampton, to whom Shakespeare dedicated two poems in 1593–4. Florio was a tutor to the Earl in the early 1590s. It is sometimes said that the pedant Holofernes in *Love's Labour's Lost* is a caricature of Florio, done for the enjoyment of the Southampton set – this overstates the case, but it is true Holofernes quotes from Florio's book of Italian proverbs, the *Gardine of Recreations* (1591).[49] At any rate, Florio is a man Shakespeare knows – for a writer in Jacobean London there is this dimension of acquaintance in his reading. The literary circuit was small and crowded; they knew one another's voices.

His reading of Montaigne seeps identifiably into the Silver Street tragicomedies. 'To embrace all the rules of our life into one', writes Montaigne, 'is at all times to will, and not to will, one same thing.' This is the shuttling, contradictory mentality of *Measure for Measure*, in which characters find themselves 'at war 'twixt will and will not'. And when Montaigne observes that 'Man all in all is but a botching and party-coloured work,' and that 'the best good I have hath some vicious taint', we hear a foretaste of the famous line in *All's Well*, 'The web of our life is of a mingled yarn, good and ill together.' The plays' shifts of tone and uncertainties of message reflect Montaigne's drastic disclaimer, 'I have nothing to say, entirely, simply and with solidity of myself, without confusion, disorder, blending, mingling.'[50]

Shakespeare read Florio's Montaigne, and may well have owned a copy, but if he did it is not the copy now in the British Library which bears on the verso of the endpaper the signature 'Willm Shakspere'. This is now held to be a forgery, though a competent one, probably dating from the late eighteenth century.[51]

Some other books which might be seen in his room on Silver Street include Richard Knolles's *History of the Turkes* (1603), used in *Othello* for detail about the Turkish invasion of Cyprus; George Whetstone's *Promos and Cassandra* (1578) and Cinthio's *Epitia* (1583), both sources of *Measure for Measure*; and an unspecified Latin edition of the works of Lucian containing the story of 'Timon the Misanthrope', originally written in Greek in the second century AD.

The chief narrative source of *All's Well* was a story from Boccaccio's *Decameron*. Shakespeare used an English translation of the story, found in William Painter's *Palace of Pleasure* (1566), a popular collection of tales. But linguistic traces suggest that for this French-set play Shakespeare also made use of a French version of the *Decameron* by Antoine de Maçon, published in 1545 and frequently reprinted.[52] The textual evidence is not conclusive, but Shakespeare's presence in a French household makes it plausible – perhaps it was a book owned by one of the Mountjoys.

Amid this small jumble of books one might note also a pair of publications, dated 1603 and 1604 – not de-luxe editions like the Montaigne folio, but rather shoddily printed quartos. The earlier of the two title-pages reads: 'THE / Tragicall Historie of / HAMLET / *Prince of Denmarke* / By William Shake-speare. / As it hath beene diverse times acted by his Highnesse ser- / vants in the Cittie of London: as also in the two U- / niversities of Cambridge and Oxford, and else-where.' This book, 'printed for N.L [Nicholas Ling] and Iohn Trundell', is the first edition of *Hamlet*. It is nowadays generally known as the 'bad quarto' (or to bibliographers, 'Q1'). It was swiftly supplanted by the 'good quarto' of 1604 ('Q2'), which is described on the title-page as 'Newly imprinted and enlarged to almost as much againe as it was, according to the true and perfect Coppie'. The latter is the play we know: the text in the First Folio ('F1') is based on it. The earlier quarto has some interesting variations, but is generally a corrupt or impoverished text, drained of much of the complex poetry and quick philosophical skirmishing which are the hallmarks of *Hamlet*. Thus Q1's version of the Prince's best-known soliloquy begins:

> To be or not to be, I there's the point.
> To die, to sleepe, is that all? I all:
> No, to sleepe, to dreame, I mary there it goes . . .

To the casual reader this may look like gibberish. It is not – 'I' was a common spelling of 'aye' – but it is clearly an inferior version of the soliloquy. The language is blunted ('there it goes' instead of 'there's the rub') and the speech is drastically truncated by the loss of seven famous lines (which should come immediately after the first), beginning 'Whether 'tis nobler in the mind to suffer . . .', and ending with that wonderful synopsis of the human condition – 'The heart-ache and the thousand natural shocks / That flesh is heir to' (3.1.58–65).

Of course, to say that Q1 has truncated a speech which 'should' be longer and richer is already to make assumptions about the relation of the two quartos. The standard hypothesis is that Q1 is a 'memorial reconstruction' by an actor who had performed in the play (possibly the one playing Marcellus). An alternative theory is that it represents an early version of the play by Shakespeare himself, with Q2 a later rewrite. There certainly was an earlier *Hamlet* (sometimes called, with a professorial twinkle, the 'Ur-*Hamlet*'). It is referred to punningly by Nashe as early as 1589 – 'he will afford you whole Hamlets, I should say handfuls, of tragical speeches' – and a performance was seen by the author Thomas Lodge at one of the Shoreditch playhouses some time before 1596.[53]

These textual mysteries make it hard to know the status of the 1603 quarto in Shakespeare's mind, but that he was irritated by its publication seems inevitable. Whether the product of an amnesiac actor or of Shakespeare's own rougher skills in his prentice-years, the text was purloined and the publication of it unauthorized. It is one of various piracies of Shakespeare play-scripts – plays such as *Romeo and Juliet* and *The Merry Wives* first appeared in corrupt editions. The supplanting of such texts was one of the guiding editorial principles of the First Folio: 'Where before you were abus'd with diverse stolne and surreptitious copies, maimed and deformed by the frauds and stealthes of iniurious imposters that expos'd [published] them, even those are now offered to your view cur'd and perfect in their limbes.'

This indignation at rapacious publishers was likely shared by Shakespeare himself. There are two reported instances of him in a temper with someone, and in each case the cause is a publication. The first, already mentioned, is the spat with Henry Chettle in 1592, further to the slurs against 'Shakescene' in *Greene's Groatsworth*. The second followed the publication of a poetry collection, *The Passionate Pilgrim*, in 1599. The title-page announced it as 'by W. Shakespeare', though only five of the poems in it were his, two of them previously unpublished sonnets and all of them printed without permission. The publisher was William Jaggard. The existence of Shakespeare's 'sugared sonnets among his private friends' had been mentioned in print the previous year, and this may have sharpened Jaggard's appetite. Shakespeare's reaction is recorded by Thomas Heywood in 1612, when a new edition of *The Passionate Pilgrim* was published, still 'by' Shakespeare – 'The author I know much offended with Mr Jaggard that (altogether unknown to him) presumed to make so bold with his name'.[54]

Publishers, said the poet Michael Drayton, 'are a company of base knaves whom I both scorn and kick at', and perhaps there were times when Shakespeare thought the same.[55] Ironically, it was the piratical Mr Jaggard who was one of the prime movers of the posthumous First Folio, and we might think he has thereby made amends for his earlier 'boldness' with Shakespeare's name. The Folio includes eighteen previously unpublished plays – among them masterpieces like *Macbeth*, *Twelfth Night* and *The Tempest* – which might otherwise have been lost for ever.

PART THREE

The Mountjoys

HELENA: *Which is the Frenchman?*
DIANA: *He – that with the plume.*
          All's Well that Ends Well, 3.5.77–8

9
Early years

We have an idea of Shakespeare's habitat in these years in Cripplegate – the furnished room, the businesslike street, the neighbours whose faces he knew, the mansions split up into tenements, the little parish church with its peal of bells – but we have so far only a passing acquaintance with the most important figures in this landscape: the family he lived with. What is their story, and how does it come to intersect with Shakespeare's?

Of the Mountjoys' origins there is only fragmentary information. We know where Christopher Mountjoy was born but not when, and we know when Marie Mountjoy was born but not where.

In his act of 'denization' or naturalization (of which more later) Christopher is described as 'a subject of the French King and born in the town of Cressey'.[1] 'Cressey' is presumably the English clerk's spelling of Crécy. There is more than one Crécy in France, but most probably Mountjoy was from Crécy-en-Ponthieu. This is certainly the Crécy that Englishmen had heard of, being the site of the famous battle of 26 August 1346, when Edward III's English archers routed the French army during the Hundred Years War. It lies in Picardie, in north-western France, in the fertile flatlands of the lower Somme, which flows into the English Channel about 12 miles west of it. Mountjoy calls it a 'town' (or perhaps this is the clerk's phrasing) but today it is little more than a large village, population about 1,500.

No record of the birth of Christophe Montjoi or Montjoie is to be found in the *registres d'état civil* for Crécy-en-Ponthieu, but the sixteenth-century registers are by no means complete.[2] For reasons I will give a little later it is likely he was born in the mid-1550s or early 1560s.

Various larger market-towns and trading centres were within easy reach of Crécy. The nearest was Abbeville, 10 miles away, but the most important one was Amiens, the regional capital of Picardie, famed for its Gothic cathedral (the largest in France) and its medieval water-gardens, Les Hortillonnages. Amiens was a centre for clothworking, part of that densely populated belt of northern France and Flanders which produced high-quality textiles: wool, cotton, silk and linen. In the 1593 'Return of Strangers', a detailed listing of foreigners in London, there are twenty-five immigrants from Amiens, living in fourteen households. All of those whose employment is given are clothworkers – the majority are silk-weavers; there are also two 'taffety-weavers', a silk-winder and a silk-twister, a dyer and a bobbin-maker. Another nearby town was Arras, famous for those embroidered hangings. From here came more silk-weavers, two wool-combers and a feltmaker.[3]

Christopher Mountjoy's future trade of tiremaking is grounded in the textile industry of his native Picardie. He doubtless served an apprenticeship, though we do not know where or in what. The creation of a head-tire involved various craft skills, among them silk-twisting, threadmaking, wire-drawing and embroidery. It also involved wigmaking, and I note the name Montois or Montoyes – possibly a variation of Montjoie – in a seventeenth-century list of *maîtres perruquiers* (master-wigmakers) in Amiens.[4]

The name could be of Norman origin, connected with the town of Montjoie in La Manche. But William Arthur's *Etymological Dictionary of Family and Christian Names* suggests a grander origin – that it may have been adopted by a French crusader, recalling a mountain near Jerusalem, which (according to that mysterious medieval globetrotter Sir John Mandeville) 'men clepen Mount-Joye, for it gevethe joye to pilgrymes hertes, because that there men seen first Jerusalem'. Arthur also suggests a military connection, for in old French dictionaries 'mont-joie' is defined as 'a heap of stones made by a French army, as a monument of victory'. Another authority tells us that 'Montjoy St Denis!' was 'the French king's war cry'.[5] Related to this, perhaps, is the fact that Montjoi(e) was from medieval times the title of the Chief Herald of France. These military and heraldic associations may suggest that Christopher Mountjoy was a descendant or offshoot of a family of substance.

In Shakespeare's *Henry V* the French herald is indeed called 'Montjoy':

> *A tucket sounds. Montjoy approaches.*
> MONTJOY: You know me by my habit [uniform].
> KING: Well then, I know thee: what shall I know of thee?
>
> KING: What is thy name? I know thy quality.
> MONTJOY: Montjoy.
> KING: Thou dost thy office fairly. (3.6.111–12, 135–7)

Some biographers have wondered about this, but as there is a purely historical reason for the name, it is hard to argue any in-joke reference to Christopher Mountjoy. There is also Shakespeare's own statement that he first knew Mountjoy in about 1602, which makes it unlikely, *prima facie*, that he referred to him in a play performed three years earlier. On the other hand, it is possible to know *of* someone without having actually met them. It is in general worth remembering that Shakespeare's statement in the Court of Requests refers only to his acquaintance with Christopher. He was not asked for, and did not volunteer, any information about how long he had known other members of the household – Marie Mountjoy, for instance.

One should not discount the presence of private allusions and in-jokes in Shakespeare. Plays like *Love's Labour's Lost*, *The Merry Wives* and *Twelfth Night*, all written for specific courtly or aristocratic audiences, are full of them. In this case it is just about possible that the 'Montjoy' of *Henry V* has some ulterior reference to the real Mr Mountjoy of Silver Street, but I doubt it.

If it does, nothing much is made of it, though there was perhaps a titter at the Globe when Henry says to him, 'Thou dost thy office fairly' – a joke at the herald's expense, in that to do one's 'office' meant to go to the privy, often called the 'house of office'.

We know nothing of the origins of Marie Mountjoy. She may have been Christopher's childhood sweetheart in Picardie, or they may have met in London, in which case she could be from another part of France entirely. We do not even know for sure she was born in France – she could have been the daughter of French immigrants already settled in England.

What we do have is her approximate date of birth. According to her own statement, made to the astrologer–physician Simon Forman, she was thirty years old in November 1597. This useful precision is rendered less precise by her statement to the same doctor two weeks later that she was twenty-nine.[6] According to the laws of arithmetic at least one of these statements is false, and that one of them is false makes me wonder ungallantly if both might be slight understatements. The older of her two ages would mean she was born in 1567 or late 1566, and perhaps we might think the latter year more likely. She was thus two or three years younger than Shakespeare, and was in her mid-thirties when he became her lodger. It is worth bearing this in mind. In the biographies she is almost invariably called 'Mrs Mountjoy', which is correct and convenient, but which tends – especially in conjunction with the faintly comic overtones of 'landlady' – to give an older image of her than is right.

New evidence, shortly to be presented, shows that the Mountjoys were a married couple by 1582. Marie was then only fifteen or sixteen, so the marriage must have been quite recent (brides under fifteen are unusual at this time, though the legal minimum age was twelve).[7] They were by then living in London, so it is possible they were married there. The marriage registers of the French Church in London might have enlightened us, but they are lost – the earliest that survive date from 1600.

The approximate date of their marriage helps to define the

otherwise unknown age of Christopher Mountjoy. As he was married by 1582 he must by then have completed his apprenticeship. The conventional age to be 'freed' of apprenticeship was twenty-one – this is variable, but I would say eighteen is a practical minimum age for a married craftsman. Mountjoy was born, therefore, no later than *c.* 1564, the same year as Shakespeare. He was probably older than this, but he cannot have been that much older, as his brother Noel was born in about 1582.[8] Allowing their mother a maximum child-bearing span of twenty-five years (and assuming Noel was not a half-brother, in which case the argument collapses) we could say speculatively that Christopher was born some time between *c.* 1557 and *c.* 1564. These are porous arguments, but I have the feeling that, like Marie, Christopher is probably rather younger than the inferred picture of him given in Shakespeare biographies. There is no real warrant for Schoenbaum calling him an 'old man' at the time of the lawsuit in 1612.

10

St Martin le Grand

*T*he Mountjoys were French Protestants, or Huguenots, and their early years were clouded by the religious storms of the late sixteenth century.[9] Inspired by the teachings of John Calvin – himself from Picardie – the Protestant movement spread rapidly through France; by the early 1560s there were some 700 Calvinist churches in the country. Opposing this was the Catholic League, led by Henri, Duc de Guise, whose political programme is summed up by Christopher Marlowe: 'There shall not a Huguenot breathe in France' (*Massacre at Paris*, 1.5). Between these irreconcilable forces the Valois monarchs – Charles IX, known as *le roi morveux* (the 'brat-king'), and his eccentric brother Henri III – vacillated feebly. Civil war broke out in 1562 and continued sporadically over thirty-five years, leaving the country scarred and bankrupt. In 1589 the Huguenot leader Henri of Navarre succeeded to the throne as Henri IV. He expediently converted to Catholicism – 'Paris vaut bien une messe' ('Paris is worth a mass') – and peace was achieved in 1598 with the Edict of Nantes, promising freedom of worship to the Huguenots.

During these decades of turmoil, thousands of Huguenots fled to England where they were officially welcomed – to begin with, at least – as Protestant friends in need. They came in the wake of terrible events, most notoriously the St Bartholomew's Day Massacre of August 1572, orchestrated by the fanatical Guise and the ageing Queen Mother, Catherine de Medici – 'Madame la Serpente' – whose black-clad presence behind the throne contributes to the psychotic tone of these years. Some 2,000–3,000 died in Paris; the Seine was choked with bodies. Out in the provinces Guisard mobs and paramilitaries moved into Huguenot areas. The overall death-count is estimated at 60,000. In England this atrocity became a byword for Catholic ruthlessness, and did much to harden Elizabethan attitudes into the aggressive anti-Catholicism of the 1580s. Among the government hawks was the Secretary of State, Sir Francis Walsingham, who had been ambassador in Paris and had witnessed the bloodbath at first hand.[10]

It is sometimes said rather loosely that Christopher Mountjoy came over to England at the time of the Massacre. This is possible but there is no evidence for it. It was a peak period of immigration – there were over 7,000 aliens in London in 1573, the highest number recorded in any of the sixteenth-century censuses – but there were other lesser peaks, and a continuous trickle between them.

Whatever the precise dates and details there is this hidden chapter of emigration in the Mountjoys' story: a chapter of upheaval and trauma. They arrive in England as asylum-seekers, indeed as boat-people, crowded into one of the over-freighted little pinnaces and fishing-boats that brought the refugees across the Channel to the south-coast ports – Dover, Rye, Newhaven, Southampton. There they were processed by the immigration officers of the day – the 'searchers', whose job was to keep a 'register of men's names to & fro'[11] – and given temporary billets. Some, hopeful of an early return, stayed on or near the coast. At Southampton a Huguenot church dedicated to St Julian (patron saint of hospitable welcome) was founded near the harbour. In Dover, seventy-eight Huguenot refugees are listed as resident in the early 1560s – twenty-five were widows; most of the men were tradesmen and craftsmen, but there were also three physicians, two preachers, two schoolmasters, two advocates, two esquires and a gardener. In Canterbury, a community of Walloons – French-speakers from Flanders – were given use of the under-croft of the cathedral, first as a weaving shed, then as a school, and finally as a church. In East Anglia the immigrants were mainly

'Dutch folk', refugees from the Spanish occupation of the Netherlands. The future pamphleteer Thomas Nashe saw them as a
young boy in Lowestoft, and left a memory, unkindly phrased,
of that 'rabble rout of outlanders' which the town had to 'provant
and victual'.[12]

In London the concentrations of Huguenot settlement were in
Southwark, St Katherine's near the Tower, East Smithfield, Blackfriars and St Martin le Grand, all of them 'liberties' – areas that
remained, by quirks and relics of old monastic rule, outside the
jurisdiction of the city authorities. The precinct of St Martin le
Grand, between Aldersgate and Cheapside, was a particular
enclave – one might even call it a ghetto. In 1574 the Privy Council
expressed concern that it was filled with 'strangers, inmates and
many lewd persons to the great noise [inconvenience] to the
governors of this city'. In 1583 there were about a hundred
immigrant families in the precinct, which does not sound a lot
but it was a small area.[13] Stow reports that on the site of the
former church, demolished during the Reformation, a 'large wine
tavern' had been built, and 'many other houses ... letten to
strangers borne': he describes the strangers there as 'artificers,
buyers and sellars' – in other words, craftsmen and tradesmen.[14]
    And it is here, in the environs of St Martin le Grand, that we
find the Mountjoys in 1582. In the subsidy roll for that year, in
the parish of St Anne and St Agnes on the north side of St Martin
le Grand, is listed the following household of 'strangers' (see
Plate 13) –

John Dewman taylor [assessed on goods value] 40s
His wyfe 4d [poll tax]
Nicholas Armesford his servant 4d
Clause Valore his servant 4d
Anthonye Dewman his servant 4d
Christofer Mongey his servant 4d
—— Mongey his wyfe 4d[15]

The last pair is almost certainly Christopher and Marie Mountjoy. Foreigners' names were spelt variously and vaguely in these documents, indeed in English writings generally, and 'Mongey' for Mountjoy is typical enough. Elsewhere their name is spelt 'Mongeoy' (by a Frenchman), 'Munjoye' (by an Englishman) and 'Monioy' (in Christopher's patent for denization). The only uncertainty, it seems to me, is with the unnamed wife. It is theoretically possible she is a previous wife of Christopher's, but we have no hint of her elsewhere, and we would quite soon have to engineer her replacement by Marie, so I will work on the assumption that this is indeed Marie Mountjoy, aged about sixteen, making her first appearance on the historical record in this rather poignantly vestigial form, '—— Mongey'. The blank is standard in the document – wives are not accorded a forename – but seems to convey also a sense of her anonymity: just another foreign face in the immigrant tenements of St Martin le Grand.

We learn from this that the Mountjoys had arrived in London some time before 1 August 1582 (which is the date of the indenture of the subsidy lists). They were living with – and in the case of Christopher, at least, working for – an immigrant tailor, John Dewman. Christopher is one of four 'servants' in Dewman's workshop. 'Servant' in this context undoubtedly means assistant or apprentice. As noted, Mountjoy's marital status argues that he had completed his apprenticeship, whether in France or England, so here he is more correctly an assistant, perhaps one with specialist expertise.

The tailor John Dewman is traceable in immigrant lists: in some he is John Dueman or Duman, and once he is Hans Du Main. He was a Dutchman, born in the Gelderland town of Lochem. He had come to England in the late 1560s, and in 1577 became a 'denizen' – a naturalized foreigner, able to purchase and bequeath property: a course Mountjoy was to follow. By 1582, as the subsidy rolls show, he was living in the parish of St Anne and St Agnes, with the Mongeys or Mountjoys among his employees. His last appearance on the record is in the 1593 Return of Strangers. He is listed with his wife, who is called

'Barbaraye', and four children, the eldest a daughter of nine; business was quieter by then, for he has only one 'stranger servant'.[16]

But in the early 1580s, when the Mountjoys were working for him, Dewman was apparently doing quite well. Four 'servants' are named in the subsidy roll, but another listing of 'estraingers' in the area, dated 6 April 1583, adds two more, William Vansutfan and Thomas Henrick, both Dutchmen.[17] The same document mentions that Dewman 'payeth tribute to the Company of the Merchant Taylors'. A workshop with half a dozen workers, and associate membership in the prestigious merchant tailors' guild: these are signs of solidity.

We need not think this means the Mountjoys themselves were doing well economically. While Dewman is assessed for the subsidy at 40 shillings, doubled as an alien to £4, his employees all pay the minimum poll tax of 4d. Against the names of both the Mountjoys is the marginal notation 'aff', standing for 'affidavit'. This signifies that the tax-collectors – in this case Marmaduke Franck, cordwainer, and John Stevens, brewer, 'petty collectors' for Aldersgate ward – had declared that the tax owed was not collectable, as the person in question had 'no distrainable goods or chattels' within the ward.[18] The purpose of the affidavit was to exonerate the collectors, not the defaulting taxpayers. It seems the Mountjoys were unable or unwilling to pay the combined sum of 8d for their poll tax. There are many possible reasons for this, as there are for Shakespeare's later and rather larger defaultings, but one notes that in this earliest documentary record of him we find Christopher Mountjoy doing precisely what he does later in the case of his daughter's dowry – not paying up.

The parish of St Anne and St Agnes lay just outside the city walls, in the north-east corner of Aldersgate ward, running up to the gate itself. The church, on the north side of Pope Lane, was also known picturesquely as St Anne in the Willows, but a note in Stow's *Survay* shows this was an image from the past – 'Some say [the name is] of willowes growing thereabouts, but now there is no such voyde place for willowes to grow, more [i.e. other] than the churchyard, wherein do grow some high ashe trees.'[19] This conveys the packed-in feel of this immigrant enclave – no open ground is left.

Living there the Mountjoys were already very close to Silver Street. St Anne's Lane (now Gresham Street) ran east from St Martin le Grand into Noble Street. If they moved directly from St Anne's to the house on Silver Street it was a journey of a few hundred yards.

Christopher Mountjoy was probably not the only member of his family to emigrate to England, and in the same subsidy rolls for 1582 there is an interesting reference to 'John Mountoye, stranger' living in the parish of St Botolph's, Bishopsgate.[20] The surname is specifically French so we can take 'stranger' to mean he is a Frenchman. He may well be related to Christopher.

John Mountjoy was a fairly prosperous man: he was assessed for the 1582 subsidy on goods valued at £10. But after this promising start the trail goes cold – he is not found in other subsidy rolls, nor in the 1593 Return of Strangers, nor in the registers of St Botolph's, written in the neat hand of the former author and controversialist Stephen Gosson, who was then the vicar. The lost registers of the French Church may have contained information on him. I was about to consider this a cul-de-sac – an interesting name and no more – when I came upon another John Mountjoy, who was of immediate interest because his occupation is given as 'tiremaker'. He lived out in the rural suburb of Stepney, east of London. He is found in the lists of marriage licences: '22 November 1610, John Montjoy of Limehouse, parish of Stepney, co Middx, tiremaker, bachelor, licensed to marry Anne Blackwood of the same parish, spinster'. They were married at St Dunstan's, Stepney six days later.[21]

Was the French John Mountjoy of Bishopsgate connected to the tiremaking John Mountjoy of Stepney? It seems likely, for by 1617 the latter was living in the former's parish of St Botolph's, Bishopsgate. On 10 April 1617 'Katherin daugh[ter] of John Mountioy & Anne' was christened there. They were still in the parish in 1621, listed in the subsidy roll as 'John Mountjoy et uxor'.[22] They were assessed to pay the poll tax of 4d per head, and so were not prospering. A William Mountjoy who married at St Botolph's in 1638 may be their son.

These John Mountjoys, recorded over nearly forty years, could be the same man: an immigrant French tiremaker who moved from Bishopsgate to Stepney and then back again, who married and had children rather late in life, and whose fortunes declined. Or it could be that the Bishopsgate householder was the father of the Stepney tiremaker. Either way, a connection with Christopher is hard to resist. Tiremaking was a very specialist craft, and to find another French tiremaker with the same name suggests family kinship. Could John Mountjoy of Bishopsgate be the brother of Christopher, and John Mountjoy of Stepney his nephew?

The presence of Mountjoys in Stepney continues. There is a Robert 'Mountioye' whose sons were baptized at St Dunstan's in the early 1630s, and a Charles Mountjoy in 1688; and at the neighbouring church of St Mary, Whitechapel (also in the parish of Stepney) an Edward Mountjoy in 1660. The name continues into the nineteenth century. And in the Stepney registers we find a further scrap of confirmation that Christopher Mountjoy was connected with this clan. In 1627, seven years after his death, his widow – his second wife, Isabel, whom we have not yet met – married again. She did so at St Dunstan's in Stepney, the church where John Mountjoy the tiremaker had been married the previous decade.[23] Perhaps Isabel was out in Stepney because some of her former husband's relatives lived there.

The spiritual and social centre of the French community in London was the French Church. Some thirty years earlier, in the time of Edward VI, Protestant immigrants had been granted the use of Austinfriars on Broad Street. They worshipped in the nave in this despoiled and dilapidated church, which had belonged to an Augustinian monastery. In the early 1560s, with the dramatic rise in the number of immigrants, the congregation had to split – the Dutch continued to worship at Austinfriars, henceforth referred to as the 'Dutch Church', and the French took over the church of St Anthony's, round the corner on Threadneedle Street (or as it was then often written, Three Needles Street, probably referring to the emblem of the Needlemakers' Company). In 1568 the Dutch Church had 2,000 members, the French Church 1,800. In 1593 the two of them together (plus the very small Italian church) had 3,325 communicants.[24] There was also a Huguenot church on Leicester Fields near Westminster, now Orange Street Chapel.

A French immigrant in London had by law to be either 'of' the French Church or of his or her local parish church. This was certainly the case from 1573, when it was decreed that anyone set down as 'of no church' in the immigrant lists should be repatriated. To some extent the choice was between Calvinist strictness and Anglican laxity. The French Church was run by a council or 'consistory' of twelve elders, who watched vigilantly over the private lives as well as the religious faith of their congregation. As the registers of the Church are extant only from 1600, we do not know if Christopher and Marie were married there in the early 1580s, or if their daughter was christened there. But those life-events in the family we do know of – two funerals and a wedding – all took place at St Olave's, Silver Street. Apart from a solitary appearance as a godfather in 1603, there is no actual evidence of the Mountjoys' involvement with the French Church at all until 1612, when judgment in the Belott–Mountjoy case was referred to the elders, and we gather from their comments then that they considered Mountjoy anything but a pillar of their community.

The Mountjoys' apparent absence from the French congregation may suggest two things. First, that they were the kind of immigrants who tried to integrate into the community rather than huddle in an expatriate enclave. Second, that to describe the Mountjoys as religious refugees does not mean they were particularly religious people. To be a Protestant in France, as elsewhere, might be as much an expression of locality, or social class, or professional grouping, as of faith; and to be a refugee might mean simply that normal life had become impossible, whether from active persecution or from the chaos and corruption attendant on civil war. This was a broad distinction recognized by the English authorities. In the 1573 census of aliens in London, over a third 'confess themselves that their coming hither was only to seek work for their living'[25] – in the parlance of today, they were economic migrants rather than asylum-seekers.

Christopher Mountjoy is in many ways a typical Huguenot refugee. He comes from north-western France, as (for obvious geographical reasons) the majority of them did. He works as a specialist 'artificer' or craftsman in the clothing and fashion industry – again typical: a breakdown of occupations in the 1593 Return of Strangers shows nearly 40 per cent involved in cloth-working and clothes-making.[26] And perhaps he is typical, too, of that sizeable minority of refugees who came over to 'seek work' – or to seek a new life – rather than for particular reasons of doctrine and worship.

11

Success and danger

H ow long the Mountjoys remained with the Dutch tailor Dewman is not known: for the rest of the 1580s their movements are obscure. There were tiremaking businesses in St Martin le Grand – a Frenchman named Morell and a Dutchman, Jonakyn Swanston, are recorded there as 'attyre-makers' – and perhaps the Mountjoys had a connection with one or other of them before setting up shop on their own.[27] The only event we can be certain of at this time is the birth of their daughter, Mary, though the date remains approximate. In 1582, Marie Mountjoy was about sixteen and recently married: this seems the earliest reasonable date for the birth of Mary. At the other end of the range, Mary was herself marriageable in 1604, so cannot have been born much after 1589. When Shakespeare took up residence at Silver Street she was perhaps in her late teens, at the most twenty-one.

The tenor of these years must be hard work and improving horizons, for by the 1590s – if not before – Christopher is an independent tiremaker, with his own workshop and apprentices. He is upwardly mobile. Perhaps there was some money around to help them – if I am right about the consanguinity of John Mountjoy of Bishopsgate, there was. There is also some luck, in that their specialist skills were increasingly in demand, as head-tiring became more fashionable, elaborate and expensive in the 1590s and 1600s. But one might also call this business acumen. Tiremaking is a nebulous sort of craft, because the 'tire' itself comes in many shapes and styles, and with many combinations of materials and effects. It is a creation more than a garment.

Thus the successful tiremaker proposes as much as reflects a fashion style – like a 'great and original writer', who (as Wordsworth says) 'must himself create the taste by which he is to be relished'.

Christopher Mountjoy does not on the whole get a good press, and this book will not do much to rehabilitate him. But one thing is clear – he was a brilliant craftsman and designer. The head-dresses that issued from his workshop were fit for a queen – a cheesy metaphor, but literally true in 1604, when Queen Anne's purchases of some Mountjoy creations are recorded in her accounts.

One also applauds the Mountjoys' success in the fashion world because of the pressures and obstacles they faced as 'strangers' setting up business in London. In late-Elizabethan London you might hear the same resentments towards immigrants that are expressed today – they took houses and jobs away from the local population; they were flooding in so numerously that they threatened 'our way of life'; they did not attempt to integrate. 'They are a commonwealth within themselves,' complained a group of petitioning Londoners in 1571. 'They keep themselves severed from us in church, in government, in trade, in language and marriage.'[28]

For the government the tide of immigration brought a mix of problems and benefits. The Tudor authorities' primary instinct was control – to keep tabs on this potentially destabilizing influx. The immigrant censuses or returns are an expression of this: there were at least ten drawn up in London between 1562 and 1593. There were also proposals for a 'free-hosting' scheme, with local citizens made officially responsible for foreigners in a neighbourhood. 'Strangers ought not to take any lodgings or houses within the city,' it was argued, 'but to abide at the tables of freehosts, and to dwell in noe other place but with the said hostes to be assigned.' But the government was also conscious of the benefits brought by the immigrants – primarily, their specialist industrial and handicraft skills, and also their money. Among the penalties of the resident foreigner was a double rate of taxation, and to this burden were added other petty tariffs and imposts.

Particularly vocal in their resentment were London's businessmen and traders, who felt their livelihoods threatened by the new competition. They organized petitions and lobbied in Parliament for protection. They were 'greeved at' the 'great number of . . . straungers settled here amongst us', and especially at two groups of them, 'marchants' and 'handycraftesmen'. Christopher Mountjoy was a skilled craftsman, and he is sometimes described as a merchant (not least in his will, which is a self-description), so these complaints, which echo on more or less unchanged for decades, precisely concern him:

They [strangers] ought not to sell any merchaundizes by retayle. Contrary heerunto many of their merchaunts are retaylers also, keep shoppes inward, and private chambers, and therein sell by whole sale and retayle, send to everyman's house, serve chapmen, send to fayres, and utter their commodities many other ways . . .

They ought to imploy the money taken for the commodities of their countryes upon the commodyties of this kingdome, which they do not, for whereas they have halfe the trade of this kingdome in importe they imploy not a twentieth part thereof, but transport the money or make it over by exchange . . .

They ought not to buy and sell merchandizes one to another, which they do freely amongst themselves, and . . . have ingrossed almost all the new draperie into their hands . . .

This indicates the conflict – on one hand, the government's half-hearted protectionism, with its restraints and regulations not properly enforced; on the other, a thriving black economy based on the high-quality workmanship which was the Huguenots' trademark, and which found a ready market among the consuming classes of Elizabethan London.[29]

There were many such petitions, never effectively addressed, and in 1593 anti-alien feeling was dangerously rekindled. It was a time of plague and war – the long-running conflict in the Low Countries, the renewed threat of Spanish invasion. The economy was stretched, inflation was running high, bad harvests drove up food prices. In London the mood was ugly, and the strangers were convenient scapegoats. 'The common people do rage against them,' wrote one observer, 'as though for their sakes so many taxes, such decay of traffic, and their being embrandled in so many wars, did ensue.'[30]

On the street, petitions having proved useless, more militant action began. In mid-April there appeared an inflammatory broadsheet, described by the Privy Council as a 'vyle ticket or placarde, set up upon some post in London, purportinge . . . violence upon the strangers'. It is addressed to 'you beastly Brutes the Belgians (or rather drunken drones) and faint-hearted Flemings, and you fraudulent Father Frenchmen'. It accuses them of 'cowardly flight from [their] natural countries', and of 'feigned hypocrisy and counterfeit shew of religion'. It complains that the Queen has permitted them 'to live here in better case and more freedom than her own people'. It issues a dire ultimatum:

Be it known to all Flemings and Frenchmen that it is best for them to depart out of the realm of England between this and the 9th of July next. If not then take that which follows, for that there shall be many a sore stripe. Apprentices will rise to the number of 2336. And all the apprentices and journeymen will down with the Flemings and strangers.[31]

The Council drafted an urgent letter to the Lord Mayor, Sir Cuthbert Buckle, ordering that those involved be 'strictlie examined' and if necessary 'punyshed by torture'. But further placards appeared – most notoriously the 'Dutch Church libel', affixed to the wall of the Dutch Church on the night of 5 May, and still picked over today because of its mysterious connections with the playwrights Thomas Kyd and Christopher Marlowe. It begins:

Ye strangers y[t] doe inhabite in this lande
Note this same writing doe it understand.
Conceit it well for savegard of your lyves,
Your goods, your children & your dearest wives.

It rehearses the usual grievances against immigrant craftsmen ('Our poor artificers starve & dye / For y^t they cannot now be sett on worke') and retailers ('Cutthroat-like in selling you undoe / us all'), but the note of rabble-rousing violence is more strident than ever –

> Expect you therefore such a fatall day
> Shortly on you & youres for to ensewe
>   As never was seene.
> Since wordes nor threates nor any other thinge
> Canne make you to avoyd this certaine ill,
> Weele cutt your throates in your temples praying
> Not Paris massacre so much blood did spill . . .[32]

This crude doggerel is signed with the *nom de guerre* 'Tamburlaine', an allusion to Marlowe's popular play, *Tamburlaine the Great* (1587), about the conquests and cruelties of the medieval Tartar warlord Timur-i-Leng.

One can guess at the feelings evoked in the immigrant community by these rabid 'placards'. A letter sent from England on 16 May to the Catholic intelligence-gatherer Richard Verstegan in Brussels, gives the following news:

The apprentices of London have dispersed many libels against all sortes of strangers, threatning severely that if they depart not spedely to massacre them all . . . Great fear is thereby conceyved by the strangers. Great companyes of them are already departed, and more daily preparing to follow, so it is thought the most part will away, our Councell not knowing how to protect them.

Verstegan himself (writing on 17 May, and thus before receiving the above) says: 'There are above 10,000 strangers determyned this somer to departe from England . . . for fear of some comotion to be made by the comon people against them.'[33] The figure is exaggerated, but no doubt those who could got out of London at this time.

It was against this backdrop of simmering xenophobia that the

1593 Return of Strangers was compiled. On 6 March, the Mayor instructed the aldermen of each ward, 'with as great secrecy as may be', to make 'diligent search' to determine:

what and how many foreigners are residing and remaining within the same; of what nation, profession, trade or occupation every of them are of . . . what or howe many servants, either men or women, doth every of them keep in their houses; how long they and every of them have been in the realm; to what church every of them resort; whether they keep any English-born people in their house or otherwise set them to work.

The aldermen were told to complete this census within four days, which expresses the urgency of the surveillance but was entirely unrealistic. The certificates were not actually returned until 4 May.[34]

Answers to all the above questions are to be found in the surviving returns, and it is a great pity, biographically speaking, that the Mountjoys do not figure among the 1,100 or so households described there. The census is a snapshot, and their absence from it shows only that they were not in London between 6 March and 4 May 1593. They had prudently moved out for a while. They could possibly have been in Brentford, where we know Mountjoy later leased a property. Or they could have been in Stepney, where we later find Mountjoy's presumed relative John, and his own widow Isabel. These villages lay outside the scope of the 1593 Return.

We know little of the Mountjoys' early years in London, but these are some of the ingredients of their experience. They are prey to the vulnerabilities of the émigré. They live with petty restrictions and swingeing taxes. They are objects of curiosity or derision, shading at times into dangerous hostility. These tensions were no doubt counter-balanced with many benefits, but they are an extenuation to be remembered when we hear the crabby tones of Christopher Mountjoy as reported by witnesses at the Court of Requests.

*

Though it seems they were out of town in the spring of 1593, it is from around this year that we get our earliest sightings of the Mountjoys in Cripplegate. Two of the deponents in the Belott–Mountjoy suit, both residents of Cripplegate, claim to have known Mountjoy at this time. Daniel Nicholas says he had known him for about twenty years. This would take us back to 1592, which is about the earliest possible date for Mountjoy's residence in Silver Street, for had he been a householder there in 1591 he would have been listed for taxation in the subsidy rolls of that year. (Thereafter there is a gap in the Cripplegate rolls until 1599, when he is listed.) Humphrey Fludd, meanwhile, says he has known Mountjoy for about eighteen years, i.e. since c. 1594. Retrospective computations by witnesses are not necessarily reliable, but Fludd's may be accurate. In about 1594, according to his own testimony, he had married Stephen Belott's mother in France, and not long afterwards he 'put' Belott 'to be the defendant's apprentice' in London. Fludd is at least likely to know in what year he was married, and his statement is fairly good evidence that the Mountjoys were in Cripplegate, in business, by about 1594.

This in turn makes it likely that Christopher is the 'Mr Munjoye' referred to in a letter of late 1593. It was written by a young Norfolk gentleman, Philip Gawdy, who sent home a number of valuably gossipy letters from London, where he was studying law. Among them are fascinating glimpses from the playhouses, such as the performance by the Admiral's Men in 1587 when a loaded musket went off onstage and killed a pregnant woman in the audience – the play was probably Marlowe's *Tamburlaine*. In his letter of 7 December 1593, Gawdy reports that he has bought his 'beloved syster' – in fact his sister-in-law, Anne – various fashion items she had requested:

her fann with the handle . . . a pair of knifes, a vardingale of the best fashion, her gold thread, her heare call [hair-caul], her pumpes, and in short there wanteth no thing she spake for but only a thing I should have had of Mr Munjoye, but he fayled me very wrongfully according to his promyse; but it is coming.[35]

It is annoying that Gawdy's very specific list becomes so vague at its point of reference to Mr Munjoye or Mountjoy, but there is little doubt that the 'thing' he had ordered was a tire or ornamental head-dress, a suitable item to go with the fan, farthingale, hair-caul and pumps which he had bought for his fashion-starved sister-in-law in Norfolk. This unsatisfied customer brings us the first of many negative comments about Christopher Mountjoy – 'he fayled me very wrongfully'. He has broken a promise to the young gentleman, as he will do later to his daughter and son-in-law.

The earliest actual documentation of the Mountjoys on Silver Street dates from early 1596. The circumstance is melancholy: the burial of an infant. The child has no name, and no gender is indicated. He or she was either stillborn or had died before baptism, usually a couple of days after birth. The burial took place on 27 February 1596. The entry in the register reads simply, 'Mrs Monjoyes childe' (see Plate 14).[36]

The wording is curious, as it is almost invariably the father who is named as the parent of a dead child, or if the mother is named she is specified as a widow. In the twenty years from 1593 to 1612 – the last decade of Elizabeth and the first of King James – there were buried at St Olave's 172 children or minors: people young enough for their parentage to be identified in the burial entry. Marie Mountjoy's child is one of only four instances where the mother is named without the explanation of widowhood. Of the others, two are definitely illegitimate children and the third probably is too. In the register of births, the pattern is even clearer. Out of several hundred baptismal entries only five name the mother, and in each case the wording shows that the child is illegitimate.[37]

The scribal conventions of the St Olave's register seem to imply that the unbaptized baby buried in February 1596 was a child of Marie Mountjoy's by someone other than her husband. It is not so easy to translate this into actuality. Why was the child not presented to the world as Christopher's even if it was not? Does it mean Marie Mountjoy had a publicly acknowledged lover? I do not think the evidence is strong enough to be sure. It remains a rumour, a whisper of scandal in the faded pages of the old parish register – but it is not the only indication of a certain sexual raciness in the Mountjoy household.

12

Dr Forman's casebook

We are prey to the randomness of historical evidence. Whole tracts of Marie Mountjoy's life are lost to us; we scrabble around for a few fragments of data, but know nothing of importance about her. She marries young; she works for a tailor; she gives birth to two children, one of whom dies. These things were important to her, of course, but they do not individuate her. What kind of person was she? What did she look like? At this more personal level she is little more to us than she was to the tax-collector who inscribed her as '—— Mongey'.

And then for a moment we catch sight of her – a chance moment of actuality, recorded and preserved. It is a Saturday evening in the late summer of 1597, and she is looking somewhat vexed as she searches in her purse. 'In Silver Street Mary Mountioy of 30 years lost out of her purse in the street as she went the 10 of Septembris last between 7 & 8 at night a gold ring, a hoop ring & a French crown.' A couple of months later, the valuables still missing, she took a course that to us seems quaint but which was then the height of fashion: she went down to Philpot Lane in Billingsgate to consult the 'cunning-man' Simon Forman – 'Oracle Forman', as Ben Jonson called him – one of whose specialities was the recovery of lost or stolen objects. It is from Dr Forman's casebook, under the date 22 November 1597, that the brief account above is taken (see Plate 15).[38]

We can sympathize with her loss. A French crown, a coin which circulated widely in England, had a value of about 7 shillings – perhaps about £70 at today's prices. Together with the two rings, one of gold and the other possibly set with precious stones, she was down, in our terms, by some hundreds of pounds. To this is now added the cost of Forman's services. He typically charged 3s 4d for a 'councell' or consultation in his surgery. (A course of medical treatment was considerably more – up to £12 – but not applicable on this occasion.)[39]

A hoop ring (or 'hop rynge' in Forman's spelling) was a single band, usually of gold or silver, and often with a romantic 'posy' or motto carved inside it. Such a ring Graziano unwisely parts with in *The Merchant of Venice* –

> a hoop of gold, a paltry ring
> That she [Nerissa] did give me, whose posy was
> For all the world like cutler's poetry
> Upon a knife: 'Love me and leave me not.' (5.1.147–50)

Mr Stephen carries one in his purse, in Jonson's *Every Man in his Humour* (1598) – a 'jet ring Mistress Mary sent me', with the posy, 'Though fancy sleep, my love is deep' – and sends her another in return, less felicitously inscribed, 'The deeper the sweeter, I'll be judged by St Peter' (2.2.33–9).

Dr Forman duly performed the astrological calculations, or 'figure casting', for which he was being paid, and these can be seen in the entry in his casebook. The figure is a grid of twelve squares, each representing a part (or 'house') of the heavens; it is an 'horary' figure, based on the position of the planets at the precise hour of the consultation. A later astrologer, William Lilly, notes that Forman was particularly 'judicious and fortunate' in 'horary questions (especially thefts)', so it seems Mrs Mountjoy had chosen well. She witnesses Forman's performance – almanacs and ephemerides, consultations and calculations, and perhaps some 'winking or tooting through a sixpenny Jacob's staff' (as Nashe irreverently puts it – a 'Jacob's staff' was a kind of sextant used by astrologers).[40] In the diary of the law student John Manningham there is an anecdote about a man who lost his purse, and – much like Marie – 'resorted unto' a cunning-man to 'helpe him to it by figur-casting'. In this case the astrologer performs a little ritual: 'he caste a paper into the chaffing dishe of coales which he placed before them' and told the customer 'he should looke in the glasse to see the visage of him that had it [the purse]'. It turns out this is a prank – the wizard is a friend in disguise – but the procedure may be authentic. A real cunning-man, Abraham Savory (whose earlier career was as an actor), claimed he could find lost or stolen goods 'with the help of a familiar spirit who appeared to him at night as a naked arm'.[41]

Another method for finding lost goods was to make a talisman or sigil, as this:

To know wher a thinge is y^t is stolen
Take vergine waxe & write upon yt Jasper + Melchiser + Balthasar + & put yt under his head to whom the good parteyneth & he shall knowe in his sleape where the thinges is become.

This appears, oddly enough, in the diary of the theatrical impresario Philip Henslowe, among the box-office receipts and cash advances to needy authors which are the diary's more customary contents. The note is from an undated section of the diary, but nearby folios have records from 1596. It is possible the instructions for this talisman were provided by Dr Forman himself, for in 1596 Henslowe consulted him about some goods stolen from his house.[42] We may tentatively add a little sequel to Marie's visit to Forman – the inscribing of words and letters on a little sigil of 'virgin wax', the placing of it under her pillow in her bedroom on Silver Street.

I do not want to add credulousness to our still-meagre list of attributes for Marie Mountjoy. Forman was consulted by Elizabethans of all walks of life (except the poorest, who could not afford his charges). His surviving casebooks, which cover nearly six years, record over 8,000 consultations.[43] We may smugly call him a charlatan, but he was genuine in his beliefs – he was not, as many were, a deliberate trickster – and probably had genuine qualities as a healer. A self-taught man, he was hounded by the Royal College of Physicians as an unlicensed practitioner. He criticized their methods, disdaining diagnosis by 'paltry pisse' (urinoscopy) and advocating moderate use of blood-letting. He speaks defiantly of his efficacy – and his courage – in treating victims of London's plague epidemics:

> Then cam the plague in sixtie thre [1603]
> Whence all theis Docters fled.
> I staid to save the lives of many
> That otherwise had bin ded.[44]

He was a small, ugly, pugnacious man with a ferocious sexual appetite, to which many women, both patients and otherwise, re- sponded. Various liaisons and seductions are discreetly recorded in the casebooks, tuned like everything else to the 'horary' dispos- ition of the planets. His codeword for sexual intercourse was 'halek', which according to Jonathan Bate 'has lexical resem- blances to the Greek for "to grind" and "to fish", both Eliza- bethan slang for having sex', but which John Bossy derives more straightforwardly from Greek *alektur*, 'cock'.[45]

The *locus classicus* of Forman studies is still A. L. Rowse's *Casebooks of Simon Forman* (1974). Though supplanted and sometimes corrected by later studies, it was the first to sample the rich, dense sociology of the casebooks, which were then little known (and which are still unpublished). It was Rowse who spotted the Mountjoy entries, which he announced in an article in *The Times*, 'The Secrets of Shakespeare's Landlady', on 23 April 1973. His chief quarry in the casebooks, however, was Emilia Lanier, the Italian-Jewish musician's daughter whom he proposed, for seemingly cogent reasons, as the 'Dark Lady' of Shakespeare's Sonnets. But Rowse's research was flawed by a certain magisterial carelessness, and it was soon pointed out that Forman had not actually described Emilia Lanier as 'brown' (dark), but as 'brave' (beautiful, with an overtone of showiness), and that he did not give her husband's forename as William (which would tie in neatly with wordplay on 'will' in the Sonnets) but as Alfonso.[46] There are also some misreadings in Rowse's in- formation on the Mountjoys. Forman resembles modern doctors in at least one respect – his handwriting can be very difficult to read.

Forman consulted the stars to locate lost objects, but would also have employed more terrestrial methods. We may suppose he asked Mrs Mountjoy something further of the circumstances, rather as a policeman or detective might do. Whom did she see around the time that the objects went missing? Was there anyone she suspected of stealing them? Some such questions, perhaps, lie behind an interesting list of three names written down by Forman immediately below the astrological symbols. They are:

Henri Wood in Colman Street
Alis Floyd w[ith] my Lady of Hunstdean
Margaret Browne that was her servant

Mr Wood of Coleman Street we will meet shortly, and find that Forman had good reason to note him down as a figure of importance in Marie's life. For the moment it is the two women, not mentioned by Rowse, who interest me.

Margaret Browne's relationship to Mrs Mountjoy is explained in Forman's note: she was an ex-servant. She is doubtless the Margery Browne who was baptized at St Olave's on 14 February 1574: a local girl. Beneath her name Forman scribbles a brief description: 'a talle wentch freckled face'. One should resist hearing a pejorative overtone in the word 'wench'; it simply meant a girl or young woman (Middle English *wenchel*, 'child'). The interest of the description is its provenance – Forman is quoting, or at least summarizing, the words of Marie Mountjoy. In the Belott–Mountjoy suit we hear her only faintly and retrospectively: she died some years before the case came to court. Here the phrasing comes from her direct. She is there in Forman's fusty consulting room, among the sinister trinketry of his trade; she speaks and he writes. If I want to summon up a sense of Marie I imagine her saying the word 'freckled' in a French accent.

The date of Margaret Browne's birth encourages the possibility that she is also the 'Mary Browne of 24 yeares' who consulted Forman a few weeks later, on 27 December 1597. (The variant forename is quite normal – John Heminges's daughter Margeret is called Mary in the marriage registers of St Mary Woolnoth; and Forman's own grandmother appears indifferently in his writings as Marian and Margery.)[47] This Mary Browne came to Forman because she thought she was pregnant. He notes, 'She hath much gravell in her Reins & heat of the back, pains stomach; she supposeth herself with child.'

If this is indeed Mrs Mountjoy's former servant, she was apparently having premarital sex, since Margery Browne of St Olave's did not marry until November 1600, nearly three years later. Perhaps she and her future husband, who lived in neighbouring Aldersgate, were already lovers. Or perhaps – equally possibly – this tall, freckled maidservant had received, willingly or otherwise, the sexual attentions of the master of the house, Mr Mountjoy. There are other instances in the casebooks of serving girls pregnant by their master.[48] As we have seen, Mountjoy would be 'censured' for exactly this, by the elders of the French Church – '[Il] fut censuré . . . d'avoir eu 2 bastardes de sa servante.' This refers to a much later liaison, when he was a widower: a different time and a different servant,[49] but adding some colour to the possibility that the pregnant maid Margaret Browne was another of Mountjoy's amorous accomplices or victims.

This is unsubstantiated tittle-tattle, just like the idea that Marie's own baby, born and buried the previous year, was illegitimate. We are in search of facts but we listen also to the whispers – and this is the second such whisper suggestive of a certain sexual looseness in the Mountjoys' marriage. The French Church elders also state that Mountjoy had been brought before a magistrate for his 'lewd acts and adulteries' (*paillardises & adultères*), but they do not say when. The word 'adultery' makes one wonder if this happened during Marie's lifetime. Probably not – the context would connect it to his later relationship with the maid and the *bastardes* produced by it. But again it throws a questioning light back on to the Mountjoys' marriage.

The other woman mentioned by Marie, 'Alis Floyd with my Lady of Huntsdean', adds a rather different frisson of interest. Alice Floyd is also a servant – that is the meaning of 'with' in this context – but she is a servant or follower of a very illustrious mistress. 'Huntsdean' is Forman's spelling of Hunsdon, as found elsewhere in the casebooks – 'my old Lord of Hunstdean that was Chamberlain'.[50] In that case he was referring to the 1st Lord Hunsdon, Henry Carey, who was Lord Chamberlain until his death in 1596. But when he writes of Lady 'Huntsdean' in November 1597, he is referring to the wife of the 2nd Lord Hunsdon, George Carey. She was Elizabeth *née* Spenser, and was noted as a patroness of writers. Among those who sing her praises were Edmund Spenser, who claimed kinship with her; Thomas Nashe, who dedicated to her his religious pamphlet of 1593, *Christ's Tears over Jerusalem*; and the musician John Dowland, whose *First Book of Songs and Ayres* – dedicated to Hunsdon, and published this year 1597 – refers to her 'singular graces towards me'.[51]

It is only a fleeting reference, but this is a first hint of contact between Marie Mountjoy and Shakespeare: an intersection of circles. George Carey, 2nd Lord Hunsdon, was the patron of Shakespeare's company, the Lord Chamberlain's Men. His father had been their first patron, when the troupe was inaugurated in 1594; George inherited both the company and, in early 1597, the Chamberlainship (which was a relief to the players, as the interim Chamberlain, Lord Cobham, was no friend to the theatre). In March 1597 the company put on Shakespeare's comedy *The Merry Wives of Windsor*, hastily written to celebrate Hunsdon's forthcoming investiture as a Knight of the Garter. It was performed before the Queen, at Whitehall Palace – Hunsdon was her cousin (he was a great-nephew of Anne Boleyn) and a favourite. According to tradition, it was she who suggested the basic theme of the play: 'Falstaff in love'.[52] Lady Hunsdon would have been a guest of honour at this gala performance, and perhaps her servant Alice Floyd was somewhere in the audience as well.

Alice herself remains elusive. She does not feature in Hunsdon's will, where the only female servant of Lady Hunsdon mentioned is 'Teesye Purdue my wives Gentlewoman'.[53] The surname is Welsh, a variant of Lloyd, and is also found as Fludd or Flood. Perhaps Marie knows her because she is a relative of Humphrey Fludd, the stepfather of their apprentice, Stephen Belott. Another Elizabethan clan was the Fludds of Bearstead, Kent. Sir Thomas Fludd was a wealthy civil servant; his son was the future philosopher Robert Fludd, currently a student at Oxford, and soon to be established as an astrologer–physician like Forman. The Jane Fludd who appears in Forman's casebooks is Robert's sister-in-law, a rather racy young lady. It is possible Alice was related to these Fludds, though she was not one of Sir Thomas's three daughters.[54]

That Marie knew Lady Hunsdon's servant Alice Floyd in 1597 does not, of course, mean that she also knew Lord Hunsdon's servant William Shakespeare in that year. We do not quite get contact, but we are close. This briefly mentioned and otherwise unknown Alice brings the two protagonists of this story into proximity with one another, and suggests the kind of courtly theatrical context in which they might have met: the tirewoman and the playmaker, not so very different in status.

Just ten days later, on 1 December 1597, Mrs Mountjoy is back in Dr Forman's consulting room. This time she has a rather different matter to discuss, for she thinks she might be pregnant. 'Videtur esse gravid x xi hebdomadas,' Forman writes – she seems to be ten or eleven weeks pregnant. He briskly notes her symptoms: 'pains head side stomach . . . swimming in the head, weakness in the legs'. He thinks she will miscarry: '7 weeks more' and then it will 'come from' her.[55]

Marie was accompanied by another woman who also 'seems to be pregnant' – Ellen Carrell or Carowle (Forman gives both spellings). The lay-out and wording of the entry shows that the two women were seen together – perhaps a precaution, given the Doctor's goatish reputation. This friend of Marie Mountjoy's leads us once again into the literary world of late Elizabethan

London. In this year 1597 there appeared on the bookstalls a collection of love-lorn sonnets entitled *Laura: The Toyes of a Traveller*, by 'R.T., gentleman'. The author was one Robert Tofte, a dilettante poet and translator who had travelled on the continent for some years. The poet bewails, in standard Petrarchan vein, the cruel indifference of his mistress, and he drops some teasing hints as to her identity. In a prefatory poem she is called 'la bellissima sua signora E.C.' – 'for thee only', he says, the ensuing sonnets 'were devisde'. This beautiful 'E.C.' – an older married woman – is further identified in some heavily signalled word-play in Sonnet 33 of *Laura*, where his passion for her:

> gainst all sense makes me of CARE and IL
> More than of good and ComfoRT to have will.

The capitalized letters spell out the surname 'Careil' and then his own initials 'R.T.'. Her name is confirmed in Tofte's follow-up, *Alba: The Months Mind of a Melancholy Lover* (1598), where a similar crossword-clue –

> Then constant CARE not comfort I do crave
> And (might I chuse) I CARE with L would have

– gives her surname as 'Carel'. (The Elizabethans, I should add, loved this sort of *à clef* stuff.)[56]

Literary historians have sought in vain for Tofte's mistress – W. C. Hazlitt thought her forename was 'Euphemia', but neglected to say why; Tofte's Victorian editor, A. B. Grosart, thought she might be connected with Sir Edward Caryll of Bedstone, Sussex, but no suitably initialled female could be found. Here, surely, she is – Ellen Carrell, accompanying Marie Mountjoy to Dr Forman's in December 1597. She has the right name; she is of the right sort of age (forty-two in 1597, according to Forman, some seven years older than her *cavaliere servente* Tofte); and she is in the right sort of social milieu. Tofte had spent three years in Europe, and his translations show him fluent both in French and Italian – he is one of those fashionably (or affectedly) continental Elizabethans who are guyed by satirists like Nashe. It would not be at all surprising if he and his 'mistress' knew the Mountjoys. Perhaps Ellen Carrell was one of their customers, as Alice Floyd and Lady Hunsdon may have been. Whether her pregnancy in December 1597 has also to do with Tofte cannot be known.

And if Marie's friend is indeed Tofte's muse, she swiftly brings us – as Alice Floyd did – to a contemporary performance of a Shakespearean comedy, for the chief reason why Tofte's outpourings have not been long ago forgotten is that a sonnet in *Alba* contains the earliest-known allusion to *Love's Labour's Lost*:

> Loves Labor Lost, I once did see
> A play ycleped so, so called to my paine,
> Which I to heare to my small joy did stay,
> Giving attendance on my froward dame,
> My misgiving mind presaging to me ill,
> Yet was I drawne to see it gainst my will.

There is, of course, no guarantee that Tofte is reporting an actual occasion, but we can at least take it as another literary clue about his troublesome ('froward') mistress, Mrs Care-ill or Carrell. She is a playgoer, and a 'pleasant conceited comedie by W. Shake-speare' – as *Love's Labours* is described in the 1598 quarto – is just the kind of play you might see her at.[57]

Tofte's fondness for semi-cryptic identifications is found else-where – in one poem he puns on the name of his landlady, Mrs Goodall; in another he calls the poet Samuel Daniel 'him that title beres of prophets twaine' – but one that catches my eye is not a literary pun but a handwritten annotation in Tofte's own copy of the 1561 folio edition of Chaucer. There, beneath the prologue to Chaucer's *Testament of Love*, Tofte wrote: 'In lode de la Madama Marie M— donzella bellessa et gentildonna' (In praise of My Lady [or Madame?] Marie M—, damsel, beauty and gentlewoman).[58] 'Damsel' and 'gentlewoman' are hardly appro-priate for her (if taken literally), but I am still tempted to wonder if the roving eye of Robert Tofte had alighted on Marie Mountjoy, the friend of Ellen Carrell. If so – and it is no more than an 'if' – we would learn for the first time that Marie was a 'beauty'.

On 7 March 1598 Marie is back with Forman – her third and last visit, and one that would have required crossing the river to Lambeth, where Forman had moved at Christmas 1597, and where he lived till his death in 1611. She comes to ask if her husband will be sick: 'Mrs Mountioy p [per] marito suo Utrum egrotet.'[59]

Marie's enthusiasm for the astrologer's skills seems to have worked on her husband, for now 'Mr Mountioy' himself appears in the casebooks, twice, asking about his apprentice. The apprentice is not Stephen Belott but a young man called Ufranke de la Cole or Coles. The first entry, on 22 March, reads simply: 'Mr Mountioy for his man qui abscurr'. The last word is a contraction of 'abscurrit' – Mountjoy's question concerns an apprentice 'who has absconded'. (Rowse tripped up here, misreading the Latin 'qui abscurr' as a name, 'Gui Asture', thus providing Mountjoy with an extra, fictitious French apprentice.) The second entry, a week later, tells us more: 'Mr Mountioy for his man Ufranke de la Coles 1598 the 29 March. Qui abscurrit. He was in St Katherine's and he came new [returned] unto Mountjoy's house about the 29 March being Friday where he was taken & committed to prison.'[60] It is not quite clear what the story is. Was Coles arrested because he had run away, thus breaking his indenture as an apprentice? Or had he run away in the first place to escape arrest for some other offence?

Coles may be related to Peter Coale, 'picture-maker', listed in the 1593 Return of Strangers. He was from Antwerp, but was French speaking, and a member of the French Church. He lived near by, in the parish of St Botolph's, Aldersgate, and was himself in prison in 1593.[61]

Part of what makes Forman's casebooks so vivid is the fact that they were written down live, on the spot, *currente calamo*. He asks, he listens, he observes, he writes. The words he writes are often formulaic – thus when a woman 'supposeth herself with child', a frequent formula, the phrase is Forman's not hers – but nonetheless these entries in his casebooks are redolent of the physical presence of Marie Mountjoy as she explains to him the small dramas of her life and her body: the lost rings, the freckled wench, the swimming in her head, the ever-present possibility of pregnancy.

And then there are the revelations about her love-life. Beneath Forman's brusque account of the missing valuables appears the name Henry Wood – a name volunteered by Marie. Was she visiting him on that September evening, when she lost those things from her purse 'as she went'? It is not unlikely, for Wood himself soon makes an appearance in Forman's casebooks, and one of his visits evokes a tremor of romance (see Plate 17) –

> Mr Wood p [per] Mari M
> Vtrum quid Amor erit
> alterd noc [nocte] 1598 the
> 20 march[62]

There is no doubt that this 'Mari M' is Marie Mountjoy. Mr Wood has come to ask 'whether her love will be altered', and we can only assume he means her love for *him*. One perceives the hint of a narrative. In December 1597 Marie fears she is pregnant, which Forman seems to confirm – she is ten or eleven weeks gone. He also predicts she will miscarry, and as there is no evidence of any child born to Marie in 1598 we might think he was right. A few months later her lover Henry is fretting that she no longer cares for him. Perhaps the 'alteration' in her feelings was precipitated by this narrow escape from the personal and practical difficulties of an illicit pregnancy – possibly not her first. This is speculation, but that Marie had some kind of affair with Wood seems fairly certain from the wording of his query.

Henry Wood, as we learn from other entries in Forman's casebooks – which concern affairs of business rather than the heart – was a 'mercer', by definition a general trader but in Elizabethan usage a trader in cloth. He was born on 18 August 1566, a punctilious piece of information (Forman usually only gives a querent's age in years) which perhaps reflects a punctiliousness of Mr Wood's. He was thus about the same age as Marie. He was himself married, so if there was an affair between them it was doubly duplicitous. The Woods lived down Swan Alley, a little sidestreet off Coleman Street too insignificant to appear on the Agas map or in Stow's *Survay*. Coleman Street itself, running up from Cheapside to Moorgate, was an important street of well-to-do merchants' houses. It could be reached from Marie's house in about ten minutes, walking east along Addle Street and across Aldermanbury.

We learn a little of Henry Wood's dealings in the import–export business. In early December 1597, while Marie worries about pregnancy, Wood sails to Amsterdam with two 'hoys' (small trading vessels), the *Paradise* and the *Griffin*. A few weeks later he is asking Forman if he will get a good price for his 'Holland cloth' in France. He also asks if he should buy a consignment of 'bay salt' (salt from the Bay of Biscay). In the summer of 1598 he has business problems: 'It seemeth that his goods will be attached [confiscated].' But perhaps the malaise is personal too – Forman divines, 'Some great enemy will proffer him friendship but treachery will follow.' Wood was a householder and a businessman, but not a very big fish: in the Coleman Street subsidy lists of 1599 he is assessed on goods valued at £3.[63]

Sometimes it is Mrs Wood who visits Forman, anxious for Henry's safety on his trips abroad. On one occasion, she fears he has been 'taken by the Dunkirkers' – pirates in the English Channel. Forman reassures: 'They away shall arrive safe, so shall himself also, & let him take heed & look well, and he shall pass very swiftly within these 3 days.' And then there is a further twist, as Mrs Wood comes to ask Forman if she should 'keep shop' with Marie Mountjoy. 'They may join,' he opines, 'but take heed they trust not out their wares much, or they shall have loss.' We can surmise that the shop would combine the cloths imported by Henry Wood with the couturier skills – and perhaps the upmarket clientele – of the Mountjoy workshop. The relationship between Henry and Marie is thus commercial as well as carnal. Mrs Wood discusses a partnership with Marie, apparently unaware of any backstairs intrigue between Marie and her husband. Marie is a deceiver in this, though of course her relationship with Henry may now be 'altered'.

On the last page of Forman's casebook for 1597 is another brief note about Marie Mountjoy (see Plate 18).[64] The contents of the page are miscellaneous – fragments of information and gossip, non-astrological, generally mundane. There are five distinct chunks of writing; the first two, which fill up most of the page, are dated early January 1598. The others, more in the nature of jottings, are not necessarily the same date, but are likely to be before 20 February, when Forman began a new casebook.

The note on Marie consists of three words, of which two are her name. Rowse comments: 'A tantalizing marginal note reads: "Mary Mountjoy alained" – which means concealed.' I am unconvinced by this reading. First, 'alain' is not a word recognized by any dictionary I have consulted, including the *OED*, which sails serenely from 'alaik' (an obsolete form of 'alack') to 'alala' (a Greek battle-cry). Second, the orthography does not support the reading. The word is hard to read because it is written in an oddly narrow, squashed-up script, and because much of it is a series of minims almost impossible to differentiate. In my view, what Forman wrote after Marie Mountjoy's name is not the tantalizing but non-existent 'alained', but something rather more prosaic – her address. The word is 'olaive', referring to her parish of St Olave.[65] Addresses feature in other memoranda on the page.

Immediately below this is another line, almost certainly written at the same time, so in effect Forman has written a short list, as follows:

mari Mountioy / olaive /
madam Kitson yellow haire /

This 'Madam Kitson' may be connected to the wealthy Catholic Sir Thomas Kitson. If so she is a relative of another woman found in conjunction with Marie in the casebooks – Lady Hunsdon,

who was Sir Thomas Kitson's niece. Sir Thomas and his wife
Elizabeth lived in a stately pile in Suffolk, Hengrave Hall, but
they were frequently in London. Their town-house was on Coleman Street, just round the corner from Marie's lover and business
partner Henry Wood. We see them in twin portraits by George
Gower, commissioned in 1573 – he black bearded and high
ruffed, she haughty and handsome with a tall plumed hat and a
fur-collared gown. They were noted patrons of music, and had
the madrigalist John Wilbye as their resident musician in Suffolk
and London.[66]

Was Elizabeth herself the 'Madam Kitson' of Forman's note?
As the wife of a knight she was correctly addressed as Lady Kitson,
so Forman's 'Madam' (= 'My Lady') would be appropriate. It
would also have been the form naturally used by a Frenchwoman:
'Madame'. But what about the 'yellow' hair? If Gower's portrait
of her is accurate, Lady Kitson's hair was ginger or auburn, and
by early 1598, when she was in her early fifties, she was most
likely grey.

But Forman's jotting does not necessarily mean that Madam
Kitson *had* yellow hair. This was my immediate interpretation,
together with a suspicion of lechery in Forman's noting of the
fact. It may rather mean that she *wanted* some yellow hair – in
other words, a blond wig or hairpiece. The use of 'hair' or 'hairs'
to mean a wig was common, as in 'a yellow hair and another like
black' which the Queen received as New Year's gifts from the
Countess of Essex.[67] Or as in this bit of London repartee from
Dekker's *Shoemaker's Holiday* (1600) –

> MARGERY: Can'st thou tell where I may buy a good hair?
> HODGE: Yes, forsooth at the poulterers in Gracious street.
> MARGERY: Thou art an ungracious wag, perdy. I mean a false hair
> for my periwig. (3.4.47–50)

This would explain Forman's apposition of Kitson's name with
Marie Mountjoy's. Head-tires of the kind made by the Mountjoys
often incorporated human hair, and the tiremaker's skills
included wigmaking. In Randall Cotgrave's French dictionary of

1611, the skills are synonymous: he defines *perruquière* as 'a woman who makes perriwigs or attires'. And it is also clear that blond hair was particularly prized in this respect. Shakespeare's own references to female wigs envisage them as 'golden'. In Sonnet 68 he writes of 'golden tresses' which 'live a second life on second head', and again, in *The Merchant of Venice*, 'crisped snaky golden locks' become 'the dowry of a second head' (3.2.92–5). Thomas Middleton refers to blond 'periwigs' worn by old courtiers, who 'take it for a pride in their bald days to wear yellow curls on their foreheads'. Also apposite, though somewhat later, is an advertisement of 1663, in which a 'perriwigge-maker' announces that 'anyone having long flaxen hayr to sell' should 'repayr unto him'.[68]

This is an odd but I believe plausible interpretation of Forman's puzzling little memorandum. Its nature is entrepreneurial. It names a supplier and a customer; it summarizes a potential little deal that will do a favour to both, and thus to Forman. The commodity in question is a quantity of blond hair – not quite the elixir of youth sought in his alchemical activities, but more immediately obtainable.

13

The ménage

The marvellous Forman material allows us a glimpse into the lives of the Mountjoys, and particularly of Marie Mountjoy, in the later 1590s. We hear something of the people with whom her life is entwined – the adulterous mercer, the pregnant maid, the sonneteer's mistress, the runaway apprentice, the charismatic magicotherapist. We hear also those names floating out from the starry realm of wealth and courtly elegance to which anyone in Marie's trade and position must aspire – Lady Hunsdon, whose servant Alice Floyd she knows; Lady Kitson, a potential customer in search of rejuvenating golden locks.

We note too a certain flurry that Marie brings with her. In that first consultation about the missing valuables she mentions three names: shortly thereafter two of them turn up as clients of Forman's. Next she brings to the consulting room Ellen Carrell, and not long afterwards her own husband consults, twice. She proves useful to Forman; favours are traded. We would call it 'networking', though to Marie a 'networke' meant only a kind of gauzy threaded material used in head-tires.

This is the world Shakespeare enters when he becomes the Mountjoys' lodger some five years later – a world of aspiration and contact-mongering, a world of amorous and commercial rendezvous.

Forman adds also to our knowledge of the Mountjoy workshop, whose activities we have yet to look into. We learn of the otherwise unknown apprentice, Ufranke de la Coles, hired at some point before March 1598. We can correlate this with what we know of Stephen Belott's apprenticeship. In his deposition at the Court of Requests, Humphrey Fludd says he 'put' Belott to be Mountjoy's apprentice shortly after his marriage to Belott's mother in about 1594. But Noel Mountjoy adds that Belott 'was a year a border in the defendant's [Mountjoy's] house before he became the defendant's apprentice'. We can thus date the beginning of Belott's apprenticeship to around 1596.

In early 1598, therefore, Christopher Mountjoy had at least two young apprentices working for him, Stephen and Ufrancke. He may well have had a third, his younger brother Noel, who was then about sixteen. Noel was certainly apprenticed at Silver Street. In his deposition, to vouch for the accuracy of his statements, he says, 'He did serve the defendant when the plaintiff served him, and knew the truth thereof.' For a period, in other words, his own apprenticeship overlapped with Stephen's. Nothing further is heard of Ufrancke after his arrest in the spring of 1598. Possibly the vacancy was filled by Stephen Belott's brother, Jean or John. The latter is described in 1612 as 'John Blott, tiremaker', and may have learned his craft alongside his brother at the Mountjoy workshop. John later emigrated to the Netherlands, where he died in about 1642. He is described in Stephen's will as 'Master John Belott, late of the city of Harlem in Holland, ffrench schoolemaster'.[69]

There is another man in the house of whom we know little more than his name. On 14 January 1601, 'Joseph Tatton, servant to Christopher Montjoye' was buried at St Olave's. In this sort of context 'servant' often means apprentice, though the household would undoubtedly have had a male servant in the more general, domestic sense, and perhaps Tatton was one such. A George Tatton, married at St Olave's in the summer of 1599, was probably a relative.[70]

This glimpse into the Mountjoy household in the later 1590s shows us eight identifiable people – father, mother and daughter, three apprentices, a manservant and a maid. The maid is a constant, though her identity changes. There was Margaret Browne, who quit (or was dismissed) in about 1597, and later there was

Joan Johnson, who said in her deposition that she had known Mountjoy for eight years, and who must therefore have started work at Silver Street in about 1604. She was at that point Joan Langforde. Although she testifies at the Court of Requests as 'Joan Johnson, wife of Thomas Johnson, basketmaker', she was not yet his wife when she entered the Mountjoys' service, nor when she observed the activities of the lodger, 'one Mr Shakespeare'. The wedding of Thomas Johnson and Joan Langforde took place at St Olave's on 8 September 1605.[71]

Thus outlined the Mountjoy ménage seems to have a compact and industrious air – a family business with some live-in employees – and this sense of solidity is confirmed by Mountjoy's appearance in the Cripplegate subsidy rolls. In 1599 'Cristofer Montioy' is assessed on goods valued at £5, a respectable sum, and the following year, now 'Xpofer Monioye', he is listed again for the same amount.[72] The Cripplegate rolls survive only partially, so this may not have been his first appearance in them. But it marks his emergence, by the end of the century, as a fully fledged householder of St Olave's. It confers on him and his family a certain substance – the more so now we can compare it with that earlier, lowlier appearance as a poll-tax payer in the 1582 subsidy, back in those difficult years of resettlement.

Mountjoy was still topographically close to St Martin le Grand, but in another sense he has come a long way from that teeming enclave. There were few 'strangers' in the small, well-to-do parishes of St Olave and St Alphege (which were combined for purposes of tax-collection). In 1599 Mountjoy is one of only two; the other is James Moore, probably a Dutchman, who pays a poll tax of 8d. In 1600 it seems the Mountjoys are the only household of foreigners in the parish.

The ménage as outlined above is broadly the household that Shakespeare comes to know in around 1603. This was a year full of momentous events – the death of Elizabeth, the soaring mortality figures of the plague, the arrival of the new Scottish king, the forging of peace with Spain – but in the narrower spotlight of this study other micro-events hold centre-stage. Stephen Belott completes his apprenticeship; there is talk of marriage with the master's daughter; there is a new lodger in the chamber upstairs.

This is the way history happens: it is measured out in days rather than epochs. Thus on 14 April 1603 – precisely in the interregnum between the death of the Queen on 17 March and the arrival of King James on 7 May; precisely at the historical fulcrum between the Elizabethan and the Jacobean Ages – Christopher Mountjoy sets out for the French Church on Threadneedle Street, there to attend the baptism of Samuel Clincquart, son of Pierre Clincquart and Marthe *née* Pieterssen. He is there as one of the godparents, so the Clincquarts are presumably friends or business associates. In the immigrant lists is a Louis 'Clinkolad', also of the French Church: given the garbling of foreign names he may be of the same family. He was a hatbandmaker from Tournai. Mountjoy had business dealings with this trade – in fact he currently owed over £2 to a bandmaker in the Blackfriars, Peter Courtois, who had supplied him with specialist embroidery work. But in this year 1603 Courtois died, and the outstanding debt was passed on to his successors.[73] Whether they ever got the money – blood out of a stone – is not recorded.

These are local events, but there is one rather unexpected international touch. Some time shortly after he completed his apprenticeship Stephen Belott made a journey to Spain. Mountjoy states that after Belott 'had served this defendant the said time of six years', he 'was desirous to travel into Spain, and this defendant did furnish him with money and other necessaries for the journey to the value of £6 or thereabouts'. Belott confirms the journey – his 'travaile into spayne' – but not, predictably, the financial contribution from Mr Mountjoy. The date of this journey must be around 1603, a time when Anglo-Spanish hostilities had relaxed but not yet concluded. I can find no clue to the nature of his voyage – possibly he joined a trading expedition; possibly he was attached in some menial way to a diplomatic retinue, in the run-up to the peace negotiations, which formally opened at Somerset House in May 1604.

We get a glimpse of broader horizons, but he is soon back on Silver Street: 'he returned from his travel unto this defendant again, and was a suitor unto this defendant's daughter to marry her'.

And so we arrive at the events of 1604 – the ones with which we began, and to which we will return: the courtship of Stephen and Mary, the intercessions of Shakespeare, the wedding at St Olave's, the non-payment of the promised 'portion' or dowry. But I want now to move on past them, and to look briefly at some later aspects of the Mountjoys' story. Within the chronological focus of this book these are events in the future, but they throw further light on the Mountjoys, and thence indirectly on Shakespeare.

In the case of Marie Mountjoy, sadly, there is not much later story to tell. She died in the autumn of 1606: her burial took place at St Olave's on 30 October (see Plate 34). We know nothing of the cause or circumstances, or indeed of Shakespeare's reaction. If the age she volunteered to Dr Forman is broadly correct she was about forty when she died.

The behaviour of her husband in the years following her death does not make very edifying reading. His intransigence on the matter of Mary's dowry we know from the lawsuit, but other evidence points up what seems a total breakdown of relations with his daughter.

First there is the matter of Mountjoy's 'denization' or naturalization. By becoming a denizen the immigrant acquired certain rights – in particular, he could buy and bequeath freehold property – but he did not attain full parity with native citizens, and he continued to be taxed at the alien's double rate. Two routes were available, both of them expensive: one could acquire a Patent of Denization, or one could get Parliament to grant an Act of Naturalization. Most foreigners did not bother with either. In the whole of Elizabeth's reign there were 1,762 patents issued, but most of those were in the early years: between 1580 and her death in 1603 there were just 293 patents, an average of about a dozen a year. Under James the numbers rose, most of the applicants being Scotsmen.

'Christofer Monioy' received his Letter of Denization on 27 May 1607. He is described in the patent roll as 'a subject of the French king and born in the town of Cressey'. He is one of thirty-one denizens created in that regnal year; also listed is another man with a connection to Shakespeare – 'Martin Droeshout, painter, born in Brabant', of whom more later.[74]

Mountjoy had by now been in England for at least twenty-five years, and one wonders what motivated him to apply for denizenship at this point. The cynical but plausible answer would connect it with the death of Marie. In late 1606 Mountjoy becomes a widower, which also means he becomes marriageable again. A few months later he acquires the rights of denizenship, including the right to buy property, thus increasing his eligibility in the marriage-market. This is in itself no more than pragmatic, but there is a further implication concerning inheritance. The denizen could bequeath any real estate he had bought, but with one broad qualification – only children born to him *after* he became a denizen were eligible to inherit. One of the implications of his denization, therefore, is a desire to disinherit his daughter Mary.

In fact it was another eight years before Mountjoy remarried. In the interim, as we learn from the scandalized comments in the ledgers of the French Church, he lived in sin with his maidservant. Mountjoy's second wife was one Isabel Dest. They were married on 21 August 1615, at another St Olave's, the one on Hart Street, possibly Isabel's parish.[75] She sounds French (probably Isabelle d'Est) but I have not found her family. A connection with the famous Italian dynasty, the d'Este of Ferrara, is extremely unlikely. It may be further to his marriage that Mountjoy left Silver Street, for when he came to draw up his will he was living outside the walls, in the neighbouring parish of St Giles, Cripplegate.

Mountjoy's will, dated 26 January 1620, survives in a contemporary register-copy; it is published here for the first time (see Plate 35). It names Isabel as his sole executrix. It makes no mention of freehold property, only his 'goods and chattels', which are unfortunately not further specified. It contains this extraordinary bequest:

Three third Parts of my goods and chattels (the whole being divided into fower third partes) I give and bequeath unto my well-beloved wife Isabel. And one other thirde part of the said fower third parts I doe hereby give and bequeath unto my daughter Mary Blott the wife of Stephen Blott.[76]

It appears that this surreal arithmetic, in which his estate is divided into four 'thirds', is designed once more to diminish the inheritance of his daughter and son-in-law. To avoid interminable contestings, the City of London customs (which charged duty on inheritances) directed that a testator should allot at least a third of his estate to his widow, and a third to his surviving children, leaving the last third to be disposed of elsewhere if he wished. Faced with the prospect of the detested son-in-law getting a third of his goods and chattels, Mountjoy and his solicitors hit on this brilliant or half-mad solution of making the thirds smaller than they should be, for the only proper definition of Mountjoy's 'thirds', since there are four of them, is that they are quarters. A quarter by any other name doth weigh the same, and these last recorded words of Christopher Mountjoy are a further attempt to defraud his own daughter. Fifteen years after the wedding, seven years after the lawsuit, he cannot climb down. It is as he had said, in the hearing of the mercer Christopher Weaver: 'he would rather rott in prison than geve them any thinge more than he had geven them before'.

These later documents confirm what both the plaintiff and the witnesses keep telling us in the lawsuit of 1612 – that Christopher Mountjoy could have paid up the dowry, and the reason that he did not was that he was a hard, mean, stubborn man: what Thomas Nashe calls a 'pinchfart penny-father'. It may be there was some specific falling-out which caused him to withhold the money in the first place, but to continue to withhold it so long and so doggedly makes him seem flint-hearted: a man incapable of giving; an uncaring father whose feelings for his daughter were subordinate to his own material comforts.

We learn a little more about Christopher Mountjoy, and none of it encourages us to like him. We might sympathize with the upheavals he has been through, we might admire him as an immigrant 'success story', we might furnish him with several layers of Gallic charm to which the record gives no clue – but as it stands we just cannot like him. This matters little to us, and even less to him – its more interesting corollary is to wonder how much Shakespeare liked him. But Shakespeare's dealings would mostly have been with his landlady. It is she, typically, who oversees the circumstances and the day-to-day requirements of the lodger; and it is she, in this particular case, who is more probably the one that Shakespeare liked.

PART FOUR

Tiremaking

Any silk, any thread,
Any toys for your head . . .
The Winter's Tale, 4.4.319–20

14
Tires and wigs

W̶e have learned something of the Mountjoys' story – such traces as remain – but what of the 'trade of Tyermakeinge' which was their livelihood? In the Belott–Mountjoy papers he is 'Christopher Mountjoy of London, tiremaker'; in the Queen's accounts she is 'Marie Mountjoy, tyrewoman'. This is their professional identity, almost as primary to them as their national identity – in contemporary eyes, the two go naturally together: they are French and they are in the fashion business.

Head-tires came in many shapes and sizes. The word 'tire' – then also written 'tyre', 'tier' and 'tyer' – is simply an abbreviated form of 'attire', and is similarly generic. Any adornment for the head that was not an actual hat or hood could be called a tire. It was a dressing for the hair, and in the original sense of the word Marie Mountjoy was a hairdresser. ('Tires' in the plural was also used in the broader sense of attire – garments, costumes, etc – which is why the dressing room of an Elizabethan theatre was called the 'tiring-house' and the man in charge of it the 'tireman'.[1] It is usually clear which sense is meant, but there are occasional ambiguities, as in Shakespeare's Sonnet 53, where 'You in Grecian tires are painted new' could refer to either robes or headgear.)

By the late sixteenth century, a particular style of head-tiring had evolved. It was a French import, associated with the glittery *cours de ballet* of the Valois court (see Plate 20): the Mountjoys were marketing a continental 'look' as much as a product.[2] The full-blown tire was an assemblage rising up some inches above the head, based on a framework of silver or gilt wire, embroidered with silk and lace and gauze and gold thread, decorated with pearls, gems and spangles, and often topped off with a feather or two. 'Tire' has no etymological link with 'tiara', though these creations could be described as complicated tiaras. It was a sumptuous and expensive item, worn by queens, noblewomen and female courtiers, and thence by imitation percolating down the social scale – as complained of by two fretful ladies of fashion onstage in 1600:

> PHILAUTIA: What? Ha' you chang'd your head-tire?
>
> PHANTASTE: Yes faith; th'other was so near the common, it had no extraordinary grace . . . I cannot abide anything that savours [of] the poor over-worn cut . . .
>
> PHILAUTIA: And yet we cannot have a new peculiar court-tire, but these retainers will have it, these suburb Sunday-waiters, these courtiers for high days, I know not what I should call 'em –
>
> PHANTASTE: O aye, they do most pitifully imitate.[3]

In texts of the day we hear of a 'tyre of gold adorned with gemmes and owches' (an 'ouch' is a gold or silver setting for a precious stone); of a 'tyer of netting'; of an 'attyre . . . in form of two little ships made of emeralds, with all the shrouds and tackling of clear saphyres'; of a 'mourning tire such as gentlewomen wear at the time of funerals'; of toweringly tall 'Turkish tires'; and, humorously, of a 'tire [of] four squirrels' tails tied in a true-love knot'.[4] The Mountjoys did not necessarily supply the gemstones that adorned the tire: these would typically be part of the wearer's own collection. When Christopher describes himself as a tiremaker he probably means he is a manufacturer of the basic unit – the delicately wrought framework into which various adornments could be fitted – though he no doubt put together complete, ready-to-wear tires as well.

The writer George Chapman laments the fate of a fashionable woman's hair – 'tortured with curling bodkins, tied up each night in knots, wearied with tires'.[5] This reminds us that the more elaborate tires must have been heavy to wear – or, by analogy, that part of the tiremaker's skill was to get volume without weight: an art of finesse, of *leggiadría*; a visual confection.

As noted, 'tiremaker' serves also to mean a wigmaker. They were not called wigmakers because the word 'wig' did not yet exist – 'periwig' (from which it comes) was still in a malleable state, and is found as 'perwycke', 'perewincle' and 'periwinke'. The fashion for wigs was associated with the French immigration: 'Perwigs ... were first devized and used in Italy by courtezans, and from thence brought into France, and there received of the best sort for gallant ornaments, and from thence they came into England about the time of the Massacre of Paris.'[6] False hair – human at best, also horse-hair and hemp – was used in the tire itself. It provided a bedding for the tire to sit on, and matched for colour it created an illusion that the whole edifice was an extension of the wearer's own hair. This bed of hair might be a 'hair-caul', which fitted close over the head, or a more substantial bouffon.[7] A periwig or peruke – a full wig completely covering the head – is not the same as a tire, but if an Elizabethan wished to purchase one, she or he might well go to the tiremaker. I have suggested that Dr Forman's note about 'Madam Kitson' proposes such a journey to Mrs Mountjoy's shop in St Olave's.

Possibly this wigmaking side of their business is referred to in a joke of Ben Jonson's. In *Epicoene* (1609) the elderly and vain Mistress Otter is described as an assemblage of artificial parts: 'All her teeth were made in the Blackfriars, both her eyebrows i' th' Strand, and her hair in Silver Street – every part of the town owns a piece of her!' (4.2.81–3). These places are named for punning purposes – her teeth are black, her eyebrows strands, her periwig silver – but there is surely a glance at the actual wigmaker of Silver Street, Christopher Mountjoy, whom Jonson undoubtedly knew through their mutual friend Shakespeare. Being mentioned – or even half mentioned – in a Jonson comedy cannot have been bad for business, though as Mrs Otter is earlier described as wearing 'a peruke that's like a pound of hemp made up in shoe-threads', the publicity is not all good.

*

No tires or wigs survive from the period of the Mountjoys' production.[8] The chief culprit is physical decomposition. Anything in contact with the head comes also into contact with human hair-oil, and material impregnated with bodily secretions is particularly attractive to moth, beetle and micro-organisms. Wigs made of human hair or horse-hair are anyway vulnerable because of natural oils in them. Over time these oils also cause an unpleasant brownish staining. For these reasons the principle of benign neglect – clothes put away in a chest in the attic and forgotten, which has resulted in some historic survivals – is less likely to happen with headwear and underwear. Another reason for the non-survival of tires is that anything embellished with costly materials was likely to be destroyed and recycled.

We cannot see an Elizabethan or Jacobean head-tire in the flesh, but we can see them in many paintings. Almost all the ceremonial portraits of Queen Elizabeth show her head lavishly attired. In the famous 'Ermine' portrait at Hatfield House (1585) she wears a tire of large pearls and coloured gems arranged in sprigs; one can see the wire framework and the padded hairpiece on which it sits. The 'Ditchley' portrait (1592) features a mighty Wurlitzer of pearls and diamonds several inches high.[9] The provenance of these tires is unclear – perhaps they were gifts. There is no mention of 'tiremakers' in the accounts and inventories of the Queen's wardrobe so meticulously analysed by the late Janet Arnold. The dressing of the royal head was one of the tasks of the Gentlewomen of the Bedchamber, better known as the 'Maids of Honour' – an account-entry shows Blanche Parry, the overseer of the Maids, receiving 'satten of sundrye colours to be used about the attyre of our hedde'. Also involved in her headwear were the Queen's 'silkmen' and 'silkwomen', of whom the most frequently mentioned are Roger Mountague and Dorothy Speckard. In 1586 Mountague was paid for 'translating [altering] & mending of an attyer for the hed of white nettworke florished with Venice silver' and for 'silver lase to edge the same rounde aboute'.[10]

We also see Elizabeth in elaborate wigs. By the mid-1580s she was greying, but her portraits continue to show her with dark-red or reddish-gold hair arranged in tight curls and waves. After an audience in 1597, the French ambassador de Maisse reported: 'On her head-tire she wore a coronet of pearls . . . and beneath it a great reddish-coloured wig with a great many spangles of gold and silver'; either side of her head 'hung two great curls of hair, almost down to her shoulders', presumably hairpieces.[11] Her wigs were also supplied by her silkmen and silkwomen. There are frequent payments to Roger Mountague:

vij [seven] heads of haire to make attiers, flowers and other devices for attiers [and] two periwigs of haire . . .
iij lardge fayre heddes of heaire [and] iiij perewigges of heaire . . .[12]

Mary Queen of Scots also used wigs – most famously the red wig she wore on the day of her death in 1587, which came off when the executioner lifted up her severed head.[13]

There is nothing to link the Mountjoys with Queen Elizabeth's headwear, but with the advent of Queen Anne or Anna, the Danish wife of King James, their fortunes rose. As mentioned, 'Marie Mountjoy, tyrewoman' received payments from Queen Anne in 1604–5 (see Plate 23); the accounts either side of this fiscal year do not survive, so it is possible she made other appearances. She is one of about thirty suppliers listed under the rubric, 'Paiments made upon severall bills of Artificers for necessaries belonging to Her Highnes Roabes and other ornamentes'. On 17 November 1604 Marie received £18 13s 7d, and on 11 March following £21 12s 10d; together with some other payments not itemized, the total sum was £59. Also receiving payment that year was her neighbour, Christopher Weaver the mercer, who would later give evidence in the Belott–Mountjoy suit; and Thomas Sheppard, perfumer, whose sister Jane will later be of interest to us.[14] That it is Marie rather than her husband named in the accounts is not unusual – roughly a third of the payees are female – but suggests what might anyway be guessed: that she was the public face of their business, the customer services department; also no doubt the one who physically fitted, adjusted, discussed and decorated the tire *in situ*, which occasionally meant in the Queen's dressing room, probably at Somerset House in the Strand, which Anne took over around this time as her private palace, renaming it Denmark House.

In this document we find the Mountjoys at their professional zenith, specialist suppliers 'by royal appointment', in company with the similarly top-drawer haberdashers, milliners, girdlers, hosiers, drapers, pinners, locksmiths, feather-makers, farthingale-makers and coffer-makers also listed in the accounts, and not so very far from those other specialist suppliers listed in royal documents at this time, the King's players.

Queen Anne wears a head-tire in the full-length portrait of her by Marcus Gheeraerts the younger, now at Woburn Abbey (see Plate 24). The painting is dated *c.* 1605–10, a range that intersects with the Queen's employment of Marie Mountjoy as her 'tyre-woman'. The tilt of her head hides some of the detail, but we see a delicate, wreath-like framework studded with pearls, a back-ground of red cloth, perhaps silk or taffeta, and a spray of white feathers. The tire is worn high on the back of her head, floating on a cloud of blondish hair which is probably in part a wig. Cool understatement is not something to which the head-tire generally aspired, but one sees a tendency to elegance and restraint in comparison to the grandiose displays favoured by Elizabeth.

It is quite possible that the headgear depicted by Gheeraerts is an actual product of the Mountjoy workshop, though as Anne wears a similar tire in a later portrait (Paul van Somer, *c.* 1617) we may have to think of it as a more generic depiction.[15] These are, at least, the type of head-tires produced by the Mountjoy workshop around the time of Shakespeare's presence upstairs.

A remarkably precise vignette of a fashionable lady putting on a head-tire is found in a language-manual printed in 1605: *The French Garden for English Ladyes and Gentlewomen* by Peter Erondell. The first dialogue in the book is 'The Rising in the Morning' (as was the norm, Erondell's manual is written in dia-logue form, with parallel texts in English and French).[16] It features a French aristocrat, Madame de Rimelaine, getting ready for the day with the help of her chambermaid Prudence, her gentlewoman Jolye and her page-boy.

'Come dress my head,' milady demands. First she must have her scalp rubbed: 'Come, Jolye, rubbe well my head, for it is very full of dandrife.' For this procedure there are 'rubbers', which the page has earlier been ordered to warm. Next she has her hair combed, but 'give me first my combing-cloth, otherwise you will fill me full of hayres'. Two combs are used, one of ivory and another 'boxen' (of boxwood), and when the combing is done, the page is ordered to clean them with 'combe-brushes' and to use 'a quill to take away the filth from them'.

Madame de Rimelaine is planning to wear her 'French hood' but Jolye tells her the weather is fine, so she resolves on a 'head attyre' instead. She calls for 'my jewels that I weare on my head'; they are in the 'long box' in her closet. She demands: 'What is become of my wyre? Where is the hair capp? Have you any ribans to make knots? Where be the laces for to bind my haires?' We again note that the tire is something assembled, rather than a ready-made artefact – a 'hair-cap' or caul to fit over the head; a wire framework in which jewels can be set; a quantity of ribbons and laces to tie things into place, as well as to decorate. Finally, 'now set on my carkanet of precious stones'.[17]

Erondell's dialogue also gives a handy vocabulary of French tire-related terms in use in 1605. The tire itself is *un atour*, though in its more general sense of head-dressing it is simply *une coiffure*.[18] The structure of wires which supports it is *un mole* (which today generally means a jetty) and the 'hair cap' is *une houppe*. These are words you would hear used in the Mountjoys' workshop.

We are close here in time, language and ambience to the Mountjoys. Erondell probably knew them within the French community of Jacobean London, and perhaps his knowledge of head-tiring owes something to their expertise in the subject. What do we know of Monsieur Erondell (or 'Mr Swallow')? He was from Normandy, and was in England by the mid-1580s, translating

Huguenot propaganda and teaching French. Thereafter nothing is heard of him till the appearance of the *French Garden*. (There is a Peter Swallow listed in the 1593 Return of Strangers, but he is a Dutch blacksmith.) One thing we do know is that Erondell was for a while French tutor to Sir Thomas Berkeley: he dedicated the *French Garden* to Berkeley's wife Elizabeth, from whom he had received 'gratuites faveurs'.[19] Not for the first time this brings up the name of the Careys, Lord and Lady Hunsdon, for Elizabeth Berkeley was their daughter – their only child. There is a venerable theory that Elizabeth's wedding to Sir Thomas Berkeley in February 1595 was the occasion of Shakespeare's nuptial fantasia, *A Midsummer Night's Dream*.

We know of two people in the Hunsdon orbit with whom Marie was acquainted at one time or another – Alice Floyd, servant to Lady Hunsdon; and William Shakespeare, poet of Lord Hunsdon's theatre troupe – and she may also have been acquainted with Peter Erondell, French tutor to the Hunsdons' son-in-law.

There is anyway a parallel between the imagined head-dressing of Erondell's *French Garden* and the actual head-dressing offered by the Mountjoys, and it is one that reminds us of their status. Mrs Mountjoy is not Madame de Rimelaine, but the one who receives the orders: Jolye the 'waiting gentlewoman'. (This is one of the definitions of 'tirewoman' given by OED – 'a woman who assists at a lady's toilet, a lady's maid', though this relates to the more general sense of 'attire'.) In 1605, the year that Erondell's manual was published, the King's Men staged the first performance of Ben Jonson's comic masterpiece *Volpone*. The affected Lady Would-be is a classic tire-wearer, and we watch her imperiously fretting with her two 'waiting-women', rather as Madame de Rimelaine does with hers –

LADY WOULD-BE: Come nearer. Is this curl
  In his right place? Or this? Why is this higher
  Than all the rest? . . . I pray you, view
  This tire, forsooth: are all things apt, or no?

WOMAN: One hair a little here sticks out, forsooth.
LADY WOULD-BE: Does't so, forsooth? . . .
   Pray you both approach and mend it. (3.2.42–53)

This is the sort of thing Marie Mountjoy had to put up with, as she attended to the tires and coiffures of her rich clientele.

Tires and wigs were worn by queens, princesses, maids of honour and grandes dames like Madame de Rimelaine and Lady Would-be – all eminently respectable. From a different angle, however, the tire was a typical instance of the sinful vanities and superfluities of female fashion. The prophet Isaiah sets the tone, foretelling the downfall of the materialistic 'daughters of Zion' – 'The Lord will take away the bravery of their tinkling ornaments about their feet, and their cauls, and their round tires like the moon' (AV, *Isaiah* 3.18).

Nashe has some strident comments in his homiletic broadside of 1593, *Christ's Tears over Jerusalem* (dedicated to the future Lady Hunsdon). He targets tires and wigs as part of a general diatribe on women's vanity:

Their heads, with their top and top-gallant lawn baby-caps, and snow-resembling silver curlings, they make a plain puppet-stage of . . .

   Thy flaring, frounzed periwigs, low dangled down with love-locks . . .

   As angels are painted in church windows with glorious golden fronts beset with sunbeams, so beset they their foreheads on either side with glorious borrowed gleamy bushes . . .

These 'borrowed gleamy bushes' are what we would call hair-extensions, also at the time called 'borders'. Nashe adds that they 'signify beauty to sell, since a bush is not hanged forth but to invite men to buy'. He is referring to the ivy bush hung outside wine-shops, but there is an obvious bawdy overtone. He suggests that this sort of elaborate headwear is associated with prostitution – beauty for sale. His friend Robert Greene refers more bluntly to 'street-walkers' in their 'quaint periwigs'.[20]

In the same year we find another writer talking of 'lascivious

Jessabells' who 'set out their broidred haire with periwigs'. They appear to be 'fine & proper women' but in reality 'live in pleasure enjoying the lust of the flesh, most filthely making a pastime thereof'.[21] If Nashe's pieties sound unconvincing, these are even more so – the writer was Dr Forman, for whom lust of the flesh was a favourite pastime. In similar vein Thomas Middleton – a disciple of Nashe, and a future collaborator with Shakespeare – describes his prototype of female vanity, 'Insolent Superbia', as a wearer of tires and wigs:

> But O her silver-framèd coronet
> With low-down dangling spangles all beset,
> Her sumptuous periwig, her curious curls . . .[22]

A visual counterpart to this depiction of tire-wearing as gaudy and immodest is Isaac Oliver's allegorical watercolour on a theme of virtue and pleasure, c. 1590–95 (see Plate 29), in which the flashily dressed figures on the right are wanton pleasure-seekers, the sprawled man reminiscent of the Prodigal Son among the harlots.[23] The central woman of this group, dressed in gold with her breasts exposed, is a vivid portrayal of a courtesan by one of the best immigrant painters in London. She wears a showy head-tire of lace and gauze, a border studded with black bugles, and tightly primped blonde hair which may well be a wig. 'Courtesan' is euphemistic: essentially one means an upmarket prostitute.

These writers and artists trail an idea that lavish tires and periwigs are a trademark of prostitutes, or anyway women of dubious reputation, and it is not surprising that we glimpse tire-wearing women among the desirable but dodgy 'dames' in the audience of the playhouse. Thus Father Orazio Busino, chaplain at the Venetian embassy, found himself at the Fortune theatre in 1617, 'amongst a bevy of young women'.[24] One of them, a 'very elegant dame', placed herself beside him, and asked him for his address 'both in French and English'. The priest 'turned a deaf ear', but not, it seems, a blind eye, for he gives an enthusiastic description of her clothing. She wore three pairs of gloves, which she took off one after the other, finally 'showing me some fine diamonds on her fingers'. He notes her yellow satin bodice, her petticoat of gold tissue with stripe, her robe of velvet with a raised pile, and finally her head-tire, which was 'heavily perfumed'.

Another 'dame' is spotted at a playhouse, probably the Blackfriars, in Henry Fitzgeoffrey's *Satyres* (1617). She too wears something fancy on her head, indeed she is identified by it –

> But stay! See heere (but newly entred),
> A Cheapside Dame, by th' tittle on her head!
> Plot, villain, plot! Let's lay our heads together.
> We may devise perchaunce to get her hither . . .
> Heer Mrs! Pox on't, she's past, she'l not come o're,
> Sure shee's bespoken for a box before.

OED gives various meanings for 'tittle' but none connected with headwear. It looks for a moment like an early version of 'titfer', but the latter is rhyming-slang (tit-for-tat: hat). Perhaps it is a jocular coinage for a head-tire.[25]

The Mountjoys' clientele included Queen Anne, and no doubt some aristocratic and courtly ladies, possibly including Ladies Hunsdon and Kitson, but it is also drawn from this more louche milieu of fashion-mad young Superbias, dolled-up dames at the playhouse, courtesans and prostitutes. Like Shakespeare and his company, the Mountjoys supply the great growth-industries of leisure and pleasure which give Jacobean London its rackety boom-town aura.

15

The 'tire-valiant'

We would see head-tires and periwigs at the playhouse, bobbing like exotic flotsam above a sea of faces, and then turning our attention back to the play itself we would find this reflected in the presence of tires and wigs onstage. This is a point of intersection in the story of Shakespeare and the Mountjoys, a common denominator. It is plausible, though probably not provable, that they came to know one another within a context of theatrical costuming.

The play-companies had a voracious appetite for costume. It has been calculated that the wardrobe of a thriving company in the early seventeenth century might be worth up to £1,000. A breakdown of purchases made by Philip Henslowe – owner of the Rose theatre, where the Lord Admiral's Men played – shows that over a six-year period (1597–1603) he paid out £561 for 'apparel and properties', the bulk being for costumes.[26] These are very large sums: the contents of the tiring-house at the Rose were probably worth more than the theatre itself. Among the costumes to be found there were the 'coat with copper lace' and 'breeches of crimson velvet' which Edward Alleyn wore as Marlowe's Tamburlaine, and 'Henry the fiftes dublet & vellet gowne', and a jerkin and cloak for Dr Faustus, and 'vi grene cotes' for the merry men in Munday's feeble Robin Hood plays.[27]

Plays were not fully costumed according to their fictional period and setting. Even in historical dramas much of the apparel onstage was contemporary Elizabethan–Jacobean wear. Hamlet is an early-medieval Danish prince but a description of him by Ophelia

(2.1.79–81) shows that Burbage played the part in doublet and hose. In the only visual record of a Shakespeare production – a drawing of *c.* 1594 showing a scene from *Titus Andronicus* – at least two of the seven figures are in Elizabethan dress (see Plate 22).[28] The look of the plays is duplicitous, as the texts themselves are – we are at once somewhere else, and in the here and now. Rather than realism, the costuming aimed for splendour and glitter: it belonged to the ancient element of spectacle. According to the Swiss tourist Thomas Platter, who saw plays at the Globe and elsewhere in 1599, 'the actors are most expensively and elaborately costumed'. Sir Henry Wotton was impressed and slightly worried by the 'pomp and majesty' of the costumes in Shakespeare and Fletcher's *Henry VIII* (1613) – 'the knights of the Order with their Georges and Garter, the guards with their embroidered coats and the like'. Their effect, he feared, was 'to make greatness very familiar, if not ridiculous'.[29]

In this sense the theatre had a symbiotic relationship with the fashion industry. It participated, both as a purchaser and as a showcase, in 'a massive capitalist development in the circulation of clothing'.[30] The Jacobean 'city comedies' brought on to the stage a precise sociology of contemporary costume. The intent was often satirical but the latest styles, the newest look, were there to be seen by an audience full of cash-rich potential shoppers.

Among the costumes would be found tires and periwigs. Wigs are a fundamental aspect of costuming – they transform, disguise, re-identify, and they would certainly be needed to turn short-haired boy-actors into long-haired women. In the sketch of *Titus Andronicus*, Queen Tamora has long fair-looking hair which is probably a wig. A famous line of Hamlet's describes an old-fashioned actor in a wig – 'It offends me to the soul to hear a robustious periwig-pated fellow tear a passion to tatters, to very rags, to split the ears of the groundlings' (3.2.8–11). We can guess that Sir Andrew Aguecheek in *Twelfth Night*, noted for his hair which 'hangs like flax on a distaff', was played by an actor in a long flaxen or blond wig. The scary wigs worn by devils in Marlowe's *Dr Faustus* were particularly memorable. In

Middleton's *Black Book* (1604) Lucifer says of the piratical old soldier Prigbeard, 'He has a head of hair like one of my devils in Doctor Faustus,' while John Melton recalls the 'shagge-haired Devils' who ran 'roaring over the stage with squibs in their mouthes' in a performance at the Fortune.[31]

Periwigs feature in a 'Sonnet' – in fact, a ballad – which describes 'the pitifull burning of the Globe playhouse' in 1613. The conflagration rages through the tiring-house, destroying both costumes and props –

> The perrywigges and drumme-heades frye,
> Like to a butter firkin;
> A woefull burning did betide
> To many a good buff jerkin.
> Then with swolne eyes like druncken Flemminges,
> Distressed stood old stuttering Heminges

This balladeer seems to have some knowledge of the company – he also mentions Burbage and Henry 'Condye' (Condell) – so he may be accurately describing Heminges's role as production-manager, having particular care of costumes and props, and thus specifically distressed by this destruction.[32]

Head-tires would also be part of the theatrical wardrobe, bedecking ladies of rank or fashion, and perhaps also more fanciful figures such as Titania in *A Midsummer Night's Dream*. The 'Queen of Fairies' at the end of the *Merry Wives* (actually Mistress Quickly in disguise) is described as having 'ribbons pendant flaring 'bout her head', which sounds like a tire of some sort. Hamlet's envisaging of a player's costume refers first to plumed headgear – 'would not this, Sir, and a forest of feathers ... get me a fellowship in a cry of players?' (3.2.263–6). These fantastical headpieces shade into the elaborate masque costumes of the early seventeenth century, which certainly featured tires. Conversely, the realistic 'city comedies' featured tires because they were a contemporary fashion or affectation. That scene in *Volpone* where Lady Would-be fusses about her tire would be played by a boy-actor wearing one – probably ridiculously ornate. And a stage-direction in Jonson, Marston and Chapman's *Eastward Ho!* (1605) has the spoilt goldsmith's daughter Gertrude entering 'in a French head-attire' (1.2, s.d.).

We find head-tires in the costume-lists of the Admiral's Men. In an inventory of 1598 there are 'vj head-tiers', and in a list of 1602 'ii hedtiers sett w^t stons'.[33] The latter were perhaps the work of a Mrs Gosen or Goossen, who appears twice in Henslowe's accounts as a supplier of head-tires –

pd at the apoyntment of the companye vnto m^{rs} gosen for
a head tyer the 22 decembr 1601 the some of . . . . xij^s [12s]

pd at the apoyntmente of the company to m^{rs}goossen for
a headtyer the 7 of febreary 1601 [i.e. 1602] the some of. . . . xij^s

This gives a going rate of 12 shillings for a head-tire in 1602; if they are the tires 'sett w^t stons', the stones must be fake, which is sufficient for stage purposes. It is possible Mrs Gosen was foreign, at any rate her married name – usually Anglicized to Gosson – is Dutch. There is an interesting clan of Gossons in London, descended from a Dutch joiner, Cornelius Gosson, who settled in Canterbury. The best known is Stephen Gosson, author and controversialist, but in 1601 he was the vicar of St Botolph's, Bishopsgate, and his wife Elizabeth is unlikely to be the woman paid by Henslowe. Perhaps the tiremaker was the wife of William Gosson, listed in the subsidy rolls for Southwark, and thus local to Henslowe's Rose theatre.[34]

Another supplier to the company was a certain Mrs Calle. On 1 January 1603 she received ten shillings for 'ij curenets [coronets] for hed tyers'.[35] This is specified as being 'for the corte', so was connected with a court entertainment rather than a public playhouse.

As previously lamented, there survives no day-to-day documentation of Shakespeare's company comparable to that of the Admiral's Men at the Rose, but there is no reason to doubt that the costume-lists of the Chamberlain's Men (or from 1603 the

King's Men) would have featured head-tires, and that their ledgers would have included payments to tiremakers for supplying them.

We lack the documentation, but if we look in the playscripts of the company's chief author we find various glancing references to tires, and one or two rather more than glancing. The earliest is in *Two Gentlemen of Verona, c.* 1590 or earlier, where Julia gazes on the portrait of the noble Silvia and says wistfully,

> I think
> If I had such a tire this face of mine
> Were full as lovely as this of hers. (4.4.182–4)

The latest is in *The Winter's Tale, c.* 1610, the 'toys' for the head which Autolycus the pedlar advertises –

> Any silk, any thread,
> Any toys for your head,
> Of the new'st and fin'st, fin'st wear-a . . . (4.4.319–21)

– being a humble reflection, for country girls, of the radiant courtly tire. There is also a reference in *Antony and Cleopatra* (*c.* 1608), where Cleopatra recalls scenes of erotic cross-dressing with Antony, but perhaps in this case 'tires' = robes:

> I drunk him to his bed,
> Then put my tires and mantles on him, whilst
> I wore his sword Philippan . . . (2.5.22–4)

The most interesting and extended references occur in two plays he wrote in 1597–8. The first is in *Merry Wives of Windsor*, when Falstaff is energetically wooing a reluctant Mistress Ford –

FALSTAFF: I would make thee my lady!

MRS FORD: I your lady, Sir John? Alas, I should be a pitiful lady.

FALSTAFF: Let the court of France show me such another! I see how thine eye would emulate the diamond. Thou hast the right arched beauty of the brow that becomes the ship-tire, the tire-valiant, or any tire of Venetian admittance.

MRS FORD: A plain kerchief, Sir John: my brows become nothing else, nor that well neither. (3.3.45–54)

The first and last of these Falstaffian head-tires can be readily explained. The 'ship-tire' is presumably a head-dress fashioned in the form of a ship, or a ship's sails. It might be something like the 'attyre ... in form of two little ships made of emeralds' described in Jorge de Montemayor's pastoral novel *Diana* (*c.* 1559), with which Shakespeare was familiar in translation; or like the tall headwear which Nashe calls 'top-gallant caps' (the 'top-gallant' being one of the sails of an Elizabethan galleon).[36] And the 'tire of Venetian admittance' simply means a head-tire elaborate enough to be acceptable in Venice, then the byword for extravagance of dress.

The puzzling item is the 'tire-valiant'. H. R. Oliver, in the Arden edition of the play, takes 'valiant' as merely intensive – something like a tire de luxe – but this seems unsatisfactory. In the 1602 quarto of the play – a corrupt text, supplanted by the longer Folio text, but incorporating some authentic material from early performances – the phrase appears as 'tire vellet'. This is a known variant of 'velvet', but this rather heavy material is not particularly associated with tires. The eighteenth-century editor George Steevens thought the phrase should be 'tire-volant', which would suggest a 'flying' tire.[37] This does not seem a bad idea, especially as the play later features Mistress Quickly wearing a head-dress with 'ribbons pendant flaring 'bout her head'. The sense of 'flaring' is precisely fluttering or flying. Another possibility not aired before is that the quarto's 'vellet' is a misreporting of 'veilèd'.

But whether this particular tire is valiant, velvet, volatile or veiled, we get from this snatch of dialogue an interesting idea of the particular contextual niche into which head-tires fit in Shakespeare's mind. They are associated with courtly French ladies; they complement the 'arched beauty' of a woman's brow; they are the antithesis of the homely 'kerchief' worn by provincial middle-class Englishwomen like Mrs Ford.

As we have seen, the *Merry Wives* was performed by the Chamberlain's Men in the spring of 1597, to celebrate the investiture of the troupe's patron, Lord Hunsdon, in the Order of the Garter. Marie Mountjoy has a known connection with the Hunsdon circle at this time, and I have wondered if she was a supplier of head-tires to Lady Hunsdon, and if this was how she came to know Shakespeare. This is conjecture, but perhaps Falstaff's little riff on tires, and on the handsome French ladies who wear them, adds to the possibility. It would be a stratum of in-joke suitable for this courtly performance in honour of the Hunsdons.

Shakespeare makes another rather specialist reference to head-tires just a year later. In *Much Ado about Nothing*, a new tire is part of Hero's wedding get-up, over which her maidservant Margaret casts a critical eye: 'I like this new tire within excellently, if the hair were a thought browner' (3.4.12–13). Margaret is saying, pickily, that she would prefer this newly purchased tire if the hair of the headpiece were a touch darker. It does not quite match Hero's own dark hair, and will therefore be discernible as false, the desired effect of the tire being an indistinguishable match.

The appearance of 'Marie Mountjoy, Tyrewoman' in the household accounts of Queen Anne in 1604 may well be a result of her contact with two of the leading figures in the King's Men – Shakespeare, who was her lodger in that year, and John Heminges, who lived close by and whose managerial role within the company may include a specific involvement in the purchasing of costume.

It is well known that Queen Anne was a devotee of court masques and spectacles in which, in the manner of the French *cour de ballet*, she and her female favourites were the principal participants. Perhaps Marie was called on to provide headwear and hairdressing for these royal entertainments. We have glimpses elsewhere of specialist female head-dressers involved in shows put on at court, including this rather piquant entry –

[For] the hyer of heares for headdes and rewards, to the French woman for her paynes and her Dawghters paynes that went to Richmond & there attended upon Mr Hunnyes his Children [the Children of the Chapel Royal, directed by William Hunnis] & dressed theire heads &c, when they played before Her Majesty.[38]

This was a generation ago – the entry is from the Revels accounts for 1573–4 – but introduces an interesting parallel: 'the French-woman and her daughter'. What more natural than that Marie Mountjoy, attending on the Queen and other ladies of rank, should be accompanied and assisted by her daughter Mary?

A string of sumptuous, state-of-the-art masques are associated with Queen Anne, of which the first two fall within the period of Marie's own brief reign as royal tiremaker. The earliest was Ben Jonson and Inigo Jones's *Masque of Blacknesse*, commissioned by Anne in 1605, but little documentation remains of this show. There is a much fuller record, both documentary and pictorial, of the *Hymenaei*, performed on 5 January 1606, probably in the Banqueting House at Whitehall, to celebrate the ill-fated wedding of the 3rd Earl of Essex to Frances Howard (later annulled on the grounds of the Earl's sexual incapacity). It was another collaboration between Jonson and Inigo Jones, the latter providing the 'design and act'; the music was by Alfonso Ferrabosco the younger, and choreography by Thomas Giles.[39]

Much of the dialogue of *Hymenaei* was delivered by actors, but the climax was a splendid tableau in which Juno, goddess of marriage, probably played by Queen Anne herself, appeared among clouds on the upper part of the stage, flanked by two groups of four ladies representing her 'Powers'. One of these ladies was Elizabeth, Countess of Rutland, the daughter of Sir Philip Sidney, and by good fortune her accounts for the period survive. They show that she paid out more than £100 for the privilege of appearing in *Hymenaei*. A few days before the performance she paid £80 'to Mr Bethall the gentleman huisher [usher] for the maske', and to this general contribution can be added the following costs for her costume:

For cutworkes [fabric cut to look like lace] bought
for my Lady at the maske per Mr Doncombe . . . . .x^{li} [£10]

To Holmeade, silkeman, for masking ware . . . . iiij^{li} viij^{s} [£4 8s]

To the tyre woman for a coronet, vi^{li}; a payer of
embrodred silke hose, iiij^{li}; a ruffe, xxx^{s}; a paire of
shoowes, xiij^{s}, for my Lady for the maske. . . . . xij^{li} iij^{s} [£12 3s]^{40}

This 'tyre woman' fulfils both types of role suggested by the term.
The chief item she provides is a piece of headgear – the lavish
'coronet' worth £6 – but she also supplies more general costume
requirements: a ruff, silk stockings, shoes. The performers would
probably have had access to royal suppliers for their costumes,
so this unnamed tirewoman may be Marie Mountjoy, the only
tirewoman named in Queen Anne's accounts of this period.

Three full-length portraits, one of them attributed to John de
Critz the elder, show ladies in masque costume from this show.
One now at Woburn Abbey (see Plate 21) is identified in a later
inscription as Lucy Harington, Countess of Bedford. Another is
at Berkeley Castle, probably in connection with Elizabeth, Lady
Berkeley – the daughter of Lord Hunsdon – who was also one of
the performers in *Hymenaei*. There is an element of the pro-
duction-line in portraits like this, and they may not be very exact
likenesses. They commemorate an occasion, the portraitist a kind
of early version of the society photographer. The costume seen in
the paintings accords with Jonson's directions for the final scene
of the masque – the 'full gathered' skirt 'of carnation striped with
silver', and 'beneath that another flowing garment of watchet [sky
blue] cloth of silver laced with blue' – though there are some
divergences of detail in the paintings, as there probably were in
the performances.^{41}

Jonson's costume notes are specific about the head-tires worn
by the 'Powers' of Juno, and here too the portraits concur. Their
hair is 'carelessly bound under the circle of a rare and rich coronet'
– £6 worth of coronet, in fact, as we know from the Countess of

Rutland's accounts – 'adorned with all variety and choice of jewels, from the top of which flowed a transparent veil down to the ground, whose verge returning up, was fastened to either side in most sprightly manner'. This headwear caught the eye of a member of the audience, John Pory, who wrote in a letter: 'The women had every one a white plume of the richest heron's feathers, and were so rich in jewels upon their heads as was most glorious.'[42] The exuberant constructions we see in these portraits would certainly merit Falstaff's commendation as 'tires-valiant'. They express to the full this theatrical aspect of the tiremaker's trade.

16

In the workshop

*T*hat the Mountjoys supplied headgear to Shakespeare's
theatre company is plausible, and may be the first connection between them. But the certain connection between them is
that Shakespeare had rooms above their workshop, so it is the
manufacturing of tires, the daily business of tiremaking, which
impinges on him.

We have some fragmentary details about the practicalities of
the Mountjoy workshop. In the preamble to litigation with his
son-in-law Mountjoy mentions that he 'did buy into the shop . . .
silvered wire and other commodities concerning their trade to the
value of £10 or thereabouts'. He is referring to the period when
he and Belott were working together as partners (he mentions it
because Belott should have contributed some of the money but
did not). This was a specific period of about six months ('half a
yeare') during 1606–7, so we might suggest outgoings of about
£20 per annum on these tiremaking 'commodities' or materials.[43]
The 'silvered wire' would be used to make the framework of the
head-tire – 'Where is my wyer?' asks Lady Rimelaine as she
prepares her tire – and would also be connected with the making
of gold and silver thread, of which more below.

We also know of another purchase, or series of purchases,
for in the will of one Peter Courtois – by the sound of him a
fellow-Frenchman – it is recorded that 'Mr Mungeoy' owed him
£2 10s 11d for 'purled work'. The will is from 1603. Courtois,
who had his business in the Blackfriars, is described as a 'bandmaker' – in other words a maker of embroidered bands for hats,

collars, cuffs, etc. The 'purled work' he supplied to Mountjoy is 'thread or cord made of twisted gold or silver wire, and used for bordering and embroidering' (*OED*).[44]

Another commodity Mountjoy bought into the workshop (because no craftsman could actually make it) was human hair. By tradition this was supplied from corpses. Such is the implication in Shakespeare's Sonnet 68 –

> The golden tresses of the dead,
> The right of sepulchres, were shorn away
> To live a second life on second head . . .

– and in *The Merchant of Venice*, where the 'golden locks' of a wig are described as 'the dowry of a second head, / The skull that bred them in the sepulchre'. It would be an exaggeration to say that all false hair was shorn from the skulls of the dead, but this is the association. The only other source is the heads of the living, which is less sinister but has an overtone of desperation. Horse-hair was also used, but not quite *de rigueur*; hemp even less so. Human hair was preferred by those who could afford it, as it is today – according to her hairdresser, Victoria Beckham spends around £6,000 a year on hair extensions, using 'real hair' from Poland, Russia and India.[45]

The silvered wire and the purled work are recorded purchases, but there is good evidence that these or related materials were also made in the workshop. One might anyway suppose so: this was a highly competitive market, and buying in expensive finished materials added further pressure to already tight profit margins. Better to make your own, where possible: 'vertical integration'.

Among the meagre items of 'houshould stuffe' which Mountjoy grudgingly gave to Stephen and Mary Belott in 1605 are the following work-related items:

An old drawing table
Two old joined stools
One wainscot cupboard

One twisting wheel of wood
Two pair of little scissors
One old trunk and a like old trunk
One bobbin box

Leaving aside the cupboard and trunks we have here a brief synopsis of the tiremaker's equipment.

The 'drawing table' looks at first glance like a table on which to do designs and templates for tires – drawing in the sense of draughtsmanship – but it is more likely to be a workbench for wire-drawing, a process which involved pulling rods of gilded silver, heated or 'annealed' for ductility, through dies of decreasing gauge until the required thinness was reached.[46] The tiremaker would not deal in the earlier stages of the process, which required equipment akin to the blacksmith's, but in more subtle renderings of fine-gauged wire. There are at least two grades used in a head-tire – the stiffer wire which forms the framework of the arrangement; and a much finer wire used for the gold and silver thread which decorates the tire. This wire-drawing activity may suggest that the workshop also produced other wired structures used in the fashion trade, such as the 'supporters' or 'underproppers' which held up heavily starched ruffs, collars, rebatos and so on. These would be made of much the same gauge of wire as the head-tire.

The wooden 'twisting wheel' donated to the fledgling tiremakers was a small spinning-wheel used for twisting or twining thin filaments of yarn to make thread. By far the most common application was silk-twisting. Thus a handbook of 1688 defines a twisting wheel as 'an engine wherewith 2, 3 or more silk threads are twisted or turned all together into one entire double thread'.[47] The slender filaments of silk to be twisted into thread were known as 'sleaves'. They were drawn out, prior to the spinning, from a bundle of coarse raw silk called 'sleave silk' or 'sley silk' (nowadays more likely be called 'silk floss'). In 1588 an ounce of 'slaye sylke' cost 8d.[48] A number of silk-twisters from Picardie are recorded in the 1593 Return of Strangers: we might think of silk-twisting as a Picard craft or industry which Mountjoy learned in his youth, and which he later applied in the more specialist area of tiremaking.

The wheel was also used for making gold or silver thread, which consists of a thin strip of flattened gold or silver, 'wrapped or laid over a thread of silk by twisting it with a wheel'.[49] ('Gold' in this context is almost always gilded silver.) These gold or silver threads could in turn be plaited into gold or silver 'twist', which is corded like a miniature rope. The 'purled work' purchased from Mr Courtois was a kind of twist; the gold twist best known today is the braiding on the sleeves of naval officers' and airline pilots' uniforms. The twisting wheel controls the tension, which must be got absolutely right. If it is too slack the cord does not hold together; if it is too tight the cord kinks.

All three products of the twisting wheel – silk thread, gold and silver thread and gold and silver twist – were used in the creation of head-tires.

An integral part of the twisting wheel was the bobbin on to which the intertwined thread or twist was wound. That 'bobbin box' donated to the newly-weds presumably contained a set of bobbins of various sizes. They were at this time wooden, but had originally been made of bone – whence 'bone lace', produced by spinning as distinct from needlework. Cotgrave's 1612 dictionary associates bobbins with gold and silver threadmaking: he defines French *bobine* as 'a quill for a spinning-wheel; also a skane or hank of gold or silver thread'.

On the evidence of the 'houshould stuffe' inventory we can say that the activities of the Silver Street workshop included fine wire-drawing and various kinds of thread-twisting. Both these are confirmed by a later document involving Stephen Belott. In 1621, Belott petitioned against the activities of the Monopolies Commission.[50] Among his complaints was that an agent of the monopolists had confiscated his 'mill', which was 'the only instrument of his living'. This mill is for wire-drawing: it is the iron or steel plate, perforated with die-holes of different diameters, through which the wire is drawn. Belott also says that for many years he has 'gotten his living by working gold and silver thread', and he describes himself as 'sometime servant to Monioye, gold wiredrawer'.

Christopher Mountjoy is elsewhere mentioned as one who practised the 'mystery' of making and working 'Venice gold and silver thread'.[51] Venice gold was another term for gold thread, though the Venetians had in turn imported the art of making it from the Middle East, and it is sometimes called 'Damask [Damascus] gold'. There is some evidence that true Venice gold involved a particular technique using strips of gilded vellum – both lighter and cheaper than wire – but the term as used in England was probably not so specific. Shakespeare refers to Venice gold in *The Taming of the Shrew* – it is part of a catalogue of exquisite and expensive materials to be seen in Gremio's 'richly furnished' town-house: 'Tyrian tapestry', 'Arras counterpoints', 'Turkey cushions bossed with pearl' and 'valance of Venice gold in needlework' (2.1.345–50). Venice gold was primarily used by embroiderers, and is frequently found in the accounts and inventories of the Queen's wardrobe.

We have at least a broad idea of the daily activities of the Mountjoy workshop – enough, perhaps, to mock up one of those informatively captioned engravings, often continental, which show us everything happening at once. In one part of the shop an apprentice sits at a table or bench, drawing wires of gilded silver through die-holes to make the fine wire suitable for gold thread. There are hammers and rollers to flatten the wire into strips ready for spinning into thread. In another part of the shop bundles of lank raw silk are being separated into 'sleaves'. A third person is working the 'twisting wheel', turning those sleaves into silk thread, and silk thread into sparkling Venice gold. Elsewhere there are women sewing and stitching, the snipping of those 'little scissors', the application of colour and glitter to beautify the wiry carapace of the tire. Here we see bales of cloth – the gauzy 'lawn' which Cotgrave calls 'toile d'atour', or tire-cloth; the satins and taffetas 'of sundry colours'. Here too are ribbons, laces, purled bands, feathers, tinsels, nets, veils, bodkins, seed-pearls, black bugles – and baskets filled with a faintly sinister cargo of human hair, also of sundry colours, yellow and silver being especially sought after. In the background, in an adjoining room, a fashionable lady receives a finished headpiece graciously proffered by the tiremaker's wife.

It is a scene of small-scale, miniaturist work: repetitive and delicate. It is hard work on the eyes, and is made more so by the law that immigrants' shops should have a 'lattice before the window' so their wares cannot be seen from the street. Metal fumes hang in the close air of the workshop, the smell of glues and dyes. Perhaps these, rather than pregnancy, were a cause of those stomach pains and 'swimming in the head' of which Marie complains to Dr Forman.

Just outside the frame of our imagined engraving – involved only in a casual, non-professional sense, but involved nonetheless – is a well-dressed gentleman of middle age who might perhaps be a merchant or mercer, but who is in fact the tiremaker's lodger, 'one Mr Shakespeare'. He passes on his way to and from the street, keeping his slightly odd hours; he is a shadow in the doorway, a footstep on the stairs. He is familiar with the scene whose outlines I have tried to construct: he observes and enquires, and what he sees and hears is stored away in that capacious and miraculously accessible memory, to be used in turn as raw material in the manufacturing of metaphors –

Thou immaterial skein of sleave-silk, thou green sarcenet flap for a sore eye, thou tassel of a prodigal's purse . . . (*Troilus and Cressida*, 5.1.29–30)

Sleep that knits up the ravell'd sleave of care . . . (*Macbeth*, 2.2.36)

Be't when she weav'd the sleided silk
With fingers long, small, white as milk . . . (*Pericles*, 4.Chor.21–2)

Breaking his oath and resolution, like
A twist of rotten silk . . . (*Coriolanus*, 5.2.96–7)

These are in approximate chronological order (the exact date of *Coriolanus* is uncertain). The earliest is Thersites' ingenious insult from *Troilus*, a play first mentioned in the Stationers' Register on 7 February 1603, and probably composed in 1602, the year in which – according to his later recollection – Shakespeare first met Christopher Mountjoy, and thus the earliest date for his sojourn on Silver Street. It is redolent of the tire-shop. The author's eye has taken in not only the skein of sleave-silk, which is 'immaterial' both visually – light, flossy, frothy – and because it is irrelevant or unusable until separated into spinnable filaments, but also the sarcanets and tassels which are part of the tiremaker's decorative arts. We find sarcenet (a fine soft silk of taffeta weave) associated with tires in Queen Elizabeth's accounts – 'sarcenets [for] tuftinge, tyringe of hedpeces, and gyrdells'.[52]

The line from *Macbeth*, composed c. 1606, is famous but often misunderstood. In the first edition of 1623 (despite its fame today the play had no separate edition before the First Folio) 'sleave' is spelt 'sleeve'; and that is the word most people hear in performance, especially in conjunction with 'knit'. The line is therefore taken to mean that the anxious mind is repaired by sleep, as a frayed sleeve is repaired by knitting.[53] This is cogent but the metaphor seems bland. We are at a moment of high psychological drama: the murder of King Duncan is done; Macbeth is confronting the trauma of guilt, which will bring in the play's insomniac visions and night-terrors: 'Methought I heard a voice cry, Sleep no more!' His state of mind is imagined not as frayed but as tangled, confused, knotted (sense 1 of 'ravel' in *OED*, 'to become entangled or confused') and most modern editors endorse the reading of 'sleave', as first proposed by George Steevens in the eighteenth century. Sleep brings order to this bundle of emotions as the hand of a silkworker unravels a tangled sheaf of sleave-silk.

In this reading the metaphor is visually linked with the simple but vivid image of the lost daughter Marina in *Pericles*, and her slender white fingers weaving 'sleided' (sleaved) silk. The play was written with George Wilkins in c. 1607–8, by which time

Shakespeare had probably moved on from Silver Street. The image may be a memory of the Mountjoy workshop – one wonders whose pale hands he is remembering.

17

The underpropper

We imagine Shakespeare on the periphery of the Mountjoy workshop, observing those details of the tiremaker's trade which surface in his texts. To see him in our mind's eye we borrow from various images of him, chief among them the engraved portrait in the First Folio, at once the most authentic and problematic of the portraits – the domed forehead, the perfunctorily stippled beard, the stiff, tray-like collar. The sombrely stylish 'Chandos' portrait is more attractive, and more theatrical, but it is the Folio engraving which has the imprimatur of Shakespeare's contemporaries – it is placed at the threshold of his Collected Works by editors who had known him for decades, and who presumably considered it a reasonable likeness.[54] And just possibly this iconic little portrait of Shakespeare has, in itself, a connection with the Silver Street workshop.

The circumstances of the portrait are mysterious. All we know for certain is to be found in the three millimetres of margin that surrounds the engraving, where a neat cursive inscription reads, 'Martin Droeshout sculpsit London'. But exactly which Martin Droeshout 'sculpted' or engraved it is not clear. The Droeshouts were a dynasty of immigrant Dutch painters and engravers – the contemporary English spelling 'Drussett' broadly conveys the correct Dutch pronunciation. There are two Martins on record, uncle and nephew, and both have their proponents as the engraver of the Folio portrait.[55]

Whichever one it was, it is more or less certain that his engraving was based, as most of them were, on an earlier portrait. It was a copy. According to Roy Strong the original portrait was a miniature, as 'evidenced in the linear terms [of the engraving] which could derive from a miniature in the Hilliard manner'. He compares William Marshall's engraving of John Donne, published in the 1630s, but based on a painted miniature of 1591. Others see no specific evidence that the original was a miniature; it could have been a line-drawing, or a 'small-scale panel or canvas painting'.[56] The fact that the engraving is a copy explains some of its technical deficiencies, particularly the disproportion of the head and body. The head and the collar go together well enough but the shoulders do not belong at all – they are too small, and are skewed at an odd angle, resulting in the meaningless physiology of the upper-right arm. A ready explanation is that the original portrait showed only the head and the collar – a common enough format in miniature portraits. These the engraver copied; the rest, for which he had no model before him, he 'infelicitously invented'.[57]

How old is the man in the picture? The first impression is of seniority – the drastic baldness, and also the greying of the hair, particularly around the left temple. (This is a deliberate engraver's effect – the lines representing the hair are discontinuous; the flecks of grey are uninked paper.) But the face looks younger than the hair would suggest; it is alert and rather fine featured. The high forehead reveals no wrinkling; those bags under his eyes seem indicative of tiredness – too much composition by candlelight, perhaps – rather than saggy with age. He certainly looks younger than the stout burgher depicted in the Stratford funeral effigy, which would show him in his last years (and may do so quite accurately, as there is some evidence that the sculptor – another immigrant artist, Gheerart Janssen junior – knew him personally). He also looks younger than the world-weary man in the 'Chandos' portrait, conventionally dated to c. 1610, when Shakespeare was in his mid-forties.[58]

These are subjective impressions but the conclusion to which they tend seems a sensible one. It is that the Droeshout engraving shows Shakespeare in early middle age, perhaps around forty or so (middle age came earlier then), still vigorous, but with signs of wear and tear. This would give us a date of *c.* 1604 for the original portrait – not a bad time for Shakespeare, newly elevated as one of the King's Men, to have his picture painted.

This is not contradicted by the dating evidence provided by the wide, stiffly starched linen collar (not, as is sometimes said, a ruff) worn by Shakespeare. It is engraved with great specificity (see Frontispiece). The arrow-shaped markings are not merely decorative, but realistically depict the 'narrow darts made on the inside of the linen band to shape it to the neck'. This conveys also the fineness of the collar's fabric, the sheer linen through which the pleating underneath is visible. If this collar or 'band' was part of the original portrait, its style could suggest a date as early as *c.* 1604. Thus Tarnya Cooper of the National Portrait Gallery: 'This type of collar with triangular sewn darts fanning out from the face appears in portraits that date from around 1604 to 1613.'[59]

The age of the sitter and the style of his neckwear broadly concur – when Shakespeare was forty that collar was newly fashionable. The evidence, such as it is, suggests that the lost portrait of him copied by Martin Droeshout was painted in or shortly after the year 1604 – precisely the period of his sojourn on Silver Street.

And perhaps the collar has something more to tell us. As well as the triangular darts fanning out from the neck there is visible a curving line running roughly parallel to the outer edge of the collar. This is not something sewn on to it. It is part of a wire supporter or 'underpropper', visible through the fabric of the collar. Formal ruffs and bands were heavily starched, and needed additional support underneath to hold them up at the back of the neck, in order to frame the face in the desired way. The Puritan pamphleteer Philip Stubbes, whose *Anatomie of Abuses* (1583) rails against contemporary vanities, and in doing so gives a detailed account of the fashions of the day, defines the under-propper as a 'certain device made of wyres ... whipped over either with gold thread, silver or silk'. It is 'applied' around the neck, 'to beare up the whole frame and body of the ruff from falling and hanging down'.[60]

We find them in Queen Elizabeth's wardrobe accounts. In 1588 her silkman Roger Mountague supplied 'one supporter of wyer whipped over with silke'. In 1601 Dorothy Speckard supplied 'a fyne ruffe pinned upon a French wire', and 'two rebata wyres' (a rebato was a collar that stood up almost vertically behind the wearer's head).[61] And Lady Rimelaine, in Erondell's *French Garden* of 1605, chooses between 'a ruffe band or a Rebato', but looking at the ruff she finds 'the supporter is so soyled' that she cannot wear it. 'Take it away, give me my Rebato of cutworke edged' – but this too is dirty: 'the wyer after the same sort as the other'.

These 'devices' of wire 'whipped over' with gold thread or silk may well have been produced in the Mountjoy workshop. They require the same materials as a tire, they use the same wire-working techniques, and they appeal to broadly the same fashion-conscious clientele.[62] It is possible, therefore, that when Shakespeare sat for his portrait, perhaps in around 1604, he did so wearing a supporter or underpropper made in the busy workshop below the rooms where he lodged.

1. The deposition. Shakespeare's statement at the Court of Requests, 11 May 1612.

2. Plaintiff and defendant in a scene from a Jacobean law-court.

3. Witness-list for the first session of the Belott–Mountjoy suit, including 'Willm Shakespeare gent'.

4. Signatures of
(a) Daniel Nicholas,
(b) William Eaton,
(c) Noel Mountjoy and
(d) Humphrey Fludd.

5. Hulda and Charles William Wallace, discoverers of the Belott–Mountjoy papers, at the Public Record Office, *c.* 1909.

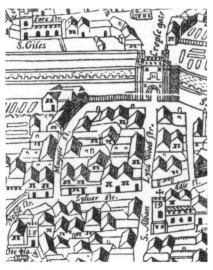

6. The house on the corner. Detail from the 'Agas' map showing Silver Street and Muggle (or Monkwell) Street.

7. The Coopers' Arms, on the site of the Mountjoys' house, from a photograph of *c.* 1910.

8. St Giles, Cripplegate, with bombed-out buildings of Silver Street in the foreground. Drawing by Dennis Flanders, 1941.

9. Commemorative stone on the site of St Olave's, Silver Street.

10. The surgeon of Silver Street. John Banister anatomizing a corpse at Barber-Surgeons' Hall, 1580.

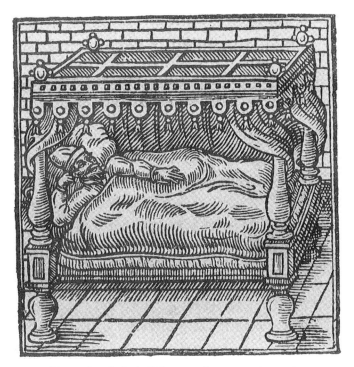

11. The author in bed. Title-page illustration from Thomas Dekker's *Dekker his Dreame (1620).*

Le Couſturier.

Apportez-moy de la beſongne,
Ie ſuis habille Couſturier,
Qui ſçait bien l'eſtoffe employer,
Autant qu'autre de la Bourgongne.

vj.

12. A Huguenot tailor at work, *c.* 1600.

13. Subsidy roll for Aldersgate ward, 1582, listing Christopher 'Mongey' and his wife as tax-payers.

14. 'Mrs Monjoyes childe'. Burial entry in the St Olave's register, 27 February 1596.

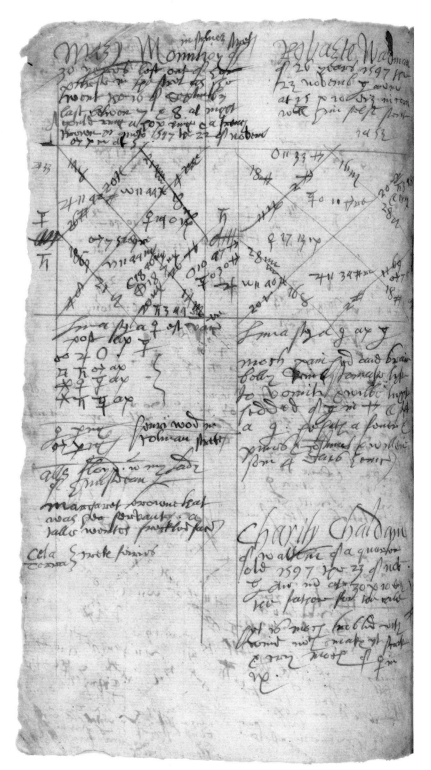

15. Marie Mountjoy consults Dr Forman about missing valuables,
22 November 1597.

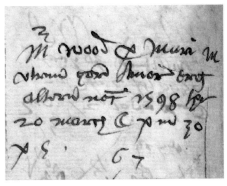

17. Henry Wood asks Forman about 'Mari M', 20 March 1598.

16. Simon Forman, astrologer, physician and serial seducer.

18. Marie and 'Madam Kitson' in a jotting by Forman, c. January 1598.

19. A woman visiting an astrologer, from a seventeenth-century woodcut.

20. A French dancer of *c.* 1580, wearing a head-tire of the sort made by the Mountjoys.

21. A lady (perhaps Lucy Harington, Countess of Bedford) costumed for the masque *Hymenaei*, 1606.

22. Theatrical headwear in Henry Peacham's sketch of a scene from *Titus Andronicus, c.* 159.

[Secretary-hand manuscript accounts, partially legible]

Maric ... Mountjoy Tyrewoman in full payment of her Bill ...

... brought in and vouched in the Attompt before mentioned and there ...

amongst the remembr of the said Attompt heere allowed and paid accordinge

to the said Bill and two ... vnder the hand of the said Maric Mountjoy ...

now brought in and rem as aforesaid thone dated the ... of November ...

1604 for the receipt of ... and thother dated the ... of March 1604

aforesaid for the receipt of ... in all as by the said ... may appeare

amountinge to ...

William ... Habberdasher in full payment of his Bille of ...

... brought in and vouched in the Attompt before mentioned and there ...

23. Payments to 'Marie Mountjoy Tyrewoman' in Queen Anne's household accounts, 1604–5.

24. Queen Anne by Marcus Gheeraerts the Younger, *c.* 1605–10.

25. Signature of George Wilkins.

THE
Miferies of Inforſt
MARIAGE.

eAs it is now playd by his Maiefties
Seruants.

Quj Alios, (feipfum) docet.

By George Wilkins.

LONDON
Printed for George Vincent, and are to be fold at his fhop in
Woodftreet. 1607.

26. First edition of Wilkins's *Miseries*,
performed by the King's Men in *c.* 1606.

27. 'A punk after supper'. Customers eating in a Jacobean brothel.

28. The famous Southwark brothel called Holland's Leaguer,
in a woodcut of 1632.

29. Tire-wearing courtesan from a painting by Isaac Oliver, c. 1590–95.

30. A wherry on the Thames near London Bridge, 1614. These water-taxis took playgoers across to the Globe and adulterers upriver to Brentford.

31. The Three Pigeons at Brentford, owned by Shakespeare's colleague John Lowin, seen here in a nineteenth-century engraving.

32. A handfasting. Detail from Gerrit van Honthorst's *Supper with Betrothal*, *c.* 1625.

33. Wedding of Stephen and Mary at St Olave's, 19 November 1604.

34. Burial of Marie Mountjoy at St Olave's, 30 October 1606.

35. Register copy of Christopher Mountjoy's will, 26 January 1620.

36. Burial of Christopher Mountjoy at St Giles, Cripplegate, 29 March 1620.

PART FIVE

Among Strangers

Écoutez: d'hand, de fingre, de nayles, d'arma,
de bilbow . . .

Henry V, 3.4.26–7

18

Blackfriars and Navarre

When he moved into the Mountjoys' house in around 1603 Shakespeare was making a choice somewhat unusual among his contemporaries – he was choosing to live with foreigners. We find him among strangers. Is this a matter of chance and convenience, or does it tell us something about him? Or – to put the question in more practical form – what else do we know about his relationship with foreigners, and particularly with French people?

One of the first foreigners Shakespeare knew in London was a Frenchwoman, Jacqueline Field, the wife of the printer and publisher Richard Field. Field has a place in literary history as the publisher of Shakespeare's first printed work, the narrative poem *Venus and Adonis* (1593); he also printed, for another publisher, Shakespeare's follow-up, *Lucrece* (1594). The connection between them went back to childhood, for Field was a Stratford man, a couple of years older than Shakespeare. They were of much the same social class, a tanner's son and a glover's son, and for a time they were schoolfellows at Stratford grammar. When he was eighteen Field left for London, and there served apprentice with the Huguenot printer Thomas Vautrollier, who had a printing-shop in the Blackfriars. By the time Shakespeare himself arrived in London, Field's circumstances were changing rapidly – in February 1587 he completed his apprenticeship; in July 1587 his master Vautrollier died; in 1588 he published his first book, in partnership with Vautrollier's widow, Jacqueline; and on 12 January 1589 he cemented this new arrangement by marrying her. It is very likely Shakespeare knew the Fields at this stage, as he certainly did in 1593 when Field became his publisher.[1]

What do we know of Jacqueline? As she had a child by Richard Field in 1590, she cannot have been born much before 1550. Her maiden name was Dutwite. Her father, James, was living in the immigrant enclave of St Martin le Grand when he died in 1591. He may have known the Mountjoys, who were living in the area in the 1580s.[2]

Jacqueline's first husband Thomas Vautrollier, a native of Troyes, was probably rather older than her. He had come to England in the late 1550s – he is first recorded working as a bookbinder – and was granted denizenship in 1562. They had at least four children. Vautrollier was a high-class printer, and business thrived: in the mid-1570s he was employing 'six woorke-men, Frenchmen or Duchemen' in his shop. He expanded his business into Scotland, and when he was away the busy Black-friars printing-shop was managed by Jacqueline. In 1581 the Stationers' Company noted that she was printing an edition of Cicero's *Epistles* 'in her husband's absence'.[3] Whether she also dallied with apprentices in her husband's absence is not known – her later marriage to Field was obviously *de convenance*, a business partnership, whatever else it was. They had a son, Richard junior, in 1590. 'Mr Field's wife', presumably Jacqueline, was buried at St Anne's, Blackfriars, on 9 March 1611.

One would like to know more, but what there is seems to suggest some similarities between Jacqueline and Marie Mount-joy. Not personal similiarities, which we cannot know, but pro-fessional ones. They are two women very much involved in their husband's business: energetic, capable, *engagées*. It is sometimes thought that Shakespeare came to know the Mountjoys through his prior acquaintance with their compatriot Jacqueline, though in my view a theatrical connection is more likely. Both women considered their husband's apprentice a good match – though in Jacqueline's case a match for herself rather than for a daughter. And both, of course, were alluringly French.[4]

*

Shakespeare's association with the Fields brought him into contact with a range of French news and views. Vautrollier had been a major producer of books in French or about French affairs. He had been encouraged in this by Lord Burghley, who saw propagandist advantage in a controlled output of French news at a time when English troops were supporting the Huguenot cause. Field inherited this role enthusiastically.[5] At the Blackfriars shop Shakespeare could read French news and French philosophy, and – on a more practical note – the French language-manuals printed by Field such as Claude Hollyband's *French Littleton* (1591) and G. de la Mothe's *French Alphabet* (1592).

Field's French connections – his wife, his authors, his publications – may be reflected in Shakespeare's early comedy, *Love's Labour's Lost*, one of three plays he set in France (the others are *As You Like It* and *All's Well*). The play's location is the royal court of Navarre in southern France. It has a king who is named Ferdinand in the play, but who inevitably calls to mind the real king, Henri of Navarre; and a visiting French princess who has elements of Henri's wife, Marguerite de Valois; and the King's three companions (Berowne, Longaville and Dumain), who are named after actual followers of Henri (the Ducs de Biron, de Longueville and d'Aumont). A series of correspondences between the play and historical events in Navarre was worked out by Abel Lefranc in 1918, and though some are tenuous, there are striking parallels. The play's 'little Achademe' of philosophical noblemen reflects Henri's own academy, to which Marguerite refers humorously in a letter of 1582, and the arrival of the Princess of France reflects real embassies from Marguerite to Henri prior to their marriage. Before one such, at Nirac in 1578, the Duc de Sully promised: 'On se livra au plaisir, aux festins et aux fêtes galantes, ne nous amusant tous qu'à rire, danser et courir la bague' (We will give ourselves up to pleasure, parties and pageantry, and do nothing but laugh, dance and gallivant).[6] This is the festive, arcadian mood of *Love's Labours*, set in a comedic version of Navarre – or rather, perhaps, set in a lost Navarre, for Henri was now King of France and the days of his 'little Achademe' were past.

Shakespeare's knowledge of the Navarre court is not particularly inside knowledge, but it must have come from somewhere. No printed source has been identified (the memoirs of Marguerite de Valois, on which Lefranc drew for some of his parallels, were not published till 1628). Perhaps the source was a place – the Fields' house in Blackfriars, where there were French people to talk to, and French books to consult, among them news pamphlets about Henri of Navarre such as the *Oration and Declaration of Henrie IV*, printed by Field in 1590.[7] *Love's Labours* is broadly dateable to *c.* 1593–5, composition thus coinciding with the printing of *Venus* and *Lucrece* at Field's shop. The 1593 quarto of *Venus* is 'exceptionally free' of misprints, which probably means the author was on hand to correct the proofs.[8]

Venus was on the bookstalls by 12 June 1593, when an elderly civil servant named Richard Stonley noted his expenditure of a shilling 'for the Survey of ffraunce with the Venus & Adhonay p[e]r Shakspere'. The book thus coupled with Shakespeare's was John Eliot's *Survay or Topographical Description of France* (1592) – more French news. It was published by John Wolfe, whose printing house in St Paul's Churchyard was another centre of foreign-interest books. Eliot was a colourful Grub Street character and passionate Francophile, who was also – like Shakespeare and Field – a native of Warwickshire. He is another plausible source for Shakespeare's interest in French affairs.[9]

One of the enigmatic jokes which litter *Love's Labour's Lost* refers to a 'French brawl' (3.1.7), and given the probable date of the play it has been suggested that this alludes to London's anti-immigrant riots of April–May 1593. Shakespeare's festive evocation of Navarre is set against the reality of London in 1593, where gangs of apprentices marched the streets chanting those murderous anti-French slogans –

> Weele cutt your throates in your temples praying
> Not Paris massacre so much blood did spill.

These commotions are exactly contemporary with the printing of *Venus and Adonis* at the Blackfriars press of Richard

Field, where the Frenchwoman Jacqueline would have felt their shockwaves.

The France of *Love's Labours* – a locus of philosophical noblemen, ingenious repartee, coquettish court ladies, over-elaborate courtesies, masques, hunts, picnics – is a kind of riposte to current anti-French hysteria. I do not suggest Shakespeare wrote it to this end, but in writing it he gives a view of the French very different from the views of the xenophobe mob, and indeed different from his own jingoistic sorties against the French in his early *Henry VI* plays. There his view was determined by historical requirements, but in comedy he is free to roam in this rose-tinted France of the imagination, where love wrangles with philosophy.

Also connected with the anti-immigrant riots are some lines attributed to Shakespeare in the 'Booke of Sir Thomas More'. This play about the great Tudor humanist and martyr, apparently never published and perhaps never performed, survives in a remarkable manuscript in the British Library, complete with marginal notes in the hand of Sir Edward Tilney, Master of the Revels, demanding cuts in the text ('Leave out ye insurrection wholy and ye causes theroff,' reads one curt instruction). The manuscript is written in six different hands, one of which – 'Hand D' – is argued on strong palaeographic evidence to be Shakespeare's. In the single scene he contributed, he shows More pacifying the rioters of the 'Ill May Day' riots of 1517. The events depicted are parallel with the riots of 1593, and the play was possibly written around that date – hence the censor's nervousness.[10]

In the scene, the leader of the aggrieved mob, John Lincoln, calls up the spectre of rising prices attributed to the influx of 'strangers'. 'He that will not see red herring at a Harry groat, butter at eleven pence a pound, meal at nine shillings a bushel, and beef at four nobles a stone, list to me.' It will come to this, another adds, 'if strangers be suffered'. Lincoln also complains about the foreigners' eating habits. They 'bring in strange roots, which is merely to the undoing of poor prentices, for what's a sorry parsnip to a good heart?' These exotic vegetables –

'pumpions' are also mentioned – are said to 'breed sore eyes', and to cause infection because they 'grow in dung'. This is both ironic and authentic: the invented grievances of racism.

More replies with a finely argued plea for tolerance. The rioters want the refugees 'removed' – the perennial rhetoric of repatriation – but More asks them to contemplate the human reality of this expulsion:

> Imagine that you see the wretched strangers,
> Their babies at their backs, with their poor luggage,
> Plodding to th' ports and coasts for transportation . . .

And he cleverly asks them to imagine what it might be like to be a 'stranger', for this is exactly what they will be when they have been banished for their riotous behaviour. Thus he draws them into sympathy and identification. What would it feel like to be rejected by 'a nation of such barbarous temper that . . . would not afford you an abode on earth'? To be subjected to acts of violence by people who 'whet their detested knives against your throats' and 'spurn you like dogs'?

> What would you think
> To be thus used? This is the strangers' case,
> And this your mountainish inhumanity.

'Mountainish' is not found elsewhere in Shakespeare, but compare Coriolanus' phrase 'mountainous error' (2.3.119), from a comparable scene in which he addresses a fractious mob; and also 'waterish' in *King Lear* (1.1.258).

Thus by a quirk of palaeographic fate, the only surviving literary manuscript by Shakespeare contains a compassionate speech on behalf of London's immigrants, just as the only surviving record of his spoken words contains a reminiscence of events in the house of an immigrant family in London.

೫

19

Shakespeare's aliens

'**P**igges and Frenchmen speake one language: awee awee!'[11] A vein of boisterous xenophobia runs through the play-house comedies of the 1590s. The French were one of the butts of this, though probably no more than the Spanish, the Dutch and the Italians. William Haughton's *Englishmen for my Money* (1598), from which the above line is taken, is a feast of stereo-types, with its story of the three daughters of an immigrant mer-chant in London, and their foiling of his plans to marry them off to rich foreigners.

Shakespeare was happy to wheel on a comic Frenchman when it suited him. Monsieur Le Bon has a walk-on part as one of Portia's suitors in *The Merchant of Venice* (*c.* 1596). Her com-ments convey an idea of the Frenchman's hyperactive sense of superiority. In Le Bon, savoir-faire is exaggerated to a pitch of highly strung competitiveness –

Why, he hath a horse better than the Neapolitan's, a better bad habit of frowning than the Count Palatine's – he is every man in no man. If a throstle sing, he falls straight a-capering. He will fence with his own shadow. If I should marry him I should marry twenty husbands. (1.2.55–60)

Shakespeare has more extensive fun with the Frenchman Dr Caius in *The Merry Wives of Windsor*. He is a blustery, touchy, belligerent character, as the French were said to be (and as Chris-topher Mountjoy seems to have been). He is also lecherous, or at least overheated, in his pursuit of the pretty young citizen's daughter Anne Page. Lechery is another stock association with the French (and again relevant to Mountjoy, at least as described by the elders of the French Church). On a more sociological note, he is a medical man: 'Master Doctor Caius, the renowned French physician'. He has an upmarket English clientele – 'de earl, de knight, de lords, de gentlemen' – to whom he administers 'the potions and the motions' (purgatives to move their bowels). This accurately reflects a fashion for French physicians, though the most famous of them, James's physician Theodore Turquet de Mayerne, had not yet arrived in England. A quack doctor satirically portrayed by Nashe in *Terrors of the Night* (1594) 'speaks nothing but broken English like a French doctor'.[12]

The comedy of Dr Caius, such as it is, lies mostly in his broken English (thus parallel with the other comic foreigner of the play, the Welshman Hugh Evans). Before his first entry his housekeeper Mistress Quickly whets the audience's appetite for this – 'Here will be an old abusing of God's patience and the King's English.' Caius' accent leads to double entendres, such as 'by my trot', where 'troth' becomes 'trot' = prostitute, and 'if there be one or two I shall make-a the turd' (3.3.219). He switches erratically from French to English, and has that hurrying tone which imperfect speakers of a language affect to cover their deficiencies – 'Vetch me in my closet *une boitine verde* – a box, a green-a box. Do intend vat I speak? A green-a box'; '*Mette le au mon* pocket – *depeche*, quickly'; ''Ods me, *que ai-je oublié?*' (1.4.41–58).

Possibly one heard this sort of immigrant patois in the Mountjoy household, though to suggest this is to collude in a stereotyping of them. In general the dialect of these Elizabethan stage-foreigners, with its impenetrable oaths and me-have-got syntax, is more comic convention than realistic representation. Caius' Franglais is echoed by later French characters like Delion in Haughton's *Englishmen for my Money,* John Fotheking in Marston's *Jack Drum's Entertainment* (1600), and Bullaker in Chapman's *Sir Giles Goosecap* (c. 1601). It is a stylized routine, equivalent to the surreal Italian-American of Chico Marx.

Dr Caius is a mere caper, in a play which (according to tradition) was cooked up in a few weeks for performance before the Queen. Traces of hurry are evident in this minor character. The speech characteristics which define him in the opening scene soon slacken off, leaving little but a funny accent. And when the play went on tour, even Caius' Frenchness becomes vague. In the 1602 quarto of *Merry Wives*, which is based on an abridged touring version of the play, Caius slips into German as well as French, suggesting that any old foreign accent or lexicon was sufficient when playing to provincial audiences. He is just 'Johnny Foreigner'.[13]

There are further comments and jokes about the French in *Henry V* (1599), though the context is historical and patriotic. Notably the play contains the only Shakespeare scene written entirely in French, and has liberal quantities of French in other scenes. His basic command of the language is clear, and at least some of the errors in the text are demonstrably the fault of incompetent copyists or compositors. The opinion of J. Dover Wilson on the French dialogue in *Henry V* is probably right: 'If we allow for Shakespeare's handwriting, for the Folio compositor's ignorance of French, for phonetic spellings to help the boy players, and for the occurrence of early modern French forms, it is doubtful whether there was originally very much wrong with Shakespeare's French.'[14] He may well have had some help from a native speaker, not impossibly Marie Mountjoy, though all that can be said for sure is that he consulted a language manual – John Eliot's lively *Ortho-epia Gallica* (1593) – when writing some of the scenes.[15] In choosing to use 'proper' French, Shakespeare departs from stage convention. It is a calculated theatrical risk – a good proportion of his audience knew no French at all – but it adds a new dimension of realism to this chronicle of events in the 'vasty fields of France'.

In one of his last plays, *Henry VIII*, written in collaboration with John Fletcher, there is a witty take on French affectations among the English – 'our travelled gallants', who come back home all Frenchified, and 'fill the court with quarrels, talk and tailors'. This is discussed by the Chamberlain and Sir Thomas Lovell. They wish 'our messieurs' would 'leave those remnants / Of fool and feather that they got in France'. Among these imported fads are enumerated 'fights and fireworks', 'tennis and tall stockings' and 'short blistered breeches' (1.2.19–31). *Henry VIII* premiered at the Globe in 1613, so this brief sally against French frivolities may have been written around the time Shakespeare was testifying on behalf of a Frenchman at the Court of Requests. 'Quarrels, talk and tailors' may just about sum up his view of the protracted wrangles of the Belott–Mountjoy case.

In these plays Shakespeare jogs along with jocular prejudice against the French – they are vain, frivolous, quarrelsome and lecherous, and they talk funny – but he does not seem to have engaged in it with much enthusiasm. In the history plays the context is jingoistic; in the comedies it is an easy laugh. What is more interesting is his tendency to challenge prejudices against immigrant aliens. We have seen it in the 'More' fragment, and we see it even more in his portrayal of Shylock the Jew.

The Merchant of Venice was written in about 1596, a time when anti-Semitism was on the public agenda. One of the *causes célèbres* of the 1590s was the execution of the Portuguese Jew Dr Roderigo Lopez on a charge of conspiring to poison the Queen. The trial featured, in default of hard evidence, a good deal of anti-Jewish propaganda.[16] It is no coincidence that the Admiral's Men played Marlowe's black tragi-farce *The Jew of Malta* so frequently at this time – a play that can be read as anti-Semitic, though full also of Marlovian undercurrents of irony which challenge that reading. In a later play by William Rowley an old usurer is described as wearing a 'visage [vizard or mask] like the artificial Jew of Malta's nose', suggesting that the actor playing Barabas wore a false nose.[17] Some have wondered if Shylock was similarly accoutred, but it seems unlikely. *The Merchant of Venice* is innovative in presenting the Jew not as a pantomime villain but as a rounded character with a mix of virtues and flaws. In a famous speech Shylock appeals to a common humanity deeper than the divide between Jew and Christian –

Hath not a Jew eyes? Hath not a Jew hands, organs, dimensions, senses, affections, passions? Fed with the same food, hurt with the same weapons, subject to the same diseases, healed by the same means, warmed and cooled by the same winter and summer as a Christian is? If you prick us do we not bleed? If you tickle us do we not laugh? If you poison us do we not die? And if you wrong us shall we not revenge? (3.1.52–60)

Our sympathy is evoked by the contemptuous treatment Shylock has received, but the effect of the play, the effect of his implacable thirst for revenge, is to stretch that sympathy taut – whether or not to breaking-point is up to each member of the audience.[18]

The apotheosis of the outsider in the Elizabethan mind was not the Jew – essentially a familiar presence – but the more exotic figure of the black African or 'blackamoor', and the apotheosis of Shakespeare's treatment of the racial outsider is *Othello*. The description of Othello as a 'Moor' has led to uncertainty about his ethnic origins – the word correctly refers to the Berber-Arab races of the Maghreb, then called Mauretania. These to the Elizabethans were 'tawny Moors' (as the Prince of Morocco is called in *The Merchant of Venice*), while black Africans were 'black Moors'. In recent times Othello has been played as an Arab by Anthony Hopkins and by Ben Kingsley, but the language of the play, with its derogatory references to his 'thick lips' and 'sooty bosom', suggests that his ethnicity is African. (His speech beginning 'Haply for I am black', often mentioned in this context, does not actually give any ethnic clue, as 'black' was then used to mean dark or swarthy. Queen Elizabeth called Archbishop Whitgift her 'little black husband'.)[19]

Black Africans were to be seen in Elizabethan London and other port cities. They were mostly West African, their presence a by-product of the transatlantic slave-trade. The slaver John Hawkins landed 300 captives from West Africa in England in the 1560s. 'Blackamoor' servants were a fashionable novelty. Alderman Paul Bayning had three black maids in his house; in a

London parish register we hear of 'John Come-quicke, a blacke-more', servant to Capt Thomas Love, and of 'a Negar [negro] whose name was supposed to be Frauncis', working for a brewer in West Smithfield. Only occasionally are their African names recorded – 'Cassangoe', 'Easfanyyo'. In 1596 the Queen told the Privy Council, 'There are lately divers blackamoores brought into this realme, of which kind of people there are allready here too manie.'[20] Another word used for them was 'Ethiops', usually in a generic sense (from the Greek root meaning 'burnt skins'), occasionally with some notion of the internal geography of Africa.

Othello is not the first of Shakespeare's Africans: there is the 'blackamoor' Aaron in *Titus Andronicus*, one of his earliest plays, perhaps composed in the late 1580s. There the equation is conventional: Aaron is black and he is a villain. His blackness is not in doubt – he is 'coal-black' and has a 'fleece of woolly hair' – and nor is his wickedness. The emblematic moment is when he holds up Titus' severed hand, gloating:

> O how this villainy
> Doth fat me with the very thoughts of it!
> Let fools do good and fair men call for grace,
> Aaron will have his soul black like his face. (3.1.201–4)

'Fat me' has an overtone of sexual arousal, and Aaron is throughout a figure of powerful erotic energy. *Titus* is virtually a homage to Marlowe – the bloodbath of the story, the fierce clarity of the treatment – and the magnetism of the evil Aaron is a typical Marlovian twist. He is the charismatic transgressor, the climbing 'over-reacher'. We get a graphic instance of his stage presence from the Peacham drawing of *Titus Andronicus* (see Plate 22), where his vividly inked-in figure draws the eye straight away.

In *Titus* the black man is the villain, exotic and evil, but a dozen or more years later, as he begins to think about *Othello*, Shakespeare's approach is more complex. Departing radically with convention, he will make the black man the hero, a 'noble Moor', and his white subordinate the villain. And it will be the hidden purpose of Iago's villainy to drag Othello back down into barbarity, to chain him once again to the 'blackamoor' stereotype. Through deceptions and stratagems – almost directorial in a theatrical sense – Iago presents Othello to the audience, and to himself, as a murderous monster.[21]

Othello has achieved prestige and status in his adopted European home, but the status is fragile. Iago works against that process of integration: he is of the class which feels embittered and excluded by the immigrant's success. Iago's is the persuasive voice of racism, and is echoed by those he influences – Desdemona's father, Brabantio, and her failed suitor, the fop Roderigo. In the opening scene Othello is denigrated (precisely the word) as 'the thick lips', 'old black ram', a 'barbary horse', a 'devil'. All this in contrast to the 'wealthy curlèd darlings' of Venice, of whom Roderigo is one. We hear of the 'rank disproportion' of a mixed marriage: Desdemona is 'in love with that she feared to look upon'. The mere formality of marriage cannot, they think, paper over this anomaly – it is 'a frail vow betwixt an erring barbarian and a super-subtle Venetian'. 'Erring' here means wandering (Latin *errare*), thus rootless, of no fixed abode. This idea is also in Iago's insinuating description of Othello as 'an extravagant and wheeling stranger / Of here and everywhere', in which 'extravagant' is also used in its Latinate sense of straying beyond bounds, while 'wheeling' conveys an idea of circling back – that return to primitivism and savagery which Iago seeks to effect in Othello. This looping retrogression is an ancient trope of tragedy. It is found in the name of Oedipus, the primal tragic hero, which is from Greek *oedipod–*, 'club-footed', a physical emblem of his heinous backward turn.

Shakespeare was at work on *Othello* in 1603–4, the years he was living in the Mountjoy household. There are many differences between a French tiremaker in Cripplegate and an African condottiere in Venice, but they share a social identity as immigrants or 'strangers'. Their status, however high, is tenuous. Their presence, however settled, remains essentially transient; they are 'strangers of here and everywhere'. Trapped in a world of stereotypes – the lecherous Frenchman, the greedy Jew, the savage African – they sometimes feel they are actors playing a part, comic or monstrous according to requirements.

20

Dark ladies

'*I*n the old age black was not counted fair . . .' There is another Shakespearean exotic we have not yet considered: the 'Dark Lady' of the Sonnets.[22] Whether or not she is based on a real woman, with whom Shakespeare had a real and guilt-ridden affair, she is certainly a character in a kind of drama, and she is given identifying physical features. Her eyes are 'raven black', her breasts are 'dun', her hair resembles 'black wires'. She is a 'woman coloured ill'. The invited visualization is of a foreign-looking woman, perhaps Mediterranean. The wiry hair could suggest a black woman, though 'dun' to describe her skin-tone suggests a brown or olive complexion. That Shakespeare talks of her as 'black' does not mean she was a negress, but gives her that frisson of dangerous otherness which the African 'blackamoor' represented in English minds.

The 'Dark Lady' is an accurate enough summary of her, though 'lady' begs some unintended questions about her social rank. It is, anyway, our name for her, not Shakespeare's. Neither word occurs in the twenty-eight sonnets about her, in which she is either addressed as 'thou' or referred to as 'my mistress' or 'my love'.

Shakespeare is again playing with stereotypes – the mistress of these poems is explicitly dark in apposition to 'fair' (and thus to the 'Fair Youth' to whom the majority of the Sonnets are addressed), and the speaker's intense sexual attraction towards her upends familiar sonneteering tropes of beauty. The opening lines of Sonnet 130 –

My mistress' eyes are nothing like the sun,
Coral is far more red than her lips' red,
If snow be white, why then her breasts are dun . . .

– are specific bouleversements of well-known bits of amorous poetry. Sir Philip Sidney's Stella has 'eyes like morning sun on snow', and Shakespeare's own Lucrece has 'coral lips' and a 'snow-white dimpled chin', and his Venus a 'sweet coral mouth'.[23] Thus the sonnet echoes canonical images from the early 1590s, including his own, in order to reverse them. Despite this woman's failure on all the clichéd romantic criteria she is irresistibly attractive to him – 'And yet by heaven I think my love as rare / As any she belied with false compare.'

The date of the 'Dark Lady' sonnets is uncertain, but at least two of them (138 and 144) had been written by 1599, when they appeared unauthorized in Jaggard's piratical collection, *The Passionate Pilgrim*. Two other sonnets in that volume were lifted bodily from the text of *Love's Labour's Lost*,[24] and it is perhaps no coincidence that this play also features an amorous dark lady, Rosaline, one of the French gentlewomen attending the Princess. Berowne falls for her hopelessly, despite his vow of abstinence. He describes her, with attempted nonchalance, as:

A whitely wanton with a velvet brow,
With two pitch-balls stuck in her face for eyes,
Ay and by heaven one that will do the deed
Though Argus were her eunuch and her guard. (3.1.191–4)

Her darkness is of colouring rather than complexion, which is 'whitely', in other words pale or sallow (see *OED* and Cotgrave, s.v. *blanchastre*). Her eyebrows and eyes are intensely black, compared to velvet and pitch, and like the 'Dark Lady' she has an air of sensuousness, of sexual appetite – 'one that will do the deed'.

Also like the 'Dark Lady', Rosaline's darkness is praised for its natural, as distinct from cosmetic, beauty:

O if in black my lady's brows be deck'd,
It mourns that painting and usurping hair
Should ravish doters with a false aspect;
And therefore is she born to make black fair.
Her favour turns the fashions of the days . . . (4.3.253–7)

This argument is very close to Sonnet 127: 'In the old age black was not counted fair . . . / But now is black beauty's successive heir.'

An extended bout of compliment and insult follows, in which Rosaline is disparaged by Berowne's friends as 'black as ebony', and is compared to 'chimney-sweepers' and 'colliers', and even to 'Ethiops' – thanks to her, says the King, 'Ethiops of their sweet complexion crack [boast].' This is comic hyperbole, but as in the 'Dark Lady' sequence there is a metaphorical linking between a dark-complexioned woman and that figure of alien danger, the blackamoor. Interestingly, the Frenchman Dr Caius is also humorously called an 'Ethiopian', which strengthens Shakespeare's playful association between French darkness and African blackness. Perhaps the actor playing Dr Caius wore a noticeably black wig and beard.

In *A Midsummer Night's Dream*, which also belongs to the mid-1590s (and perhaps specifically to the wedding of Elizabeth Carey to Sir Thomas Berkeley), the contrast between two girls, one tall and fair (Helena) and one small and dark (Hermia), again links to the Sonnets. Hermia is called a 'tawny Tartar', a 'raven', and (again) an 'Ethiop'. Each girl gets her man, but not before a mix-up with love-potions causes midsummer mayhem. As in *Love's Labours* there is bantering debate on the relative merits of brunettes and blondes. To Duke Theseus it seems a kind of madness – the madness of infatuation – to prefer the dark lady:

Lovers and madmen have such seething brains . . .
One sees more devils than vast hell can hold –
That is the madman. The lover all as frantic,
Sees Helen's beauty in a brow of Egypt . . . (5.1.4–11)

The last line offers a double opposition – between fair Helena and gipsy-like Hermia ('gipsy' = Egyptian), and between Helen of Troy and Cleopatra.

These genial comedies of the 1590s discuss the delights of sultry black-browed women, and their exciting difference from conventional ideals of fairness – ideas explored more sourly and obsessively in the 'Dark Lady' sequence. Is this a genuine predilection of Shakespeare's? The 'I' of the Sonnets is not exactly William Shakespeare, and the poems are not just a protracted emotional diary, but to divest them of all personal meaning makes them a bloodless set of literary variations, which they are palpably not.[25] Then there is Cleopatra herself, the embodiment of sultriness, described as 'tawny' and 'gipsy' and 'riggish' (highly sexed) in the late tragedy *Antony and Cleopatra* (*c.* 1607–8) – now an ageing 'Dark Lady', but still full of erotic 'witchcraft'. And it seems that, in the author's imagination, the impeccably English Alice Ford in the *Merry Wives* is also dark-haired, for Falstaff woos her somewhat indelicately as 'my white doe with the black scut'. The scut is the hindquarters of a female deer, and here stands for the triangle of pubic hair.

We seem to find that Shakespeare was sexually drawn to dark, foreign-looking women, and one could say that the idea of foreignness was sparky and exciting to him in other ways.

There is a question in the quiz-game Trivial Pursuit: 'What is the most common name in the plays of Shakespeare?' The answer is Antonio, which occurs seven times. It is a curious fact about the greatest playwright of Elizabethan and Jacobean England that not a single one of his thirty-seven canonical plays is set in Elizabethan or Jacobean England. There are plays set in ancient Britain (*Lear*, *Cymbeline*), and the histories are perforce set in medieval and early Tudor England, though they come no nearer in time than the birth of the future Queen Elizabeth, which occurred in 1533, a generation before Shakespeare's birth. Otherwise they are set abroad, or as the Elizabethans would say, 'beyond sea'. They are set in Verona (twice), Venice (twice) and

Sicily (twice), in Athens and Vienna, in Navarre and Roussillon, in Illyria, Bohemia and Denmark. *As You Like It* is partly set in the Forest of Arden, which is a real English location – the family of Shakespeare's mother, Mary *née* Arden, was from there – but this 'Arden' is textually the Ardennes, for the play (following its chief source, Thomas Lodge's *Rosalynde*) is nominally set in northern France, and has minor characters called Le Beau and Amiens, and the melancholy Jaques, whom the metre demands that we pronounce bisyllabically ('Jay-quis' or possibly 'Jah-quis') but who is really no more than a Jacques.

In another sense, of course, *all* these plays are set in contemporary England. The characters speak Elizabethan English, display a spectrum of contemporary attitudes and foibles, wear contemporary English costume, and are as likely to have English names as foreign ones. Shakespeare's Hamlet is not really Danish, and Sir Toby Belch not a jot Illyrian (i.e. Croatian).

In Shakespeare, and particularly in Shakespearean comedy, real English life as it was experienced by his audience was shown to them through a prism of foreignness, by which process it was subtly distorted and magnified. In this sense the foreign – the 'strange' – is an imaginative key for Shakespeare: it opens up fresher and freer ways of seeing the people and things which daily reality dulled with familiarity. It is his way into the dream world of comedy. He did not, as far as we know, ever leave the shores of England. Attempts to argue that his Italian settings were the product of first-hand knowledge founder precisely on the vagueness and carelessness of those settings. He travels in imagination. 'Verona' is not a place but a magical name, an 'Open Sesame' to a liberating idea of difference. In Shakespeare's mind, one might say, a foreign country was a kind of working synonym for the theatre itself – a place of tonic exaggerations and transformations; a place where you walk in through a door in Southwark and find yourself beached up on the shores of Illyria.

In the great melting-pot of London Shakespeare could hear half the languages of Europe in half an hour's stroll through the dockyards. But to breathe this tonic air of difference, what better ploy than to live in a house full of foreigners? Their voices float up into the thin-walled room, adding a touch of strangeness to the familiar sounds of the street. 'Then begins a journey in my head . . .'

PART SIX

Sex & the City

Some rise by sin and some by virtue fall . . .
　　　　　　　　Measure for Measure, 2.1.38

21

Enter George Wilkins

Among the witnesses called on behalf of Stephen Belott in the early summer of 1612 was George Wilkins, 'victualler', of the parish of St Sepulchre. He gives his age as thirty-six; he says he has known the plaintiff and the defendant, Belott and Mountjoy, 'about seaven yeares' – that is, since *c.* 1605. His appearance is brief: he has no knowledge of the events leading up to the wedding, and is not questioned on those points. The purpose of his testimony, it seems, is to confirm the poor quality of those items of 'houshould stuffe' which Mountjoy had given the newly-weds. This Wilkins duly does. 'This deponent sayth' – writes the clerk –

that after the plaintiff was married wth Marye the defendant's daughter he and his wyffe came to dwell in this deponents house in one of his chambers. And brought wth them a fewe goodes or houshould stuffe whch by report the defendant her father gave them, for which this deponent would not have geven above ffyve poundes yf he had bene to have bought the same.

This opens up another episode in the story. After their marriage Stephen and Mary left the house on Silver Street, and lived in a 'chamber' at the house of George Wilkins. Wilkins dates this to 1605, and we find this corroborated by Christopher Mountjoy in his original answer to Belott's bill of complaint, where he notes that after their marriage 'the Complainant and his wife had stayed in the house of this defendant the space of halfe a yeare or thereabouts', and then 'did depart'. Relations had deteriorated to the point where Belott 'refused to stay there any longer, and would need take other courses for his better preferment, as he then pretended'. They remained away for a year or so: 'After the Complainant was gone from the house of this defendant about a yeare, this defendaunts wife dyed, and then the Complainant and his wife came again and lived with this Defendant as partners in their said trade of Tyeringe.'

From these corroborating statements we infer that Stephen and Mary were absent from Silver Street between the summer of 1605 ('half a year' after the wedding) and the autumn of 1606 (death of Marie Mountjoy), and that for at least part of that time, and perhaps for all of it, they were living in the house of George Wilkins. This may be an act of hospitable friendship on Wilkins's part, but I doubt it. As the word 'victualler' implies, and as other evidence confirms, Wilkins kept a tavern. He is known to have had an establishment on Cow Cross Street, on the edge of the notorious brothel quarter of Clerkenwell, but the earliest record of this is in 1610. Other evidence shows that prior to this Wilkins was living in the parish of St Giles, Cripplegate. It was probably there that the Belotts moved, in 1605, into a rented chamber in what may well have been some kind of lodging-house. It was a convenient location – close enough to the Mountjoys, and even closer to Belott's family, his stepfather Humphrey Fludd (and other Fludds) being resident in St Giles parish.[1]

This addition to the Belott–Mountjoy story comes freighted with curious significance. As we know, the 'victualler' George Wilkins was also a writer. He was, or became, a literary associate of Shakespeare – for a while a collaborator with Shakespeare – and so his brief appearance at the Court of Requests opens up something rather rare: a specific biographical context for a Shakespeare play.

The play is *Pericles*, probably first performed in early 1608, and published the following year. The broad consensus among literary historians is that Wilkins wrote most of the first two acts and Shakespeare almost all of the rest. (Other authors have been proposed as the collaborator – notably John Day, who himself collaborated with Wilkins on other plays – but the evidence is overwhelmingly in Wilkins's favour.)[2] It has always been thought rather odd that a mediocre writer like Wilkins should have made such a large contribution to this late Shakespeare play – large enough for it to be excluded from the First Folio of 1623, though later instated in the more capacious Third Folio of 1664. In my view Wilkins's best writing is better than most critics allow, but I am thinking of certain lines or images, certain intensities of atmosphere, particularly 'low-life' atmosphere; overall, in broader terms of character, structure, insight and so on, he is pedestrian – a voluble but unsophisticated hack.

It is also the case that Wilkins's career as a writer was very brief. All his extant work appeared on the page or the stage within a three-year span, 1606–8, so it seems he was unpublished – a would-be writer – when the Belotts came to stay in 1605. Only three single-authored works are definitely his: an undistinguished pamphlet, *Three Miseries of Barbary* (c. 1606); a play which might just about be called a tragicomedy, *The Miseries of Enforced Marriage* (1607); and a novelized version of *Pericles*, published in 1608 while the play was still onstage. He may also be the 'G.W.' who wrote a translation from Justinian, *The Historie of Justine* (1606) – some doubt that he knew enough Latin to be the translator, but the fact that much of the volume is plagiarized from an earlier translation by Arthur Golding sounds more like him. To these can be added his collaborations – a jest-book, *Jests to Make you Merrie* (1607), written with Thomas Dekker; a picturesque play, *The Travells of the Three English Brothers* (1607), with John Day and William Rowley; and *Pericles*, with Shakespeare. He may also have contributed to John Day's *Law Tricks* (1608).[3]

The bibliographical ins and outs of the *Pericles* text have been closely studied elsewhere. My interest here is in teasing out a biographical context, a vestigial pathway that leads up to the text, so let us stick for a moment with George Wilkins the victualler or tavern-keeper, the landlord for a while of the newishly wed

Stephen and Mary Belott, and perhaps through this very connection first known to Shakespeare.

In his deposition at the Court of Requests Wilkins gives his age
as '36 years or thereabouts', but in another deposition two years
later he says he is about forty. The best we can say is that he was
born in the mid-1570s, and was at least ten years Shakespeare's
junior. He could possibly be George son of Walter Wilkins, baptized at St Botolph's without Aldgate on 2 March 1577, but a
more attractive proposition is that he was the son of 'George
Wilkins the poet', who lived on Holywell Street in Shoreditch,
and who was buried at St Leonard's, Shoreditch, on 19 August
1603. This is plausible in itself, and is made more so by the
younger George's echoing description of himself, at the baptism
of his own son, as 'George Wilkens, Poett'. There is no trace of
any printed work by George Wilkins senior – was he perhaps a
'poet' in the oral tradition: a balladeer or tavern entertainer? No
trace of him, either, in the Shoreditch subsidy rolls, so he was not
apparently a householder.[4]

In early 1602, in his mid-twenties, Wilkins married one Katherine Fowler. It is also in this year that his first tangle with the law
is recorded: he was bound over to keep the peace, further to
what we might call 'threatening behaviour' – a minor matter but
prophetic of later delinquencies. His father's death the following
year may have brought him something, for by 1605 he has a
house, in a chamber of which the Belotts are living. This was
probably in St Giles, Cripplegate, where the parish register
records the baptism of Wilkins's daughter Mary on 13 December
1607, and her burial on 11 September 1609, and the baptism of
his son Thomas on 11 February 1610. Wilkins's briefly prolific
literary career belongs to these years at St Giles. He is begetting
children, and he is hectically writing.

The abrupt curtailment of his literary career – for reasons we
do not know but which I will later guess at – does not remove
him from view, however. Various later episodes in his life are
known, though they are always a particular kind of episode,

because they are recorded in the rolls and registers of the Middlesex Sessions – essentially the magistrates' court – before which he appeared frequently, usually in the dock facing charges, and sometimes as a witness or surety for someone else facing charges.[5] The earliest such record is from 1610, but one should resist the tempting narrative arc which suggests that Wilkins's criminal career begins *after* his literary career stops. For various reasons there are few detailed Sessions records prior to 1608, so there may have been earlier cases against Wilkins of which no record remains. One needs only to glance at his *Miseries of Enforced Marriage*, written in late 1605, to know that the murky milieu in which his police-record places him was one he already knew intimately.

Here is a bald summary of George Wilkins in the magistrates' court, usually in Clerkenwell and sometimes at the Old Bailey:

4 April 1610 – Wilkins is bound over to keep the peace towards Anne Plesington, elsewhere described as a 'noted queane' and 'comon harborer of lewd persons' – in other words, a prostitute.

22 April 1610 – Wilkins puts up surety of £10 for John Fisher, 'cordwainer' (leather-worker), who had 'unlawfullye begotten one Grace Saville with child'.

23 September 1610 – Wilkins ['Wilkeson'] gives surety for Thomas Cutts, butcher, bound over for 'woundinge one John Ball in the head with a Welshe hooke'.

3 March 1611 – Wilkins is charged with 'abusing one Randall Berkes and kicking a woman on the belly which was then great with childe'. It is the gruesome act of violence which catches the eye, but it is also worth noting a couple of literary connections in this case. Berkes, whom Wilkins abused, was a bookseller. And one of Wilkins's sureties for bail was 'Henry Gosson of St Lawrence Poulteney, gent', who was the publisher of Wilkins's *Three Miseries of Barbary*, and more recently of the Shakespeare–Wilkins *Pericles*, issued in 1609, and now, in 1611, reprinting for a new edition.

2 September 1611 – Wilkins is bound over to answer charges of compounding a felony by 'convayinge away of Mawline Sames

who committed the fellonye'. Magdalen Sames or Samways was accused of 'the felonious stealing of 50s from one William Usurer'. She is referred to by her maiden name though she was married to a glover named Thomas Morris. Earlier in 1611 she was in gaol for living 'incontinently' with another man; in later cases she is charged with being a cutpurse and a whore. In a fascinating twist we learn that she had recently borrowed money from the theatrical impresario Philip Henslowe.[6] Her last repayment to him was due around the time of her alleged theft from the moneylender called William.

20 September 1611 – Wilkins is bound over 'for abusing Mr Barnes, constable of Clerkenwell, in the execution of his office'. Perhaps this is connected with the Samways affair – in the earlier charge he had 'conveyed' her away (helped her to escape) and now perhaps he is obstructing a policeman trying to arrest her.

26 March 1612 – Wilkins is charged with another act of violence: 'he hath outrageously beaten one Judyth Walton & stamped upon her, so that she was caryed home in chayre'. This woman is elsewhere described as a 'common bawd'.

2 July 1612 – Wilkins is accused of an 'extreame outrage' – a physical attack – on Martin Fetherbye, 'headborough' or constable of Charterhouse Lane. This perhaps occurred at Wilkins's tavern, since it resulted in the loss of his licence: 'imposterim non cusodet tabernam' (in future he may not keep a tavern). He is 'put downe from victualling', though this loss of business proves temporary. One notes that his appearance at the Court of Requests on behalf of Stephen Belott (19 June 1612) comes sandwiched between these two court appearances for acts of violence.

25 August 1614 – Wilkins's wife Katherine sues a neighbour, Joyce Patrick, for slander. Joyce had called her a 'bawd' and said, 'Thy husband may goe horne by horne with his neighbours' (meaning he was a cuckold). Among the insults Joyce hurled at her, in 'angry and vehement manner', was this: 'You, Mistress Sweetmeat, you will do more with an inche of candell then some will doe with a whole pound – Wilkinses wiefe I speak to thee.' A witness on Katherine's behalf says she had 'never byn reputed

or accounted a bawd', but another says their house is frequented by 'lewd women', and that he has sometimes spent twenty shillings in one night there.

3 December 1614 – Wilkins is again accused of abusing an officer of the law, this time John Sherley, constable of Clerkenwell.

21 December 1614 – Wilkins testifies in a Chancery suit in which a moneylender, Thomas Harris, is accused of defrauding a dissolute young heir, John Bonner, now deceased. This is not a charge against Wilkins, though he witnessed their dealings, probably at his tavern, and his collusion with the crooked Harris is not unlikely. His testimony allows us to eavesdrop for a moment. He heard Bonner accuse Harris of selling him 'a nagge or geldinge for the sum of xx^{tie} markes [£13 6s 8d]' though it was 'not worth half the money', and of having 'cosened and over reached him' in various 'bargens passed betwixt them'. Harris, he says, 'answered little or nothing to the contrary, but hath often in laughing sort confessed soe much'.

5 September 1616 – Wilkins is 'charged to have taken a cloke and a hatt from the person of John Parker feloniously'. The cloak was valued at 30 shillings, and the 'blacke felt hatt' at 3s 4d. Parker was said to have been 'in great fear and peril of his life' (though this is formulaic).

6 August 1618 – Wilkins is charged with having 'feloniously received, harboured and comforted Anne Badham, against the King's Peace and dignity'. He did so knowing she had committed a felony – she had picked a man's pocket, and 'carried off 55 shillings and fourpence halfpenny which was in the pocket'. Both the theft and Wilkins's harbouring of her are said to have taken place 'at Cow Cross', which probably means at Wilkins's tavern. This case echoes the earlier one involving Magdalen Samways. Perhaps Anne was a prostitute working in the tavern, who stole from one of her clients, and did so with the connivance of the tavern-keeper Wilkins.

This last case moved slowly. Wilkins appeared on 3 September, but the trial was remanded. A month later, on 2 October, the clerk of the sessions recorded that Wilkins was discharged from the obligations of his bail because he was dead – 'exoneratus q[uia] mortuus est'. An appropriate epitaph, in that it appears in the crabbed Latin of the law-courts, where Wilkins was such a familiar face. He was in his early forties when he died.

Two themes emerge with obsessive regularity from Wilkins's police-record: violence and prostitution, and sometimes they combine in acts of violence against women who are said or inferred to be prostitutes. Even his wife Katherine is accused of being a 'bawd', though of course she denies it. Those vicious assaults on women – the 'kicking' and 'stamping on' – are characteristic of the pimp who asserts his authority with physical aggression. This atmosphere of violence is found in his writings. Here is the profligate young gallant Sir Frank Ilford bullying his new wife (whom he has been tricked into marrying) to give him her jewels –

> ILFORD: Nay, 'sfoot, give 'em me, or I'll kick else.
> WIFE: Good, sweet –
> ILFORD: Sweet with a pox, you stink in my nose. Give me your jewels! Nay, bracelets too.
> WIFE: Oh me, most miserable!
> ILFORD: Out of my sight, aye and out of my doors, for now what's within this house is mine. (*Miseries*, 2185–91)

The threat to kick, and the whole aggressive timbre, sounds much like the real-life cases glimpsed through the Sessions records.[7] A graphologist might note a further echo of all this in the curiously boot-shaped formation seen in Wilkins's signature (see Plate 25).

In many of these records Wilkins is specified as 'victualler', as he also is in the Court of Requests. His establishment is usually described as on Cow Cross Street and sometimes on Turnmill Street, and was perhaps at the junction of those two streets – a house on the corner like the Mountjoys'. Turnmill (often Turnbull) Street was axiomatically associated with brothels. It is mentioned in Shakespeare's 2 *Henry IV*, when Shallow prates of 'the wildness of his youth, and the feats he has done about Turnbull Street' (3.2.288–300), and is described succinctly in

Sugden's *Topographical Dictionary* as 'the most disreputable street in London, a haunt of thieves and loose women'.[8]

All the evidence points to Wilkins's establishment being some kind of a brothel. That word is not always helpful: the vaguer legalistic formula, a 'bawdy house', might be better. The dedicated brothel with a woman's face in every window certainly existed, but as always prostitution was in the main less formalized, more diffuse and opportunistic.[9] At Wilkins's tavern, let us say, there were women available, as there was food, wine, dice and tobacco, and there were 'chambers' upstairs or near by which could be hired for the business of pleasure. It is a situation familiar to commentators such as the playwright-turned-preacher Stephen Gosson:

Every vaulter [prostitute] in one blind taverne or other is tenant at will, to which she tolleth resorte, and plays the stale to utter their victualls, and to help them empty their musty cakes. There she is so entreated with wordes and received with curtesie that every back-roome in the house is at her commaundement.[10]

This connection between sex and snacks is also described by Robert Greene, who knew whereof he spoke. In his *Disputation between a He-connycatcher and a She-connycatcher* (1592), a tart called Nan explains how they encourage customers to eat the overpriced sweetmeats in the 'trugging-house' or brothel –

First we feign ourselves hungry, for the benefit of the house, although our bellies were never so full; and no doubt the good pandar or bawd she comes forth like a sober matron, and sets store of cates [sweetmeats] on the table, and then I fall aboard on them, and though I can eat little, yet I make havoc of all. And let him be sure every dish is well-sauced, for he shall pay for a pippin-pie that cost in the market fourpence, at one of the trugging-houses eighteen pence.[11]

That name given disparagingly to Katherine Wilkins, 'Mistress Sweetmeat', may contain a pun on 'cate' and Kate; it may also refer to her serving of sweetmeats in the Wilkins brothel.

Law-reports confirm the set-up. Margaret Barnes, a Westminster prostitute known for her statuesque physique as 'Long Meg', also ran a tavern or 'victualling house' in Rotherhithe where prostitutes plied their trade. There, on a day in 1562, were discovered a scrivener from Westminster and a broker from Holborn, 'who makinge merye at dinner had eche of them a chamber and a woman'. The trouble arose when a young man called Zachary Marshall fell in love with one of Meg's girls, Ellen Remnaunt, and proposed to her. Marshall was, ironically, the son of the matron of Bridewell, the correctional institute for prostitutes and vagrants, a place known for savage punishment and endemic sexual corruption.[12] A writer of Jacobean 'city comedies' could not have invented a better plot.

This gives us pretty clearly the business-profile of 'George Wilkins, victualler'. One might fare at Wilkins's much as Fustigo does in Dekker's *Honest Whore* (1605) – 'Troth, for sixpence a meal, wench, as well as heart can wish, with calves chaldrom and chitterlings, besides I have a punk after supper, as good as a roasted apple' (3.1.12–13). A pungent menu – 'chaldrom' or chawdron is a spiced dish of calves' entrails, 'chitterlings' are fried pigs' intestines, and the 'punk' is, of course, a prostitute.

22

The Miseries

This was George Wilkins, the man in whose house Stephen and Mary Belott came to live, in the summer of 1605, bringing with them that meagre cartload of 'houshould stuffe' for which – he later asserted – he would not have given a fiver. We do not know if he already ran the tavern-cum-brothel on Turnmill Street, which is first referred to in 1610: it is anyway unlikely that the Belotts would be lodged there. The more likely location, for reasons already given, is St Giles parish (which was only ten minutes' walk from Clerkenwell – all this story is tightly confined). But, wherever it was, we have a strong suspicion it was a seedy or shady sort of house where women of negotiable virtue could be found and hired.

The arrival of the Belotts in Wilkins's house marks the first known connection between Wilkins and Shakespeare. They may have known one another before, but this is the first visible link. The connection is a simple, human one. Two young people well known to Shakespeare – his landlord's apprentice, his landlady's daughter – have gone to live with Wilkins. But it has complications. They are young people in whose welfare Shakespeare has been involved. The circumstances are unhappy. One thinks particularly of Mary, exiled from her family home, caught in this terrific cross-fire of antagonism between her father and husband, and now insalubriously lodged in the house of a pimp.

And here is a synchronicity. It is more or less exactly at this time, in the summer of 1605, that there begins an identifiable literary connection between Wilkins and Shakespeare. At this point, as far as the evidence remains, Wilkins was an unknown and unpublished author. But some time in or shortly after June 1605 he began work on a play for Shakespeare's company, the King's Men.

The play was Wilkins's best and most characteristic work, *The Miseries of Enforced Marriage* (see Plate 26). We can be fairly sure about the dating because the play was based on real events – a shocking murder-case in Yorkshire, in which two young children were killed by their father, Walter Calverley, a well-born man who had spiralled into debt and dissipation and, it seems, insanity. Calverley also attempted to murder his wife, Philippa, but she survived. The killings happened on 23 April 1605, and public interest in the case was further whetted by a news-pamphlet, *Two Unnatural Murthers*, which gave a detailed account of the affair.[13] This pamphlet, registered at Stationers' Hall on 12 June and published shortly afterwards, was certainly used by Wilkins when writing the *Miseries*.

One of the things that emerged from the *Unnatural Murthers* pamphlet was that as a young man Calverley had been betrothed, but had been unwillingly forced by his guardian to marry another woman. Thus the glimmerings of a love-story lie behind the grim facts of his decline and fall. In the final version of Wilkins's play – there was more than one – it is this back-story which holds centre-stage. It becomes a study (if that is not too spruce a term for a Wilkins play) of a man sinking into drunkenness and vice to escape the 'miseries' of an unhappy and enforced marriage.[14]

Wilkins wrote fast (and, as some bungled lines in the printed text suggest, none too legibly). The play was probably onstage at the Globe in early 1606. In May of that year an Act to Restrain Abuses of Players came into force, forbidding use of the names of God, Christ, etc, onstage. Oaths and casual blasphemies are scattered liberally through the *Miseries*, suggesting that it had been performed before this clean-up.[15] The play was apparently still packing them in when it was published the following year – the title-page of the 1607 quarto reads, 'The Miseries of Inforst

Mariage. As it is now playd by his Maiesties Servants'. This long run shows it was a success, and three further editions (1611, 1629, 1637) show that it continued to be popular.

The *Miseries* is one of a series of hotly topical plays of the time which gave the stage an edge of journalistic reportage. And it seems the King's Men had a particular interest in the Calverley case – or thought their public would have a particular interest in it – for there is another dramatic treatment of it in their repertoire, the brief and bleak *Yorkshire Tragedy*. This was published in 1608. It belongs in lists of the 'Shakespeare apocrypha', being ascribed to him on the title-page of two early editions, and in the entries relating to them in the Stationers' Register. The publisher, Thomas Pavier, was a noted pirate, and the play was not included in the Folio, so this attribution is not generally credited. Shakespeare may have added some touches, but the main authorship was not his. Various authors have been proposed – Thomas Heywood, John Day, Wilkins himself – but the most plausible candidate is Thomas Middleton, who was collaborating with Shakespeare on *Timon* in *c.* 1605.[16]

The *Miseries* does not have the intensity of the *Yorkshire Tragedy* but its lack of artistry makes it valuable in another sense – we hear Wilkins and his world throughout it. The central character is not so much the Calverley figure, William Scarborrow (Scarborough), as the parasitic 'gallant' Sir Francis Ilford, one who, in his own words, 'live[s] by the fall of young heirs as swine by the dropping of acorns' (1054–5). There is every sign that the play was printed from Wilkins's 'foul papers' – his working draft of the play – and so I give a representative scene in original spelling – Wilkins's spelling. It is a tavern scene, nominally in the Mitre in Bread Street, but it has the rough timbre of Wilkins's own tavern as we discern it in those court cases listed above. This is how Sir Frank Ilford orders his drinks –

ILFORD: Where be these Rogues here: what, shall we have no Wine here?

DRAWER: Anon, anon, sir.

ILFORD: Anon, goodman Rascall, must wee stay your leysure? Gee't
us by and by, with apoxe to you.

SCARBORROW: O do not hurt the fellow.

Exit Drawer

ILFORD: Hurt him, hang him, Scape-trencher, star-waren [stair-
warden?], Wine spiller, mettle-clancer, Rogue by generation. Why,
dost thou heare Will? If thou dost not use these Grape-spillers as
you doe theyr pottle-pots, quoit em down stayres three or fouyre
times at a supper, theyle grow as sawcy with you as Sergeants, and
make bils more unconscionable than Taylors.

Enter Drawer

DRAWER: Heres the pure and neat grape Gent. I hate [have it] for
you.

ILFORD: Fill up: what ha you brought here, goodman Roge?

DRAWER: The pure element of Claret sir.

ILFORD: Ha you so, and did not I call for Rhenish you Mungrell?
Throws the wine in the Drawers face.

SCARBORROW: Thou needst no wine, I prithee be more mild.

ILFORD: Be mild in a Taverne? Tis treason to the red Lettyce, enemy
to their signe post, and slave to humor:
Prethee, lets be mad,
Then fill our heads with wine, till every pate be drunke,
Then pisse i' the street, jussell all you meet, and with a Punke,
As thou wilt, do now and then. (1057–84)

There are hints in this scene that Wilkins has seen or read the
Falstaff comedies,[17] but for the most part no literary influence
needs to be invoked. This is Wilkins *in propria persona*, writing
what he knows best: the rough badinage of alcohol and violence,
the jostling and pissing of drunken young hoorays. He knows it
from the inside, and there is a poignant self-reflection in Scarborrow's words –

> Thus, like a Fever that doth shake a man
> From strength to weakness, I consume myself.
> I know this company, their custom vilde,
> Hated, abhorr'd of good men, yet like a child

By reason's rule instructed how to know
Evil from good, I to the worser go ... (1118–23)

And on the title-page of the *Miseries* he appends a hopeful Latin tag: 'Qui alios seipsum docet' – he who teaches others teaches himself.

23

Prostitutes and players

What are we to make of this association between the gentle-manly Mr Shakespeare and the vicious Wilkins? There are two answers to this question, one general and one specific.

To be summed up accurately enough as 'the pimp and playwright George Wilkins' makes him an unusual figure, perhaps unique, but in another sense his twin careers fit together quite easily, because prostitution and the theatre were closely associated. The theatre of Shakespeare's day was part of London's vast entertainment industry, and the playhouses stood amid other venues of leisure and pleasure – baiting-rings and cock-pits, bowling-alleys and dicing-houses, taverns and brothels. These places were typically found in the old 'liberties' of the city, beyond the writ of the civic authorities. The Liberty of the Clink in Southwark, where the Globe stood, was a brothel quarter from time immemorial; the prostitutes were called 'Winchester geese', as the liberty was administered by the Bishop of Winchester.[18]

A stone's throw from the Globe stood the celebrated brothel called Holland's Leaguer, run by Elizabeth Holland. A seventeenth-century woodcut (see Plate 28) shows a formidable, moated little fortress on the riverbank. A wooden jetty leads to a tall studded gate, beside which stands a bouncer armed with a tall pike; a small square hatch in the gate permits the vetting of visitors.[19] This hatch was a common feature of brothels: it is probably the origin of Pickt-hatch ('pickt' = spiked), a zone of the red-light district in Clerkenwell of which Wilkins's Cow Cross Street establishment was part. Another architectural feature of the brothel is the latticed window, which is both a security arrangement and a form of enticement – the girls half glimpsed within, in provocative states of undress: 'those milk-paps / That through the window-bars bore at men's eyes' (*Timon*, 4.3.117–18).[20]

If the moralizers are to be believed, the theatre itself was little more than an annexe to the brothel, and sexual assignations were as much part of the entertainment as the play itself. In that 'chappel of Satan, I meane the Theatre', says Anthony Munday, you will see 'harlots utterlie past all shame, who press to the forefront of the scaffolde . . . to be as an object to all mens eies'. According to Thomas Dekker, prostitutes were so frequently in the theatre that they knew the plays word for word – 'every punck and her squire, like the interpreter and his puppet, can rand [rant] out by heart' the speeches they have heard. A generation later, in the 1630s, William Prynne notes the proximity of theatres and brothels – 'the Cock-pit and Drury Lane; Blackfriars play-house and Duke Humfries; the Red Bull and Turnball street; the Globe and Bankside brothel houses'. Hence 'common strumpets and adulteresses, after our stage-plays ended, are often-times prostituted near our playhouses, if not in them (as they may easily be, since many players, if reports be true, are common pandars)'.[21]

Trulls, trots, molls, punks, queans, drabs, stales, nuns, hack-neys, vaulters, wagtails – in a word, whores – were everywhere, but professional prostitution was only part of it. According to the same writers the theatres were a general free-for-all of assigna-tions, pick-ups and uninhibited flirtations, a place where 'light & lewd disposed persons' congregated for 'actes and bargains of incontinencie'. We have already noted that 'Cheapside dame' spotted by Henry Fitzgeoffrey, and that seductive lady whose heavily perfumed head-tire gave Father Busino such palpitations. They are not tarts, but they are women on the look-out for fun and sex:

Citizens wives . . . have received at those spectacles such filthie infections [moral corruption] and have turned their minds from chaste cogitations, and made them of honest women light huswives . . . There is the practising with married wives to traine them from their husbands, and places appointed for meeting and conference.

A minor poet writing in 1600 particularly associates the Globe ('the Bank-side's round-house') with this sort of promiscuity – it is a place where 'light-tayld huswives' come 'in open sight themselves to show and vaunt'. The Elizabethan spelling 'huswife' reminds us that a housewife could also be, etymologically at least, a 'hussy'.[22]

The theatre is also a place where a man brought his mistress rather than his wife – thus Dekker's lovely image in *Satiromastix* (*c.* 1601) of a well-breeched citizen sitting 'in your penny-bench theatre with his squirrel by his side cracking nuts'.

Stephen Gosson, a playwright who became a moral scourge of the theatre, describes the procedures of a pick-up –

In the playhouses at London it is the fashion of youthes to go first into the yarde, and to carry theire eye through every gallery, then like unto ravens, where they spy the carrion, thither they flye, and presse as near to the fairest as they can . . . They give them pippines, they dally with their garments to passe the time, they minister talke upon all occasions, & either bring them home to theire houses on small acquaintance, or slip into tavernes when the plaies are done.[23]

Thus Wilkins the theatre man, doubtless a playgoer as well as a playwright, relates directly and perhaps profitably to his other career in the sex-trade. His is just the sort of tavern one might 'slip into . . . when the plaies are done', though in his case it would be the northern playhouses – and especially the Red Bull in Clerkenwell, in business from *c.* 1604 – which would supply this clientele.

The association between the playhouse and prostitution is perennial, but in the years 1604–5 we find a particular concentration of interest in prostitution on the stage. In this brief period there were three plays onstage featuring prostitutes in the title-role –

John Marston's *The Dutch Courtesan*, 'playd in the Blacke-Friars by the Children of her Maiesties Revels' in *c.* 1604 and published in 1605; and Thomas Dekker's two-part drama, *The Honest Whore*, the first with contributions by Thomas Middleton, performed by Prince Henry's Men (the former Admiral's Men) in 1604, and the sequel performed by the same company in 1605. Middleton, meanwhile, as well as contributing scenes to *The Honest Whore*, published two prose-pamphlets in 1604, of which one (*The Black Book*) is largely set in the brothel-quarter of Pickt-hatch, and the other (*Father Hubberd's Tales*) frequently features prostitutes. Another 'courtesan', Frank Gullman, appears in his *A Mad World, my Masters* (*c.* 1605).

In Marston's *The Dutch Courtesan* a young gallant, Freevill, is about to marry, and must break off his long liaison with the eponymous 'courtesan' Franceschina. The jilted prostitute is furious, and when Freevill's high-minded friend Malheureux conceives an unexpected passion for her – 'That I should love a strumpet! I, a man of snow!' – Franceschina promises herself to him, but only if he will kill Freevill. The two friends hatch a plot: Freevill goes into hiding so Malheureux can pretend he has killed him. So successful is the pretence, however, that Malheureux is arrested for murder. Freevill reappears in time to save him; his stratagem, he claims, was to cure Malheureux of his unseemly passion for the prostitute. Franceschina is condemned to be whipped and imprisoned.

Though punitive at the end, the play derives much of its energy from the sexual frisson of Franceschina. She is variously called a 'pretty, nimble-ey'd Dutch Tanakin', a 'soft, plump, round-cheek'd froe [Dutch *frow*, woman]', a 'plump-rumped wench with a breast softer than a courtier's tongue', an 'honest pole-cat of a clean instep, sound leg, smooth thigh, and the nimble devil in her buttock', and so on. She is the epitome of the high-class tart, the Christine Keeler or Heidi Fleiss *de ses jours*. When Malheureux refers to her as a whore, Freevill reproaches him: 'Whore? Fie, whore! You may call her a courtesan . . .'Tis not in fashion to call things by their right names.' She plays on the lute and the cithern, singing songs with suggestive lyrics about nightingales sleeping next to 'prickles'. She has an enchanting if silly foreign accent – 'Vill you not stay in my bosom tonight, love?'; 'O mine aderliver [Dutch *alderliefest* = dearest] love vat sall me do?' – but she seems more hybrid 'continental' than merely Dutch. Her name is Italian, and her language contains many French inflections ('my shambra' for chamber, and 'Foutra 'pon you'). Her clientele is also cosmopolitan: she consorts 'with the Spaniard Don Skirtoll, with the Italian Master Beieroane, with the Irish Lord Sir Patrick, with the Dutch merchant Haunce Flap-dragon, and specially with the greatest French'. Some of her clients are 'wealthy knights and most rare bountiful lords', and some are upright citizens – her 'custom' is 'not of swaggering Ireland captains, nor of two shilling Inns o' Court men, but with honest flat-caps, wealthy flat-caps [London tradesmen]' (2.2.13–17, 28–30).

A similar characterization of the upmarket prostitute is found in Middleton's pamphlets of 1604, evoked with a certain lip-smacking relish:

He kept his most delicate drab of three hundred [pounds] a year, some unthrifty gentleman's daughter ... She could run upon the lute very well, which in others would have appeared virtuous but in her lascivious ... She had likewise the gift of singing very deliciously, able to charm the hearer, which so bewitched our young master's money that he might have kept seven noise of musicians for less charges ... She had a humour to lisp often, like a flattering wanton, and talk childish like a parson's daughter ... He would swear she spake nothing but sweetmeats, and her breath then sent forth such a delicious odour that it perfumed his white satin doublet better than sixteen milliners.[24]

In Dekker's *Honest Whore* – nominally set in Italy but with much that is particular to London, not least the powerful scenes in Bedlam and Bridewell (probably Middleton's work) – the eponymous whore is Bellafront ('pretty face'). In Part 1 she is converted to 'honesty' by Count Hippolito, but when she declares herself in love with him he rejects her. Hippolito marries the daughter of the Duke of Milan, and Bellafront is married, unhappily, to the worthless Matheo. The play was a big success, and Dekker obliged with a rapidly written sequel, in which the bleakly ironic development of her marriage is that Matheo wants her to return to prostitution to pay for his extravagant lifestyle. She meets Hippolito again, now a widower: this time it is he who falls in love with her, and tries to seduce her; and this time it is she who virtuously resists. The play ends with a coda described on the title-page as 'Comicall passages from an Italian Bridewell', in which various prostitutes are paraded before being taken away for hard labour or whipping. One of these, Katarina Bountinall, comments ironically on the idea of a whore turning honest: 'Foh! Honest? Burnt [deflowered] at fourteen, seven times whipped, six times carted, nine times duck'd, search'd by some hundred and fifty constables, and yet you are honest? Honest Mistress Horseleech, is this world a world to keep bawds and whores honest?' (2778–81).

The play of Shakespeare's which belongs to this time, and which mirrors these preoccupations, is *Measure for Measure*. Its first recorded performance was at court in December 1604; it had possibly played at the Globe shortly before this. It is a play which confronts many difficult social issues, but one of its central concerns is the control of prostitution – or rather the impossibility of this: 'Does your honour mean to geld and splay all the youth of the city?' – and it features a comic duo in the brothel business, the bawd Mistress Overdone and the pimp Pompey Bum. The setting is Vienna, but in all respects other than its name is London in 1604.

Its central story concerns the attempted seduction by the acting governor of the city, Angelo, of the virtuous and virginal Isabella, a novice nun, in return for the life of her brother, who has been condemned to death for 'lechery' under new harsh laws enacted by the same Angelo. These new laws have a counterpart in reality. On 16 September 1603, a royal proclamation ordered the demolition of houses and rooms in the suburbs frequented by 'dissolute and idle persons': ostensibly a precaution against the further spread of the plague, but in effect an edict against the brothels of the suburbs.[25] This is precisely reflected in the opening of the play, where Mistress Overdone receives the dire news from her pimp:

> POMPEY: You have not heard of the proclamation, have you?
>
> MRS OVERDONE: What proclamation, man?
>
> POMPEY: All houses in the suburbs of Vienna must be plucked down.
>
> MRS OVERDONE: And what shall become of those in the city?
>
> POMPEY: They shall stand for seed – they had gone down too but that a wise burgher put in for them.
>
> MRS OVERDONE: But shall all our houses of resort in the suburbs be pulled down?
>
> POMPEY: To the ground, Mistress.
>
> MRS OVERDONE: Why here's a change indeed in the commonwealth! What shall become of me? (1.2.85–97)

Pompey's comments about the city brothels are typical of the play's constant bawdy undertone. 'Stand for seed' ostensibly means they are left standing like seed-corn, but within the brothel context 'stand' and 'seed' refer to erections and ejaculations. Also characteristic is the world-weary observation of profiteering in high places: a 'wise burgher', one in the know, has bought up these condemned properties on the cheap.

For Overdone this is a disaster to cap a bad year, for 'what with the war, what with the sweat, what with the gallows, and what with poverty, I am custom-shrunk'. Editors gloss this as a close reflection of events of 1603 – the continuing war with Spain, the plague, the bout of executions further to Jesuit-linked plots against King James (the 'Main' and 'Bye' plots), and the slackness of trade in the deserted city. In Middleton's *Black Book*, entered on the Stationers' Register in March 1604, the pimp Prigbeard similarly complains 'of their bad takings all the last plaguy summer' when they were 'undone for want of doings'.[26]

The brothel world of Mistress Overdone and Pompey Bum is concisely drawn. Overdone (also called 'Madam Mitigation' –

she 'mitigates' the pangs of sexual desire) is described as a 'bawd of eleven years continuance', and prior to that she was doubtless a prostitute herself. 'You that have worn your eyes out in the service' probably refers to her suffering from the optical atrophy which is a symptom of advanced syphilis. Her brothel in the suburbs 'plucked down', she moves into the city and opens up another. She calls it a 'hot-house' – originally a *bagno* or bath-house, but now just a synonym for a brothel: another word was 'stew-house', from which the familiar Jacobean term 'the stews' to mean a red-light district. 'I have seen corruption boil and bubble till it o'errun the stews,' says the Duke at the beginning of *Measure*.

We enter this 'hot-house' or brothel only in the words of others – mostly Pompey and one of his customers, Master Froth. It is in appearance a tavern. Pompey is its 'tapster' or 'drawer' – as we would say the barman – who is also a pimp: a 'parcel [part-time] bawd'. The place serves food and drink, though the only victuals we actually hear of are 'stewed prunes', sitting in a 'fruit dish' which the garrulous Pompey specifies as 'a dish of some three pence'. Prunes are often associated with brothels: possibly they were considered aphrodisiac. Pistol, an habitué of bawdy houses, 'lives upon mouldy stewed prunes and dried cakes' (2 *Henry IV*, 2.4.155).[27] The house has an 'open room' called the Bunch of Grapes (the rooms of taverns were named, as at the Boar's Head in East Cheap, where there were rooms called the 'Half Moon' and the 'Pomgarnet', or Pomegranate). This open room is something like a public bar. A fire burns in the grate – the room is 'good for winter'. Elsewhere there are private rooms, booths and snugs. Here we might find Master Froth, 'a man of fourscore pound a year, whose father died at Hallowmas', sitting in a 'lower chair'; and the prattling gallant Lucio who had earlier got Kate Keepdown with child; and a selection of the other customers listed by Pompey, all of them 'great doers in our trade'. There is Master Caper in 'a suit of peach-coloured satin', purchased on credit from Master Three-pile the mercer; and 'young Master Deep-vow, and Master Copperspur, and Master Starve-Lackey the rapier and dagger man, and young Drop-heir that killed lusty Pudding, and Master Forthright the tilter, and brave Master Shootie [Shoe-tie] the great traveller, and wild Half-can that stabbed pots . . .' (4.3.9–18). These are the gallants and men-about-town who are Mistress Overdone's clients at her tavern-cum-brothel in the city.[28]

In *Measure for Measure* we find Shakespeare in the city-comedy terrain of Marston, Middleton and Dekker – the topical tone, the interest in prostitution, the louche, scoffing gallant Lucio and his cronies. But the play is also very different. With its awkward conundrums and knotted verse-style – that 'special density of broken wit', as Barbara Everett calls it[29] – *Measure* was hardly a crowd-pleaser in the way that Dekker's *Honest Whore* was. No sequel was rushed out to satisfy public interest or titillation, and there was no published edition of the play before the First Folio.

So here is a question that might have been aired among the 'sharers' of the King's Men around the beginning of 1605. How well is their chief poet Shakespeare keeping up with the new brash fashion of the city comedies? Can he deliver this blend of sex, satire and sharp urban reportage for which the public is clamouring? If *Measure for Measure* is an attempt to do so, it may have been judged a failure. It is a work of great sublety and intellectual power, but is it also bums on seats? Business is business, at the Globe and elsewhere, and the answer is probably not.

In this scenario we might find a more specific context for Shakespeare's association with the redoubtable Wilkins, who swims into his view in the early summer of 1605. In Wilkins, he finds not only intimations of literary talent, not only the chafing ambition of the unpublished writer – he finds also a man who knows this seedy brothel world from the inside, a man who lives this world which the other writers only look in on. He is the real thing. What Shakespeare likes about George Wilkins – 'likes' in a purely professional, talent-spotting sense – is precisely that double curriculum vitae: the playwright and the pimp rolled into one. If the company wants 'Sex and the City' plays, this is the man to write them.

The detail can only be invented, but we have some ingredients for the scene. The location: a lodging-house of low repute outside Cripplegate. The characters: the shady landlord Wilkins; his new lodgers Stephen and Mary; and their friend Mr Shakespeare, a famous man of the theatre. Wilkins, improbably but factually, nurses ambitions to be a poet; Mr Shakespeare is on the look-out for new talent. On the table we see some cups of wine, a dish of fly-blown pippin pie, and a copy of a new pamphlet, *Two Unnatural Murthers*, with its true story of drunkenness, degradation and senseless violence just crying out to be adapted for the stage by someone – Mr Shakespeare glances around the dingy parlour; from an upstairs chamber come shouts and shrill laughter – by someone who understands these things.

However it really was, we know that Wilkins wrote his play, and the King's Men performed it in 1606. It uses the Calverley story but also rewrites it with an abruptly manufactured happy ending – a tragicomedy of sorts, as the fashion required and as the success of the play doubtless justified.

This skeletal and partly speculative narrative – a story of mutual literary opportunism – is a kind of prelude to *Pericles*, for it was doubtless the success of the *Miseries*, still onstage in 1607, that led to Wilkins's collaboration with Shakespeare on *Pericles*. The play is based on the story of Apollonius of Tyre, as told in John Gower's medieval poem *Confessio Amantis* and more recently in Lawrence Twine's *Patterne of Painefull Adventures* (1576). A new edition of Twine's book appeared in 1607, and was perhaps the particular spur, though the authors' debt to Gower is advertised by putting him onstage as the play's Chorus. They had completed the play some time before 20 May 1608, when it was registered at Stationers' Hall.

As noted, the consensus view of *Pericles* – backed up more recently by computer-aided 'stylometric' studies – is that Wilkins was responsible for the first two acts, and Shakespeare for most of the rest. It is not known whether Wilkins wrote a whole play which Shakespeare decided partly to rewrite, or whether

Shakespeare took over the play at the point where the story interested him. He comes in at a pivotal moment of high drama – Pericles on the 'storm-tost' ship bound for Tyre; the death of his wife Thaisa in childbirth, and her burial at sea:

> A terrible childbed hast thou had, my dear.
> No light, no fire: th'unfriendly elements
> Forgot thee utterly. Nor have I time
> To give thee hallow'd to thy grave, but straight
> Must cast thee scarcely coffin'd in the ooze,
> Where for a monument upon thy bones
> And e'er remaining lamps, the belching whale
> And humming water must o'erwhelm thy corpse,
> Lying with simple shells . . . (3.1.56–64)

After the dull but efficient scaffolding of the Wilkins acts, the play is injected with rich Shakespearean melody.[30]

This being the kind of story it is – a 'romance', as it is generally called; a 'mouldy tale', as Ben Jonson called it – Thaisa is not really dead, and will be reunited with Pericles; and their daughter Marina, 'whom for she was born at sea I have nam'd so', will suffer many vicissitudes before she too is found again by her father. Among her tribulations she is captured by pirates and sold into prostitution in Myteline, an episode much expanded by Shakespeare from the sources (or perhaps expanded by Wilkins and rewritten by Shakespeare). Part of Act 4 is set in the brothel – uniquely in Shakespeare: the brothel in *Measure* is only reported to us.[31] The scenes feature an unnamed bawd and pandar, and the pandar's servant, Boult. At odds with the generally stylized tone of the play, the brothel is evoked in a brisk, businesslike way, and one might think the expertise of Wilkins is a contributory factor in this. It is a low-grade place with three resident girls well past their best –

BAWD: We were never so much out of creatures. We have but poor three . . . and they with continual action are even as good as rotten.

PANDAR: Therefore let's have fresh ones, whate'er we pay for
them . . .

BOULT: Shall I search the market?

BAWD: What else, man? The stuff we have, a strong wind will blow
it to pieces, they are so pitifully sodden.

PANDAR: Thou say'st true. There's two unwholesome, a'conscience.
The poor Transylvanian is dead that lay with the little baggage.
(4.2.6–21)

The solution to their problems, they hope, is the beautiful and
virginal Marina, sold to them by the pirates. But this is romance,
and her virtue triumphs over the customers' desires – 'Fie upon
her! She's able to freeze the god Priapus and undo a whole generation . . . She would make a Puritan of the devil if he would
cheapen a kiss of her.'

We are back in the fictive brothel-world of *Measure* and the city
comedies, which is also the real world of Shakespeare's co-author
Wilkins. But the vulnerable and virtuous presence of the romance-
princess Marina casts a different light over it. It occurs to me that
Marina in the bawdy house at Myteline might have some traces
of a real person in a real situation – Mary Belott in the house
of Wilkins. Her arrival there marks the first known connection
between Shakespeare and Wilkins, and her presence there may
have had a similar aspect of sexual vulnerability, of innocence
cast among the wolves – or anyway may have been construed
that way by Shakespeare, who cared about her and who perhaps
felt some pangs of avuncular anxiety about the rackety circumstances in which she now found herself.

Stephen and Mary Belott began this excursion into the Wilkins–
Shakespeare partnership, and we can follow their lives a little at
this point. They were probably not living with Wilkins in 1607–
8, when *Pericles* was being written, but they were his neighbours
in St Giles. As we saw, they had returned to Silver Street in late
1606, after the death of Marie Mountjoy, and Stephen had
worked with his father-in-law 'as partners in their said trade of

Tyeringe'. But this rapprochement did not last, and after about six months they packed up once more and left, probably for the last time. They set up business on their own, and took on an apprentice, William Eaton, who deposed at the Court of Requests that he had known Belott since 1607. All further records of the couple, up into the 1620s, show they were living in St Giles – quite possibly with Belott's stepfather, Humphrey Fludd.

The first such record is a happy event.[32] On 23 October 1608 their daughter Anne was baptized at St Giles. This is the first child of the marriage that we know of – she comes nearly four years after the wedding. Another daughter, Jane, was baptized just over a year later, 17 December 1609. A few weeks later George and Katherine Wilkins were at the church to baptize their son Thomas. Also living at St Giles, probably in partnership with Stephen, was his brother John, who appears in the register in 1612 and is described as a 'tiremaker'.

The Belotts settle into anonymity: another artisan family in the narrow lanes of St Giles. But the faint aroma of sexual scandal which hangs over this everyday story of tiremakers, pimps and playwrights is not entirely absent from the Belotts' lives either. Looking through the registers of St Giles I was interested – indeed startled – to see the name Mary Byllett: interested because 'Byllett' could easily be a variation of Belott, and startled because she appears there as the mother of an illegitimate child, 'Anne Byllet daughter of Edward Skemish and Mary Byllett', baptized 16 May 1610. Could she be Mary Belott *née* Mountjoy? It soon becomes apparent she is not: her child was born only five months after Mary Belott's daughter Jane; also, Mary Byllett must have been single, for a few months later, on 30 January 1611, she was at the altar at St Giles getting married. She was not, therefore, the wife of Stephen Belott, but she could have been his sister. This possibility is somewhat strengthened by the fact that her husband was one Richard Eaton, who is later described as a 'bodymaker' (bodicemaker), and who may well be related to Stephen Belott's apprentice, William Eaton. A possible scenario from this: Stephen's sister, a fallen woman with an illegitimate child, is married off to his apprentice's brother, thus relieving her of a difficulty faced by many young women in Jacobean London, bluntly defined by the Bawd in *Pericles* as 'the bringing up of poor bastards'.

As for Wilkins, we might call *Pericles* the apex of his literary career – his most prestigious piece of work, though not his best. The play was extremely popular, but his response to its popularity is characteristically erratic. In 1608 he issued a novelized treatment of the story, *The Painfull Adventures of Pericles*, which he advertises on the title-page as 'the true history of the play of Pericles, as it was lately presented'. Part of the book is lifted bodily from one of the source-books, Twine's *Patterne of Painefull Adventures*, and part of it is based on the play – though whatever source Wilkins used for these sections, it was often rather different in its phrasing from the copy used for the first printed edition of the play, which appeared the following year. This printing of the play was probably unauthorized, and is full of textual fudgings and corruptions: it is another 'bad quarto', but as the play was not included in the Folio it is the only text of *Pericles* we have.

We are on the edge of a bibliographical minefield which I do not wish to enter. The details are obscure, but there is an undeniable whiff of underhand dealing. Playscripts were owned by the company which performed them, so in legal terms these unauthorized texts of *Pericles* are thefts or misappropriations of property belonging to the King's Men. Wilkins's novelization is a grey area: it is not quite a piracy, perhaps, but it involves some plagiarism of his co-author's work. (This has a positive side, for sometimes Wilkins records a Shakespearean phrase not found in the 1609 quarto: the resonant 'poor inch of nature', describing the baby Marina in the storm, is almost certainly Shakespeare's and is reinstated in modern editions of the play.)[33] It is probable Wilkins also had something to do with the unauthorized quarto of *Pericles*. Its publisher, Henry Gosson, had earlier published Wilkins's *Three Miseries of Barbary*, and in 1611, two years after the appearance of *Pericles*, we find him providing sureties for Wilkins in one of his scrapes with the law. In short, both *The*

Painfull Adventures of Pericles and the 1609 *Pericles* contain stolen literary goods with Wilkins's fingerprints all over them.

We have seen before that Shakespeare grew testy when his work was purloined – those 'stolne and surreptitious copies' to which the Folio editors refer. The *Painfull Adventures of Pericles* is Wilkins's last known work. After a brief swagger of literary success a chill settles over his career, and the next we hear of him is at the Middlesex Sessions in Clerkenwell, bound over for aggression towards the 'quean' or prostitute Anne Plesington – and so begins the dark and violent tragicomedy inscribed in his police-record.[34]

24

Customer satisfaction

S omewhere between the 'sixpenny drab' in the backstreets
and the high-class 'courtesan' cruising for custom in her
new-fangled coach, there was a hinterland of what one might
almost call 'genteel prostitution', in which respectable-looking
young – and not so young – women traded sexual favours for
money or goods.

We have seen these women at the playhouse – the 'Cheapside
dame', the 'light huswife' and others – on the look-out for sexual
assignations that may or may not be also commercial ones. We
find them also in these plays and pamphlets of 1604–5. Thus
Middleton tells us that the discerning young gallant of 1604 likes
his 'harlot' to be a woman of class: 'They should be none of these
common Molls neither, but discontented and unfortunate gentlewomen . . . poor squalls with a little money which cannot hold
out long without some comings-in; but they will rather venture a
maidenhead than want a head-tire' (the tire here epitomizing – as it
often does – the expensive and unnecessary fashion-accessory).[35]
And in Marston's *Dutch Courtesan*, the broad-minded Freevill
speaks sympathetically of wives who seek paid sex as a solution
to economic problems –

A poor decayed mechanical man's wife: her husband is laid up, may not
she lawfully be laid down, when her husband's only rising is by her
falling? A captain's wife wants means: her commander lies in open field
abroad, may not she lie in civil arms at home? A waiting gentlewoman
that had wont to take say [a kind of fine cloth] to her lady, miscarries

or so: the court misfortune throws her down, may not the city courtesy take her up? Do you know no alderman would pity such a woman's case? (1.1.102–9)

These amateurs were viewed with predictable suspicion by professional working girls. In Dekker's *Honest Whore 2*, the upmarket Penelope Whorehound, who pretends to gentility – 'I come of the Whorehounds' – and wears a 'costly gown', says: 'If I go amongst citizens' wives, they jeer at me; if I go among the loose-bodied gowns [prostitutes] they cry a pox on me because I go civilly attired, and swear their trade was a good trade till such as I am took it out of their hands' (2729–32). And in Jonson's *Bartholomew Fair* (1614) the prostitute Alice – 'your punk of Turnbull, Ramping Alice', a true 'mistress of the game' – complains to the flirtatious Mrs Overdo the judge's wife (who is not to be confused with Shakespeare's Mistress Overdone): 'A mischief on you, they are such as you that undo us and take our trade from us, with your tuff-taffety haunches . . . The poor common whores can ha' no traffic for the privy rich ones. Your caps and hoods of velvet call away our customers, and lick the fat from us' (4.3.283–9).

A particular aspect of this is the idea of tradesmen's and shop-keepers' wives who offer sexual favours, or least promising flirtations, to customers. We find this with Mistresses Mulligrub and Burnish, the wives respectively of a vintner and a goldsmith, in Marston's *Dutch Courtesan*. Here is what Mistress M says of Mistress B –

I know her very well. I have been inward with her and so has many more . . . She has been as proper a woman as any in Cheap. She paints [uses cosmetics] now, and yet she keeps her husband's old customers to him still. In truth, a fine fac'd wife in a wainscot carved seat is a worthy ornament to a tradesman's shop, and an attractive, I warrant. Her husband shall find it in the custom of his ware, I'll assure him.

The word 'inward' is used doubly: the line broadly means, 'I have been socially intimate with her and others sexually intimate with her.'[36] 'Proper' in the next sentence is probably also duplicitous. No longer in the first blush of youth, Mrs Burnish continues to use her physical charms as an 'attractive' to her husband's male customers. And Mrs Mulligrub, it seems, does much the same – 'I do keep as gallant and as good company, though I say it, as any she in London. Squires, gentlemen and knights diet at my table.' She offers them credit, and perhaps something more: 'Full many fine men go upon my score, as simple as I stand here . . . [They] promise fair, and give me very good words, and a piece of flesh when time of year serves . . . My silly husband, alas, he knows nothing of it; 'tis I that bear, 'tis I that must bear a brain for all.' (3.3.2–13, 17–27). There is more Marstonian innuendo in this. That 'piece of flesh' which her favoured customers offer her is ostensibly a joint of meat for feast days like Christmas, but has an obvious bawdy reading as well. And ' 'tis I that bear' puns on 'bear' = carry the weight of a man on top, and perhaps also on 'bare'.[37]

The same idea is expressed from the opposite angle in Middleton's satire, *The Family of Love*, c. 1602–4, where the apothecary Purge is complacent about his wife's infidelities because they help business along –

He that tends well his shop, and hath an alluring wife with a graceful 'what d'ye lack', shall be sure to have good doings, and good doings is that that crowns so many citizens with the horns of abundance . . . I smile to myself to hear our knights and gallants say how they gull us citizens, when indeed we gull them, or rather they gull themselves. Here they come in term-time, hire chambers, and perhaps kiss our wives: well, what lose I by that? God's blessing on's heart, I say still, that makes much of my wife; for they were very hard-favoured that none could find in's heart to love but ourselves . . . Tut, jealousy is a hell, and they that will thrive must utter their wares as they can, and wink at small faults. (2.1.2–10)

The implication of that last sentence is that this apothecary's wife is herself one of his 'wares'.

Another complacent apothecary is the subject of a jest in Wilkins and Dekker's *Jests to Make you Merrie* (1607):

An apothecary that had a gallant creature to his wife, was wondred at, that shee (especially) and himselfe could be so rich in apparell, and so expensive in dyet, hauing no customers resorting to their shop for any phisicall stuffe, but onely a few gentlemen that came to take pipes of the divine smoake. Whereupon some of his neighbors giving up their credit, that this geere could not last long, oh (said one of them) you are all deceived in that man, it is not possible he should sinke, hee is so well held up by the heade [by his cuckold's horns].

And in Wilkins's *Miseries*, when Butler plans an assignation with Wentloe and Bartley near Goldsmith's Row, he instructs them, 'Ask not for me, only walk to and fro, and to avoid suspicion you may spend some conference with the shop-keepers' wives; they have seats built a-purpose for such familiar entertainment' (1820–23). This is the same arrangement mentioned by Marston: 'a fine fac'd wife in a wainscot carved seat is a worthy ornament to a tradesman's shop'.

Women in shops enticing potential male purchasers are also mentioned in the anonymous *Pasquin's Palinodia* (1619). Speaking of the tradesmen in the upmarket Jacobean shopping-mall called the New Exchange, the author says:

> Thy shops with pretty wenches swarm,
> Which for thy custom are a kind of charm.

These girls are customers rather than shopkeepers, but it is the same nexus of sex and money which is the terrain of Jacobean city-comedians, and which was defined by them as an aspect of the period's social instability. London was a hive of retail activity: conspicuous consumption was its by-word, and increasingly it was an area in which women were in control. For their menfolk, says Ian Archer, 'shopping becomes a locus of anxieties ... The apparent availability of women in the shops and the desire of city women for consumer goods threatened the patriarchal order on which the authority of citizen husbands rested.'[38] The Cheapside dame cruising for company at the theatre, the pretty girls out shopping at the New Exchange, the fine-faced wife offering cosy chats in the wainscot seat – these are all females enthusiastically engaged in a free-market economy in which they can be sellers and buyers and indeed the commodity itself.

The shop as a locus of sexual assignation or anyway promise – how much does this touch a chord with the Mountjoys of Silver Street? We have hints of the climate there. There are those shenanigans reported in, or inferred from, Simon Forman's casebook, in which Marie's relationship with Henry Wood the mercer seems precisely a mix of business and sexual dalliance ('amor' is the word written down by Forman, so presumably Mr Wood called it 'love', but one suspects that dalliance is what it was). There is that dead baby whose father is not named, and that pregnant maid Margaret Browne, and then later (and more substantial) those two illegitimate children of Christopher's by another maid, and those statements that he had been up before the bench for 'lewd acts and adulteries'.

One remembers also that the head-tire and the periwig were among the most characteristic wear for prostitutes – those 'borrowed gleamy bushes' which 'signify beauty to sell', those 'quaint periwigs' worn by 'street-walkers', those 'lascivious Jessabells' who 'set out their broidred haire with periwigs'. We see that glittery confection of gold and gauze on the courtesan's head in Isaac Oliver's allegorical study of pleasure. She is a decade or so earlier, but this is more or less how the Franceschinas and Bellafronts of Jacobean London looked and dressed. The woman in the painting and the courtesans onstage are fictions, but they are accurate portrayals of real women in that trade or situation – and it is perfectly likely, on a strictly retailing basis, that these women were sometimes to be found in the Mountjoys' shop, buying something special 'with low-down dangling spangles all beset' for that promising assignation with some bountiful lord or wealthy flat-cap.

In these ways a certain dodgy glamour attaches to the Mountjoys' shop, above which Shakespeare sits writing his mirthless comedy about a city obsessed and corrupted with sex – a city he calls 'Vienna' but which is really London.

25

To Brainforde

A universally overlooked detail of the Belott–Mountjoy depositions is that as well as the house on Silver Street Christopher Mountjoy leased a property 'at Brainforde'. It is mentioned by Noel Mountjoy and Christopher Weaver, the two deponents who know most about Mountjoy's financial standing. As they speak of his income from the property, we infer that in 1612, at least, he was sub-letting it.

What the deponents called 'Brainforde', a common spelling at the time, is today the pleasant West London suburb of Brentford. Jacobean Brentford straggled between two village clusters – Old Brentford was part of Ealing parish; New Brentford (or West Brentford) was part of Hanwell parish. These two villages, also known as the Upper Side and Lower Side, were not united as a parish in their own right until 1828. Lying close to the north bank of the Thames, some 8 miles upstream from London, it was a rustic place among fields and marshy meadows, with a famous cattle-fair every July. To the west it abutted on to the great estates of Syon House, seat of the Earls of Northumberland.[39] It sounds a pleasant, faintly pastoral escape from this world of pimps and courtesans and sexual predation in which we have found ourselves – but it is not.

You would not think so, walking its neat streets today, but in Shakespeare's time Brentford had a lurid reputation. It was 'a place of resort' for Londoners and had numerous prostitutes. It is alluded to in various plays and pamphlets of the period, almost invariably as a place for a dirty night or weekend. Thus in Dekker and Webster's *Westward Ho!*, written *c.* 1605–6, three gallants consider their options for a 'merry midsummer night' on the razzle with three citizens' wives –

> WHIRLPOOL: We'll take a coach and ride to Ham or so.
>
> TENTERHOOK: O fie upon't, a coach – I cannot abide to be jolted.
>
> MABEL: Yet most of your citizens' wives love jolting!
>
> GOZLIN: What say you to Blackwall or Limehouse?
>
> JUDITH: Every room there smells too much of tar.
>
> LINSTOCK: Let's to mine host Dogbolt's at Brainford, then. There you are out of eyes, out of ears: private rooms, sweet linen, winking attendance, and what cheer you will!
>
> ALL: Content! To Brainford!
>
> MABEL: Ay, ay, let's go by water. (2.2.322–30)

These are the typical connotations of Brentford – a place of amorous truancy, an escape into illicit pleasure; a place where no questions are asked, because everyone else is up to much the same thing, and where suitable accommodation is ready and waiting – private rooms, scented linen and 'winking attendance' (in other words, discreet service: to 'wink at' something was deliberately not to see it). Thus one went to 'make merry at Brainford'.

This is the idea also in Middleton and Dekker's *Roaring Girl* (1612) –

> LAXTON: Prithee, sweet plump Moll, when shall thee and I go out a' town together?
>
> MOLL: Whither? . . .
>
> LAXTON: To Brainford, Staines or Ware.
>
> MOLL: What to do there?
>
> LAXTON: Nothing but be merry and be together. (3.1.181–6)

Again Brentford is one of various choices, and again it is Brentford which wins – they go there: Laxton calls it a 'lecherous voyage'.

Here is the trip from London to Brentford as taken by the adulterous couples of *Westward Ho!* They meet at eight in the morning at the Greyhound in Blackfriars – 'an excellent rendez-vous', fulfilling two criteria: 'a tavern near the water-side that's private'. Thence, hoping not to be seen, they 'whip forth, two first and two next, on a sudden, and take a boat at Bridewell dock, most privately'. An alternative starting-off point is mentioned in Middleton's *Chaste maid in Cheapside*:

> Let's e'en go to the Checker
> In Queenhive [Queen Hithe], and roast the loin of mutton
> Till young flood, then send the child to Branford. (2.2)

This adds a practical detail: one waited till 'young flood', when the tide begins to flow up the river (and presumably waited at the other end for the ebb-tide). The journey would be delightful, rowed upstream in a wherry or water-taxi (see Plate 30). It was also possible to go by land, via Fulham and Hammersmith, but the roads were in poor condition, and the invariable connotation of an outing to Brentford – indeed part of the fun – is going there by river.[40]

Once there you might find it, as one of the characters does in *Westward Ho!*, a 'lousy town'. No sooner have you arrived but a 'consort' of local fiddlers appears 'under the wenches' comical window'. They will expect a crown (5 shillings) for their entertainment, added to the innkeeper's 'bill of items'. Sir Gozlin complains: 'Ud's [God's] daggers! Cannot sin be set ashore once in a reign upon your country quarters, but it must have fiddling? ... Cannot the shaking of the sheets be danced without your town piping?'

In these riverside houses and cottages converted into pleasure-dens, the idling gallants consider their options – 'sit up at cards all night', or 'drink burnt wine and eggs', or have a hot 'sack-posset' and a 'pipe of tobacco', or visit the 'hot-house'. And easily the expensive gratifications turn sour – 'I'm accursed to spend money in this town of iniquity. There's no good thing ever comes out of it. And it stands upon such musty ground by reason of the river, that I cannot see how a tender woman can do well in't.'

We hear of Brentford again, in the same context of amorous escape, in Jonson's *The Alchemist* (1610). As the plot unravels in the final act, Dr Subtle deserts his partner in crime Face, and tries to get his girlfriend, Doll Common, to run away with him –

> We will turn our course
> To Brainford westward, if thou sayest the word,
> And take our leaves of this overweening rascal.
> . . .   My fine flittermouse,
> My bird of the night, we'll tickle it at the Pigeons
> When we have all . . . (5.2.85–99)

That last comment is a reference to the famous inn in Old Brentford, the Three Pigeons. This inn has a Shakespearean connection, as it was owned by a colleague in the King's Men, John Lowin. Lowin acted alongside Shakespeare in Jonson's *Sejanus* in 1603, and was a company 'sharer' by 1604. He is listed in the First Folio, as one of the 'principall actors' in Shakespeare's plays. According to an early-eighteenth-century account he played the title-role in Shakespeare and Fletcher's *Henry VIII* (1613) – 'The part of the King was so rightly and justly done by Mr [Thomas] Betterton, he being instructed in it by Sir William [Davenant], who had it from old Mr Lowen, that had his instructions from Mr Shakespeare himself' – a genealogy akin to the studio lineages of Italian Renaissance painting. Lowin later lived in Southwark, and 'carried memories of Shakespeare down to the closing of the theatres in 1642'.[41]

It is not known when Lowin became owner of the Three Pigeons. Another of Shakespeare's colleagues, Augustine Phillips, owned a house at nearby Mortlake, just across the river on the south bank. This house seems to have served as a base for the company in the summer of 1603, when the plague was at its height in the city. It is quite likely Shakespeare knew the Three Pigeons, and not impossible he knew the Mountjoys' house in Brentford. The inn was associated with the playwright George Peele – or at least with his avatar in *The Merrie Conceited Jests of George Peele* (c. 1605) – 'Honest George . . . is now merry at the Three Pigeons in Brainford, with sack and sugar, not any wine wanting, the musicians playing, my host drinking, my hostess dancing.' It remained famous or infamous through the centuries: part of Oliver Goldsmith's *She Stoops to Conquer* (1773) is set there. Nineteenth-century engravings show a rambling, teetering old building with tall chimneys and a range of rickety stables out back (see Plate 31). It was demolished in 1911.[42]

Court records give us the reality of this little good-time town beloved of the London playwrights. Various women in trouble with the law are identified in the records as 'late of London, spinster', which probably means they are prostitutes of one hue or another transiently set up here. Thus at 'Brayneford' on 8 November 1571, Isabell Cornewall 'late of London, spinster' broke into the house of Joan Parker, widow, and stole a silver ring and a purse containing 3s 8d. She pleaded guilty but asked for clemency as she was pregnant: if so, another unmarried mother. And sometimes the story is grim, as this: in the early afternoon of 12 December 1598, 'in a room of the dwelling house of James Lovegrove at Braneford, co Middx . . . Agnes Charche, late of London, spinster, gave birth to a male infant, living at the time of birth, and forthwith then and there with her hands twisted and broke the neck of the said infant'.[43]

And with the prostitutes come the thieves, such as Richard Heyward, 'late of London', charged in 1601 with stealing 30 pounds of feathers worth 40 shillings from Michael Goodyeare of Brainford, and John Anderton 'late of London, yeoman', who stole various items from a woman in New Brentford, including a 'woollen cloak of tobacco colour' and a linen cap 'wrought with gold and silke'. And in July 1612, just a few weeks after the Belott–Mountjoy depositions, Edward Flood of New Brentford was charged with possession of a cloak 'feloniously taken out of the howse of the Lady Keligway without Aldgate'. One of his sureties in posting bail was one Ninus Layne 'of St Olive's in the city of London' – possibly a neighbour of Christopher Mountjoy (though 'St Olive's' could also refer to St Olave's, Hart Street).[44]

We know, broadly speaking, why Christopher Mountjoy leased a property in Brentford. He did so to make money by sub-letting it. Thus Noel Mountjoy: 'He hath but the lease of two houses: one lease of the house wherein he dwelleth, divided into two tenements, and a lease of a house in Brainforde, by which leases he gaineth an overplus of rent more than he payeth.' How much he made from it is not vouchsafed – from the two properties combined he received rents of about £35 per annum. Roughly half of this covered the annual cost of the two leases, and the other half was profit 'de claro'.

We do not know what kind of house it was, or what it was used for, but on the whole it would not be surprising if it offered chambers with sweet linen where well-breeched Londoners could 'fleet the time carelessly' with other men's wives, or indeed with professional ladies of the kind who bought their 'quaint periwigs' and head-tires at the shop on Silver Street. There is another possibility. In her deposition in 1612, the Mountjoys' former maidservant Joan Johnson gives her address as the 'parish of Ealing in the county of Middlesex'. Old Brentford was part of Ealing parish, so it is possible that Joan and her husband Thomas the basketmaker were now Mountjoy's tenants in Brentford.[45]

These possibilities are not mutually exclusive – to be a basketmaker's wife does not at all disqualify a woman from running a 'house of resort'. And so Joan Johnson – or Joan Langford as she was when Shakespeare knew her at Silver Street – becomes another of the Mountjoys' maids to be touched with this aura of assignations and adulteries which seems a feature of life *chez* Mountjoy. But as so often in this book these are question-marks only – what, in another type of enquiry, would be called hunches.

26

'At his game'

*W*e have an idea of the simmering randiness of the age – the pliant dames at the playhouse, the prostitutes scattered through the suburbs, the 'fine-faced' shopkeepers' wives in their wainscot seats, the jaunts upriver to the fleshpots of Brentford. And we have seen something of how this impinges on Shakespeare. The fictive brothels and bawds of *Measure for Measure* and *Pericles* are in part a product of literary necessity, of competitive playhouse modernity, but they are also connected with the real-life brothel-world of George Wilkins, the tavern-keeper and pimp who becomes – briefly and more or less simultaneously – a landlord of the Belotts and a playmaker for the King's Men. With Wilkins we touch on violence and squalor. He beats up prostitutes; he receives stolen goods from them; his own wife is called a bawd in the street. These particular events occur after Shakespeare's known involvement with him, but the kicker of women and the penner of the *Miseries* are demonstrably one and the same man.

This remains a literary relationship, a brief and ultimately unsatisfactory collaboration with a promising but deeply unstable young writer. But one wonders about the more personal side. What did Shakespeare think of Wilkins? Or more broadly – because that specific question is unanswerable – what was Shakespeare's own relationship to the Wilkinsian world of low taverns and punks; or to the slinkier demi-monde of those upmarket courtesans with foreign accents; or indeed to that more decorously erotic milieu of desperate housewives and flirtatious shopkeepers to which his landlady might be thought to belong? What, in short, was Shakespeare's love-life like, during the long months he spent in London, far from a marriage-bed which had anyway – if the tradition is to be believed – long ago turned cold?

Here is one answer, proposed by a young law-student at the Middle Temple, John Manningham, who on 13 March 1602 wrote down the following story in his diary:

Upon a tyme when Burbidge played Rich. 3 there was a citizen greue soe farr in liking with him, that before shee went from the play shee appointed him to come that night unto hir by the name of Ri: the 3. Shakespeare overhearing their conclusion went before, was intertained and at his game err Burbidge came. The message being brought that Rich. the 3d was at the dore, Shakespeare caused returne to be made that William the Conquerour was before Rich. the 3.

Beneath this Manningham adds helpfully: 'Shakespeare's name William', and then the name, 'Mr Curle', signifying that he got the story from his fellow-student at the Temple, Edward Curle.[46]

It is a wonderful story and of course quite unverifiable: the neatness of the punchline tends to argue against its being true, yet it was obviously 'true' enough in another sense – credible, typical, backgrounded – to the teller of the story. It remains at the anecdotal level of the 'jest-book', where apocryphal stories are fathered on to real people (Dick Tarlton, George Peele, Mary Frith et al.).

That the players participated in the sexual opportunities on offer in the theatres is hardly to be doubted. The Manningham anecdote is part of a general lore about the sexual attractiveness of players to their female audience. The women did not scream and faint, or throw their underwear onstage like girls at the height of Beatlemania, but the charisma of the stage is perennial. 'O my troth,' cries Frank Gullman in Middleton's *A Mad World*, as she watches the handsome Follywit deliver the prologue of a play-within-the-play called *The Slip*, an' I were not married, I could find in my heart to fall in love with that player now, and send for him to a supper. I know some i' th' town that have done as much, and there took such a good conceit of their parts into th' two-penny room that the actors have been found i' th' morning in less compass than their stage, tho' 'twere ne'er so full of gentlemen ... (5.2.33–9)

There are the standard bawdy equivoques in 'parts', 'room' and 'compass'.

The character-writer John Earle also notes the charisma of the actor: 'the waiting-women spectators are over-eares in love with [him], and Ladies send for him to act in their chambers'.[47] And we have hints of an actual affair between the Countess of Argyll and the player–poet Nathan Field, for a gossipy letter of 1619 relates that the Earl of Argyll 'was privy to the paiment of 15 or 16 poundes ... for the noursing of a childe which the worlde sayes is daughter to My Lady and N. Feild the player'. There is a portrait of Field: darkly handsome, with the look of a languid pirate. A similar frisson may be behind a reminiscence of Ben Jonson's, recorded by William Drummond: 'Ben being one day at table with my Lady Rutland, her husband coming in accused her that she kept table to poets.'[48] (An occasion for this might be around 1606, when the Countess performed in Jonson's masque *Hymenaei*, perhaps wearing a Mountjoy head-tire.)

Manningham's anecdote places Shakespeare and Burbage in this world of actors and their stage-struck 'groupies', which is also a milieu of homosocial competitiveness in which such women are trophies. In the story Shakespeare is rather laddish: he is 'at his game' before Burbage gets there. It is not quite clear from the story whether the 'citizen' has cheerfully accepted the arrival of Shakespeare at her door, and in her bed, or whether she is still under the illusion that the visitor is Burbage. If the latter – the 'bed-trick', as used in various Shakespeare plays – the story would have an added biographical touch, suggesting that Shakespeare was of broadly similar build to Burbage – in other words, quite short.[49]

*

The Manningham anecdote is a well-informed topical jest, but Shakespeare's name is linked more specifically with a woman called Jane (or Jennet) Davenant. She was the wife of a vintner in Oxford, John Davenant, and the mother of the future poet laureate Sir William Davenant. It is to the latter, ultimately, that we owe the information about Shakespeare and Mrs Davenant, though the conduit of the story is the indispensable but sometimes unreliable John Aubrey, who writes:

Sir William [Davenant] would sometimes when he was pleasant over a glass of wine with his most intimate friends, e.g. Sam: Butler (author of Hudibras) &c, say that it seemed to him that he writt with the very spirit that Shakespeare [*sc* did], and seemd contendended [*sic*] enough to be thought his son . . .

One interpretation of this is that Davenant meant he was Shakespeare's godson, or perhaps only his 'son' in a metaphorical sense of poetic inheritance. But this was not Aubrey's immediate interpretation, for he continued the sentence, 'in which way his mother had a very light report, whereby she was called a whore' – but he, or someone else, crossed this out. A later seventeenth-century embroidery of the story had the young William Davenant running to see his 'godfather' Shakespeare whenever he came to Oxford, and being told 'not to take the name of God in vain'.[50]

Jane Davenant was, according to Aubrey, 'a very beautiful woman, & of a very good witt and of conversation extremely agreable'. (Aubrey might be expected to say this of Shakespeare's putative lover, but he had many Oxford connections, and was writing within living memory of her, so it may well be true.) She was born Jane Sheppard, baptized at St Margaret's, Westminster on 1 November 1568. Her father, Robert, was probably in minor court service, as her brothers would later be. From the will of her uncle William, we learn that she was known in the family as 'Jennet'. She married John Davenant in about 1593, in her mid-twenties. The Davenants were a successful family of wine-merchants, importing direct from Bordeaux and Gascony. They lived close to the Thames, in St James Garlickhithe, near the

Three Cranes Wharf where their casks of claret and 'butts and pipes of sweet wynes' were unloaded. After a string of dead babies we find Jane in the consulting room of Dr Forman, in January 1598: 'she supposeth herself with child', Forman wrote – as he had of Marie Mountjoy a month earlier – 'but yt is not soe'. In about 1600 the Davenants moved to Oxford, where they ran a large, four-storey wine-tavern, later in the century known as the Crown, part of which still stands at No. 3 Cornmarket. They ran the place for twenty years, had seven healthy children, and died within a few weeks of each other in the spring of 1622. In an echo of the Mountjoys, Davenant's will expressed the hope that his apprentice would marry his daughter.[51]

There is much to commend the idea that Shakespeare knew the Davenants, and it is possible he did so through the Mountjoys. There is the French connection: Davenant's wine-business, in which he deals with French exporters, and no doubt has French clients like Mountjoy keen to enjoy the wines of his homeland. There is also a connection with Jane's brother, Thomas Sheppard, who was a glover and perfumer, employed at court. He appears in the lists of the Coronation progress of 1604, under 'artificers', as Shakespeare does under 'falconers, etc', both with the rank of Grooms of the Chamber. And in Queen Anne's household accounts for 1604–5, Sheppard appears as a supplier of perfumes alongside Marie Mountjoy, 'tyrewoman'.[52] These are connections that might bring Shakespeare and Jennet Davenant together, though of course there are many others.

Sir William Davenant was plausibly Shakespeare's godson, named after him, and was 'contented' to be thought his illegitimate son. He was born in March 1606, so, if we take him literally, Shakespeare and Jennet made 'the beast with two backs' in the summer of 1605, a likely time for Shakespeare to be en route to his family in Stratford. She was then in her late thirties, and had borne eight children.

One would be tempted to dismiss this as an exaggeration of Davenant's, were it not for an unnoticed hint of the affair in Marston's *Dutch Courtesan*, performed in 1604. As we have seen, the play features a flirtatious vintner's wife, Mrs Mulligrub, who has certain gentlemen 'at [her] table', and who sometimes receives from them a 'piece of flesh', a situation of which her 'silly husband . . . knows nothing'. I think this may be an in-joke allusion to the real vintner's wife, Mrs Davenant, and her liaison with Marston's literary rival, Shakespeare. This perhaps explains why the cuckolded husband Mr Mulligrub is told a rather laboured joke about 'jennets' (= young horses) that 'dance the old measures' (2.3.65–8). He finds it very amusing, and repeats it back – 'Ha, ha, ha . . . Jennets to dance the old measures . . . Dost take me for an ass?' But he is indeed an ass, for the joke is told by a conman disguised as a barber, who is shaving Mulligrub so he can also 'shave' or fleece him of a bag of money. This deceiver of the vintner is described as a 'thick, elderly, stub-bearded fellow', which may just about be an unflattering description of Mr Shakespeare in 1604. 'Thick' means portly, 'elderly' would refer to his baldness, and a 'stub' or stubble beard is precisely what Shakespeare has in the Droeshout engraving, based on an original portrait dating from around this time. Personal hits of this sort are characteristic of Marston, who was one of the squabbling poets in the earlier 'War of the Theatres'.

The unnamed 'citizen' of the Manningham anecdote; the vintner's wife Jennet Davenant – two women (or conceivably the same woman?) said to have had adulterous affairs with Shakespeare – would perhaps echo Emilia in *Othello*, with her worldly-wise view of extramarital flings:

DESDEMONA: Would thou do such a deed for all the world?
EMILIA: The world's a huge thing. It is a great price for a small vice.
DESDEMONA: In truth I think thou wouldst not.
EMILIA: In truth I think I should, and undo't when I had done.

On the matter of infidelity Emilia knows where the blame lies: 'I do think it is their husbands' faults / If wives so fall.' First, there is the husband's loss of sexual interest –

'Tis not a year or two shows us a man.
They are all but stomachs, and we all but food.
They eat us hungrily, and when they are full,
They belch us. (3.4.100–103)

Then there are the husbands' own strayings – 'They slack their duties, / And pour our treasures into foreign laps' – and their domestic tyrannies: they 'break out in peevish jealousies' and 'strike us' and 'scant our former having [reduce our allowance]'. Women have not only an equal right to be unfaithful, but an equal taste for sexual adventure –

What is it that they [husbands] do
When they change us for others? Is it sport?
I think it is. And doth affection breed it?
I think it doth. Is't frailty that thus errs?
It is so, too. And have not we affections,
Desires for sport, and frailty, as men have?
Then let them use us well, else let them know:
The ills we do, their ills instruct us so . . . (4.3.87–103)

These words are spoken in the privacy of female companionship ('us'), free from the subservience which conventional morality demanded of a wife. They are also spoken in the playhouse, where morality can be knocked around a bit, and where amorous 'sport and frailty' are a popular diversion, onstage and off. Upright citizens – virtually an endangered species, according to the city comedies, but still vocal – would call Emilia 'loose' or 'light', but the playgoer of 1604 could enjoy, as we do, her easygoing pragmatism on the subject.[53]

One person who would understand Emilia's words is Marie Mountjoy, in whose house they may well have been written. Relations with her crabby, tight-fisted husband may have been bad. His treatment of their only child – an alienation he pursued long after Marie's death, indeed until his own death – does not suggest a loving family man. In the only recorded conversation between them, Marie entreats him to be more generous to their daughter and is brusquely rejected – 'He would never promise them anything, because he knew not what he should need himself' (deposition of Christopher Weaver). He was probably unfaithful to her – 'paillardises & adultères' – and on the evidence of the Forman casebooks it seems likely she was unfaithful to him.

A question has hovered in my mind while writing this book. It has no real answer, but scraps of evidence and speculation keep leading me back to it. What did this apparently amorous and adulterous Frenchwoman mean to Shakespeare, and he to her?

The only relationship between them that we know for sure is that Marie Mountjoy was his landlady. Thus phrased, the relationship has a humdrum, faintly comic connotation. But we also know that she asked him – and it is Shakespeare's own statement that *she* asked him – to persuade Stephen Belott to marry her daughter. And when he had successfully done this, he was also asked to 'contract' the young couple in a formal betrothal. Neither of these roles requires any deep personal relationship, but they at least suggest he was someone she trusted.

Was there more? In a novelistic sense the circumstances would seem quite propitious – the celebrated player–poet and the sparky French costumière. It would be pertinent to add 'dark-eyed' to her attractions, but the fact is we have no idea what Marie looked like. Shakespeare thinks of Frenchwomen as dark, and dark women as sexy: she may have been both, or neither.

In the absence of evidence one weighs probabilities. Conducting an affair with a married woman while living in her husband's house sounds complicated and tiring. In the city-comedy world this sort of thing goes on all the time – 'Here they come in term-time, hire chambers, and perhaps kiss our wives: well, what lose I by that?' says Purge the apothecary in Middleton's *Family of Love*[54] – and we have a fairly strong sense that the Mountjoy household was more a place of sexual freedom than of restraint. But what argues against it in the real world is inconvenience and emotional claustrophobia.

Of the two Shakespearean extramarital encounters we hear about, one is a one-night stand and the other is with a woman in distant Oxford. They are merely anecdotal, especially the first, but even when inaccurate a contemporary anecdote carries information about what is likely or credible. The first is casual sex, the second is occasional sex; a third category, not evidenced but certainly contextualized in these chapters, is paid sex.[55] Any or all of these may resolve the question of Shakespeare's love-life in London better than the idea of a long-running sexual companionship with a 'mistress'. The only person he actually describes as his mistress is the enigmatic 'Dark Lady' of the Sonnets, and the poems are full of a desire to escape his entanglement with her. The relationship is described as a confinement, a cage – 'Prison my heart in thy steel bosom's ward', 'I being pent in thee / Perforce am thine' (133) – or as a kind of debilitating sexual addiction:

> My love is as a fever, longing still
> For that which longer nurseth the disease,
> Feeding on that which doth preserve the ill,
> Th'uncertain sickly appetite to please. (147)

The Sonnets, we are constantly reminded, are not autobiography, but the 'I' who speaks in them is a jaded lover who wants to be shot of the whole affair.

Do we look through that metaphorical window in Silver Street and see the middle-aged Shakespeare 'at his game' with the landlady? The answer must be no – not because it definitely never happened, but because we cannot know if it happened. An aura of sexual intrigue hangs about the house, a frisson which various hints – illegitimate children, the affair with Henry Wood, the clientele of courtesans, the house in Brentford – have suggested is intrinsic to these particular people with whom he lived. This tells us something about Shakespeare's circumstances, and about his choice of circumstances, but nothing about his involvement in them. 'Let not the creaking of shoes nor the rustling of silk betray thy heart to women,' warns crazy Tom in *King Lear* – words Shakespeare wrote in around 1605, possibly in this very house which seems so full of exactly these dangers.

After a fair amount of snooping I can find no evidence of

impropriety. If I had to sum up the relationship between Shake-speare and Marie Mountjoy I would say only that she was his friend – a description of her at once bland and deeply resonant. If there was something more, it remains a secret between them.

PART SEVEN
Making Sure

Vows are but breath and breath a vapour is . . .
Love's Labour's Lost, 4.3.65

27

A handfasting

We have come some way from that carton of old papers at the National Archives which began this enquiry. We have learned something of the physical and personal circumstances of Shakespeare on Silver Street – the industrious, quarrelsome, somewhat rackety family of immigrants with whom he lodged; the workshop with its wire-mills and twisting-wheels, and its clientele which included royalty and aristocracy as well as prostitutes and players. We have some new facts about the Mountjoys, and some new speculations about them. But one thing we do know for sure – on his own sworn evidence and that of others – is that some time in 1604 Shakespeare 'persuaded' Stephen Belott to marry Mary Mountjoy, and I conclude by returning once more to the micro-story of marital ups and downs narrated in the depositions of the Belott–Mountjoy suit, and to Shakespeare's involvement in it.

What did Shakespeare do? His own phrasing of the matter – or rather the legal statement which in some part records his phrasing – is as follows:

Mr Mountjoy 'willingly offered' his daughter Mary in marriage to Stephen Belott, should he 'seem to be content and well like thereof'.
Shakespeare was 'entreated' by Mrs Mountjoy to 'move and persuade' Stephen to 'effect the said marriage', and 'accordingly' did so.
Mountjoy 'promised' to give Stephen 'a portion in marriage

with Mary his daughter', but what sum it was Shakespeare 'remembereth not'.

Stephen 'was dwelling with' Mountjoy, 'in his house', and 'they had amongst themselves many conferences about their marriage'.

'Afterwards' the marriage was 'consummated and solemnized'

Other deponents in the case echo Shakespeare's statement pretty closely. Belott's apprentice William Eaton says Shakespeare was 'sent' to 'move the plaintiff to have a marriage [with] Mary', and 'was wished by the defendant to make proffer of a certain sum that the defendant said he would give'. And Noel Mountjoy says 'Mr Shakespeare was employed by the defendant about that business', and was asked 'to make a motion to him [Belott] of a marriage'. But, regrettably, 'in what manner and to what effect' Shakespeare did this, Noel 'knoweth not'.

In all this Shakespeare is given an oddly factorial role – he is 'sent' to the former apprentice to 'move' him; he is asked to 'make proffer of' a sum of money; he is 'employed about that business'. He has the status of an agent, a go-between, a broker of marriage. We can see how he might be an ideal choice as the persuader of Stephen Belott. He has the required authority: a parent, a gentleman, a servant of His Majesty. There is also a more personal element. He liked Belott – he thought him an 'honest fellow' – and we can suppose that Belott liked and respected him. And then, as a kind of added bonus to all this, he is Shakespeare, a man uniquely eloquent in affairs of the heart. All in all, a useful person to have on hand should you wish to 'persuade' someone to marry your daughter.

The fullest account of Shakespeare's actions is that of Daniel Nicholas, the friend of Belott, the son of the charitable mayor Sir Ambrose Nicholas, and the only deponent besides Shakespeare to be described as a 'gentleman'. In his first deposition of 11 May 1612, Nicholas refers, as the others do, to Shakespeare being sent to Belott on his mission of persuasion. But in his second deposition, of 19 June, he adds a further aspect to Shakespeare's role, indeed a culmination of it –

In regard Mr Shakespeare had told them that they should have a sum of money for a portion from the father, they were made sure by Mr Shakespeare by giving their consent, and agreed to marry, [giving each other's hand to the hand *deleted*], and did marry.

Those words scored through in the original are the particular clue. They were deleted as inadmissible, perhaps because Nicholas was describing something he had not actually witnessed, or perhaps because the circumstances of the marriage itself were not at issue. I reinstate them because this is not a court of law, because Nicholas is a good deal closer to the event than we are, and because the phrasing he uses tells us fairly precisely what it was that Shakespeare did, or 'moved' Stephen and Mary to do, on that day in 1604.

What Nicholas is describing is what the Elizabethans and Jacobeans called a 'troth-plight' or a 'handfasting', and what was legally called *sponsalia per verba*, or 'betrothal by words'. When Nicholas says the couple was 'made sure' by Shakespeare he is using a specific term associated with betrothals – 'In matrimonie there is a contract or makyng sure, there is a coupling or handfasting of eyther partie, and finally marriage.'[1] The Mountjoys themselves might have used the word *accorder* – Cotgrave's French dictionary gives '*Accorder une fille* – to handfast, affiance, betroath himself unto a maiden'.

   These betrothals were taken seriously, indeed were considered a binding contract. There were two kinds of contract, *de praesenti* and *de futuro*. The *de praesenti* was an agreement to become man and wife as of the present time. According to Pollock and Maitland's *History of English Law*, it 'established a bond which could not be dissolved except under exceptional circumstances, and not at all if *copula carnalis* had taken place'. The *de futuro* contract was a promise to wed in the future – roughly the equivalent of a modern engagement. It could be broken off by either party, 'unless *copula carnalis* had occurred, in which case the betrothal was automatically converted into *de iure* marriage'.[2]

Nicholas's phrasing tends to suggest the full *de praesenti* troth-plight: Stephen and Mary 'agreed to marry, giving each other's hand to the hand, and did marry'. The last clause may refer to their subsequent wedding in church, or it may mean they were married there and then, by the contractual force of their 'consent'. That the handfasting in itself constituted a marriage is made clear by the Elizabethan expert on the subject, Henry Swinburne, whose *Treatise of Spousals*, written in about 1600, was the fruit of his long years as a judge at the Prerogative Court in York. Those who 'have contracted spousals *de praesenti*', he writes, 'are reputed man and wife . . . For spousals *de praesenti*, though not consummate, be in truth and substance very matrimony.'[3] The same idea is expressed more poetically in John Webster's *The Duchess of Malfi* (*c.* 1612) –

> I have heard lawyers say a contract in a chamber
> *Per verba presenti* is absolute marriage.
> Bless, heaven, this sacred gordian which let violence
> Never untwine! . . .
> How can the church build faster?
> We are now man and wife, and 'tis the church
> That must but echo this. (1.2.18–35)

It would perhaps have been one of Shakespeare's tasks to remind the couple of the binding nature of the betrothal, as did a certain William Addison in a similar situation, as recorded in a case before the London Consistory Court in *c.* 1610.[4] He warned Joan Waters to 'take heed what she did . . . for it was a contract which was not for a day or a month but for term of life', and Joan 'answered she knew what she did'.

Cases of disputed marriage at the Consistory Court, also known more sinisterly as 'matrimonial enforcement suits', have been meticulously studied by Loreen Giese and others.[5] They contain many accounts of troth-plightings, and these give us some broad contexts for the one at Silver Street. Most of the contracts take place in a room (sometimes specified – hall, kitchen, chamber, etc) in a house connected with one of the spouses, though taverns and 'victualling houses' were also a popular venue (see Plate 32), and sometimes, weather permitting, they were performed al fresco, in a garden or orchard, or even 'on horseback'. One young woman named Susan Fidgett went to 'the ffeildes to dry clothes' and came back betrothed.[6] But these were exceptions, and it is likely the handfasting of Stephen and Mary took place at the house on Silver Street.

There was no rigid verbal formula, but we hear set phrases familiar to us from the wedding-service in the 1662 Book of Common Prayer, such as 'With this ring I thee wed' and 'Till death us do part' (or more commonly 'depart'). In a case of 1598 John Griffin explained the correct wording to an intending husband: 'I John take thee Jane to my wedded wife, till death us depart, and thereto I plight thee my troth; and then the woman to say the like words again.' These words, he assured him, 'do make folks sure together'. Here are some other variations.

[Thomas] holding her by the right hand said: I Thomas take thee Grace to my wife, and I will have thee to my wife and no other woman, and thereto I plight thee my troth. And then they loosing hands, Grace took Thomas by the right hand, saying: I Grace take thee Thomas to my husband [etc] . . .

[Elizabeth took Martin] by the hand and said unto him these very words and none other: Here is my hand, in faith forever, whether my mother will or no. And then the said Martin answered: There is my hand and my faith forever, and I will never forsake thee . . .[7]

Gifts would often be exchanged in token of the betrothal – typically, as today, rings. In one case, the man having brought no ring, a witness 'stooped down and made a ring of a rush, and would have given it them'. Sometimes the ring is specified – 'a seal ring of gold with the picture of a white dog upon it, with the ears tipped with silver'. Hoop rings are also mentioned, like the one Marie lost out of her purse, and the double-hooped 'gimmel' ring, symbolic of clasped hands, was popular. On a gold gimmel ring of *c.* 1600, now in the Museum of London, is engraved a handfasting motto:

> As handes doe shut
> So hart be knit

Almost as popular as rings was the spouses' exchange of a piece or coin of gold, broken in half between them. Many other betrothal gifts are itemized – a pair of gloves 'worth 2s 6d', a petticoat, a 'peece of crimson rybbyn knitt in a square knott wch she called a treww lovers knott', a 'jewell called an aggat', a prayer book, 'a French crowne and a tothepiker [toothpick] of silver', and so on.[8]

These reports of handfastings in Elizabethan and Jacobean London help us to gauge something of the scene at Silver Street. It is a brief, well-worn ceremony, balanced between a certain *ad hoc* casualness and a touching formality. This is a folk-rooted society, at ease with ritual. Shakespeare is not exactly officiating – the ceremony is precisely private rather than official: a 'contract in a chamber'. Legally speaking, he is no more than a witness of an oral contract. But often in these accounts there is someone obviously in charge, a master (or occasionally mistress) of cere-monies, and the phrasing of Daniel Nicholas's statement – 'they were made sure by Mr Shakespeare' – clearly suggests this. His role might indeed be summed up as 'directorial'. It is a scene to be acted out. There are lines to be spoken, and gestures to be got right, and props to be handled. It is not necessary that anyone else was present – a single witness was sufficient – but doubtless her parents were there, and perhaps others such as the maid Joan Langford, and Belott's mother and stepfather, the Fludds (but not, it seems, Mary's uncle Noel, who said he did not know the 'manner' or 'effect' of Shakespeare's involvement). And so for a few moments the Mountjoys' shadowy parlour becomes a little theatre, and a hush falls as Stephen and Mary take hands and speak their vows.

*

When was Shakespeare knitting the young couple's hearts in this way? The actual wedding took place at St Olave's on 19 November 1604 (see Plate 33). The troth-plighting would probably have been a few weeks before this. Church regulations required the calling of the banns on three successive Sundays before the marriage could be 'solemnized' in church. The 19th fell on a Monday, so if the banns were observed – and there is no reason to think they were not – the latest date for the betrothal of Stephen and Mary would be Saturday 3 November, or at a pinch early on Sunday the 4th.

It does not need to be quite so hurried, of course, but it is unlikely there was a very long gap. In her study of courtship in Shakespearean England, Anne Jennalie Cook finds that 'betrothals usually lasted a month or so'. The official Church view was that the wedding should follow fairly quickly after the betrothal, to avoid the temptations of premarital sex. Thus Heinrich Bullinger, the great Calvinist preacher whose sermons were very popular in England: 'After the handfasting & making of the contract, the churchgoing & wedding should not be deferred too long, lest the wicked sew his ungracious seed in the mean season.'[9]

There is also the question of Shakespeare's presence. He was probably out of London during the summer – the 'tedious dead vacation' when the law-courts closed, and the royal entourage decamped, and the play-companies went on tour (or, in the case of Shakespeare, went back to his family and his garden at New Place in Stratford). The end of the long summer break was signalled by the feast of Michaelmas (29 September), and the city got back to business in early October: the new law-term, the new theatrical season.

It was perhaps around then, back in London in the dying fall of the summer, that Shakespeare was asked by Marie Mountjoy to have a quiet word with the reluctant or hesitant suitor Stephen Belott. He did what she asked, and won Belott's consent, and afterwards presided over the betrothal. In his original bill of complaint Belott says that on the basis of Mountjoy's 'offers' and 'persuasions' he 'did shortly after entermarry with the said Mary'.

This is vague, and it is not quite clear if 'entermarry' refers to the betrothal or the wedding, but again it suggests things moved quite quickly.

None of this is infallible – one of the Consistory Court cases refers to a wedding performed two years after the contract – but these are the conventions, and the vestigial narrative recoverable from the lawsuit seems to fit with them well enough. The probable date of the Silver Street betrothal was October 1604.

28

'They have married me!'

The troth-plighting ceremony has a natural homespun theatricality, to which the playwright and matchmaker Mr Shakespeare would surely have responded on that day in October 1604. And not long after the betrothal of Stephen and Mary, there was a troth-plighting scene being played at the Globe theatre:

> SCARBORROW: This hand thus takes thee as my loving wife.
> CLARE: For better, for worse.
> SCARBORROW: Aye, till death us depart, love.
> CLARE: Why then I thank you Sir, and now I am like to have what I long looked for – a husband.

The scene is from *The Miseries of Enforced Marriage* by George Wilkins (242–6). It was written in the latter part of 1605, precisely when Stephen and Mary were lodging with Wilkins in St Giles. The formulae of troth-plighting were common knowledge, so one cannot argue any direct connection or intended reference. But the proximity is tantalizing.

Later in the play, learning the news of Scarborrow's subsequent marriage to another woman (the 'enforced marriage' of the title, which reflects the facts of the Calverley case on which the play is based), Clare speaks poignantly of the 'wrong / Done to a troth-plight virgin like my self':

> O perjury, within the hearts of men
> Thy feasts are kept . . .
> He was contracted mine, yet he unjust

Hath married to another: what's my estate then?
A wretched maid, not fit for any man,
For being united his with plighted faiths,
Whoever sues to me commits a sin
. . . Who'ere shall marry me
I am but his whore, live in adultery. (800–822)

This is not a reflection of the Belotts, though the opening sentence may well be a reflection of Shakespeare (by which I mean it sounds like Wilkins trying to sound like Shakespeare). And the unhappy paradox of Clare's situation – she is both married and unmarried; she must remain a virgin or else be a whore – has a touch of the Shakespearean problem plays. The paradox is probably faulty: the contract has been broken by Scarborrow, so she need no longer be bound by it.[10] But Wilkins was not a writer to trouble over details.

The play also contains a more humorous (and more typically Wilkinsian) version of a betrothal, as described by the reprobate Sir Frank Ilford. A father is anxious to make a match for his daughter, and having discussed the possibility with an eligible young man, he sets the charms of the daughter herself to work on him:

Then putting you and the young pug to, in a close room together . . . where the young puppet, having the lesson before from the old fox [her father], give thee some half a dozen warm kisses, which after her father's oaths takes such impression in thee, thou straight call'st: By Jesu, mistress, I love you. When she has the wit to ask: But sir, will you marry me? And thou in thy cox-sparrow humour, replyest: Aye, before God, as I am a gentleman will I, which the father overhearing, leaps in, takes you at your word, swear[s] he is glad to see this, nay he will have you contracted straight, and for a need makes a priest of himself. (101–13)

This is Wilkins at his best – emphatic, rapid, scarcely grammatical: a little sketch of a young man trapped inadvisedly into marriage. It is written just as he might tell it, in his cups, to assembled cronies and molls in the tavern. Again one senses a refraction of reality – a kind of slapstick version of Stephen Belott, coerced by the Mountjoys and Shakespeare into marriage: 'nay he will have you contracted straight'.

Every contact leaves traces, and these passages from the *Miseries* seem to be traces of the known contact between Wilkins, the Belotts and Shakespeare. They are not references or in-jokes, as such, but they come to us direct from Cripplegate in 1605, from a space where the legible world of authors and texts coincides with the usually unrecorded world of lodgers and neighbours and wives and in-laws.

Clare as 'troth-plight virgin' touches on a more genuine question of the time – was it permissible for a plighted couple to have sex? When the preacher Bullinger fulminates about the sowing of 'ungracious seed' – in other words, prenuptial sex – he is expressing the godly Protestant view that betrothed couples should abstain from sex until after the church wedding. But this was a precept often 'honoured in the breach'. A study of the subject shows a 'wide spectrum of opinion on the question of sexual relations between espoused couples', and some evidence that attitudes split along both class and gender lines, the upper classes and women being more resistant to the idea of sex before the wedding, while 'young men [and] the lower ranks' were more likely to approve it.[11] At the heart of the question was an inherent contradiction. If a betrothal constituted a binding marital contract – if it was, in effect, a marriage – then why was it not permissible to enjoy conjugal relations immediately? The trend to a more relaxed view is disapprovingly observed by Bullinger. Too often, he says, 'wicked uses and customs' prevail. 'At the handfasting there is made a great feast and superfluous bancket, even the same night are the two handfasted persons brought and layed together, yea, certain weeks afore they go to the church.'

What Shakespeare's view was we do not know, though some lines in the late romance *The Winter's Tale* (*c.* 1610) are suggestive. Ranting about his wife's supposed infidelities, Leontes says:

> My wife's a hobby horse, deserves a name
> As rank as any flax-wench that puts to
> Before her troth-plight . . . (1.2.276–8)

The 'flax-wench' – the flax-worker, who combed and spun the plant for linen and thrashed it for linseed – is here a general pejorative for a low, sluttish girl. She has a bad reputation because she 'puts to' – has sex – before her troth-plight. The logic of the phrasing suggests that having sex *after* her troth-plight would have been acceptable. Many families interpreted it this way, and what we know of the Mountjoys does not suggest they would be sticklers for sexual abstinence.[12]

A particular phrasing in Shakespeare's deposition may reflect on this. He says that 'afterwards' – in other words, after the betrothal – the marriage of Stephen and Mary was 'consummated and solemnized'. The order of those two verbs could suggest that sexual consummation preceded the church wedding. So perhaps there was a 'bancket' that night in Silver Street – Mr Mountjoy's narrow-necked purse permitting – and afterwards Stephen and Mary were 'layed together' in a chamber upstairs, quite possibly in that 'old feather-bed' which was later part of their meagre inventory of household goods.

The play of Shakespeare's which reflects precisely on this matter of prenuptial sex is *Measure for Measure*, which we know Shakespeare was writing in 1604, and which was first performed at court on St Stephen's Night, 26 December 1604, a few weeks after the wedding of Stephen and Mary at St Olave's. In *Measure* there are two troth-plights; they both occur before the action of the play begins, but they are both important fulcrums of the plot, and like so much in the play they balance each other out. The first is between Claudio and Julietta. As Claudio is dragged off to prison under the new morality-laws of Vienna, he complains of injustice because his supposed crime of 'lechery' was actually committed with his betrothed fiancée:

> Upon a true contract
> I got possession of Julietta's bed:

> She is fast my wife
> Save that we do the denunciation lack
> Of outward order: this we came not to
> Only for propagation of a dower
> Remaining in the coffer of her friends. (1.2.134–40)

Claudio's crime is precisely that he has sexually consummated a *de praesenti* contract before it was solemnized by a church wedding. This particular twist was introduced by Shakespeare – the equivalent couple in his source-plays was not betrothed – and is ideal for his purposes, since it makes Claudio technically but not morally guilty. Many in the audience would sympathize with his view that he was married to Julietta in all but the 'outward order' of the church wedding, and was therefore free to take 'possession' of her bed.[13]

At the other end of the play, the hypocritical Deputy, Angelo, having attempted to get Isabella to give him sex in return for her brother's pardon, is tricked into bed with his own former fiancée, Mariana, to whom he was plighted some while previously. He is Mariana's 'husband on a pre-contract', the Duke explains, and this is confirmed by the lady herself: 'I am affianced this man's wife as strongly / As words could make up vows'; and, speaking to Angelo himself, 'This is the hand which with a vow'd contract / Was fast belock'd in thine.' He is forced to marry her at the end, having rendered their *de futuro* contract indissoluble by his unwitting consummation of it.

The language of these scenes – 'contract', 'affianced', 'hand . . . fast', 'vows' – is precisely the language Shakespeare was using at Silver Street in his role as marriage-broker and betrother. One notes also the 'dower remaining in the coffer' – faintly prophetic of the withheld dowry that will dog the marriage of Stephen and Mary.

All's Well that Ends Well is linked in theme and tone with *Measure* and was probably written shortly after it in *c.* 1604–5. This is in many ways the classic Silver Street play – subtle, haunting, ambiguous, autumnal. It is set in southern France – the old Navarre romance again – and centres on the relationship between Bertram, the young Count of Roussillon, and the physician's daughter Helena, a lowly figure in his household. Her love for him is hidden until, having healed the dying King with an old 'recipe' of her father's, she is rewarded with a free choice of the young beaux at court for a husband. She chooses Bertram, to his horror, and despite his reluctance they are betrothed immediately by the King. This is not just a play which uses a betrothal as a plot-fulcrum. It is a play wholly about the betrothal – it is the story of what leads up to it, of how it comes about, of how it is tested to the utmost, and degraded, and finally – through complex entanglements and trickeries: that 'fictive knot' of tragicomedy – of how it leads to a true loving union.

I remarked earlier that a play which features a young French-man being pressed into marriage, written at a time when the author was himself pressing a young Frenchman into marriage, is likely to carry some kind of resonance between the fictional and the biographical. In the play it is the King who persuades Bertram to marry, and who performs the handfasting of the young couple. (A contemporary speaks of Shakespeare playing 'kingly parts',[14] so it is not impossible he actually played the King in *All's Well*.) His words are a compressed poetic synopsis of actual words spoken by Shakespeare in the late summer of 1604 –

> Here, take her hand,
> Proud, scornful boy, unworthy this good gift,
> That dost in vile misprision shackle up
> My love and her desert . . .
>   Check thy contempt.
> Obey our will which travails in thy good.
> . . .
> Take her by the hand
> And tell her she is thine.

And the scornful boy complies unwillingly: 'I take her hand.' The couple are thus betrothed or plighted –

Good fortune and the favour of the King
Smile upon this contract, whose ceremony
Shall seem expedient on the now-born brief,
And be perform'd tonight . . . (2.3.150–82)[15]

'O my Parolles,' cries Bertram afterwards to his dubious hanger-on, Monsieur Parolles. 'They have married me!'

Around this central betrothal runs an undercurrent of more dubious marriage-advice supplied by the wonderfully dreadful Parolles. To Helena he offers the demeaning but not entirely unrealistic counsel that it is better to get herself a husband while she is young, and her virginity is still 'vendible'.

Keep it not; you cannot choose but lose by't. Out with't! Within the year it will make itself two, which is a goodly increase, and the principal itself not much the worse . . .'Tis a commodity will lose the gloss with lying; the longer kept, the less worth. Off with't while 'tis vendible; answer the time of request. Virginity like an old courtier wears her cap out of fashion, richly suited but unsuitable . . . Your old virginity is like one of our French wither'd pears: it looks ill, it eats drily – marry, 'tis a wither'd pear: it was formerly better. (1.1.143–58)

The extended comic metaphor of her virginity as capital, and sex as a productive investment of it (a very city-comedy formulation), shades uncomfortably into an imagery of desiccated female genitalia. He concludes bluntly, 'Get thee a good husband and use him as he uses you.'

But to Bertram Parolles is a counsellor against marriage. He quotes the old proverb, 'A young man married is a man that's marred,' and (with more off-colour vaginal imagery) speaks in favour of the manly pursuits of soldiery:

PAROLLES: He wears his honour in a box unseen
That hugs his kicky-wicky here at home,
Spending his manly marrow in her arms

. . .

To other regions!
France is a stable, we that dwell in't jades.

> Therefore to th' war!
> BERTRAM: It shall be so . . .
> Wars is no strife
> To the dark house and the detested wife. (2.3.275–88)

Then later Parolles is a broker and witness of Bertram's false offer of marriage to Diana – 'I did go between them . . . I was in that credit with them, at that time, that I knew of their going to bed, and of other motions, as promising her marriage' (5.3.253–9). Compare the phrasing used by Noel Mountjoy: 'Mr Shakespeare was employed . . . to make a motion to him of a marriage.'

This 'equivocal companion' Parolles, discoursing with cynical eloquence on the pro and contra of marriage, is another reflection of Shakespeare's role as a marriage counsellor in the Mountjoy household – a somewhat sour version of it.[16]

Parolles is pure Shakespeare – there is not a trace of him in the source-books. As Dr Johnson notes, he 'has many of the lineaments of Falstaff and seems to be the character which Shakespeare delighted to draw, a fellow that had more wit than virtue'.[17] He is an elaboration of the braggart or *miles gloriosus* of the old Roman comedies – a phoney, vacuous, meddling figure, yet like the cynical wastrel Lucio in *Measure* he seems central to the play, or rather to our involvement in it. These rogues have a charm which is deliberately withheld from the protagonists; they express the 'mingled yarn' of experience. Our first introduction to Parolles suggests this idea, as Helena says:

> I know him a notorious liar,
> Think him a great way fool, solely a coward,
> And yet these fix'd evils sit so fit in him
> That they take place where virtue's steely bones
> Looks bleak i' th' cold wind. (1.1.98–102)

Parolles is indeed exposed as a liar, fool and coward. The scene of his shaming is painful, but is swiftly cancelled by his defiantly resilient soliloquy at the end of it –

> If my heart were great
> 'Twould burst at this. Captain I'll be no more,
> But I will eat and drink and sleep as soft
> As captain shall. Simply the thing I am
> Shall make me live . . . (4.4.319–23)

This Monsieur Parolles – 'Mr Words' – is a man of loud opinions and big gestures, but no substance. As Lafeu says of him, 'There can be no kernel in this light nut: the soul of this man is in his clothes – trust him not.' I sometimes think he is Shakespeare's own mocking self-portrait: the actor with nothing inside him.[18]

29

Losing a daughter

*A*utumn comes in. The stars are for a moment in benevolent alignment over Silver Street. On 1 November the King's Men begin their winter season at court with a performance of *Othello* at the Banqueting House at Whitehall. On 17 November Marie Mountjoy receives payment of £18 13s 7d from the Queen's accountants. On 19 November, the young couple 'made sure' by Mr Shakespeare are married at St Olave's, the little parish church which Stow calls 'a small thing without any noteworthy monuments'. Perhaps Shakespeare was present. Perhaps there was a peal of bells, though it was just a Monday in November, nothing special.

> Good fortune and the favour of the King
> Smile upon this contract . . .

But this good fortune will not last. All will not end well. Within a few months relations have broken down within the house. The father and the son-in-law at loggerheads, and between them the daughter, caught up in the warfare. Shouted words float upstairs to the chamber where Shakespeare writes. He is at work on *King Lear*. The deluded father, blind to the meaning of affection, rages at his daughter Cordelia, 'Better thou hadst not been born than not to have pleased me better.' More precisely, the father vents his displeasure by withholding the daughter's promised dowry. Cordelia's 'price has fallen', he tells her suitor, the Duke of Burgundy. She is now 'dowered with our curse' and nothing more. This 'dowerless daughter' is taken instead by her other suitor, the

King of France: 'she is herself a dowry,' he says (1.1.187–241). Again we hear the echoes of Silver Street, the sublimation into high drama of what is casually there at hand. The Duke's plaintive plea to Lear, 'Give but that portion which yourself proposed', is virtually a synopsis of the argument going on downstairs in the early months of 1605, and later picked over, with Shakespeare's assistance, at the Court of Requests.

Shakespeare had daughters himself, back in Stratford. They were around the same age as Mary – Susanna born in 1583, and Judith, the twin of the lost boy Hamnet, in 1585. As his elder daughter reaches the age of twenty-one, the nominal and legal age of adulthood, the question of her marriage prospects starts to gnaw at him. For a man without a son, for a man seemingly tense about his social status, his substance as one who lived and worked in the insubstantial realm of the theatre, it is a worry. Susanna turned twenty-one in late May 1604, very close to the time her father was negotiating this other marriage down in London. Whether she had already met her future husband, Dr John Hall, is not certain – they would be married in 1607.[19]

Perhaps the troth-plighting of Mary Mountjoy carried some psychological freight in the mind of Mr Shakespeare, himself the father of marriageable but unmarried daughters. Perhaps there was an aspect of wish-fulfilment in it – even a kind of dramatic enactment. The brief ritual of the Silver Street betrothal becomes a little piece of theatre – let us call it 'The Handfasting' – in which the daughter is betrothed to an 'honest fellow' with prospects, and all is 'made sure by Mr Shakespeare'. (This in ironic contrast to the actual plays he was writing at the time, which pursue the Montaignian agenda of making everyone unsure about things.)[20]

In his later plays Shakespeare keeps returning to the theme of the daughter. More precisely the daughter lost or banished, then arduously found: a rhythm of breakdown and reconciliation, expressed in the magico-mystical imagery which is the language of the late plays or 'romances'. Helena in *All's Well* is a kind of prologue to this. She is not the King's daughter, yet in her healing of the King, in her steadfastness through 'dismal' difficulties, and in the imagery of regeneration which surrounds her, with a sudden and heart-wrenching shift of tone, at the end of the play –

> DIANA: Dead though she be, she feels her young one kick.
> So there's my riddle: one that's dead is quick.
> And now behold the meaning.
> *Enter Helena*

– she prefigures the father–daughter relations of the later plays: Lear and Cordelia, Pericles and Marina, Cymbeline and Imogen, Leontes and Perdita, Prospero and Miranda.

I have been teased by the possibilities of Shakespeare's relationship with the charming Mrs Mountjoy, but perhaps the person at the heart of the story is her daughter Mary, of whom we know next to nothing until she steps into the limelight of the Belott–Mountjoy suit. Her life touches Shakespeare's in this circumstantial way, but seems also to touch his imagination. She is betrothed to a reluctant husband, as Helena is in *All's Well*; she is banished 'dowerless' by her father, as Cordelia is in *King Lear*; she is lodged in the house of a pimp, as Marina is in *Pericles*. She is not the 'model' for these characters, any more than Stephen is the model for the recalcitrant bridegroom Bertram, but there are traces of her in them: a real young woman, living in the house where Shakespeare writes, and in the house of his co-author Wilkins. Was it Mary's hands Shakespeare saw in his mind's eye when he wrote in *Pericles* of a girl weaving silk 'with fingers long, small, white as milk'?

I have spoken of Shakespeare's 'opportunism' but the word is perhaps too pragmatic. What one means is his capacity to include so much, all the allusions and associations that are somehow drawn down into the dramatic moment, some instantly recognizable, some explained by scholarly exegesis, but much of it remaining as a kind of mist of ulterior meanings, too vaporous – and too personal to the author – for us to catch, though partly recoverable in this case from the recesses of the Belott–Mountjoy papers.

*

I look again through the depositions given at the Court of Requests in 1612, and my eye alights not on the brusque testimony of Mr Shakespeare himself, but on that account of the visit to Shakespeare by Daniel Nicholas, made some time before the case came to court, perhaps around 1610 or so. Here once again is what Nicholas says:

> The plaintiff did request him this deponent to go with his wife to Shakespeare, to understand the truth how much and what the defendant did promise to bestow on his daughter in marriage with him the plaintiff, who did so. And asking Shakespeare thereof, he answered that he [Mountjoy] promised if the plaintiff would marry with Mary his only daughter, he would by his promise, as he [Shakespeare] remembered, give the plaintiff with her in marriage about the sum of fifty pounds in money and certain household stuff.

I note Nicholas's wonderfully unwitting phrase – he went 'to Shakespeare to understand the truth': something that many have done since, though not quite in the sense he means it.

But there is something else, an unnoticed clue – indeed unnoticeable without recourse to the original document. 'The plaintiff did request him this deponent to go with his wife to Shakespeare . . .' In Wallace's transcription it sounds like Daniel Nicholas was accompanied by his own wife when he visited Shakespeare. But in the original one sees that the clerk first wrote, 'The plaintiff did requeste him this deponent to goe with him to Shakespeare,' but then – presumably corrected by Nicholas – changed that last 'him' to 'his wyffe'. It is clear, therefore, that the person who accompanied Daniel Nicholas on his visit to Shakespeare was not the otherwise unmentioned Mrs Nicholas, but Mary Belott. Indeed Nicholas now takes a subsidiary role in this little scene, which is essentially a meeting between Shakespeare and Mary, this girl whom he once knew well, and whom he handfasted to her husband, for better or worse, and who is now in need of his help.

And then there is that troubling discrepancy which I mentioned at the beginning of the book. When Daniel Nicholas (or, as we might now think, Mary Belott) asked him what dowry Mountjoy had promised the couple, Shakespeare said it was about £50. But when he was asked the same question in court, he claimed he could not remember the figure. A sum was promised, he says, 'but what certain portion he remembereth not'. The reason he gives for his ignorance is that he had not been privy to the financial discussions at the time of the marriage. He says, 'The plaintiff was dwelling with the defendant in his house, and they had amongest themselves many conferences about their marriadge' – implying that he was not present at these 'conferences'. Nonetheless the anomaly remains: his story has changed.

This seems to imbue his deposition with a note of betrayal, a refusal to involve himself. He was probably the only person who could swing the court – he was a gentleman, he was broadly impartial, and he had been personally involved in the negotiations. How much he would have pleased Mary if he had told the court what he had earlier told her and Daniel Nicholas – that Mountjoy had promised the sum of £50.

But he does not. Caution prevails: a man must be careful what he says in a court of law. In his failure to remember, his shrug of non-involvement, he sides with the unforgiving father and against the spurned daughter. And so the deposition, a unique record of Shakespeare speaking, contains also this faintly sour note of silence. He follows the example of his own Parolles, that creature of the Silver Street nights, whose last words are, 'I will not speak what I know.'

'Mr Words' has spoken enough.

He appends the hurried, perfunctory signature which one sees at the bottom of the paper. The pen blotches on the *k* and tails off: 'Willm Shaks'. It will do. It will get him out of that courtroom, away from all these questions and quarrels, the interminable loose ends of other people's lives, like a 'ravell'd sleave' of silk whose tangles can never be unpicked. The signature attests his presence at that moment, but in his mind he is already leaving. After a last few formalities he bids good day to the Mountjoys and the Belotts.

He walks down to the wharf at Westminster Stairs to catch a boat downriver. He does not know if he will see them again, and we do not know if he did.

Epilogue

The characters who have populated this little corner of Shakespeare's life now slip back into the shadows briefly penetrated by the Belott–Mountjoy suit.

Other than his marriage to Isabel d'Est, in the summer of 1615, nothing further is heard of Christopher Mountjoy. When he drew up his will on 26 January 1620 (see Plate 35) he was living in St Giles, Cripplegate. It would be nice to think this betokens some reconciliation with his daughter and son-in-law, who also lived in the parish, but the financial contortions of the will itself seem to argue against this. The will has a faint connection with Mr Mountjoy's erstwhile lodger – one of its overseers was a man called Thomas Seaman, who would later perform the same service for Elizabeth Condell, widow of Shakespeare's old colleague Henry Condell. In her will she bequeathed Seaman £10 and 'all her books' – the latter probably including a copy of the First Folio of Shakespeare's plays, of which Condell had been co-editor.[1]

The burial register of St Giles records the funeral of 'Christopher Mountioie Tyremaker' on 29 March 1620 (see Plate 36). Administration of his goods was granted to Isabel on 5 April. His grieving widow did not remain so for long, however, for on 17 July she was married at St Giles to one William Broxon. He is described elsewhere as a 'smith', and was himself recently widowed. We might perceive in Isabel a penchant for elderly husbands, for within a few years Broxon was also dead, and she was at the altar for (at least) the third time, at

St Dunstan's in Stepney, where she married John Fisher on
1 May 1627.

The Bellotts continued to live in St Giles at least until the early
1620s. They had six children – all daughters – of whom two died
in infancy. Three were later married: Anne, the eldest, to William
Haier or Hayer, 'wiredrawer'; Jane to Francis Overing, a glover;
and Hester – or, as Stephen Belott wrote it, 'Easter' – to a Christopher Bates.[2] The husbands sound English, their professions
artisan; the wiredrawing son-in-law may be a partner in the tiremaking business. Of their youngest daughter Elizabeth, born in
1621, there is no further record, and she is not mentioned in
Belott's will. Perhaps she died young, or perhaps – families being
one of the chief ways in which history repeats itself – she is
another shunned daughter.

In 1619 Belott was at loggerheads with the new monopoly on
gold and silver thread. Strict production quotas were imposed on
the thread-workers, who had to pay nearly 60 per cent of their
earnings to the commissioners. At the apex of this pyramid of
royally licensed robbery was the notorious Sir Giles Mompesson,
who made huge profits until protests led to his investigation and
impeachment; he is caricatured as the greedy schemer Sir Giles
Overreach in Philip Massinger's New Way to Pay Old Debts
(c. 1621). Belott was one of many who suffered violent intimi-
dation from the monopolists' heavies, and as we know he was
not a man to leave offences unanswered. His petition for redress,
dated 20 March 1621, survives in the House of Lords Record
Office, a stone's throw from the former site of the Court of
Requests. 'About two yeares since,' he complains, a 'pursuivant'
named Ireland 'did forciblie enter' his house,

and going into an upper room, where the chamber door was locked, the
said Ireland did violentlie breake open the said doore & tooke out of
the chamber the peticioners mill, the onlie instrument of his living, and
caried away the same ... wherebie the peticioner his wife & children
are utterlie undone.[3]

Another upstairs room in Cripplegate, another faint glimpse of Mary, shielding her frightened children as the men rifle through the chamber. Whether Belott ever got the 'recompense' he craved we do not know.

The last record of Mary Belott *née* Mountjoy is the baptism of her daughter Elizabeth on 21 September 1621. I have not found any record of her burial. She was dead when Stephen Belott drew up his will in July 1646. He had by then a second wife, Thomasine, though no children by her. Their address was 'the Bowling Alley neere Long Lane'. The street ran down from Aldersgate to Smithfield. Stow describes it as 'builded on both the sides with tenements for brokers, tipplers, and such like'; John Taylor the water-poet associates it with pawnshops.[4] The neighbourhood has a down-at-heel air.

Belott bequeathed money to Thomasine and his three married daughters, but the money was inconveniently overseas, in Holland – 900 guilders, then worth £90, left to him by his brother John, who had died in Haarlem: another pot of cash just out of reach. Stephen Belott died in early 1647, probably in his mid-sixties.[5]

And what of Mr Shakespeare? These others all outlived him. When he walked out of that courtroom in the early summer of 1612 he had just under four years left. In literary terms he was already coasting downhill. The only plays later than this date are his three collaborations with John Fletcher. Two of them – *Henry VIII* and the lost *Cardenio* – were performed by the King's Men in 1613; and the last, *The Two Noble Kinsmen*, probably in 1614.

He was sometimes to be seen in London – indeed he became, for the first time, a property-owner in the city. The Blackfriars Gatehouse, which he bought in March 1613, was a rambling old house near the river, with 'sundry back-dores and bye-ways', and was probably a pied-à-terre as well as an investment. But most of what we know of these last years belongs to his life in Stratford: a well-off gentleman in well-earned retirement, surrounded by his family and his fruit-trees at New Place, though not entirely free of the small vexations that come with respectability. There was a brief but embarrassing court case, when his daughter Susanna Hall sued a man who said she had 'bin naught with [had sex with] Rafe Smith' and had 'the runinge of the raynes [gonorrhea]'. There was the threat of enclosure in the Welcombe area, where he owned land – 'My cosen Shakspeare' (wrote the town clerk, Thomas Greene, in his diary) 'told me that they assured him they ment to enclose noe further then to Gospell Bushe, and so upp straight . . . [to] Clopton Hedge.'[6]

And then there was the matter of his younger daughter Judith, who turned thirty in 1615 – one last piece of matrimonial business to be arranged. She was married at Holy Trinity church on 10 February 1616. Her husband was a feckless young man, Thomas Quiney, who had recently sired an illegitimate child. His business ventures would fail, his children by Judith would die young.[7] Not quite an 'honest fellow', perhaps: a match made in haste rather than heaven. Six weeks later, already sick, Shakespeare drew up his will, and on 23 April 1616 he died.

Half a century later, a Stratford vicar obligingly offered a cause of death – Shakespeare had over-indulged at a 'merry meeting' with fellow-poets Drayton and Jonson. 'It seems [they] drank too hard, for Shakespeare died of a fever there contracted.' This Parnassian binge is certainly too good to be true. Neither Shakespeare nor Drayton has any reputation for roistering, and Jonson (who could drink enough for all three of them) is not known to have visited Stratford. A more sober conjecture is that Shakespeare died of typhoid fever. The spring of 1616 was unseasonably warm and wet, favourable to water-borne infections. The mortality rate in Stratford was high that year, nearly 50 per cent up on recent years.[8] He died in the company not of poets, but of his fellow-townspeople – one among many.

In his last sole-authored play, *The Tempest* (1611), Prospero's great speeches of recantation are often taken as Shakespeare's farewell to the stage: 'This rough magic I here abjure . . .'; 'Our revels now are ended . . .'; and most poignantly in the Epilogue, also spoken by Prospero –

> Now my charms are all o'erthrown,
> And what strength I have's my own,
> Which is most faint.

But though these lines may be, in part, Shakespeare's swansong, they are not his last words on the stage. These are to be found in the little-read and seldom performed *Two Noble Kinsmen* of *c.* 1614. The play, an elegant tragicomedy set in ancient Athens, has more Fletcher and less Shakespeare than *Henry VIII*, and was not included in the Folio, but the final act is demonstrably his.

A speech by Theseus – one of those 'kingly parts' that Shakespeare himself used to take – brings the play to a close.[9] Its concluding lines, addressed to the 'gods', are the nearest we have to Shakespeare's last words – oddly unfamous, quietly spoken, serenely puzzling:

> O you heavenly charmers,
> What things you make of us! For what we lack
> We laugh; for what we have are sorry; still
> Are children in some kind. Let us be thankful
> For that which is, and with you leave dispute
> That are above our question. Let's go off
> And bear us like the time. (5.6.131–7)

The stage direction calls for a 'flourish' of music before the characters walk off.

Appendix:
The Belott–Mountjoy Papers

The chief documents relating to the Belott–Mountjoy case are here transcribed in full, arranged as follows:

Pleadings (Complaint, Answer, Replication and Rejoinder; January–May 1612)

Depositions (witness statements at three sessions of the Court of Requests; May–June 1612)

Arbitration (referral from the Court of Requests and deliberations of the French Church; June 1612–February 1614)

I also give, under the heading **Other Documents**, some later papers not connected with the lawsuit – Mountjoy's will (January 1620), Belott's petition to the House of Lords (March 1621) and Belott's will (July 1646).

Most of these documents were first published by Charles William Wallace in 1910 (*University of Nebraska Studies* 10/4, 8–44). The scarcity of that volume makes this reprint desirable. His transcripts, checked against the originals at the National Archives and the French Church of London, are remarkably accurate. Mountjoy's will and Belott's petition are published here for the first time, from manuscripts at the Guildhall Library and the House of Lords Record Office.

I. PLEADINGS

a. Stephen Belott's Bill of Complaint, 28 January 1612
[TNA PRO REQ 4/1/3/1]

To the King*es* moste Excellent Ma^{ty}

In all humblenes Complayninge sheweth vnto yor moste excellent Ma:^{tie} yor highnes poore and faythfull and obedient subpliant Stephen Belott of

London Tyermaker, That whereas yor Suppliant aboute nyne yeares sithence laste paste beinge then a Servant vnto one Christopher Mountioye of London Tyer maker [did] well Carry and behaue himselfe in the tyme of his saide service wth the saide Christopher bothe iustly & to the greate proffitt and advantage of the [said] Christopher, as that thereby yor saide Suppliant in all outwarde appearance did obtayne the good will and affecion of him the saide Christopher in suche sorte as hee then offered vnto yor saide Suppliant, that yf hee would accept in marriage one Marie Mountioye beinge his daughter and only Child that then hee would giue in Marriage wth his saide daughter vnto yor saide Suppliant the somme of three scoore poundes or thereaboutes for a porcion vppon yor saide Suppliantes daye of Marriage or shortlie after and would likewise at the tyme of his deceasse leaue vnto yor said Suppliant and his saide daughter the somme of two hundred pounds more vppon wch offers of ye saide Compt.^{lt} and vppon his perswacions yor said Supp.^{lt} did shortly after entermarry wth the saide Mary and haue liued togeather by the space of theis five yeares and haue had diuers Children betwixt them to the greate encrease of theire Chardge and are likelie to haue manie more so that theire poore trade is not able to giue them maintenance and yor saide Suppliant lent the saide Christopher the somme of fortie shillinges wch hee denies to paye or to performe his former promise, But so it is may it please yor moste excellent Matie. that yor said Suppliant growinge since his saide entermarriage wth the saide Mary into some want and necessitie by the reason of the encrease of his Chardge as a fore saide yor saide Supp.^{lt} therefore repaired vnto him the saide Christopher desiringe him to satisfy and paye vnto yor saide Supp.^{lt} the said somme of three scoore poundes soe promised by him vnto yor saide Supp.^{lt} as all so to putt in suertyes to leaue yor Supp.^{lt} and his wiffe two hundred poundes att his deathe, who all together forgettinge his ffatherlie promisses nor pityinge the distressed poore estate of yor said poore Subiecte and his greate Chardge verie vnnaturally dothe not only nowe deny his said promisse and refuse to paye the said somme of three scoore poundes but likewise denieth the payment of the saide somme of ffortie shillinges so lent him as a fore said. As allso hath sithence giuen forthe diuers tymes to diuers persons, that hee intendeth not to leaue vnto yor Supp.^{lt} his wiffe nor Children the vallue of one penny when soever hee shall departe this naturall lyffe, beinge not onlie to the greate [hurt] and hinderance of yor said Supp.^{lt} his wiffe & famyly but alsoe to theire vtter vndoeinge yf they bee not releiued by the iustice of this honorable Courte, & beinge a man of good estat & wthout charge. In Tender Consideracion whereof and for asmuche as by ye strict Course of the Common lawes of this Realme yor said pore subiecte is remediles either to recover the said three scoore poundes soe promissed as

aforesaid or to Compell him the saide Cristopher Mountioye to putt in
suretyes to leaue tow hundred poundes to yor highnes poore subject & his
wiffe at his death beinge of late inclyned to waste his estate for that yor said
subject cannott prove the saide promisses in soe strict manner as by the
Common lawe is required or yf hee Could yet hath not yor said subject by
the said Common lawes of this Realme ffitt or apt remedy neither is yor
saide loyall subject able to proove the loane of the said fforty shillinges
to ye said Christopher Mountioye but perswadeth himselfe that the said
Christopher either to dischardge a good Conscience as knowinge periurye
is a moste damnable sinn or to avoide the punishment inflicted on such as
comit the saide sinn, may it therefore please yor highnes the premisses
Considered, To graunt vnto yor subject yor highnes moste gracious writt of
privie seale to be directed vnto the said Christopher Mountioy Commaund-
inge him thereby at a Certayne day and vnder a Certayne payne therein to
be directed personally to appeare before yor highnes in yor highness Courte
of White Hall Comonlie called the Court of Requestes Then & there to
make a direct answer to the premisses and to stande to suche further order
& direction therein as by yor highnes or yor said Counsell shalbe thought
meete to stand wth equity & good conscience, And yor said loyall subjecte
accordinge to his bounden dutye shall hartely pray to god to prolonge yor
highness happy Raigne and lyfe longe to Contynewe./

Raf: Wormlaighton.

b. Christopher Mountjoy's Answer, 3 February 1612 [ibid./2]

The Answeare of Christopher Mountioy to the Bill of Complainte of
Stephen Belott Compl^t

This defendante All advantages of exception to the Insufficiencie and Incer-
tainty of the sayd Bill nowe and at all times saved vnto him for answeare
thervnto and for the manifest declaration of the truth saith That about ten
yeares last past the defendante was Contentented [*sic*] at the Entreaty of the
sayd Complainauntes friendes to accept of the Complainaunte to serve him
as a prentise to learne his trade being a Tyremaker his said frendes promis-
singe to finde him Convenient apparrell while he shoulde so Continue
in this deffendauntes service, and the said Complainaunte did serve this
defendaunte as a Prentice to learne his trade the space of six yeares or
thereaboutes. But dueringe all the time of his sayd service neither the Complaynaunte nor any of his friendes did according to theire promise fynde

him any apparrell att all savinge Linen but this Defendaunte was enforced to finde him all the Residue of his apparrell duering all the sayd time neither had the Complainaunte duering all the sayd time of six yeares any further or other releefe or oth^r maintenaunce from any of his friend*es* but was duering all the saide time wholy and solye mayntayned by this Defendaunte. And after the said Complainaunt had served this Defendaunte as aforesayd the said time of six yeares then the said Complainaunte was desierus to travell into spaine and this Defendaunte did furnish him wth mony and other necessaryes for the Iorney to the vallue of six pound*es* or therabout*es* after which time the sayd Complaynaunte returned from his travell vnto this Defendaunte againe and was a suter vnto this Defendaunt*es* daughter to marry her and to that purpose did move this Defendaunte and his then wife for theire Concent*es* for the marriage which this Defendaunte and his sayd wyfe being poore and able to bestowe lyttle or nothinge wth their sayd Daughter in marryage (save y^t this Defendante had then brought her to a good perfection in his sayd trade of Tyermakeinge) was Contented to yeelde vnto: though the said Complainaunte neither then had nor ever sithence to the knowledge of this Defendaunte any mony, or other valluable good*es* or land*es* whatsoever from his sayd friend*es* nor any other thinge whatsoever but what he had gotten in this Defendaunt*es* service and by the trade that this Defendaunte had learned him. And afterward*es* vid. about five yeares past the sayd Complainaunte was marryed to the sayd Daughter of this Defendaunte at which mariyage it was agreed betweene the said Complainaunte and this Defendaunte that if the sayd Complainaunte with his wife shoulde Continue and worcke in theire trade to the benefitt of this Defendaunte in the house of this Defendaunte duering the space of twoe yeares or thereabout*es* after the said Marriage this Defendaunte giveinge them Conveniente housrome and dayate Convenient for them so that this Defendaunte might only haue the benifitt of theire laboures. Then this Defendaunte at the end of the sayd twoe yeares would give vnto the sayd Complainaunte fiftie pound*es* or to that effect as this Defend^t nowe remembreth aft^r which time the sayd Complaynaunte did for a little time remayne in the house of this Defendaunte accordingly. But after the sayd Complaynaunte and his wife had stayed in the house of this Defendaunte as aforesayd the space of halfe a yeare or there about*es* he refused to stay there any longer and would need*es* take oth^r Courses for his better p*re*fermente as he then p*re*tended And at the end of the sayd halfe yeare when the said Compl^t Did departt from the house of this Defendaunte out of his love to the sayd Complainaunte and his wife (beinge no other way Compellable thervnto) did bestowe on them a good proportion of houshoulde stuffe and the thing*es* Concerninge theire trade according to this Defendaunt*es* poore ability being

to the vallue of Twenty pound*es* or thereabout*es* and lykewyse ten pound*es*
of ready mony to put into theire pursse and did hartely desier theire welfare
and lykwise did Intende to leave vnto the sayd Complaynaunte and his wife
beinge the only chylde of this Defendaunte all or the moste parte of that
estate which god should have blessed them with at the time of his Death.
And allso in his fath*er*ly love to have ben helpfull to them from time to time
accordinge to his poore ability After which time (y^t the said Complainaunt
was gon from the house of this Defendaunt) about a yeare This
Defendaunt*es* wife dyed and then the said Complaynaunte and his wife
Came againe and lived wth this Deffendaunte as p*artner*es in ther sayd
trade of Tyeringe about the space of half a yeare dueringe which time
this Defendaunte had in his hand*es* the summe of forty shilling*es* of the
Complaynaunt*es* mony and at the end of the said Halfe yeare & about the
time of the Complaynaunt*es* depareture from this def^{tes} house the sayd
Complaynaunte being Indebted vnto a Bruer the summe of three pound*es*
desiered this Defendaunt to pay it for him to the sayd Bruer which sayd
somm of three pound*es* this Defendaunte payed for the sayd Complaynaunte
accordingly but this def^t was nev^r sithen*es* repaide the s*aid* 3^{11}. or any p*arte*
therof other the*n* the s*aid* 40^s as aforsaid, and dueringe the sayd half
yeare that the Complaynaunt was with this Defendaunte as aforesayd this
Defendaunte did buy into the shopp with his owne mony silvered wyer and
oth^r Comodyties Concerninge theire trade to the vallue of Ten pound*es* or
therabout*es* for which the sayd Complainaunte should by agreemente have
payd halfe but did pay never a peny And this Defendaunte absolutely
denyeth that he did ever to his knowledge offer vnto the sayd Complaynaunte in marryage wth his daughter the summe of Threescore pound*es* or
any portion or other som*me* whatsoever other than the sayd summe of ffifty
pound*es* at the end of the foresayd three yeares and vpon the Considderation
as before is expressed. And this Defendante lykewyse denyeth that he did
ever p*ro*mise to leave to the sayd Complainaunte and his wife at his Death
the some of two hundred pound*es* or any other Certaine summe but as
aforesayd did Intende to deale with the Complaynaunt and his wife at the
time of his Death as it is fitting for a fath*er* to deale with his only Chylde
But this Defendaunte neither then Coulde nor yet Canne set dowe any
Certaynty thereof for that this def^t, both then was and yet is a poore man
and knows not howe it will please god to blesse him in his estate at the time
of his Death nor how the sayd Complaynaunte and his wife will behave
themselves toward*es* this Defendaunte In his life time wherby they may
deserve this Defendaunt*es* either more or lesse affection and love toward*es*
them. And this defendaunt lykewyse denyeth that he to his knowledge
doth owe the Complaynaunte forty shilling*es* or any other former somme

of Mony whatsoever otherwyse than as before is expressed An this Defendaunte further saith that he did about a month sythence earnestly request the sayd Complaynaunte in the presence of his neighboures to account wth him for the sayd Reckoninge betweene them at which time the sayd Complaynaunte did give this Defendaunte Ill Languages and bid him Come by his mony howe he Coulde Without that that any other matter or thing Contained in the sayd Bill of Complaynt materiall or effectuall to be answered vnto and not heerin sufficiently Confessed and avoyded denyed or traversed is true All which matters this Defendante is ready to averr and prove as this most honorable Court shall award and humbly prayeth to be dismissed out of the same with his reasonable Chardges in this behalfe most wrongfully sustayned/

Geo: Hartoppe

c. Belott's Replication, 5 May 1612 [ibid./3]

The Replicacion of Stephen Belot Comp^lt to the Answer of Christopher Mountioye def^t.

The said Comp^lt not Confessinge or acknowledginge anie matter or thinge materiall or effectuall in the said def^tes Answer conteyned to be true in suche sorte manner or forme as in and by the said bill they are sett forthe and declared sayth that the said Answer is in all or the moste parte thereof vntrue incerteyne and insufficient to be replyed vnto for manie imperfeccions in the same appearinge. All the advantages of excepcion to thincertaintyes and insufficiencies whereof nowe and at all tymes hereafter to this Comp^lt, saued, This Comp^lt, for Replicacion sayeth in all thinges as in his said Bill of Complainte he hathe sayed, and doth and will auer maynteyne iustyfie and proue his said Bill of Comp^lt, and euerie matter article and allegacion therein Conteyned to bee true Certayne and sufficient to be answered vnto set forthe and declared w^thout that that this Comp^ltes ffrends at the tyme of his Commynge to bee Apprentice wth the said def^t did promise to finde this Comp^lt. Convenient apparrell while he shoulde Contynewe in the said def^tes service. Or that the said def^t at the tyme of this Comp^ltes trauaile into spayne did furnishe this Comp^lt. wth six poundes or wth any other somme of Money but that this Comp^lt, was only therein furnished by himselfe w^thout that that allsoe this Comp^lt. moved the said def^t or his wyffe for theire Consentes to the Mariage of the said Mary but that this Comp^lt, was only drawen therevnto by the said def^t, And w^thout that that after the Marriage of this Comp^lt. wth the said Mary there was any suche Conclusion or agreement made betwixt the said def^t and this Comp^{lt}, euer receuied any good*es* or howsehold stuffe of the said def^t or any things Concerninge theire trade, or desiered the said def^t to pay the somme of three poundes or any other somme to the Brewer, or was soe indebted vnto the said Brewer as by the said Answere all soe is alleadged, wth that that the said def^t did p*r*omise vnto this Comp^{lt}, the somme of threscore pounds in mariadge wth the said Mary his daughter and did likewise p*r*omise to leave vnto this Comp^{lt}, and his wyffe the some of two hundred poundes or thereabout*es* after his deceasse, And that the said def^t is truely indebted vnto this Comp^{lt}. in the somme of fforty shillinges wthout that that this Comp^{lt}. was desiered by the said def^t to come to anie accompte or gaue the said def^t any ill languages as in & by the said Answere is allsoe Alleadged, And wthout that that any other matter thinge or thinges Clause sentence, Article or allegacion in the said Answere Conteyned materiall or effectuall in the lawe to be replyed vnto, and not heerein sufficiently replyed vnto Confessed and avoyded denyed or trauersed is true, All and euery wch matters hee this Comp^{lt}. is ready to averr iustify mayntayne and proue as this honorable Courte shall award, And humbly prayeth as hee before by his said Bill of Complaynte hathe allready prayed./

Raf Wormlaighton

d. Mountjoy's Rejoinder, undated [ibid./4]

The reioy*nd*^r of Christopher Mountioy defend*n*^t to the Replica*cion* of Stephen Belot Compl*ainant*

The sayd Defendaunte not acknowledgeing any thing in the sayd Replec-ation materially alledged to be trew in such sort as in and by the sayd Replication is aledged for reioy*nd*^r thervnto sayth in all thing*es* as in his Aunsweare he hath sayd and doth and will averr mayntayne and prove his sayd Aunsweare and every matter Artickle and thinge therein Contayned to be true Certaine and sufficient to be Replyed vnto in manner and fo*r*me as therein is sett forth affirmed and Declared with that that this Defendaunt will mayntaine and prove that the sayd Complainnant*es* frend*es* did promis to fynde the sayd Complaynaunte apparrell as in and by this Defendaunt*es* ausweare is affirmed and that this Defendaunt did furnish the sayd Com-plainaunte with mony at the time of his travell*es* into Spayne and that this Defendaunte and his then wife was then moved and and earnestly solisited by the sayd Complaynaunte to Consente to his Marynge of theire Daughter and the Complainanaunte not drawene therevnto by this Defendaunte, and that this Defendaunte did give vnto the sayd Complainaunte houshould stuffe and oth^r good*es* and Did make such Conclusion*es* and agreement*es* wth the sayd Compla*ina*nte as in and by the sayd aunsweare is truly affirmed and this Defendaunte was also desiered by the Complaynaunte to pay vnto the Bruer three pound*es* for the Debt of the sayd Complaynaunt and payd it as in his sayd Defendaunt*es* Aunswer is lykewyse most truly affirmed wthout that that this Defendaunte did ev^r promise three score pound*es* or any other somes of mony vnto the sayd Complainaunte eith^r in marriage with his sayd Daughter or after his Death or is indebted vnto the Complaynaunte in the somme of fforty pound*es* or any other some what soever as in and by the sayd Bill and Replication is falsly surmysed all which matters this Defendaunte is ready to averr mayntayne and prove as this Honorable Courte shall award and humbly prayeth as in his sayd Answeare he hath prayed.

George Hartoppe

2. DEPOSITIONS

a. First session, 11 May 1612 [TNA PRO REQ 4/1/4/1]

Interrogatories to bee mynistred to Wittnesses to bee produced on the parte and behalf of Stephen Belott Complt. against Christopher Mountioye Deft.

1 Imprimis whether doe you knowe the parties plt. and deft. and howe longe haue you knowne them and either of them.

2 Item whether did you knowe the Complt when he was servant wth the said deft howe and in what sort did he behaue himselfe in the service of the said deft and whether did not the said deft. Confesse that hee had got great profitt and Comodytie by the service of the said Complt.

3 Item whether did not the said deft seeme to beare great good will and affec*ci*one towards the said Complt during the time of his said service and what report did he then giue of the said Complt touching his said service and whether did not the said deft make a mo*ci*on vnto the said Complt of marriage wth the said Mary in the Bill men*ci*oned being the said deft*es* sole Child and daughter and willingly offer to performe the same yf the said Complt. should seeme to be content and well lyke thereof. and whether did not hee lykewise send anie person or noe to perswade the said Complt. to the same, declare the truthe of yor knowledge herin.

4 Item what some or somes of moneye did the said deft promise to giue the said Complt. for a por*ci*on in marriage wth the said Marye his daughter whether the some of threscore pownd*es* or what other somme as you knowe or haue hard and when was the same to be paied whether at the

daie of Marriage of the said Complt and the said Marye or whath other tyme and what further porcion did the said deft promise to giue vnto the said Complt wth the said Marye at the tyme of his decease whether the some twoe hundred poundes or what other somes and whether vppon the said perswaciones and promisses of the said deft. did not the said Complt shortly after marrye wth her the said Marye declare the truthe herein as you knowe verylie believe or haue Credybly hard.

5/ Item what parcells of goodes or houshold stuffe did the defendt promise to geue vnto the complainant in Marriadge wth his said wiefe And what parcells of goodes did he geue him in Marriage wth his said wyffe did he not geue them these parcels (vizt.) One ould ffetherbed, one oulde ffether boulster, A flocke boulster, a thine greene Rugg, two ordanarie blanckettes woven, two paire sheetes, A dozine of napkines of Course Dyaper, twoe short table Clothes, six short Towelles & one longe one, An ould drawinge table, two ould Joyned stooles, one Wainscott Cubberd, one Twistinge wheele of woode, twoe paire of litle Scyssers, one ould Truncke and a like ould Truncke./ One Bobbine box: And what doe youe thincke in yor Conscyence all these said parcelles might be woorthe at the tyme when they weare deliuered by the defendauntes appoyntm^t, vnto the plaintiffes declare the truthe hearein at lardge./

DEPOSITION OF JOAN JOHNSON

Johane Johnsone the wyffe of Thomas Johnsone of the parishe of Elinge in the Countye of Middlesex Baskettmaker of the Age of ffortye yeres or th'aboutes sworne and examyned the daye and yere abouesaid deposeth and say[th]

1/ To the ffirst Interrogatory this deponent sayth she knoweth the plaintiff and [hath] knowne him about Eight yeres./ and the deft about Eight yeres./

2/ To the seconde Interr this depont sayth shee did knowe the plaintiff when he served the deft, And sayth he behaved him selfe well and in good sorte when he served the defendt for shee was servant to the deft at the tyme./ but shee never herd the deft confesse and saye that he had greate proffitt and Comoddytie by the plaintiffes service./ And more shee cannot depose.

3/ To the thirde Interrogatory this deponent sayth that the defendt seemed to beare greate good will and affection towardes the plaintiff when he served him, geuinge him reporte to be A verry good servaunte for pl[ ] his service./ But that the deft moved the plaintiff to Marrye wth his daughter Marye she knoweth not./. But sayth that there was a shewe of goodwill betweene the plaintiff and deftes daughter Marye wch the deftes wyffe did geue Countenaunce vnto and thinke well of./ And as shee Remembereth the deft did send and perswade one Mr Shakespeare that laye in the house to perswade the plaintiff to the same Marriadge./ And more shee cannott depose

4/ To the iiij^{th} Interrogatory this deponent sayth shee never herd her [M^r] the defendant proffer the plaintiff any some of money in Marriadge [w^{th}] his daughter Marye. but yt was Reported in the house that the plaintiff was to haue wth her in marriadge the some of ffyftye poundes. but what tyme of paym^t was th^rof appoynted or agreed vppon shee knoweth not, nor of any promise of any other or furth^r porcion to be payed the plaintiff eyther at the tyme of marriadge between them, or at the tyme of the deftes deceas[e] but [that] they after married togeathe^r./And more shee cannott [depose]

5/ To the vth Interr this deponent sayth shee knoweth not what parcelles of goodes and houshould stuffe the defendt promissed to geue vnto the plaintiff in marriadge wth his wyffe./ But sayth the deft gaue in marriadge wth her to the defendant [sic] the seuerall parcells [of] goodes in the Interrogatory mencioned./ but the valewe of them she certaynlie knoweth not, but thinketh they were woorth some Eight poundes./ or thereaboutes./ And more shee cannot depose./

X [Her Mark]

DEPOSITION OF DANIEL NICHOLAS

Danyell Nycholas of the parishe of S^{ct}: Olphadge w^{th}in Criplegate London gent of the Age of ffyftye twoe yeres or th^raboutes sworne and examyned the daye and yere aboue said depòseth and sayth

1/ To the ffirste Interr this deponent sayth he hath knowne the plaintiff about twenty yeres and deft about twelue yeres*

2/ To the seconde Interrogatory this deponent sayth he knewe the plaintiff servaunte vnto the defendant who behaved him selfe verry well in the defendantes service for any thinge he euer herd to the contrary. And hath herd that the deft profitted well by the pltes service wth him. And more he Cannott depose./

3 To the thirde Interrogatory this deponent sayth he herd one W^m: Shakespeare saye that the deft did beare A good opinnion of the plaintiff and

---

* In Nicholas's second deposition (19 June) these computations are, more plausibly, given the other way round.

affected him well when he served him, And did move the plaintiff by him the said Shakespeare to haue [a] marriadge betweene his daughter Marye Mountioye [and] the plaintiff. And for that purpose sent him the said Sh[akespeare] to the plaintiff to perswade the plaintiff to the same, as Shakespere tould him this deponent wch was effected and Solempnized vppon promise of a porcion wth her./ And more he cannott depose./

4 To the iiijth Interrogatory this deponnt sayth that the plaintiff did Requeste him this deponnt to goe wth [him deleted] his wyffe to Shakespe[are] to vnd^{r}stande the truthe howe muche and what the defendant did promise [to] bestowe on his daughter in marriadge wth him the plaintiff, who did sòe./ And askinge Shakespeare th^{r}of, he Answered that he promissed yf the plaintiff would marrye wth Marye his the deftes onlye daughter, he the defendt would by his promise as he Remembered geue the plaintiff wth her in marriadge about the some of ffyftye poundes in money and Certayne Houshould stuffe./ And more he cannott depose touchinge the said Interrogatory to his Rememberaunce for he remembereth not any daye sett downe for paym^t of the porcion or deliuerye of the houshould Stuffe. but only that he would geue her soe much at the tyme of her marriadge./

5/ To the vth Interrogatory this deponent Can saye nothinge more then he hath alreddye deposed./

Daniell Nicholas

DEPOSITION OF WILLIAM SHAKESPEARE

William Shakespeare of Stratford vpon Aven in the Countye of Warwicke gentleman of the Age of xlviij yeres or thereaboutes sworne and examined the daye and yere abouesaid deposethe & sayethe

1 To the first Interrogatory this deponent sayethe he knowethe the partyes plaintiff and deffendt and hathe know [ne] them bothe as he now remembrethe for the space of tenne yeres or thereaboutes./

2 To the second Interrogatory this deponent sayeth he did know the comp^t when he was servant wth the deffendant, and that duringe the tyme of his the compltes service wth the said deffendt he the said Complt to this deponentes knowledge did well and honestly behaue himselfe, but to this depontes remembrance he hath not heard the deffendt confesse that he had gott any great proffitt and comodytye by the service of the said complainant, but this deponent saith he verely thinckethe that the said complainant was a very good and industrious servant in the said service. And more he canott depose to the said Interrogatory:/

3/ To the third Interrogatory this deponent sayethe that it did evydentlye appeare that the said deft did all the tyme of the said compltes service wth him beare and shew great good will and affeccion towardes the said complt, and that he hath hard the defft and his wyefe diuerse and sundry tymes saye and reporte that the said complt was a very honest fellowe: And this depont sayethe that the said deffendant did make a mocion vnto the complainant of marriadge wth the said Mary in the bill mencioned beinge the said defftes sole chyld and daughter and willinglye offered to performe the same yf the said Complainant shold seeme to be content and well like thereof: And further this deponent sayethe that the said defftes wyeffe did sollicitt and entreat this deponent to moue and per-swade the said Complainant to effect the said Marriadge and accordingly this deponent did moue and perswade the complainant thervnto: And more to this Interrogatorye he cannott depose:/

4/ To the ffourth Interr this deponent sayth that the defendt promissed to geue the said Complainant a porcion [*of monie and goodes* deleted] in Marriadg[e] wth Marye his daughter./ but what certayne porcion he Rememberithe not./ nor when to be payed [*yf any some weare promissed*, deleted] nor knoweth that the defendant promissed the [*defendt* deleted] plaintiff twoe hundered poundes wth his daughter Marye at the tyme of his decease./ But sayth that the plaintiff was dwellinge wth the defendant in his house. And they had Amongeste themselues manye Conferences about there Marriadge w^ch [afterwardes] was Consumated and Solemp-nized. And more he cann [ott depose./]

5/ To the vth Interrogatory this deponent sayth he can saye noth[inge] touchinge any parte or poynte of the same Interrogatory for he knoweth not what Implen^tes and necessaries of househould stuffe the defendant gaue the plaintiff in Marriadge wth his daughter Marye./

Willm Shaks

b. Second session, 19 June 1612 [ibid./2]

Inter to bee mynistred to witnesses to bee produced on the parte and behalfe of Stephen Bellott Comp^lt againste Christopher Mountioy def^t.

1 Inprimis whether doe you knowe the parties p^lt. and def^t and howe longe haue you knowen them and ither of them?

2 Itm of what estate or ability is the said def^t accompted to bee of and what Lease or Leases of howses or tenementes hathe hee, and where doe the said howses or tenementes lye, and what is the yeerely vallue thereof?

and what tyme or tymes are to come in the said Leases and whether doe you not thinke that the said def^t receiueth fforty pound*es* per ann*um* de claro by his said Leases? or howe muche dothe hee receiue by the same as you haue Credibly heard or verily beleeue in yor Conscience *to* bee true, and whether hathe not the said def^t giuen forthe speaches that hee will rott in prison before hee will giue any thinge vnto the said Comp^{lt} yf the Cause should bee decreed agaynste him in this honorable Courte declare the truthe of yor knowledge herein as you knowe verily beleeue or haue Credibly heard./

3 Itm who apparelled the said Comp^{lt}. duringe the tyme of his seruice wth the said def^t? whether not the ffrends of the said Comp^{lt}. and for howe longe tyme did the said Comp^{ltes} ffrend*es* soe fynde him wth apparell? whether not duringe the terme of two yeares or howe muche longer declare the truthe of yor knowledge therein.

4 Itm whether did not the said def^t or some other by his appointment send you or any other p*er*son to yor. knowledge vnto the said Comp^{lt}. to make a mo*ci*on of marriadge betwixt the said Comp^{lt}. and the said Mary Mountioy beinge the def^{tes} sole Childe and daughter, and what word*es* did the said def^t vse vnto you or to any other to yor. knowledge touching the marryage of the said Comp^{lt}. wth the said Mary? whether did not the def^t then say that yf shee the said Mary did not marry the said Comp^{lt}., that shee the said Mary should not Coste him *n*or haue a groate from him, and whether did not the said def^t likewise promise that yf the Comp^{lt}. and the said Mary did marry together then hee would giue a por*ci*on wth the said Mary vnto the said Comp^{lt}.? howe muche was the said por*ci*on that hee then promised, whether not the somme of threescore pounds or what other somme as you thinke in yor. Conscience to bee true? and before whome did the said def^t soe promise the same, whether before you or any other to yor. knowledge, and whether vppon the said promisses and per-swa*ci*ons did not the said Comp^{lt}. Contracte himselfe wth the said Mary?

5 Itm whether after the marriadge betwixt the said Comp^{lt}. and the said Mary did the said def^t giue any goods or howsehold stuffe to the said Comp^{lt}. and his wyffe? yf yea, to what vallue did the said goods or howsehold stuffe amounte vnto, whether vnto the somme of ffiue pounds or to what other somme declare the truthe of yor. knowledge herein./*

---

* In the margin beside Interrogatories 3, 4 and 5 are written the names, respectively, of Humphrey Fludd, William Shakespeare and George Wilkins. They were
expected to testify on these particular questions – but Shakespeare did not appear
at the second session. Interrogatory 4 has phrasings attributed to Shakespeare by
Daniel Nicholas.

SECOND DEPOSITION OF DANIEL NICHOLAS

Dannyell Nicholas of the parishe of S^{ct}: Alphadge wthin Criplegate London gent of the Age of threeschore and twoe yeares or thereaboutes swoorne and examyned the daye and yeare abouesaid deposeth and saythe./

1/ To the ffirste Interr this deponent sayth he hath knowne the plaintiff twelue yeares, and the defendt about twentye yeares.

2/ To the seconde Interr this deponent sayth that the defendt is Amongest his neighboures thought to be a Suffitient man in estate and abillitie, and Reporte is amongste the neighboures that he hath Diuerse leases neere about wheare he dwelleth and at Braynforde woorthe by reporte thirtye poundes per Annum or thereaboutes. And by reporte he hath latelie takne newe leases of them./ but what yeares are yett to come in them his leases this deponent knoweth not./ And sayth he thinketh in his Conscyence the defendt Receiveth about thirtye poundes yerely Rent de Claro for the same houses/ And sayth he herd one Christopher Weaver saye that the defendt hadd A good estate to paye euerye man his owne and to geue the plaintiff his porcion yf he pleased./ but the defendt hadd made an othe that Althoughe the Lawe gaue him the plaintiff his porcion, he the deft would Rott in prison before he would geue the plaintiff any one groate thereof./ And more he Cannott depose

3/ To the thirde Interr this deponent sayth that the pltes ffath^r in Lawe Humphrey ffludd, reported in this deponentes presentes & the presentes of others that he the plaintiff was often and seuerall tymes Apparrelled by him the said Homphrey ffludd and the plaintiffes mother and others of the plaintiffes ffrendes, duringe the moste parte of the tyme of his service wth the defendt./ And more he cannott depose touchinge the same Interr./

4 To the iiijth Interr this deponnt sayth that the defendt did never send him this deponnt vnto the Complainant to make mocion of Marriadge betwixte the Complainant and the said Marye Mountioye beinge the defendtes sole daughter and Childe but M^r: William Shakespeare tould him this deponent that the defendt sent him the said Mr Shakespeare to the plaintiff about suche a marriadge to be hadd betweene them, And Shakespeare tould this deponent that the defendt tould him that yf the plaintiff would Marrye the said Marye his daughter he would geue hime the plaintiff A some of money wth her for A porcion in Marriadge wth her./ And that yf he the plaintiff did not marry wth her the said Marye and shee wth the plaintiff shee should never coste him the deft her ffather

A groat, wherevppon And in Regard Mr Shakespeare hadd tould them that they should haue A some of money for a porcion from the fath^r they weare made suer by Mr Shakespeare by geuinge there Consent, and agreed to Marrye, [*geuinge eache others hand to the hande* deleted]. And did marrye./ But what some yt was that M^r [*Shake* deleted] Mountyoye promissed to geue them he the said Mr Shakespeare could not remember, but said yt was ffyftye pound*es* or th^rabout*es* to his beste Rememberaunce./ And as he Rememb*er*ith Mr Shakespeare said he pro*m*issed to geue them A porcion of his good*es*: but what, or to what valewe he Rememberithe not./ And more he Cannott depose./

5 To the vth Interr this depon*en*t sayth that after the Marriadge Solempnized betweene the pl*aintiff* and Marye, one George Wilkins tould him this depon*en*t that the defendt gaue them some Implem^{tes} belonginge to househould, wch good*es* weare in his the said Wilkins Custody, wch good*es* the said Wilkins Reported he would not haue geuen ffyve pound*es* ffor./ And more he cannott depose

Daniell Nicholas

DEPOSITION OF WILLIAM EATON

William Eaton apprentice wth the Compl*ainan*t of the Age of nynteene yeres or th^rabout*es* sworne and examyned the daye and yere abouesaid deposeth and saythe./

1/ To the ffirste Interr this deponnt sayth he hath knowne the plt ffyve yeres or th^rabout*es*. And the def*endan*t about ffoure yeares and A halfe./

2/ To the seconde Interr this depon*en*t sayth he cannot c*er*taynlie depose any thinge touching the deft*es* estate or habillitie, only sayth he knoweth the deft hath A house in Muggle streete & in Silver Streete London and another at Branforde, but what they are woorth by the yeare he knoweth not./ nor hath herd the deft vse any such speeches as in the Interro*gatory* is vrdged./ And more he Cannott depose.

3 To the thirde Interr this depon*en*t Can saye nothinge./

4 To the iiijth Interr this depon*en*t sayth he hath herd one Mr Shakspeare saye that he was sent by the defendt to the pl*aintiff* to moue the pl*aintiff* to haue A marriage betweene them the pl*aintiff* and the defendt*es* daughter Marye Mountioye, And herd Mr Shakespeare saye that he was wished by the deft to make pr*o*ffer of A certayne some that the defendt said he would geue the pl*aintiff* wth his daughter Marye Mountioye in Marriadge, but he had forgott the some./ And [*m^r Shakespeare tould the*

plt deleted] more he cannott depose touchinge the same Interr*ogatory*./
5/ To the vth Interr this deponnt Can saye nothinge of his owne knowledge nor by Credible reporte./

william Eyton

DEPOSITION OF GEORGE WILKINS

George Wilkins of the p*a*rishe of S^ct. Sepulchers London Victuler of the Age of thirtye Syxe yeres or th^raboute*s* sworne and examyned the daye and yere abouesaid deposeth and saythe./

1/ To the ffirste Interr this deponent sayth he hath knowne the pl*aintiff* about Seaven yeres and the deft as longe./

2. 3. 4/ To the second, third and ffourth Interr this deponent is not examyned at the Requeste of the pl*aintiff*./

5 To the vth Interr this deponent sayth that after the plt was married wth Marye the deft*es* daughter he the pl*aintiff* and his wyffe came to dwell in this deponnt*es* house in one of his Chambers. And brought wth them A fewe good*es* or household stuffe wch by Reporte the defendt her fath^r gaue them, ffor wch this deponent would not haue geuen Aboue ffyve pound*es* yf he had bene to haue bought the same./ And more he cannott depose touchinge the same Interr:/

George Wilkins

DEPOSITION OF HUMPHREY FLUDD

Humfrey ffludd of the p*a*rishe of S^ct: Gyles W^thout Criplegate one of his Ma^tse: Trumpetores of the Age of ffyftye three yeres or th^raboute*s* sworne and examyned the daye and yere abouesaid deposeth and saythe

1/ To the ffirste Interr this deponent sayth he hath knowne the pl*aintiff* about Eighteene yeares for he married his mother in ffraunce And the defendt he hath knowne about Eighteene yeres for he put the pl*aintiff* to be the defendt*es* apprentice./

2/ To the seconde Interr this deponent is not examyned at the Requeste of the plt./

3/ To the thirde Interr this deponnt sayth that whileste the pl*aintiff* was in service wth the defendt, this deponent gaue the pl*aintiff* three suyt*es* of Apparrell vz twoe Cloak*es*, And three suyt*es* of Apparrell. And his mother gaue him good store of Lynnen wch apparrell and lynnen Could not serve him lesse than three yeres, besides the deft was so Stricte vnto him that he this deponent and the plaintiffes mother weare fayne manye tymes to geue him monney and to paye the Barber for Cuttinge the hayr of his heade./ And more he cannott depose./

4. 5/ To the iiijth and vth Interr this deponent is not examined at the Requeste of the plaintiff./

Homfrey Fludd

DEPOSITION OF CHRISTOPHER WEAVER

Christopher Weaver of the parishe of S^{ct}: Olaves in Sylver Streete London mercer of the Age of thirty Eight yeres or thereaboutes sworne and examyned the daye and yeare abouesaid deposith and sayth

1/ To the ffirste Interr this deponnt sayth he hath knowne the plaintiff about twelue yeres and the deft about Syxteene yeares./

2/ To the seconde Interr this deponent sayth he knoweth not the deftes Estate, but sayth he hath the lease of his house wherin he dwelleth. And A lease of A house in Braynford in the County of Middlesex. But he knoweth the deft hath lyen at Intereste these three or ffoure yeres for twenty poundes in one place, and hath neyther payed the principalle nor Interest money due for the same./ And lykewise hath takne vpp other monney, And soulde his plate and some houshold stuffe./ And furth^r sayth that he herd that the deft payeth yerelye Rent for those leases some Seaventeene poundes per Annum./ And sayth that he thinketh the deft Receaveth some Eighteene poundes per Annum de Claro besides his owne dwellinge and hath A Soiourner in his house wth him but what proffitt he maketh th^rby he knoweth not./ And sayth the deft hath said in this deponntes hereinge that in Regard the plaintiff and his daughter had vsed him so vnkindlie, And in Regard he promissed them nothinge he would Rather Rott in prison then geue them any thinge more then he had geuen them before./ And more he cannot depose./

3 To the thirde Interr this deponent sayth he hath herd the deft saye that after the plaintiff came to be his apprentice he ffound the plaintiff all his wearinge apparrell. And oth^rwise he Cannott depose touchinge the same Interr./

4 To the iiijth Interr this deponent sayth he was never made an Instrum^t between the plaintiff and the deft by the deftes appoyntm^t for the moveinge of A marriage betweene the plaintiff and deftes daughter.

And more he cannot depose touchinge any parte of the same Interr for that he never herd the deft promise the plaintiff any some of monney or other thinge wth his daughter Mary in Marriadge wth the plaintiff nor saye that yf she married not the plaintiff shee should not coste him A groate/

5 To the vth Interr this deponent sayth he hath herd the deft and his wyffe saye that they gaue the plaintiff wth there daughter Marye in marriadge the some of ten poundes in monney and houshould Stuffe of moste sortes somthinge viz in monney and goodes to the valewe of thirtye poundes And more he Cannot depose to his Rememberaunce/

Chr: Weauer:

DEPOSITION OF NOEL MOUNTJOY

Nowell Mountioye of the parishe of S.^{ct} Olaves in Sylver Streete London Tyremaker of the Age of thirtye yeares or th^raboutes sworne and examyned the daye and yeare abouesaid deposith and saythe./

1/ To the ffirste Interr this deponent sayth he hath knowne the plaintiff about ffyfteene yeres and the deft longer for he is this deponentes brother./

2/ To the seconde Interr this deponent sayth that his broth^r the deftes estate is not muche ffor he hath but the lease of twoe houses one lease of the house wherein he dwelleth devided into twoe tenementes and a lease of a house in Brainforde by wch leases he gaineth An ouerplus of Rent more then he payeth to the valewe of about nyntene or Seaventeene poundes per Ann./ And hath A tyme in his lease of the howse wherein he dweleth of some thirty yeres to come wch he renewed but latelie, but howe longe tyme he hath to come in the house he hath at Brainford he knoweth not./ Albeyt the deft is much in debte, And sould or pawned his plaite A greate whileste sync so that his estate cannot be verry greate./ And sayth that he herd his brother the deft saye that yf he weare Condempned in this suyte vndeserved he would lye in prison before he would gyve the plaintiff any thinge./ And more he Cannot depose.

3/ To the thirde Interr this deponent sayth that the plaintiff was A yeare A boorder in the deftes house before he became the deftes Apprentice duringe wch tyme he beleveth the deft did not apparrell the plaintiff: but after the plaintiff became the deftes seruaunte the deft apparrelled him. Albeyt his ffrindes might send him somtymes A Cloake or payre of Stockinges or such a thinge./ wch he knoweth to be true for that he did serve the deft when the plt served him. And knewe the truth th^{r}of: And more he Cannott depose./

4/ To the iiij^{the} Interr this deponent sayth he was never sent by the deft vnto the Complt to make A mocon to him of A marriadge to be hadd betwixte the Complainant and Marye Mountioy the deftes sole Child and daughter, nor knoweth of any other that was by the defendt sent vnto the plaintiff vppon that messaiege: but the plt tould this deponnt that one Mr Shakespeare was Imployed by the deft about that buysnes: in what mann^r: or to what effecte he knoweth not: And sayth he never herd the deft saye that yf his daughter Mary married not wth the plaintiff shee should neve^r haue groate from him./ nor knoweth that the defendant promissed to geue the plaintiff Any porcion of monney wth his daughter Mary in marriadge nor howe much he promissed yf he promissed any, nor knoweth vppon what promise the Complt contracted him selfe wth the said Marye/. And more he Cannott depose.

5/ To the ffyfte Interr this deponnt sayth that after the plaintiffes marriadge wth the said Marye, he this deponent went to see them, And the plaintiff vppon some speeches betweene this deponent and the plaintiff the plaintiff tould him that the defendant had geuen him wth his daughter in marriadge the some of ten poundes and Certayne houshould stuffe, but the valewe of the houshould stuffe he knoweth not./ And more he Cannott depose./

Nouel Montioi

c. Third session, 23 June 1612 [ibid./3]

Interrogatories to be ministred vnto witnesses produced on the parte and behalf of Christopher Mountioy defendant to the bill of Complaynt of Stephen Bellott Comp.^{lt}./

1. Inprimis whether do yo^u knowe the parties plaintiffes and defend^t./

2 Item whether did yo^u not heare or knowe that Mary the late wief of Christopher Mountioy the def^t did in her life tyme vrdge the said defend^t to give somthinge more vnto Bellott the plt./ and his wief then he had donn, and did not the said Mountioye the defend^t aunswere her that he would never promise them anie thinge: because he knewe not what he should neede himselfe? or what other speaches to that purpose did you heare her or anie other speake and when were they spoken declare the whole truth therein accordinge to yor remembrance

3 Item have you not heard the late wief of Christopher Mountioy the defend^t declare what her then husband the said Christopher Mountioy

and shee had given the said Complt and his wief after theire Marriage and that shee would have had the said Christopher Mountioy her then husband to have given them more but he vtterly refused and would not or what other speaches have yo^u heard her say touchinge that matter declare the whole truth in particuler as yo^u remember?

4 Item do yo^u knowe or haue yo^u heard of anie monie or other good*es* wch the said Comp.^{lt} Bellott hath receaved of the said Christopher Mountioy the defend^t or his late wief and whether were those som*m*es of monie or other good*es* delivered to them and what was the vallewe of them declare yor whole knowledge herein?/

5 Itm hath not the Complaynant Stephen Bellott vrdged or *per*swaded yò^u to Conceale yor knowledge or otherwise to depose or speake somthinge Concerninge the matter nowe in question betweene him and the said Mountioy the defend^t wch yo^u knowe not to be truee and what speaches hath he lately vsed, or spoken vnto yo^u to that or anie such purpose and when did he speake them declare the *pre*misses hereof according to yor knowledge?/

6 Item whether did yo^u heare or knowe that the said Christopher Mountioy the defend^t did by himselfe or anie from him desire the said Stephen Bellott the Comp^{lt} to reccon wth him about the monie and other things due betweene them and what aunswere did the said Bellott make therevnto and whether do yo^u knowe or haue heard that the said Bellott hath Confessed that he did owe the said Mountioy anie monie or other thing*es* and what was that monie and other thinges and when did he Confesse it and what speaches have yo^u heard the said Bellott speake Concerninge the Reconinge or difference betweene the said Mountioy and him and when did he speake them declare yor whole truthe herein?/

7 Item did not yo^u of yor voluntary will and disposition to make the pl^t. and defend^t frend*es* goe to the pl^t. about three week*es* since and tould the pl.^{t} that he tooke a wronge Course to sue his Father in Lawe And that it weare better they weare kinde and Lovinge frend*es* and what aunswere made the plantiff vpon yor Conference wth him thereabout declare yor knowledge?/

SECOND DEPOSITION OF CHRISTOPHER WEAVER

Christopher Weaver of the p*ar*ishe of S^{ct} Olaves in Sylver Streete London m*er*cer of the Age of thirtye Syxe yeres or th^{r}about*es* sworne and examyned the daye and yere abouesaid deposith and saythe

1/ To the ffirste Interr this deponent sayth he knoweth the plaintiff and defendant./

2/3/4/5/ To the ij.^{d} iij.^{d} iiij.th v.th and vjth Interr this deponent is not examined at the Request of the deft

7/ To the vijth Interr this deponent sayth that about three weekes synce he this deponent wishinge well to bothe the plaintiff and deft went of his owne voluntary will and disposition to talke wth the plaintiff and to see yf he could bringe them to be frindes And Questioninge wth the plaintiff About the same vnkindnes and shewinge him that he tooke A wronge Course to sue his ffath^r in Lawe, the plaintiff Answered him this deponent that he would never haue sued his ffath^r in Lawe yf his ffath^r in Lawe would haue bene willinge to haue hadd his Companye in ffamilliar mann^r as at his table./ And said further he Could be contented the matter should be Ended betwixte them, so that his ffath^r would lett him dwell in one of his houses, w^{oh} was nexte to his owne dwellinge house payinge some Rent for yt, And furth^r said he could leave his wyffe in better estate then he ffound her whensoeuer god should be pleased to calle him, vnto w^{oh} this deponent said he was gladd of yt, And said he this deponent would make yt knowne to the deft his father. And do what he could to make them ffrindes or woordes to that effecte And so did, but the def^t yt seemed had taken such an vnkinnes at his sonne in lawes vsage towardes him that he said he would never geue him Any more, As before he hath deposed in his Answeare to the pltes Interr. And more he Cannott depose.

Chr: Weauer

SECOND DEPOSITION OF NOEL MOUNTJOY

Nowell Mountioy of the parishe of S^{ct}: Olaves in Sylver Streete London Tyremaker of the Age of thirtye yeres or th^{r}aboutes sworne and examyned the daye and yere abouesaid deposeth and saythe

1/ To the ffirste Interr this deponent sayth he knoweth the plaintiff and defendant./

2/3/ To the seconde and third Interr this deponent Can saye nothinge touchinge any parte of the same Interr

4/ To the iiijth Interr this deponent sayth that the plaintiff since his marriadge wth the deftes daughter Marye tould this deponent that the deft had geuen them the plaintiff and his wyffe the some of ten poundes in monney and Certayne houshould stuffe but the valewe of the houshould stuffe he

cannot declare, for that he did not see the househould stuffe deliuered./
And more he Cannott depose

5 To the ffyfte Interr this deponent sayth that the plaintiff sent for him this
deponent about A yere since wch he thinketh is neere about or synce this
suyte beganne. And asked this deponent yf he knewe of the tenn poundes
the deft his ffath^r in lawe gaue him and his wyffe synce there Marriadge./
And this deponent tould the plaintiff he did knowe of yt, wherevppon
the plaintiff tould him this deponent that yf when he was called to
Answeare wherefore yt was geuen them, he this deponent might doe him
the plaintiff good yf he this deponent would Answeare that he the plaintiff
Receaved yt of the deffendant for woorke donne for him, sayinge to this
deponent that he the plaintiff was lykelie to be A better ffrind to this
deponent then the deft would be, vrdginge that the deft was all for him
selfe./ And furth^r that synce that tyme the pltes mayd lykewise vrdged
this deponent that shee herd him saye that he herd the deft saye that he
gaue the plaintiff that ten poundes aforesaid for woorke: wch was ffalse:
ffor wch this deponent Rebuked the mayde. And more he Cannott depose./

6/ To the vjth Interr this deponnt sayth that the plt tould him that the deft
came vnto him And desired him to Reccon wth him About monney And
other thinges betweene them/ And the plaintiff tould this deponent that
he Answeared him the deft that he would not Reccon wth him any thinge,
sayinge he was sorry he hadd not more in his handes to Reccon wth him
for then he hadd sayinge he saies I owe him three poundes, & he oweth
me fforty shillinges, yf all come to all tis but twenty shillinges difference./
And more he cannott depose touchinge the said Interr to his Rememberaunce./

7/ To the vijth Interr this deponent is not examyned at the Requeste of the
defendant

Nouel Montioi

DEPOSITION OF THOMAS FLOWER

Thomas fflower of the parishe of S^{ct} Albans in Woddstreete London mer-
chaunttaylo^r of the Age of thirtye Eight yeres or th^raboutes sworne and
examed the daye and yere abouesaid deposith and saythe/

1/ To the ffirste Interr this deponent sayth he knoweth the plaintiff and deft
2/ To the seconde Interr this deponent sayth that he hath often herd Marye
the defendtes wyffe did often in her lyffe tyme vrdge her husbond the deft
to geue somthynge more vnto the plaintiff and his wyffe then he had

donne before wherevnto the deft Mountioye would comonlye answeare her that he would not promise them any thinge because he knewe not what he should neede him selfe./ And soe he hath herd the deft often saye he would promise nothinge for feare of wantinge him selfe or woordes to the lyke effecte./ And more he Cannott depose./

3/ To the third Interr this deponent sayth he hath herd the deftes wyffe in her lyffe tyme saye that her husbonde and shee hadd geuen her daughter Marye and her husbond the plaintiff synce there marriadge togeath^r the some of ten poundes in Monney And Certayne Implem^{tes} of houshould stuffe, And that shee would haue had her husbond Mountioye haue geuen them more./ but he would not sayinge he knewe not what he him selfe might want or wordes to the lyke effecte. And more he Cannott depose/

4 To the iiijth Interr this deponent sayth that he herd as aforesaid that the plaintiff Receaved of the deft ten poundes in monney and Certayne househould stuffe./ but the valewe of the houshould stuffe he knoweth not./ And furth^r sayth that synce the plaintiffes goinge from the deft the deft sent this deponent to the plaintiff to desire him to Reccon wth him for some Monney and other thinges wch he had takne wth him when he went Awaye./ And the plaintiff did answeare this deponent that he had but some fewe trifles of his wch he would not confesse in particuler nor deliuer. And more he Cannott depose/

5 To the vth Interr this deponent sayth the plaintiff hath not at any tyme vrdged nor perswaded this deponent to conceale his knowledge nor otherwise to depose and speake Any thinge concerninge the matt^r nowe in Question betweene them./ And more he cannot depose./

6/ To the vjth Interr this deponent sayth that by him this deponent the defendt did longe synce desire the plaintiff to Reccon wth him the defendant about monney And other thinges due betweene them, wherevppon this deponnt moved him to A Recconinge, who Answeared in mann^r ffollowinge vz wheare I haue a penniwoorth of Any thinge, I would I hadd more of his. I haue nothinge but that wch I will keepe And yf I owe him Any monney lett him com by yt as he Can./ wch Answeare this deponent retorned the deft. And more he cannot depose.

7 To the vijth Interr this deponent is not examned at requeste of the defendant./

Thomas fflowers

3. ARBITRATION

a. Referral from the Court of Requests to the French Church, 30 June 1612 [TNA PRO REQ 1/26, fol. 421]

In the matter of varyance brought before the King*es* ma^{tie} and his highenes Counsaill in his ma^{tes} ho: Court of Whitehall by Stephen Bellot compl*ainant* against Xpofer Mountioy def^{t}, the said compl*ainant* by his bill seeking to be releived touching A promise supposed by the said bill to be by him the said def^{t} Mountioy made for the payment vnto the said compl*ainan*^{t} of the som*me* of threescore pound*es* or theareaboute*s* vpon the day of the said compl*ainan*^{tes} marriage wth Mary Mountioy daughter of the said def^{t} & now wief of the compl^{t}, And for the leaving to the said compl*ainan*^{t} & Mary his wief the some of CC^{l} more at the tyme of his the said def^{tes} decease, As in & by the said bill of complaynt more at lardge appeareth. Vnto wch bill the said def^{t} appeared & answered, witnesses on both p*artes* were exami*ne*d and A day of hearing appoynted. Vpon opening whereof It is by his ma^{tes} said Counsaill of this Court in p*re*sence of the said p*ar*ties and of Counsaill learned on both sydes ordered by and wth the full consent of the saide p*ar*ties, that the same matter shalbe referred to the hearing ordering & finall determina*ci*on of the Reverend & grave overseers and Elders of the french Church in London aucthorising them hereby to call before them both the saide p*ar*ties, And vpon considera*ci*on had of the state of the same cause & the circumstanc*es* of the same, to heare Order & finally determine the said matter touching the promise as to their discre*ci*ons & wisdomes shall seeme convenient, And such order as shalbe herein determined by the said Committees this court will confirme establishe & decree./

b. Entries in the Act-book of the French Church, 1612–14 [*Les Actes du Consistoire de l'Eglise Françoise de Londres, 1589–1615*; FPC MS 4]

30 July 1612 [fol. 495]. Cretophle Montioye ayant esté mis en p*ro*ces p*ar* son gendre Etiene Belot, p*our* q^{1}q^{e} argent de son mariage q^{e} p*re*tendoit luy deuoir vz: 10. li. dont n' auoit preuve, ne tesmoings. La Court p*ar* lett*re* nous pria de le mettre en Arbitre, ce qui fut fait, dont furent elleus, Abraham Hardret, Gedeon de Laune, *pour* Monioye: Et Dauid Carp*er*au & Pierre Beauuais p*our* Belot. tous 2. pere & gendre desbauchéz.

(Christopher Montjoye having been sued by his son-in-law Etienne Belot for a certain marriage portion which he claims is owed to him, viz. £10, for which he has neither proof nor witness, the Court requested us by letter to put the case to arbitration, which was done, for which purpose were elected Abraham Hardret and Gideon de Laune for Monjoye, and David Carperau and Pierre Beauvais for Belot. Both the father and son-in law are debauched.) 13 September 1612 [fol. 498]. Etienne Belot, redemandant le mereau, dont il s'est absteint de long temps a raison de atroverses [?] auec son beau pere, Cretophle Montioye. On veillera sur luy. & la Cene de 10–bre. &-c.

(Etienne Belot asking for the sign [i.e. the sacrament] again, from which he has long abstained because of his quarrel [?] with his father-in-law, Cretophle Montioye, we will watch over him at the Communion of October)

6 May 1613 [fol. 501]. Cretophle Montioye, entré, fut censuré de ce q^l ne payoit les 20. Nobles a son gendre, ordonné p*ar* les Arbitres, plaida poureté, bien q^e luy baillera des dettes, p*our* les receuoir. Et d'auoir eu 2. bastards. de sa seruante, a quoy il ne respondit p*ertinam*^{t} Aussi Michel Art son Ancien Leuicta de serm^t faux en la Court spirituelle q^l n'auoit couché avec elle. Ne se trouua preuue suffisante. Suspendu.

(Cretophle Montjoye, coming before us, was censured for not paying his son-in-law the 20 nobles ordered by the Arbritators; he pleaded poverty, although he will find the money by borrowing it. And [*sc* he was censured] for having had two bastards by his maidservant, to which makes no pertinent response. Also Michel Art, his elder, convicted him of falsely swearing in the Spiritual Court that he had not slept with her. There was not sufficient proof. Suspended.)

2 September 1613 [fol. 505].* Cristopher Monjoie ha estes appelles 2 fois et ha dict qu'l ne setient point des n*o*tres p*ar*tant de aduiser en plus grande Compaingnie de sa rebellion.

(Cristopher Monjoie has been summoned twice, and has said that he does not recognize our authority. We intend to advise the full Company [i.e. congregation?] of his rebellion.)

27 February 1614 [fol. 511]. Cretophle Montioye, ayant souuent esté exhorté, en p*ar*ticulier & Consistoire d'estre pieux, de sa vie desreglée, & desbordée, & suspendu sans fruict, estant endurci, ayant esté tiré au Magistrat p*our* ses paillardises, & adulteres; N'ayant voulu venir au Consistoire y estant appellé. Ne fréquantant ceste Eglize, suspendu publiquem^t p*our* ces

---

* This entry is written in what Wallace calls a 'flourished court-hand of Gothic-Roman very difficult to read'. I have followed his transcription and given a rather speculative translation.

scandalles. Exhortons de prier Dieu p*our* luy, de luy toucher le coeur, *luy* donant vraye rescipiscence.

(Cretophile Montjoye, having often been exhorted both in private and in the Consistory to be pious, because of his irregular and outlandish life; and having been suspended without any effect, becoming more hardened; and having been brought before the Magistrate for his lewd acts and adulteries; and having not wished to come to the Consistory when summoned; and not frequenting the church, was publicly suspended for these scandals. Let us pray for him, that God may touch his heart and give him true repentance.)

4. OTHER DOCUMENTS

a. Will of Christopher Mountjoy, 26 January 1620 [Peculiar Court of the Dean & Chapter of St Paul's, *Registrum Testamentorum 1608–33*; GL MS 25626/4, fol. 179]

In the name of God Amen, the Six & twentith day of January *Anno Dm secundum computacionem Ecclesiae Anglicanae* 1619 [i.e. 1620] . . . I Christopher Mountjoy of London, Marchant, beinge sicke & weake in body but of perfect mind & memory (thankes bee given to almightie God therefore) doe make & ordeyne this my last will and Testament in manner & forme followinge (that is to say): *ffirst* I give & bequeath my soule unto almightie God my maker and Creator, trustinge & assuredly beleivinge y^t by the merritte of *Jesus Christ my Saviour* I have and shall have free & cleire remission of all my sinnes & that after this transitory life ended I shall be pertaker of that heavenly rest wch God hath prepared for his elect. *Item* I will my body to be Christianlike buried at the discrecon of myne Executrix herein after named. *Item* my will and minde is that all such Goods & Chattells as God hath bestowed upon mee shall, after my debtes paid & funeralls discharged, bee given & disposed of in manner & forme following (that is to say) Three Third partes of my goods & Chattells (the whole being devided into ffower Third partes) I give & bequeath unto my welbeloved wief Isabell. *And* one other thirde part of the said ffower Third parts I doe hereby give & bequeath unto my daughter Mary Blott the wief of Stephen Blott. *And* my will & minde is that all & everie my said goods and Chattells shall, assoone after my decease as conveniently may bee, bee equally devided betweene my said wife & daughter according unto my severall bequests herin before menconed by two indifferent persons to be nominated & elected betweene them. *And* I doe hereby make & appoint the said Isabell my wief the full & sole Executrix of this my last will & testament. *In witness whereof* I the said Christopher Mountjoy have to this my last will & testament sett my hande & seale the daie & yeares first above written. *Par moy Christopher Mountjoy.* Sealed & delivered by the said Christopher Mountjoy & by him published & pronounced in the presence of Raphe Merifeild *Ed: Dendye Thomas Seman Robert Walker.*

b. Petition of Stephen Belott, 20 March 1621 [HLRO PO/JO/10/1/16, item 5]

To the right noble Assemblie the upper house of Parlament The humble peticon of Stephen Bellott sometime servant to one Monjoye Gould wyredrawer: sworne before the right hono^{ble} the Assemblie of the upper house of parlyament the 20th daie of march 1620 [i.e. 1621]

Humblie shewing that the petioconer hath for many years gotten his living by the art of working gold and silver thredd, and thereby onlie mainteyned his wife and children.

That about twoe yeares since Mr ffowles under collor of his patent sent out Ireland his pursevant whoe did forciblie enter into the peticoners house and going up into an upper roome where the chamber doore was lockt, the said Ireland did violentlie breake open the said door & tooke out of the chamber the peticoners mill the onlie instrument of his living, and caried away the same to Mr ffowles whoe doth hitherto deteine the same, whereby the peticoner his wife & children are utterlie undone.

he humblie beseecheth your honorable consideracons of their wronge. And that the periconer may have recompense for the same as yor honors shall think meet. And he shall dailie praie &c

stephen bellott

c. Will of Stephen Bellott, 25 July 1646 [TNA PRO PROB 11/99, fol. 227]

In the name of God Amen I Stephen Belott of the Bowleing Alley neere Long Lane in the parish of Sepulchers without Newgate London Tyer maker: Being at this present Sick in body but of Sound and perfectt memorie, Lawd and praise be therfor giuen to Almightye God, Calling to minde my yeares and my infirmities, The ffrailtie of this Transitorie life and the vncertentye of the hower of death: doe make and Ordaine this my last will and Testament: And first and Principallie I Commend my Soule into the handes of Almightie God my Creator, Hopeing and Stedfastlie beleeuing that by and through the Meritts of the death and passion and pretious blood shedd vppon the Crosse of Jesus Christ, his onely Sonne and my alone Sauiour and Redeemer, I haue and shall haue full and ffree Remission Pardon and fforgiuenes of all my Sinns and Offences; And to be saued vnto life euerlasting./ My body I Committ to the earth from whence it came to be decentlie buried, in assured Hope of the Resurrection thereof at the Gennerall Judgement day vnto life eternall: And touching such worldly goods and Estate as it hath pleased God of his greatt goodness and mercie to blesse me withall, I doe hereby giue deuise and bequeath the same in manner and forme following: That is to say, Inprimis whereas my late brother Master John Belott, late of the Citty of Harlem in Holland ffrench Schoolemaster deceased, in and by his last will and Testament beareing date the Third day of October, Anno Domini One Thousand six hundred ffortie and Twoe, hath giuen left and bequeathed vnto me the said Stephen Belott, the Summe of Nyne hundred Gilders, Being fowerscore and Tenn poundes English: To be paid after the decease of my sister in lawe Mistris Maijlie van Regemuorter late wife of my said brother Master John Belott deceased, As in and by his said Last will and Testament more at lardge doth and may appeare: And which said Legacie or summe of Nyne Hundred Gilders I haue Constituted authorized and appointed the Elders and deacons of the ffrench Reformed Church in Harlem, for the vse and behoofe of me my Executors and Administrators, to Aske Leauy sue for recouer and receaue the same, of and against the heires Executors and Administrators of my said sister in lawe Mistris Maijlie van Reemuorter after her decease As in and by the said writeing of deputation (Relation thereto being had) more at lardge doth and may appeare; And now my will and minde is, And I doe hereby will deuise and dispose the said Legacic of Nyne hundred Gilders being in English fowerscore and Tenn poundes in manner following: And first I giue and bequeath vnto my daughter Ann now the wife of William Haier wyer drawer, the somme of Twentie poundes thereof: Item I giue and bequeath vnto my daughter Jane now the wife of ffrancis Ouering, Glouer, the like Summe of Twentye poundes thereof: Item I giue and bequeath vnto my daughter Easter now the wife of Christopher Baytes, other Twentie poundes thereof: Item I giue and bequeath vnto my loueing wife Thomazine Belott Twentie poundes more thereof; And the other Tenn poundes my will is shalbe for the satisfieing of That Tenn poundes which I borrowed and receaued of my said sister in lawe Mistris Maijlie van Regemuater when I was with her in Harlem: Item I giue and bequeath vnto the poore of the Reformed Church in Harlem the summe of fforty shillings; And my will and desire is, That my loueing wife Thomazine Belott, and my daughter

Jane Oueringe shall goe over togeather vnto Harlem in Holland; and there receaue and bring over the said moneys at such time and when as the same shall become due and payable after the decease of my said sister in lawe; And my will and minde is that my said loueing wife and my said three daughters shall be at, beare and allow euery one of them fower and equall parte portion and share towards the charges and expences of their Journey and trauelling ouer vnto Harlem, and for and about the recouering Changeing Transporting and returning and bringing ouer the said monies to deuide the said moneys to and amongst my said wife and my Three daughters equallie for the satisfieing of their said seuerall Legacies (euery one of them beareing and allowing an equall ffowerth parte of all expences and Chardges of fetching and bringing ouer the same as aforesaid according to the true meaneing of this my last Will and Testament; The rest and residue of all and singuler my Goods, Chattells Houshould stuffe Apparrell Bedding Lynnen Wollen, Brasse Pewter Bonds Bills, writings Specialties debtes Ready monyes and all other my goods and estate whatsoeuer vnbequeathed (My debtes and legacies paid and my ffunerell expences dischardged) I doe fully and freely giue and bequeath vnto my said loueing wife Thomazine Belott whome I make and ordaine my full and sole Executrix of this my last Will and Testament; desireing her to execute and performe the same in and by all things according to my true intent and meaning herein before specified and declared; And I doe hereby Reuoke and disanull all former and other Wills by me at any time heretofore made; And I doe pronounce and declare this and none other to stand and be my last Will and Testament: In Witnes whereof I the said Stephen Belott to this my last Will and Testament (Contained in fower sheets of Paper) haue sett my hand and Seale, The fiue and Twentieth day of July Anno Domini One thousand six hundred ffortie six: And in the twoe and twentieth yeare of the Raigne of our Soueraig Lord King Charles &c

Par moy Etiene Belot.

Sealed and Subscribed by the Testator, and acknowledged Published and declared to stand and be his last Will and Testament in the presence of vs Roger Goude: Richard Gill Scr./

Notes

1. The deposition

1. The other signatures are two relating to his purchase of the Blackfriars Gatehouse (conveyance, 10 March 1613, Guildhall Library; mortgage-deed, 11 March 1613, BL Egerton MS 1787); and three on his will, 25 March 1616 (PRO Prob 1/4). On various spurious autographs see SRI 93–109.

2. A comparable text is the reported conversation about land-enclosures in the diary of Thomas Greene, Stratford town clerk, 17 November 1614: 'My cosen Shakespeare . . . told me that they assured him they ment to enclose noe further then to Gospell Bushe [etc]' (SRI no. 37). But this is more a précis than a recording of what Shakespeare said. His will doubtless relates to oral instructions but cannot usefully be called a record of his spoken words.

3. Izaak Walton, *Life of Sir Henry Wotton* (1651), in *Lives* (1956), 120–21. The *bon mot* was recorded 'at his first going ambassador into Italy', i.e. in 1604. A clown's punning reply to the question 'Does Master Scarberow lie here?' (Wilkins 1607, A2v) may be a feeble reminiscence of the exchange in *Othello*.

4. For the earlier finds (Keyser v Burbage et al., Court of Requests, February 1610; Ostler v Heminges, King's Bench, October 1615; Witter v Heminges and Condell, Court of Requests, April 1619) see Wallace 1910b, EKC 2.52–71.

5. Schoenbaum 1970, 645–56.

6. Wallace 1910a, 490.

7. Huntington Library, San Marino, Calif., Wallace Papers Box 11, Envelope 27; Schoenbaum 1970, 650–51.

8. Both submissions describe Belott's marriage (19 November 1604) as 'about five yeares past'. However, Noel Mountjoy's deposition (23 June 1612) refers to a meeting with Belott 'about a yere since, wch he thinketh is neere about or since this suyte began'. With a little stretching these approximations meet to suggest a date around late 1610 or early 1611 for the initiation of the suit.

9. Stow 1908, 2.118–20. Belott's Bill also refers to 'Yr Highnes Court of White Hall, comonlie called the Court of Request'. This White Hall (or White Chamber) was part of Westminster Palace, and has no connection with the nearby Whitehall Palace.

10. For Belott's will (25 July 1646) see Appendix 4.

11. FPC MS 4; see Appendix 3.

12. Wallace 1910a, 489; SDL 213.

13. L. Hotson, 'Not of an Age', *Sewanee Review* 39 (1941), reprinted in Hotson 1949, 161–84; it was originally a lecture at the Folger Shakespeare Library, 23 April 1940. A. L. Rowse, 'The Secrets of Shakespeare's Landlady', *The Times*, 23 April 1973, expanded in Rowse 1976, 107–10.

14. That *Pericles* was only partly Shakespeare's was noted in the prologue to George Lillo's adaptation, *Marina* (1738): 'We dare not charge the whole unequal play / Of Pericles on him.' On evidence both external (see Chapters 21–23) and internal (see Jackson 2001, Vickers 2002) Wilkins is overwhelmingly the most plausible co-author, though F. Hoeniger (Arden edn, 1963, lii–lxiii and Appendix B) mounts a case for John Day, himself a collaborator with Wilkins. For biographical and critical sources on Wilkins see Part Six, note 3 below.

15. Formulated by the Lyonnais investigator Dr Edmond Locard in his *Manuel de technique policière* (Paris, 1923), ch 3.

2. Turning forty

16. Dulwich College MS I/49; Foakes 1977, vol. 2, no. 49. The eighteenth-century scholar Edmund Malone possessed a 'curious document' which he thought afforded the 'strongest presumptive evidence' that Shakespeare was living in Southwark in 1608 (*An Inquiry into the Authenticity of certain Miscellaneous Papers* (1796), 215; EKC 2.88). He intended to publish it in his *Life* of Shakespeare, but died before he reached that stage of the story. This mysterious item may have been a copy of the poor-relief list of 1609, though the dates do not quite match. Malone refers to another document (also unidentified) which showed that Shakespeare was in Southwark in 1598 – this was perhaps the Pipe Rolls entry relating to his unpaid tax

(see note 65 below). Malone's inference that Shakespeare lived continuously in Southwark between 1598 and 1608 is invalidated by the sojourn on Silver Street, which he did not know about.

17. According to traditional reckoning, Shakespeare's fortieth birthday fell on 23 April 1604. In fact his birthdate is not known: he was baptized on 25 April 1564, and so may have been born on any day between about 20 and 24 April; the choice of the 23rd – St George's Day – is a jingoistic convenience, first mooted in the early eighteenth century. Thomas De Quincey suggested that the wedding-day of Shakespeare's granddaughter Elizabeth, 22 April 1627, commemorated his birthday. See SDL 20–24.

18. EKC 2.323–7. William Lambarde records the Queen's dramatic utterance a few months later: 'I am Richard II, know ye not that?' (326). Blair Worden questions whether the play was Shakespeare's ('Which Play was Performed at the Globe Theatre on 7 February 1601?', *LRB* 25, 10 July 2003).

19. Jonson refers to these travails in conversations with the Scottish poet William Drummond, 1618–19: see Patterson 1923, 25–7. The offending play was *Eastward Ho!* Letters written from prison by Jonson and his co-author George Chapman survive in contemporary copies. The authors were 'hurried to bondage and fetters', Jonson says, 'without examining, without hearing, or without any proof but malicious rumour' (C. Petter, ed., *Eastward Ho!* (1973), Appendix 3). Jonson was also imprisoned in the Marshalsea in 1597, as part-author (with Thomas Nashe) of the lost satire *The Isle of Dogs* (Nicholl 1984, 243–9); and in Newgate in 1598, charged with killing the actor Gabriel Spenser in a swordfight on Hoxton Fields (Riggs 1989, 49–53).

20. Leishman 1949, 369–71. The plays were performed at St John's College, Cambridge, *c.* 1598–1602; the author was possibly Edmund Rishton, a student at St John's (BA 1599, MA 1602), whose name appears on the outer leaf of the extant MS (Bod., Rawlinson MS D.398). On the War of the Theatres or Poetomachia ('Poets' Quarrel') of *c.* 1599–1602, see Steggle 1998. On the Shakespearean 'purge' see Honigmann 1987, 42–9; Riggs 1989, 63–85; Duncan-Jones 2001, 118–25.

21. SDL doc. 157.

22. For the dates see the section on George Carey in Wallace T. MacCaffrey, 'Henry Carey, 1st Baron Hunsdon', *ODNB* 2004. For the disease see the anonymous court lampoon on him – 'Fool hath he ever bin / With his Joan Silverpin. / Quicksilver's in his head / But his wit's as dull as lead' (C. C. Stopes, *Life of Henry, Third Earl of Southampton* (1922), 235–7). Joan Silverpin was a generic name for a prostitute, and mercury preparations a supposed cure for syphilis.

23. Accounts of Sir George Home, Master of the Great Wardrobe, for the 'royall proceeding through the Citie of London', 15 May 1604 (PRO LC2/4/5, fol. 78). Each of the named players received 4 yards of red cloth for a cloak.

24. PRO SC6/JASI/1646, fol. 28r (original numbering) or 29r (new numbering).

25. SDL 148–50, citing eighteenth-century sources (Nicholas Rowe's 1709 edn of Shakespeare for Hamlet senior, Samuel Johnson and George Steevens's 1778 edn for Adam). John Davies (note 28 below) says Shakespeare played 'kingly parts'. Cast lists in Ben Jonson's *Works* (1616) name Shakespeare as an actor in *Everyman in his Humour* (1598) and *Sejanus* (1603) but do not specify the parts.

26. For an overview of the portraits, including recent technical analyses, see Cooper 2006, 48–75. On the lost original of the Droeshout engraving see Chapter 17.

27. On the Shakespeare coat of arms and attendant controversies, see Duncan-Jones 2001, 85–103; Cooper 2006, 138–42. 'Not without mustard': Ben Jonson, *Every Man out of his Humour* (1600), 3.1.205, though the phrase was current earlier (Nashe 1958, 1.171). 'Shakespeare ye player' is in a list drawn up in 1602 by Ralph Brooke, York Herald (Folger Library, Washington, MS V.a.350, fol. 28).

28. John Davies, 'To our English Terence, Mr Will. Shake-speare', in *The Scourge of Folly* (*c.* 1610), Epigram 159.

29. EKC 2.67–71, 95–127; SDL 155–6; Honan 1998, 236–44, 290–94.

30. *Ratsey's Ghost* (Shakespeare Association Facsimiles 10, 1935), sigs B1–B1v. The book was the sequel to *The Life and Death of Gamaliel Ratsey* (1605). Ratsey, a highwayman, was executed at Bedford on 26 March 1605; the pamphlets recount his supposed 'madde prankes and robberies'.

31. Hamnet was named after his godfather, Hamnet or Hamlet Sadler, a Stratford baker and lifelong friend of Shakespeare's. The forename, a diminutive of the Norman name Hamon, is found elsewhere in the Stratford registers (EKC 2.3–4). It has no etymological connection with the fictional Hamlet (an Anglicized form of the Scandinavian Amleth) but there is surely an emotional assonance, especially if (as Rowe asserts) Shakespeare played Hamlet's father.

32. *Kind Harts Dreame* (1592), sig. A4.

33. On Chettle's possible authorship see W. B. Austin, *A Computer-aided Technique for Stylistic Discrimination: The Authorship of 'Greene's Groatsworth of Wit'* (Washington, DC, 1969); John Jowett, 'Notes on Henry Chettle', *RES* 45 (1994), 385–8. The 'upstart crow' (*Groatsworth*, 1592, sig. F1v) refers to Shakespeare as a mimic, i.e. actor, but carries also the

imputation of plagiarism. In the *Epistles* of Horace a plagiarizing poet is described as a 'little crow' decked with 'stolen colours'. As Chettle's phrasing shows, Shakespeare felt his 'honesty' had been impugned, as well as his 'art'.

34. *Microcosmos* (1603), 215. 'Generous' carries an overtone of *generosus*, the legal Latin term for a gentleman.

35. Scoloker 1604, 'Epistle', sig. E4v. The author's name is a bibliographic convenience. The poem was formerly attributed to Anthony Scoloker or 'Skolykers', an immigrant printer and translator, but the discovery that he died in 1593 makes this unlikely; his son, also Anthony, predeceased him. There is actually no reason to associate 'An. Sc.' with this family at all. See Janet Ing Freeman, 'Anthony Scoloker, translator' and P. J. Finkelpearl, 'Anthony Scoloker, poet' (*ODNB* 2004).

36. Aubrey 1949, 85; Edmond 1987, 13–21.

37. J. L. Borges, 'Todo y nada', in *El Hacedor* (Buenos Aires, 1960), trans. J. E. Irby, 'Everything and Nothing', in *Labyrinths* (1970), 284–5.

3. Sugar and gall

38. *Othello* 1.3 takes information about the Turkish invasion of Cyprus from Richard Knolles's *History of the Turks* (SR 30 September 1603). On *Measure*'s topical allusions referring to 1603–4 see J. W. Lever, Arden edn (1965), xxxi–xxxv, and Chapter 23 above.

39. *All's Well* is dated *c.* 1603 by Alexander Leggatt (New Cambridge edn, 2003, 11); *c.* 1603–4 by G. K. Hunter (Arden edn, 1959, xviii–xxv); and *c.* 1604–5 by Susan Snyder (Oxford edn, 1993, 24). Schrickx 1988 argues that political alliances mentioned in the play point to a performance during celebrations of the Anglo-Spanish peace treaty (July–August 1604). The frequency of rhymed couplets (a feature of Shakespeare's early work) may suggest he reworked an earlier version of the play. The mysterious 'Loves Labours Wonne', mentioned in a list of Shakespeare's plays in 1598 (Francis Meres, *Palladis Tamia*, fol. 282r), could conceivably be a reference to it.

40. G. B. Shaw, *Plays Pleasant and Unpleasant* (1898), Preface, ix.

41. Wilson 1932, 119; Rossiter 1961, 117. Rossiter also finds this grating wit in the 'indecent sonnets' (i.e. chiefly the 'Dark Lady' sequence). Some of the sonnets (first published in 1609) probably belong to the Silver Street years. Stylometric analysis assigns nos 104–26 to the early seventeenth century, and two of this group have allusions to the succession and coronation of James I (1603–4). See MacDonald Jackson, 'Rhyme in Shakespeare's Sonnets: Evidence of Date of Composition', *NQ* 46 (1999), 213–19.

42. G. B. Guarini, *Compendio della poesia tragicomica* (1601). Cinthio's

Epitia (1583) was a source, via English versions, for the plot-line of *Measure for Measure*. It is described by Cinthio as a 'tragedia di lieto fin' (a potential tragedy with a 'pleasant' ending) – what Sir Philip Sidney called 'mungrell Tragy-comedy' (*Apologie for Poetry*, 1581).

43. For some other responses to *Hamlet* in *Diaphantus* see Duncan-Jones 2001, 179–81.

44. Sypher 1955, 115–17, 152–3. He discerns in *Measure* the hallmarks of Mannerism defined by Panowski as *Spannung* ('tension'), *Streckung* ('elasticity') and *Flucht ohne Ziel* ('projection without climax'). Elizabeth Yearling describes the 'devices' of Jacobean tragicomedy as 'tonal contrasts, protean characters, ambiguous language and self-conscious theatricality' (*RES* 34 (1983), 214).

45. An ongoing repartee between Marston and Shakespeare is discernible in *c.* 1600–1601: Marston's *Antonio's Revenge* has parallels with *Hamlet*, and his *What You Will* with *Twelfth Night* (itself subtitled 'What You Will', and performed at the Middle Temple, where Marston was a member, in February 1601). Both writers appended 'Poeticall Essaies' to Robert Chester's *Love's Martyr* (1601); Shakespeare's contribution, 'The Phoenix and the Turtle', is praised by Marston as a 'moving *epicedium*'. See W. Reavley Gair, ed., *Antonio's Revenge* (Manchester 1978); Duncan-Jones 2001, 137–56; Steggle 1998, 40–48.

46. On the *Timon* collaboration see Wells 2006, 184–8; John Jowett, Oxford edn (2004), 1–3; Gary Taylor, 'Thomas Middleton' (*ODNB* 2004). Almost all of Act 3 is generally ascribed to Middleton, plus 1.2 and parts of 2.2, 4.2 and 4.3.

47. On Nashe see *1 Henry VI*, ed. J. Dover Wilson (Cambridge, 1952), xxi–xxxi, though the parallels adduced are not necessarily the result of collaboration. On Peele and Shakespeare see Vickers 2002. On 'The Booke of Sir Thomas More' (BL Harley MS 7368) see Part Five, note 10 below.

48. Sylvia Feldman, ed., *A Yorkshire Tragedy* (Malone Society, 1973), v–xvi. The entry in SR, 2 May 1608 (Arber 1875, 3.337) also describes it as 'written by William Shakespere'. The publisher, Thomas Pavier, later produced a series of unauthorized Shakespeare quartos, some misleadingly dated.

49. Sisson 1935; John Berryman, 'Shakespeare's Reality' (1971), in Haffenden 2001, 347. Colin Burrow tilts wittily at the windmill of 'literary biography', where 'explanations of literary activity . . . tend to be made up from a dash of Freud, a handful of social aspiration, a scratching from Foucault's armpit, and a willingness to entertain simple one-to-one correspondences between fiction and life' ('Who Wouldn't Buy It?', *LRB* 27, 20 January 2005).

50. Tillyard 1965, 152.

4. Shakespeare in London

51. Ben Jonson, 'To the memory of my Beloved, the Author Mr William Shakespeare' (1623), line 71, in *Complete Poems*, ed. George Parfitt (1975, 265).
52. Aubrey 1949, 255.
53. William Dunbar (attrib.), 'In Honour of the City of London' (late fifteenth century); Nashe, *Christs Teares* (1593), sig. X3 (Nashe 1958, 2.158–9). Nashe's diatribe earned him a brief spell in Newgate, and was substituted with a toned-down version in the 2nd edn of 1594.
54. 'harey the vi', marked as a new play, first appears in Henslowe's diary on 3 March 1592 (Foakes 2002, 16). The *Groatsworth* was published within a few weeks of Greene's death on 3 September 1592 (Nicholl 1984, 135, 301).
55. The 'lost years' and their legends are summarized in SDL 77–90, Sams 1995. For the Catholic narrative (which in part depends on a player in Lancashire called William Shakeshafte being the sixteen-year-old Shake-speare) see E. A. J. Honigmann, *Shakespeare: The Lost Years* (1985); Richard Wilson, *Secret Shakespeare: Studies in Theatre, Religion and Resistance* (2004).
56. Diary of Thomas Greene, 17 November 1614: see note 2 above. The Blackfriars Gatehouse, purchased by Shakespeare in March 1613, was an investment rather than a residence, but may have served as a London pied-à-terre (Honan 1998, 378–9).
57. Bod., Aubrey MS 8, fol. 45v. The lay-out of the page (see EKC 2.252) is confused, but the view that Aubrey's interlineated note is about Beeston himself, rather than Shakespeare, deprives us unnecessarily. Beeston's birthdate is not known: it could be as early as 1603 (his parents married in 1602), which would make him thirteen when Shakespeare died. Beeston was recommended to Aubrey by another old stager, John Lacey, who also provided him with material on Shakespeare. Lacey, born in Yorkshire in about 1615, cannot have known Shakespeare personally, but he had worked with Ben Jonson (d. 1637), furnishing northern dialect terms for his late play *The Tale of a Tub*.
58. On literary Shoreditch see Mark Eccles, *Christopher Marlowe in London* (1934), 122–6; Nicholl 1984, 39–40; and the second of Gabriel Harvey's *Four Letters* (1592). Various Balls (but not Em) feature in the Shoreditch registers.
59. PRO E179/146/354; EKC 2.87–90; Giuseppi 1929. For an introduction to the subsidy rolls see Lang 1993. Some London rolls are available online on

Alan Nelson's website (http://socrates.berkeley.edu/ ~ahnelson/SUBSIDY/ subs.html).

60. Hazlitt 1864, 2.317. John Manningham notes in his diary (November 1602; Sorlien 1976, 123): 'a common phrase of subsidies and such taxes: the greate ones will not, the little ones cannot, the meane [middle-ranking] men must pay for all.'

61. Shakespeare's second assessment (PRO E179/146/369) resulted in a tax liability of 13s 4d; this was a new subsidy and the tax-rate was higher.

62. Honan 1998, 322; Michael Foster, 'Thomas Morley' (*ODNB* 2004).

63. On Maunder as Messenger of the Chamber see Nicholl 2002, 53–4, 206. Henry Maunder of St Helen's was alive in 1603, when a man is described as his servant (*Registers of St Helen's, Bishopsgate*, Harleian Society 31 (1904), 260), but was probably dead by 1608 when 'Isabell Maunder, widow' was buried (ibid., 271). 'Anne Maunder al[ia]s Bedwell', a godmother in 1612 (ibid., 418), is probably his married daughter.

64. Ibid., 260; Scouloudi 1985, 182.

65. PRO E372/444 (Residuum London, 6 October 1599) and 445 (Residuum Sussex, 6 October 1600).

66. Shakespeare is called 'honey-tongued' by both Francis Meres (*Palladis Tamia*, 1598) and John Weever ('Ad Gulielmum Shakespeare' in *Epigrammes*, 1599, 4.22). 'O sweet Master Shakespeare', spoken by a foppish fan, Gullio, in anon, *Returne to Parnassus* pt 1 (*c*. 1599), 3.1.1054–5. Manningham: see Part Six, note 46 below.

67. HMC Salisbury 3.148; EKC 2.332; Elizabeth Allen, 'Sir Walter Cope' (*ODNB* 2004).

PART TWO: *SILVER STREET*

5. The house on the corner

1. For the 'Agas' map see Prockter and Taylor 1979. 'Muddled truth': Peter Campbell, 'In Russell Square', *LRB* 28, 30 November 2006; cf. H. G. Wells on London as a 'stupendous' city formed of 'incidental and multitudinous littleness' (*The New Machiavelli*, 1911).

2. Byrne 1925, 55–8. On Islington: Nashe 1958, 2.224, 4.262.

3. Wood 2003, 267, but with no source. I cannot find it in P. Jones and T. Reddaway, *Surveys of Building Sites in the City of London after the Great Fire* (3 vols, London Topographical Society Publications 97–9, 1962–6), though the work is only partly indexed. There is a corner house with an 18-foot frontage on Silver Street (1.112), but it is on the corner with

Wood Street. The surveys indicate pre-Fire property boundaries, and do not necessarily refer to individual houses. A frontage of 63 feet would suggest a substantial house, similar to the known measurements of nearby Dudley Court (note 13 below). The stretch of Silver Street between Wood Street and Monkwell Street was about 75 metres (228 feet) long (Howe and Lakin 2004, Fig. 68).

4. In 1850, the Coopers' Arms is listed as one of seventeen public houses in Cripplegate Ward Within (Baddeley 1921, 213–14). The property was leased, somewhat ironically, from the United Kingdom Temperance and General Provident Institution, which in turn leased it from New College, Oxford (Wallace 1910a, 506). In the Silver Street ratebooks for 1890 every building but one is a warehouse (Baddeley 1921, 77–8): the exception, rated at £38, is presumably the Coopers' Arms, though it is described as a 'dwelling house'. The Coopers' Company had their livery hall not far away, between Aldermanbury and Basinghall Street.

5. Stow 1908, 1.299, 2.344.

6. William Maitland, *History of London* (1753–6), 2.905–6.

7. On Greene's lodgings see Gabriel Harvey, *Four Letters* (1592), in *Works*, ed. A. B. Grosart (1884), 1.170–3; his landlady, a Mrs Isam, was said to be a 'big fatte lusty wench' with an 'arme like an Amazon' (Nashe 1958, 1.289). Jonson: Aubrey 1949, 178; this is not the Elephant and Castle south of the river, but one 'outside Temple Bar'. Roydon's address is given in a Star Chamber deposition of 1593 (see note 27 below). Nashe refers to his lodgings in *Have with you to Saffron Walden* (1596): 'all the time I have lyne in her [Mrs Danter's] house' (Nashe 1958, 3.114–15; Nicholl 1984, 224–6).

8. Weaver adds that from these two properties Mountjoy 'receiveth some eighteen pounds per annum de claro besides his own dwelling'; this is corroborated by Noel Mountjoy, who says Mountjoy 'gaineth an over-plus of rent more than he payeth to the value of about nineteen or seventeen pounds per annum'. Thus Mountjoy sub-let part of the Silver Street property and the whole of the Brentford property for a combined total of about £35 per annum, resulting in a net profit ('de claro') of about £18 per annum.

9. Stow 1908, 1.208, citing a 'presentment' listing 150 'households of strangers' in Billingsgate ward. His comment is formulaic: cf. the 'Complaynt' of London citizens, 1571: 'the merchant straungers take upp the fairest houses in the citty, devide & fitt them for their severall uses, take into them several lodgers & dwellers' (PRO SP12/81/29; Tawney and Power 1924, 1.308–10).

10. Janet S. Loengard, ed., *London Viewers and their Certificates, 1508–*

1558 (London Record Society, 1989), No. 207, 1 April 1547. The 'viewers' were a group of four men commissioned to adjudicate property disputes in the city.

11. Harington 1927, 86–7.

12. Orlin 2000b, 350–51.

13. GL MS 12805, Evidence Book 7; Schofield 1987, 112–13.

14. On Jacobean privies, see Schofield 1987, 22–4; Symonds 1952, 86–9. Schofield distinguishes the privy, 'a small chamber with structural connections to below-ground cesspits', from 'temporary partitions, close-stools or other non-structural and more mobile arrangements'. They were often set into an upstairs chimney, with the updraught of the flue acting as a ventilator, though Harington notes that an 'unruly' wind will instead 'force the il ayres down the chimneis' and into the lower rooms. Nashe frequently refers to the printed page ending up in the privy. The full title of *Strange Newes* (1592), one of his pamphlets against Dr Harvey, reads: *Strange Newes of the Intercepting Certaine Letters and a Convoy of Verses* [Harvey's recently published *Four Letters*] *as they were going privilie to victuall the Low Countries* (i.e. to be used as toilet paper).

6. The neighbourhood

15. Windsor House: Stow 1908, 1.312, 315, 2.344; Milne and Cohen 2001, 40–9. Entries in the St Olave's parish register (GL MS 6534) are indexed in Webb 1995, vol. 6, and transcribed (up to 1625) by Alan Nelson (GL MS 52/77/3, typescript, 2000). Alice Blague: Rowse 1976, 139. Sir David Fowles's ownership of Windsor House is inferred from the parish register, 9 February 1607 (Webb 1995, 4.541, but misread as 'Fowler'): 'Henry son of David Fowles, knight, baptized at the house of the said David'. All other home baptisms recorded in the register refer to Windsor House. On Fowles or Foulis, a Scottish favourite of King James, see Fiona Pogson, 'Sir David Foulis' (*ODNB* 2004).

16. Milne and Cohen 2001, 45, and figs 47–50, 56–62.

17. H. Harben, *A Dictionary of London* (1918), s.v. Olave; Milne and Cohen 2001, 126. It was from medieval times the guild-church of the Silversmiths' Company (G. Huelin, *Vanished Churches of the City of London* (Guildhall Library, 1966), 22).

18. Stow 1908, 1.306; Baddeley 1921, 43.

19. GL MS 6534, fol. 1v. Flint's transcript covers the years 1561–93; the entries continue thereafter in his hand till 1609, when the new incumbent,

Thomas Booth, took over. Flint matriculated at Cambridge as a 'gentleman pensioner' in March 1583, proceeded BA 1587 and MA 1590 (Venn 1922–7, 1.2, 51).

20. Diary fol. 15–15v, February 1601; Sorlien 1976, 52–3.

21. On Barbers' Hall see Young 1890; http://www.barberscompany.org.uk. The earliest record of the Hall is from the 1480s; the current building was opened in 1969.

22. Andrew Griffin, 'John Banister' (*ODNB* 2004), and see note 42 below. He was buried at St Olave's on 16 January 1599 (Webb 1995, 4.684).

23. Norman Moore and Sarah Bakewell, 'Richard Palmer' (*ODNB* 2004). For his property on Monkwell Street see Schofield 1987, 97–9.

24. See Marcus Woodward, ed., *Gerard's Herball* (1985); Marja Smolenaars, 'John Gerard' (*ODNB* 2004).

25. See H. N. Ellacombe, *Plant-lore and Garden-craft in Shakespeare* (1878). Iago's appositions (hyssop/thyme; nettles/lettuce) accord with contemporary ideas of 'dry' and 'moist' plants being mutually beneficial. Shakespeare writes often of the therapeutic power of herbs: 'O mickle is the powerful grace that lies / In plants, herbs, stones, and their true qualities' (*Romeo and Juliet*, 2.2.15–16); 'Not poppy nor mandragora, / Nor all the drowsy syrups of the world / Shall ever medicine thee' (*Othello*, 3.3.334–6). And see Ophelia's famous catalogue, 'There's rosemary, that's for remembrance [etc]' (*Hamlet*, 4.5.175–83).

26. Hotson 1949, 125–7. After Savage's death in 1607 his son Richard sold the Silver Street house to Shakespeare's colleague John Heminges: see Eccles 1991–3, s.v. Heminges.

27. Henry Bannister appears in the 1599 rolls for Farringdon ward (PRO E179/146/390a, fol. 1), living either in the western part of St Olave's or in one of the three small adjoining parishes grouped with it for tax-collection purposes. I conjecture that he is the same as the goldsmith Henry Bannister, who is linked with Skeres in a loan to the poet Matthew Roydon (PRO Close Roll 1144/24, 6 January 1582; G. C. Moore-Smith, 'Matthew Roydon', *MLR* 9 (1914), 97–8). Wolfall and Skeres: PRO STAC 5, bundle S9/8, 26 April 1593; Nicholl 2002, 28–31, 467. Though 'of Silver Street' in 1593, Wolfall may be the 'Jhon Woolfall' whose children were baptized at nearby St Mary Aldermanbury in 1580–81 (*Registers*, ed. W. B. Bannerman (Harleian Society 61, 1931), 44–5).

28. Stow 1908, 1.299. We learn from Nicholas's will (PRO Prob 11/60, 31 May 1578) that Daniel Nicholas was a younger son. He stood to inherit certain 'messuages and tenements' on Bread Street in the event of his elder brother John dying without issue.

29. Jonson's second son, Joseph, was baptized at St Giles on 9 December

1599 (Riggs 1989, 54); Dekker is probably the Thomas Dicker or Dykers whose three daughters were baptized there between 1594 and 1602 (F. P. Wilson, 'Three Notes on Thomas Dekker', *MLR* 15 (1920), 82); on Wilkins in St Giles see Part Six above. Richard Hathaway, part-author of *Sir John Oldcastle* (1600), written for the Admiral's Men as a riposte to Shakespeare's *Henry IV*, is doubtless the 'Richard Hathway, Poett' who appears in the St Giles register in March 1601, and probably the 'scholemaster' and 'Master of Arts' of the same name who features earlier, though no record remains of his university career (MacManaway 1958, 562). On Edmund Shakespeare see EKC 2.18: 'Edward' is an erroneous repetition of his son's name ('Edward sonne of Edward Shackspeere'). He died aged twenty-seven, and was buried at St Saviour's, Southwark, on 31 December 1607, 'with a forenoone knell of the great bell' for which someone (by tradition his brother) paid 20 shillings.

30. Also at St Mary Aldermanbury lived the Digges family: the mathematician Thomas Digges had died in 1595, but Shakespeare knew his son Leonard, who later contributed a prefatory poem, 'To the Memorie of the deceased Authour, Maister W. Shakespeare', to the First Folio.

31. Nelson's literary works included a verse epitaph on Sir Francis Walsingham, and an account of the annual pageant of the Fishmongers' company (Eleri Larkum, 'Thomas Nelson', *ODNB* 2004). A later literary resident was the metaphysical poet Francis Quarles, buried at St Olave's 11 September 1644.

32. On Giffard see Foster 1891, 1.1, 563. He and Palmer treated the Prince with an infusion of *Teucrium scordium* (Sarah Bakewell, 'Richard Palmer', *ODNB* 2004). This plant (the water germander) 'was at one time esteemed as an antidote for poisons, and also as an antiseptic and anthelmintic' (Plants for a Future database, http://www.pfaf.org).

33. Schofield 1987, 135.

34. Baddeley 1921, 210–15. The last mail-coach left the Two Swans, bound for Dover, in 1844, and the inn was demolished in 1856 to be replaced by a depot for rail-freight.

35. John Taylor, *The Carriers Cosmographie*, sig. C2: 'The carriers of Worcester doe lodge at the Castle in Woodstreet, their dayes are Fridaies and Saturdaies.' For Evesham, sig. B2v. Stratford itself is not in Taylor's list.

36. On Greenaway see Shapiro 2005, 260–61. The letter he carried was from Richard Quiney, a Stratford man then in London, to Abraham Sturley, who refers to it in his reply of 4 November 1598 (EKC 2.103). Greenaway doubtless carried others in the correspondence, though not Quiney's earlier letter to Shakespeare (25 October 1598; Cooper 2006, no. 58) which is the

only item of Shakespeare's correspondence to survive: this was sent from Quiney's London lodgings, the Bell in Carter Lane, and did not leave London. The sum they wished to borrow from their 'loveinge contreyman' was £30.
37. Stow 1908, 1.206, 290, 2.311.
38. Ibid., 1.115, 2.285; Salgãdo 1977, 163–82. Wilkins 1607, 1177–9, describes accommodation at the Poultry Counter: 'the featherbed in the Maisters side . . . the flock-bed in the Knights warde . . . the straw-bed in the Hole'.
39. Nelson 2006, 63.

7. 'Houshould stuffe'

40. Milne and Cohen 2001, 1–8; Howe and Lakin 2004.
41. Howe and Lakin 2004, 95–8, and fig. 88 showing the location of the sites.
42. On the transmission of Paracelsian ideas into England see Nicholl 1980, 65–9. Among early advocates of the controversial 'chymicall physick' was the Silver Street surgeon John Banister (C. Webster, 'Alchemical and Paracelsian medicine', in Webster 1979, 327).

8. The chamber

43. 'T. M.', *The Blacke Booke* (1604), in Middleton 1886, 8.24–6.
44. Donne 1912, 1.11.
45. John Dickinson, *Greene in Conceipt*, 1598, t–p; Aubrey 1949, 178.
46. Francis Beaumont, 'To Mr B:J' (Ben Jonson), 15–21, first printed in EKC 2.224 from a MS in Pierpont Morgan Library, New York.
47. Frank Kermode, ed., *The Tempest* (Arden edn, 1954), 147–50; Baldwin 1944, 2.443–52. Middleton has a version of the Ovid passage, spoken by Hecate, in *The Witch*, c. 1616 (Middleton 1886, 5.443).
48. On Shakespeare's use of Harsnett see John Murphy, *Darkness and Devils: Exorcism and* King Lear (Athens, Ohio, 1984). Many of the devils' names come from the testimony of Sara Williams, a chambermaid in a Catholic household, whose supposed possession in 1586 was investigated by Harsnett (Murphy 1984, 182 ff).
49. Florio's connection with the play was first mooted by William Warburton, *Works of Shakespear*, 1747, 2.227–8, and explored by Frances Yates, *A Study of* Love's Labour's Lost (1936).
50. Montaigne 1603, 2.184, 195, 185. Taylor 1925 finds hundreds of

echoes in plays subsequent to 1603, though some are tenuous. See also Robert Ellrodt, 'Self-consciousness in Shakespeare and Montaigne', *Shakespeare Survey* 28 (1975), 37–50. Gonzalo's ideal commonwealth (*Tempest*, 2.1.143–64) is closely based on Montaigne's essay 'On Cannibals'. Hugh Grady, *Shakespeare, Machiavelli and Montaigne: Power and Subjectivity from* Richard II *to* Hamlet (Oxford, 2002) argues Montaigne's influence prior to the Florio translation, an influence certainly found in Francis Bacon's *Essays* (1597) and William Cornwallis's *Essays* (1600).

51. BL shelfmark C.21.e.17; SRI 102–4. Ben Jonson's copy of the book does survive, with an inscription dated 1604; it cost 7 shillings. Jonson also knew Florio, and inscribed a copy of *Volpone*, 'To his loving Father & worthy Freind Mr John Florio: the Ayde of his Muses, Ben: Jonson seales this testemony of Freindship & Love'. See David Mcpherson, 'Ben Jonson's Library and Marginalia', *Studies in Philology* 71 (1974), 72–3.

52. H. G. Wright, 'How Did Shakespeare Come to Know the *Decameron?*' (*MLR* 50 (1955), 45–8), argues his use of Maçon's version. See also Howard Cole, *The 'All's Well' Story from Boccaccio to Shakespeare* (Urbana, Ill., 1981).

53. Nashe's preface, 'To the Gentleman students', in Robert Greene, *Menaphon* (1589): Nashe 1958, 3.312. Thomas Lodge, *Wit's Miserie* (1596), sig. H4v: 'as pale as the vizard of the ghost which cried so miserably at the Theator, like an oister wife, Hamlet, revenge'. The 'revision' theory championed by Eric Sams (Sams 1995, 121–35, and 'Taboo or Not Taboo? The Text, Dating and Authorship of *Hamlet*, 1589–1623', *Hamlet Studies* 10, (1988), 12–46) is not generally accepted, though questions remain about 'memorial reconstruction' as the source of bad quartos: see Maurice Charney, ed., *'Bad' Shakespeare: Revaluations of the Shakespeare Canon* (Rutherford, NJ, 1988).

54. Thomas Heywood, *Apologie for Actors*, 1612; EKC 2.218.

55. Letter to William Drummond, 14 April 1619, referring to problems with the printing of the second part of *Poly-Olbion* (Anne Lake Prescott, 'Michael Drayton', *ODNB* 2004).

PART THREE: *THE MOUNTJOYS*

9. Early years

1. PRO C66/1750 (Patent Rolls 5 Jas I, Roll 30); Shaw 1911, 11.

2. Information provided by Frédérique Hamm, Director of the Archives Départementales de la Somme, Amiens.

3. Scouloudi 1985, 223–31, lists places of origin stated in the 1593 return, cross-referrable to her index of named individuals (147–221).

4. Bibliothèque Municipale, Amiens, MS HH 749; I am grateful to the archivist, Thomas Dumont, for this reference. Some vaguer genealogical trawling finds a Monguiot family living in Le Harcourt in 1612; a Pierre Montjoie at Aubervilliers in 1658; and several Montjoies in Namur, Belgium, in the eighteenth century.

5. W. Arthur, *Etymological Dictionary of Family and Christian Names* (New York, 1857), s.v. Mountjoy. He notes that the name 'is still retained in a division of the hundred of Battle, not far from the remains of the majestic pile reared by William the Conqueror'. War cry: T. Wylie, *The Reign of Henry V* (1914–29), 2.178.

6. Bod., Ashmole MS 226, fols 254v, 263v; see Chapter 12.

7. On Elizabethan marrying ages, see Ralph Houlbrooke, *The English Family, 1450–1700* (1984), 63ff.; Laurence Stone, *Crisis of the Aristocracy* (1965), 656–7. Shakespeare's Juliet is fourteen, and her father thinks 'two more summers' should pass before she is 'ripe to be a bride' (*Romeo and Juliet*, 1.2.9–11); cf. Bruce Young, 'Haste, Consent, and Age at Marriage: Some Implications of Social History for *Romeo and Juliet*', *Iowa State Journal of Research* 62 (1987), 459–74. In Samuel Rowlands's *'Tis merry when gossips meet* (1602) a fifteen-year-old 'mayde' is urged to marry: 'Your mother is to blame / To wish so womanly a wench to stay. / She knows fifteene may husband justlie clame' (sig. D3). Rebecca Edwards was fourteen when she married the actor William Knell, and a widow at fifteen; she subsequently married John Heminges, and was a long-term acquaintance of Shakespeare. The average marriage age was, of course, much higher. Houlbrooke gives twenty-six as the mean age for Elizabethan women, twenty-eight for men; the figures were similar across western Europe.

8. In his deposition of 1612 Noel gives his age as 'thirty years or thereabouts'.

10. St Martin le Grand

9. The origin of 'Huguenot' is debated: an early form, 'eiguenot', found in the *Chronique de Genève* (1550), suggests a derivation from German *Eidgenosz*, 'confederate'.

10. Alfred Sornan, ed., *The Massacre of St Bartholomew: Reappraisals and Documents* (1974); Leonie Frieda, *Catherine de Medici* (2003), 248–72. Among those sheltered at the English embassy were Sir Philip Sidney and Timothy Bright; the latter relived their experience, 'which my mind shudders to recall and flees from in grief', in a letter to Sidney in 1584 (Alan Stewart, *Sir Philip Sidney* (2000), 86–8).

11. Henry Gaymer of Rye is thus described, when in 1586 he detained the assassin of the Queen of Navarre, René or Renato, trying to enter the country (BL Lansdowne MS 48, no. 70).

12. Nashe 1958, 3.158.

13. Scouloudi 1985, 80, 129. On Huguenots in London see also Scouloudi 1987; Yungblut 1996; Picard 2003, 123–37.

14. Stow 1908, 1.308, 2.342–3.

15. PRO E179/251/16, fols 23–4.

16. Kirk 1910, 2.338, 410; Scouloudi 1985, 173. Harman Dewman, tailor, also living in St Anne's in 1582, is probably a brother.

17. Hatfield House, Cecil MS 208/8; Kirk 1910, 2.349–50.

18. Lang 1993, xlii–li.

19. Stow 1908, 1.307.

20. PRO E179/146/390; Kirk 1910, 2.244.

21. Foster 1887, 951.

22. GL MS 4515/1; PRO E179/147/494.

23. St Dunstan's marriage register (LMA Mf X024/068), 1 May 1627. Later Mountjoys in Stepney are recorded in IGI.

24. On the French Church see Beeman 1905; Lindeboom 1950, 7ff. It remained on Threadneedle Street until 1840. The current church at Soho Square, designed by Aston Webb in 'late Franco-Flemish Gothic with Romanesque overtones' (N. Pevsner, *London* (1952), 6.394), opened in 1893.

25. Picard 2003, 128.

26. Scouloudi 1985, 81, 233–7.

11. Success and danger

27. Scouloudi 1985, 196–7, 209. She considers Daniel Morrell and Samuel Morrell (listed one after the other in the 1593 return, with identical attributes) to be the same man erroneously duplicated. He had come to England in *c.* 1584; in 1593 he had no servants or apprentices. Swanston's was a larger operation, employing five 'stranger women' and five English workers.
28. PRO SP12/81/29; Tawney and Power 1924, 1.308–10.
29. For the statutory restrictions invoked by the petitioners, see Scouloudi 1985, 49–50. For attempts to encourage immigrants in trades not practised by locals (e.g. silk-working) see Luu 2005.
30. Richard Verstegan to Robert Persons, 27 [i.e. 17] May 1593; Petti 1959, 155. Verstegan uses continental dating ('stilo novo'), ten days later than English reckoning.
31. Strype 1824, 4.167. 'Vyle ticket': Privy Council directive to Mayor of London, 16 April 1593 (Dasent 1890–97, 24.187).
32. Arthur Freeman, 'Marlowe, Kyd and the Dutch Church Libel', *English Literary Renaissance* 3 (1973), 44–52; Nicholl 2002, 47–53, 347–52. The full text of the libel, in a copy of *c.* 1600, was discovered in 1971 among the 'residual' MSS of the nineteenth-century collector Sir Thomas Phillips.
33. Petti 1959, 155, 163. Verstegan's unnamed correspondent in England was probably the Jesuit Henry Garnet.
34. Scouloudi 1985, 73–80; Strype 1824, 4, no. 107. Detailed returns survive in a MS owned by the Dugdale family (Merevale Hall, Warwickshire): it is damaged from being used as scrap-paper by Sir William Dugdale when compiling his *Antiquities of Warwickshire* (1656). Extracts and summaries of the census are in Huntington Library, Ellesmere MS 2514, and BL Lansdowne MS 74/31.
35. BL Egerton MS 2804, fol. 90; Jeayes 1906, 77–8. The letter is addressed to Gawdy's elder brother Bassingbourne.
36. GL MS 6534, fol. 106.
37. In the burial register the other three are: '—— Seamer, child of Joan Seamer' (24 September 1593); 'an infant murdered by the mother, a servant to J. Sayers' (14 November 1599); '—— Pierte, infant of Elizabeth, in Jonas Scot's house, imputed to the E of Desmond' (11 May 1602). In the baptismal register (where the naming of the parent is only standard from 1600 onwards) the five entries are: 'Lawrence Morrise, son of Olive by one Laurence Williams in Coleman Street' (22 April 1604); 'Sarah Hely, daughter of Ann, widow, illegitimate' (3 October 1604); 'Judith Gardner, daughter of Elizabeth or as was said one William Gardner in J. Gates's house' (19 June

1605); 'Thomasine Gaber, daughter of Elizabeth with Mr Buckle' (10 January 1605); 'Jane Basket daughter of Jane, sojourner with Nicholas Terrell' (30 March 1606).

12. Dr Forman's casebook

38. Bod., Ashmole MS 226, fol. 254r. I read the date of the incident as 10 September (rather than the 16th, as read by Rowse and repeated by others). Forman's zero has an embryonic upstroke where the pen completes the circle; his actual '6' is much more pronounced. On Forman see Kassell 2005, Traister 2000 and (more generically) Melton 1620.

39. Bod., Ashmole MS 411, fols 101–2. Other charges were 2s for a 'purge', 3s for a 'comfortable drink', 5s for a call-out, and 20 nobles (£6 13s 4d) for a regime ('the Diet') lasting twenty-four days. Payment was sometimes dependent on results: in 1601 a patient agreed to pay £6 down and the same again when cured, but 'if she be not well at all I must give her £5 again' (Rowse 1976, 215).

40. W. Lilly, *History of his Life and Times* (1715), 16; Nashe 1958, 3.83. Nashe's satirical portrait of the cunning-man in *Terrors of the Night* (1594) is in part suggestive of Forman: see Nashe 1958, 1.363–7; Nicholl 1984, 197–200.

41. The story in Manningham's diary (June 1602; Sorlien 1976, 77) was from 'Ch Da', i.e. Charles Danvers, a Wiltshire gentleman almost certainly acquainted with Forman. His father had intervened on Forman's behalf in 1586: 'The Bishop [of Salisbury] and I were made friends by . . . Sir John Danvers' (Rowse 1976, 47). On Savory see Eccles 1991–3, s.v.

42. Foakes 2002, 39 (Diary, fol. 17); Cerasano 1993, 150–53. Henslowe consulted Forman on 6 August 1596 (Bod., Ashmole MS 234, fol. 85), and again on 5 February 1597 (Ashmole MS 226, fol. 13v), suffering from 'pain in the reins [kidneys]' and 'water in the stomach', for which he was pre-scribed a purgative. Forman had other theatre people in his clientele, and was a keen playgoer. His 'Bock of plaies' (Ashmole MS 208, fols 200–213; SRI 3–20) describes productions of *Macbeth*, *Cymbeline* and *The Winter's Tale* seen at the Globe in 1611; he also saw a *Richard II* but it does not seem to be Shakespeare's version.

43. The six extant casebooks provide a continuous record from March 1596 to November 1601. Statistical analysis of the first two (Kassell 2005, 129–30) shows 2,760 consultations, of which 60 per cent were by women.

44. Bod., Ashmole MS 802, fol. 133; Kassell 2005, 98.

45. Jonathan Bate, *Daily Telegraph*, 10 February 2001; John Bossy,

'Haleking', *LRB* 23, 22 February 2006. Kassell (2005, 130–1) counts fifty-six records of sexual intercourse in Forman's papers. A similar overtone of predation is found in the case of a surgeon, Tristram Lyde: 'He would have caused the women to have stript themselves naked in his presence, and himselfe would have annoynted them [with quicksilver]' (Manningham's diary, February 1601; Sorlien 1976, 53). In 1599, aged forty-seven, Forman married the sixteen-year-old Anne Baker, whom he refers to in sexual notes as 'Tronco'.

46. These errors (Rowse 1973, 106) were pointed out by Stanley Wells (*TLS* 11 May 1973) and silently revised in later editions.

47. Bod., Ashmole MS 226, fol. 278v. Variant forenames: see Mary Edmond, 'John Heminges', *ODNB* 2004; Rowse 1976, 306. Thomas Middleton's wife Magdalen *née* Marbeck, is also sometimes documented as Mary.

48. E.g. 'Joan, servant of Mr Borace of Radcliffe', who was pregnant by him when she consulted Forman in 1598, and feared he was trying to poison or bewitch her 'that she should die' (Bod., Ashmole MS 195; Rowse 1976, 213). Margery Browne's husband was Christopher Laughlin of St Botolph's, Aldersgate (Webb 1995, 4.644).

49. Schoenbaum erroneously names her as Michelle Art (SRI 39). The entry relating to her and Mountjoy (FPC MS 4, fol. 501) refers to 'Michel Art son ancien'. He was the church elder responsible for Mountjoy, and it was his evidence which led to Mountjoy being 'censured'. See Appendix 3.

50. Bod., Ashmole MS 226, 17 May 1597, reproduced in Rowse 1973.

51. The widow of the 1st Lord Hunsdon, Lady Anne, was still alive, but Forman would have distinguished her as the 'old' Lady Hunsdon (as her husband is 'my old Lord' in the reference above). On Elizabeth Carey, see Wallace T. MacCaffrey, 'Henry Carey, 1st Baron Hunsdon', *ODNB* 2004; Nicholl 1984, 182–4. Nashe calls her an 'excellent accomplisht court-glorifying lady'; Dowland's tune, 'My Lady Hunsdon's Puffe', was written for her. Forman himself had been patronized by Carey: 'the 22nd of December [1587] I rode to Sir George Carey's' (Rowse 1976, 289). On the intellectual ambience of the family see Katherine Duncan-Jones, 'Bess Carey's Petrarch' (*RES* 50 (1990), 304–19), 'Bess' being the Hunsdons' daughter Elizabeth, later Lady Berkeley.

52. Hotson 1931, 111–22; H. J. Oliver, ed., *Merry Wives* (Arden edn, 1971), xliv–lii. The plausible but undocumented tradition that the play was a royal command is first mentioned in the preface to John Dennis's adaptation, *The Comical Gallant* (1702). That Shakespeare wrote it fast is also plausible, though Dennis's 'fourteen days' is surely an exaggeration.

53. PRO PROB 11/102, 10 May 1599. 'Teesye' is probably a diminutive of Prothesia.

54. William Huffman, *Robert Fludd and the End of the Renaissance* (1988), 4–8; Rowse 1976, 29–30, 251–2.

55. Bod., Ashmole MS 226, fol. 263v.

56. *Laura*, sigs A4v, D1; *Alba*, sig. E3v. On the life and writings of Tofte (1562–1620) see A. B. Grosart's edn of *Alba* (1880); Williams 1937; L. G. Kelly, 'Robert Tofte' (*ODNB* 2004). I am very grateful to Matt Steggle for alerting me to the possibilities explored here.

57. *Love's Labours* was written earlier (perhaps *c.* 1593–4: see Chapter 18), but the 1598 quarto is described as 'newly corrected and augmented'. The play was performed before the Queen during Christmas 1597–8, but there is nothing to suggest that Tofte moved in courtly circles, or that the performance remembered or imagined in *Alba* was a royal one. There are Carrells in the subsidy rolls, any (or none) of which might be connected with Ellen. One is the seriously wealthy Edward Carrell, esq, who is assessed on £200 in lands and fees in 1599 (PRO E179/146/393, fol. 6). He lived near the Mountjoys at St Botolph's, Aldersgate.

58. The book was seen and described by the Tofte expert Franklin Williams in the 1930s. Though it has marginalia in his hand, and the cropped remains of his signature, an inscription on the title-page shows that in 1597 the book was given by Lady Margaret Radcliff to Sir George Buc, the future Master of the Revels; it is not known whether Tofte owned it before or after this, so his praise of 'Marie M—' cannot be dated (Williams 1937, 296). Tofte lived in the parish of St Andrew's, Holborn; his landlady, whom he mentions in *The Blazon of Jealousie* (1615), was the wife of a barber-surgeon, Thomas Goodall.

59. Bod., Ashmole MS 195, fol. 8.

60. Ibid., fols 16, 24. It is hard to tell if the final mark in the name is an *s* or an oblique punctuation. 'Gui d' Asture' was exorcized by R. E. Alton (*NQ* 223 (1978), 456–7).

61. Scouloudi 1985, 160.

62. Bod., Ashmole MS 195, fol. 15v.

63. Bod., Ashmole MS 226, fol. 258; Rowse 1976, 192; PRO E179/146/325, fol. 2.

64. Bod., Ashmole MS 226, fol. 310v.

65. 'Alained': Rowse 1976, 109. The initial letter, unconnected to the others, is too blotted to read with any certainty, but compare the poorly formed *o* of 'yellow' in the line below. The tall ungainly upstroke which follows is not Forman's usual *l* (which has a pronounced rightward curve, somewhat like a modern capital C), but there is a parallel formation on the same page ('lefte' in the top line of the second piece of writing), and also in the *l* of 'glob[e]' in Forman's report of a performance of *Richard II* (see note 42

above). The fifth letter could be *n*, as Rowse reads it, but Forman's *n*, invariably open at the top, is identical with his *u* (see the juxtaposed *u* and *n* of 'Mountioy'), and in the orthographic convention of the time *u* and *v* are the same, so it could as well be a *v*. The last letter is not a *d*. Forman uses an Italic-type *d* with a pronounced looping curve. In my view it is a poorly formed secretary *e*, paralleled by the equally loose *e* of 'dore' a couple of lines above. The formation is echoed at the end of 'Madam' in the line below, but there it is a gratuitous upstroke after the final *m*. I have wondered if the word is 'olavum' (referring to the Latin name of the parish, 'Sanctus Olavus') but 'olaive' is the more likely reading.

66. Joy Rowe, 'Kitson family', *ODNB* 2004; Hearn 1995, nos 53–4; John Gage, *History and Antiquities of Hengrave* (1822), 175–85. A spirited glimpse of Lady Kitson is in a letter of Philip Gawdy, *c.* 1594: 'My L. Kytson is well recovered & in token of thankesgyving danced all this last night as long as she was able to go' (Jeayes 1906, 79–80). Two of her cousins were frequent visitors to Forman in the late 1590s: Anne Brock *née* Jerningham, who was the niece and namesake of Lady Kitson's mother; and Anne's daughter, Alice Blague, wife of the Dean of Rochester. Mrs Blague was a particular confidante, and for a while the lover, of Forman. She recruited clients for him, including, in 1601, Lady Kitson's father, Sir Thomas Cornwallis. Among her friends at court were Lord Hunsdon's sisters, Lady Hoby and Lady Scrope, and she doubtless knew Lady Hunsdon as well. She visited Forman at least twice in January 1598, the probable date of Forman's memo concerning 'Madam Kitson'.

67. New Year's Gift Roll 1578, in Nichols 1823, 2.68.

68. *The Blacke Booke* (1604), Middleton 1886, 8.37. 'Flaxen hayr to sell': George Gray, news-sheet advertisement, 4 February 1663, cited in *OED* s.v. periwig 3.

13. The ménage

69. Registers of St Giles, Cripplegate (GL MS 6419/2), 5 April 1612: baptism of 'Martha daughter of John Blott, tiremaker'. In his will of 3 October 1642 he left Stephen 900 guilders to be paid after the death of his widow, Maijlie.

70. Webb 1995, 4.684, 644.

71. Ibid., 4.646. Her husband may be the Scottish basketmaker Thomas 'Johnsonne', a native of Moffat, who came to London in about 1590, and was living in the Castle Baynard district of the city in 1593 (Scouloudi 1985, 186). If this is the same man he was a widower when he married

Joan, for in 1593 he had a wife, Isabel. But the name is extremely common.
72. PRO E179/146/390, fol. 32 (1599); E179/146/409, fol. 3 (1600) On his nominal assets of £5 he has to pay tax of 26s 8d: the double tax-rate for foreigners in Shakespeare's London.
73. Mountjoy as godfather. FPC, Marriage Register 1600–39, fol. 43; Moens 1896, 48. Clinkolad: Scouloudi 1985, 160. Courtois: Whitebrook 1932, 93.
74. Mountjoy's denization: see note 1 above. For denization figures see Scouloudi 1985, 5; Shaw 1911.
75. W. Bruce Bannerman, ed., *Registers of St Olave, Hart Street 1563–1700*, Harleian Society Registers 46 (1916), 260.
76. See Appendix 4.

PART FOUR: *TIREMAKING*
14. Tires and wigs

1. The tireman of the Globe, unnamed, is humorously presented onstage in the prologue written by John Webster for Marston's *The Malcontent* (1604). More generally *OED* gives 'tireman' = a dresser or valet, or a tailor; and 'tirewoman' = a lady's maid, or a dress-maker or costumier. The tiring-house is shown (marked 'mimorum aedes') in the De Witt sketch of the Swan theatre (1596); it was also used for backstage effects: 'drummers make thunder in the tiring house' (Melton 1620, sig. E4r), referring to a production of *Dr Faustus*.
2. The French courtly head-tire in turn echoed Renaissance Italian costume for *feste* and pageants, on which see Newton 1975. The influence is discernible in Vecellio 1598, a handbook of French and Italian costume written by the brother of the painter Titian. Extravagant tires designed by Inigo Jones for the *Masque of Queenes* (1610) were adapted from René Boyvin's engravings of head-dress designs by Rosso Fiorentino for court festivals at Fontainebleau in the 1530s (Peacock 1984; Hearn 1995, 161).
3. Ben Jonson, *Cynthia's Revels* (1601), 2.4.51–61. Phantaste's new head-tire is also based on continental models: ''Tis after the Italian print we look'd on t'other night.' See also Jonson's *Alchemist* (1610): one of the 'pleasures of a countess' is to have 'citizens gape at her and praise her tires' (4.2.50–51). Those tires could be robes, however.
4. 'Tyre of gold': Edmund Spenser, *Faerie Queene* (1590), 1.10.32. 'Tyer of netting': Michael Drayton, *Muses Elisium* (1630), 2.113. 'Ship tire': Jorge de Montemayor, *Diana*, trans. Bartholomew Yong (1598), in Hotson 1949,

178. 'Mourning tire': will of 1639 in *Wills and Inventories of Bury St Edmunds 1470–1650* (Camden Society, 1850), 183. 'Turkish tires': John Hall, *Paradoxes* (1650), 67. 'Squirrels' tails': John Marston, *Histriomastix* (1599), 2.117. In Jonson's *Everyman in his Humour* (1598), 3.2.37–8, Kitely's decree that his wife 'shall no more / Wear three-pil'd acorns to make my horns ache [cuckold him]' certainly refers to headgear and perhaps to a head-tire.

5. George Chapman, *A Justification of a Strange Act of Nero* (1629), in M. R. Ridley, ed., *Antony and Cleopatra* (Arden edn, 1954), 67n.

6. John Stow, *Annales*, ed. E. Howe (1631), 1038; Stow's spelling 'perwig' is also found in *Hamlet* Q1. Joseph Hall has 'th' unruly winde blowes off his periwinke' (*Satires*, 1598, 3.5 line 8). For other spellings see *OED*, s.v. periwig. Philemon Holland uses 'perrucke' in his translation of Suetonius (*Historie of Twelve Caesars*, 1606); his marginal explanation ('a counterfeit cappe of false hair') suggests the word was still unfamiliar.

7. On hair-cauls ('nets made of knotted human hair') see Arnold 1988, 204. One decorated with pearls is visible in a portrait of Queen Elizabeth (Pollok House, Glasgow, *c.* 1590; Arnold 1988, figs 46, 296). Her hoodmaker, Margaret Sketts or Schetz, supplied these items. The tiremaker would also use 'rolls': tightly packed hair held together inside nets, used to bolster up the natural hair.

8. I am grateful to Susan North, Curator of seventeenth- and eighteenth-century fashion at the Victoria and Albert Museum, London, for information in this paragraph and elsewhere.

9. In the 'Armada' portrait (1588) she wears a 'halo of pearls' surrounding a 'bodkin topped with feathers and a diamond fleur de lys' (Scarisbrick 1995, 15). See also head-tires in portraits of Mary Fitton (*c.* 1585, Arbury Hall); Princess Elizabeth (Robert Peake, 1603, National Maritime Museum); and the Countess of Arundel (Daniel Mytens, *c.* 1618, NPG).

10. Maids of Honour: Arnold 1988, 202. The same document records one of the Maids, Dorothy Abington, receiving lengths of black and orange sarcenet 'to lyne cawles'. Mountague's payment: BL Egerton 2806, fol. 216, 27 September 1586.

11. Norris 1938, 2.609. The German traveller Leopold von Wedel, who saw her at Hampton Court in 1585, writes: 'on either side of her crisp hair hung a great pearl as large as a hazel-nut' (Klarwill 1928, 322–3). This 'crisp' or curled hair was a wig. An earlier report (Pierre Ronsard, *Le Boccage royal*, 1567) refers to her 'longues tresses blondes', but these may have been her own tresses.

12. PRO LC5/36, fols 212–13, 6 June 1592; LC5/37, fol. 90, 29 April 1595. Cf. LC5/37, fols 222, 257, 288. The 'heads of hair' are distinct from

periwigs; they were conveniently sheaved bundles of hair to be used for making hair-cauls, hair-lace, etc.

13. Mary wore wigs twenty years earlier, as witnessed by Sir Francis Knollys: 'Mystres Marye Ceaton [Seaton], who is . . . the fynest dresser of a woman's heade and heare that is to be seen in any countrye . . . did sett sotche a curled heare upon the Queen [Mary] that was said to be a perewycke that shoed very delicately' (letter to Sir William Cecil, 28 June 1568, BL Stowe MS 560, fol. 24v). Knollys seems to have been particularly taken with this, for early the following year Nicholas White wrote of Mary: 'Her hair of itself is black, and yet Mr Knollys told me that she wears hair of sundry colours' (Norris 1938, 3.2.515–16).

14. Marie's payment: see Part One, note 24. Weaver had already known the Mountjoys for some time (since c. 1596 according to his Court of Requests deposition). On the Sheppards see Chapter 26.

15. The headwear shown by Van Somer (NPG) is 'an attire of royal pear-shaped pearls standing up at the back of her head on a wire covered with red ribbon', set off by a large 'table-cut diamond bodkin in the centre of her head, with pear-pearl and ruby drops hanging from it, and a tuft of feathers behind' (Scarisbrick 1995, 21, 67).

16. Erondell 1605, sigs E1v–E3v.

17. The carcanet, often a collar or necklace, is here a head-ornament (cf. Cotgrave 1611, s.v. fermaillet: 'a carkanet or border of gold etc such as Gentlewomen wear about their heads'). Erondell's last dialogue, 'Of the going to bed', has more on Madame de Rimelaine's headwear: a 'white hayre-lace to binde my haires', a 'white fillet [hair-band] for to raise up my haires', a 'little linnen coyffe', and an under-cap.

18. In modern French atour is used mainly in the plural, and with a jocular note: a woman dans ses atours = dressed up in her finery.

19. Byrne 1930, xiii–xv; J. Maclean, Lives of the Berkeleys (1883).

20. Christs Teares, sigs S3–S4v; Nashe 1958, 2.137–40. 'Frounzed' = frizzed, curled (OED 'frounce', sense 2). 'Streetwalkers': Robert Greene, A Notable discovery of cozenage (1591), in Salgādo 1972, 180.

21. Bod., Ashmole MS 208, fol. 121v, c. 1593; Kassell 2005, 160.

22. Microcynicon, 1599, Satire 3; Middleton 1886, 8.123–7. He refers again to hair-extensions in A Mad World, my Masters (c. 1605), where women who 'wear half-moons made of another's hair' are said to be 'against kind' (i.e. unnatural).

23. Statens Museum for Kunst, Copenhagen; Hearn 1995, no. 78 (cat. entry by Tabitha Barber); Strong 1983, 155–7.

24. CSP Venetian 1617–19, 67–8.

25. Satyres and Satyricall Epigrams, with certain Observations at

Blackfryers (1617), sig E8v; Gurr 1987, 231. However, the 'tittle' may be a small hat, or even (as Matthew Steggle suggests to me) a beauty spot. Wearing expensive headgear to the theatre had its dangers, as in Sir John Harington's vivid anecdote (*c.* 1595) in which two muggers try to snatch a jewelled 'border' off a woman's head as she walks up the 'dark and private' playhouse stairs (*Letters and Epigrams*, ed. Norman McLure (1930), 245–6; Gurr 1987, 210).

15. The 'tire-valiant'

26. Chambers 1923, 1.372. On the costs and logistics of theatrical costuming see also Cerasano 1994; Bentley 1984; Carson 1988, 35.

27. Two inventories of Admiral's Men costumes survive: one dated 10 March 1598, transcribed from a lost original by Edmund Malone in his 1790 edn of Shakespeare (Wells 2006, 234–6); and one *c.* 1602 (Dulwich College MS1/90; Cooper 2006, no. 35).

28. Longleat House, Wilts., Portland Papers 1, fol. 159. The folio, which also contains an elegantly scripted excerpt from the play, is signed 'Henricus Peacham'; the date, in abbreviated Latin, may be 1594 or 1595. *Titus* was in repertoire at the Rose, performed by Sussex's Men, in the winter of 1593–4. Peacham, later the author of *The Art of Drawing* (1606) and *The Compleat Gentleman* (1623), was then a sixteen-year-old student at Cambridge. The costuming implications of the sketch are discussed in Cerasano 1994. See also June Schlueter, 'Rereading the Peacham Drawing', *SQ* 50 (1999), 171–84, though her central thesis (that the sketch is not of Shakespeare's play, but of a scene from the anonymous *Tragaedia von Tito Andronico*, performed in Germany by English actors, and known only in a German translation published in 1620) may struggle for acceptance.

29. Platter 1937, 166–95; Wotton to Edmund Bacon, 2 July 1613, in L. Pearsall Smith, ed., *Life and Letters of Henry Wotton* (1907), 2.32.

30. Stallybrass 1996, 295.

31. *The Blacke Booke* (1604), in Middleton 1886, 8.13; Melton 1620, sig. E4r. For a general survey of headgear worn onstage see Linthicum 1936, 216–37.

32. The author is sometimes identified as William Parrat. Two ballads on the burning of the Globe were registered the day after the fire (SR 26 July 1613; Arber 1875–94, 3.528), one of them by Parrat, but it does not have the same title as this one, which was first published in 1816 (*Gentleman's Magazine* 86, 114) from a MS found in York. See Chambers 1923, 2.420; Peter Beale, 'The Burning of the Globe', *TLS* 20 June 1986. On Heminges's managerial role, see Mary Edmond, 'John Heminges' (*ODNB* 2004).

33. See note 27 above.

34. Foakes 2002, 185, 198 (Diary, fols 95v, 104). William Gosson of St Olave's, Southwark, is listed in subsidy rolls from 1593 (PRO E179/146/ 349 etc); he may or may not be Stephen Gosson's brother of that name, later described as 'gentleman and drum-major to James I'. Another possible husband for Mrs Gosen is Lianard Gawson, a Polish tailor from Danzig (Gdansk) listed in the 1593 return (Scouloudi 1985, 178), though he was at that point unmarried.

35. Foakes 2002, 221 (Diary, fol. 118v).

36. The story of Proteus and Julia in *Two Gentlemen of Verona* (*c.* 1590) suggests Shakespeare's knowledge of *Diana*. It was translated from the Spanish by Bartholomew Yong in the early 1580s; possibly Shakespeare knew this translation in MS, as it was not published till 1598.

37. *Merry Wives* (1602), sig. D4v: 'The arched bent of thy brow / Would become the ship tire, the tire vellet, / Or anie Venetian tire.' On the Quarto text see Gerald Johnson, '*The Merry Wives of Windsor* Q1: Provincial Touring and Adapted Texts' (*SQ* 38 (1987), 154–65). 'Tire-volant': see Steevens's edn of Shakespeare (1793), vol. 3.

38. Feuillerat 1908, 241; Korda 2002, 212–14. Also in the 1573–4 accounts are an 'Italian woman' and her daughter, paid £1 13s 4d for 'hier of womens heares for the Children', and for attending the Children 'to dresse their heades'; and a 'Mistris Swegoo', who also sounds foreign, paid to 'garnishe ix heades . . . for the ix Muzes' (Feuillerat 1908, 219, 156).

39. Jonson 1925–51, 7.205–41; Orgel and Strong 1973, 1.101–5; Hearn 1995, 190.

40. Belvoir Castle accounts, 4 March and 18 May 1606 (HMC Rutland 4.457–8). The other 'Powers of Juno' were the Countesses of Bedford and Montgomery, Ladies Berkeley and Knollys, and three Maids of Honour, Dorothy Hastings, Blanche Somerset and Cecily Sackville. The earlier *Masque of Blackness* (described in the Revels accounts as the Queen's 'Maske of Moures') had parts for eleven 'Ladies of Honour', who 'came in great shows of Devises wch they satt in, wth exzselent Musike' (PRO AO3/ 908/13, fol. 2v; Streitberger 1986, 9).

41. For Jonson's costume notes see Jonson 1925–51, 7.230–31; for a discussion of the paintings, see ibid., xv–xix. The third painting (Welbeck Abbey; Hearn 1995, no. 129) was first catalogued at Titchfield House in 1731 as 'A Turkish Lady'. One of Inigo Jones's earliest surviving costume designs (Chatsworth House; Hearn 1995, no. 106) has similarities to these costumes and may be for *Hymenaei*; the head-tire has been compared to Italian models in a Florentine *intermezzo* of 1589 and in Vercellio 1598.

42. Pory to Sir Robert Cotton, 7 January 1606 (BL Cotton MS Jul Caes 3, fols 301–2); Jonson 1925–51, 10.466.

16. In the workshop

43. See Mountjoy's 'Answer' (Appendix 1). On the movements of Stephen and Mary Belott in the years after their marriage see Chapter 21. There was a similar disagreement over an unpaid brewer's bill.

44. Whitebrook 1932, 93. A more precise explanation of Courtois's 'purled work' is found in the unlikely location of Henry Ainsworth's *Annotations on the Book of Psalms* (1622). Glossing Psalm 45.13–14, 'Her clothing is of wrought gold ... [a] raiment of needlework', Ainsworth suggests the garment is made of 'purled works or grounds, closures of gold such as precious stones are set in'. This would be apt for Mountjoy's requirements: a form of gilded embroidery to house the gems that featured in a tire.

45. Sleny Georghiou, quoted in *Sunday Times* ('Talking Heads', 2 July 2006). Cf. Victoria Beckham on 'bad extensions': 'You can see the glue holding the bonds in at the scalp, [and] the extensions themselves look all frizzy because they're made out of nylon instead of real hair' (*That Extra Half an Inch*, 2006, 290). Such or similar disasters were doubtless avoided by the expert stylists of Silver Street.

46. Glover 1979, 1–12.

47. Randle Holme, *The Academy of Armory* (1688), 3.21.

48. *OED*, s.v. sleave silk. *Webster's Dictionary* defines it as '(a) The knotted or entangled part of silk or thread. (b) Silk not yet twisted; floss'. 'Sleave' is cognate with Swedish *slejf* and German *Schleife*, a knot. Fishing flies were made out of it: 'Sleave-silk flies / Bewitch poor fishes' wand'ring eyes' (John Donne, 'The Bait', 23–4; Donne 1912, 1.47).

49. Chamber's *Cyclopaedia* 1727–41, s.v. See Gina M. Barrett, 'Metallic Threads: A Background to their Use in Textile Work' (http://www.et-tu.com/soper-lane).

50. See Epilogue and Appendix 4. The petition is mentioned (misdated and with no source) in Hotson 1949, 179; I am grateful to James Travers for his help in tracking it down.

51. This document, also mentioned without source in Hotson 1949, 179, and described only as 'a lawsuit', remains elusive.

52. Cunnington 1970, 224; Feuillerat 1908, 23, 82.

53. For 'ravelled' = frayed, see *OED*, s.v. ravel, citing Bishop Fuller, 'To hem the end of our history so it ravel not out . . .'.

17. The underpropper

54. In a commendatory poem opposite the engraving in F1 (below it in editions subsequent to F3, 1664), Ben Jonson writes: 'This figure that thou here seest put, / It was for gentle Shakespeare cut; / Wherein the Graver had a strife / With Nature, to out-doo the life.' That Jonson really thought the portrait accurate and expressive (or that he had even seen it when he wrote the poem) cannot be guaranteed. See Spielmann 1924, 27.

55. On the identity of the engraver see Edmond 1991, Schuckman 1991. Martin Droeshout senior, born in Brussels in the late 1560s, came to England in about 1584 (Kirk 1910, 3.179, 183; Edmond 1991, 341). He was created denizen in 1608, appearing on the same patent roll as Mountjoy (Shaw 1911, 11), and was a freeman of the Painter-Stainers' company. He is last heard of, living at St Olave's, Hart Street, in 1641. Martin Droeshout junior, son of Michael and nephew of Martin senior, was born in London in 1601. It has been thought that he was the engraver, primarily because Martin senior is described in contemporary documents as a 'painter' or 'limner' (miniature portraitist) but never as an engraver. This line of reasoning is challenged by Edmond: the word 'painter', she shows, was used loosely to convey a general idea of 'picture-maker'. The Dutch artist Remegius Hogenberg, who was certainly an engraver, appears eight times in the register of St Giles, Cripplegate: only once is he described as a 'graver'; on all the other occasions he is called a 'picture-maker' or 'painter'. The nomenclature, in short, does not preclude the painter Martin senior from also being the 'graver' of Shakespeare's portrait.

56. Strong 1969, 283; Cooper 2006, 48. Some thought the original was the 'Flower' portrait (Royal Shakespeare Company, Stratford; formerly owned by Edgar Flower), an atmospheric oil-portrait, demonstrably similar to the Droeshout, and inscribed with the date 1609. However, recent technical analysis (2005; Cooper 2006, 72–5) has shown that, as many suspected, it is a nineteenth-century fabrication.

57. Spielmann 1924, 34–5. The poor quality of this prestigious commission is mysterious: Richard Vaughan's portrait of Ben Jonson (c. 1622–7) shows how much more vivid and expressive an engraving could be (Riggs 1989, 281). One plausible conjecture is that the editors of F1 were obliged to commission Droeshout, because it was he who had painted the original portrait on which the engraving was based (Honigmann 1985, 146–8). Honigmann is one of the engraving's apologists: its 'withdrawn and fastidious features' convey 'the thoughtfulness of a reserved and private man, not the tavern-haunting, overflowing poet of popular mythology'.

58. On the Stratford monument see SRI 158–63. The Janssen family, Dutch immigrant sculptors and 'tomb-makers', have various connections with Shakespeare: their workshop was in Southwark, close to the Globe; their clientele included the Earls of Southampton and Rutland, both patrons of Shakespeare, and the Combe family of Stratford, his neighbours.

59. Cooper 2006, 48. The style of the doublet is after *c.* 1610, tending to confirm its absence from the original portrait.

60. Stubbes 1879, 1.52. 'The underpropper or supportasse was a wire frame ... spread out behind from the doublet collar, to which it was fixed, supporting the ruff, which was pinned to it' (Cunnington 1970, 113). *OED* notes that 'supportasse', found only in Stubbes, may derive from a printer's error. It was also known as a 'pickadil' (originally a cutwork border for a collar, and probably the origin of the London street name, Piccadilly). Some underproppers were made of stiffened card, pasteboard, etc; an example in the Victoria and Albert Museum (Accession no. 192–1900) is discussed by Susan North in Cooper 2006, 120.

61. Arnold 1988, 226.

62. The supporter is associated with wigs and tires by William Warner: 'Buskes, perriwigs, maskes, plumes of feathers fram'd, supporters' (*Albion's England*, 1592, 9.47).

PART FIVE: *AMONG STRANGERS*

18. Blackfriars and Navarre

1. Kirwood 1931; David Kathman, 'Richard Field', *ODNB* 2004. It has been suggested that Field was a source of books used by Shakespeare, such as Holinshed's *Chronicles* (1587), Ovid's *Metamorphoses* (1589) and North's translation of Plutarch's *Lives* (1595), in all of which he had a hand as printer or publisher.

2. In his will (8 June 1591, PRO Prob 11/77; PCC Sainberbe) Dutwite calls himself a merchant. He is not listed among the 'strangers' of St Martin le Grand in 1582 (see Part Three, note 15), unless he is James 'Detewe', taxed on £3 and described as a 'bugler' (probably a maker of bugles, 'tube-shaped glass beads' for decorating garments, rather than a musician). A James Detwitt, pursemaker, became a denizen in 1550 (Kirk 1910, 2.350): if he was Jacqueline's father it is likely she was born in England.

3. Greg and Boswell 1930, 11. See W. R. Lefanu, 'Thomas Vautrollier, Printer and Bookseller', *HSL Proceedings* 20 (1964), 12–25; Andrew Pettegree, 'Thomas Vautrollier', *ODNB* 2004. Two of their four sons

(Manassas and James) were alive in 1624, when they are mentioned in Field's will.

4. Another possible Frenchwoman known to Shakespeare was 'Dorothy Soer, wife of John Soer', named in a legal document of 1596 in which William Wayte swore out 'sureties of the peace' against her and three others, one of them Shakespeare (Hotson 1931). French families named Soeur, Soir, Soyer, Sohier, etc, are found in immigrant lists of the period (Honigmann 1985, 150–51) but Dorothy has not yet been identified.

5. Burghley was probably behind Field's first publication, *The Copie of a Letter Sent out of England to Don Bernardin Mendoza* (1588): this piece of anti-Spanish propaganda was ostensibly the work of a Catholic priest, Richard Leigh, but manuscripts survive in Burghley's hand (Pettegree, 'Thomas Vautrollier', *ODNB* 2004). The following year Field wrote a fulsome dedication to Burghley, calling himself 'a printer alwaies ready and desirous to be at your Honourable commaundement' (George Puttenham, *Arte of English Poesie*, 1589, sig. A3v).

6. *Love's Labour's Lost*, ed. R. David (Arden edn, 1956), xxix–xxx; A. Lefranc, *Sous le masque de William Shakespeare* (1918).

7. The Huguenot language-teacher G. de la Mothe, whose *French Alphabet* was published by Field in 1592, may have been a conduit of information. For what little is known of him see Lambley 1920, 161–2; Frances Yates, *A Study of Love's Labour's Lost* (1936), 61–4. He may possibly be the De la Mothe found by Lefranc in a contemporary list of Navarre court officials.

8. SDL 130. The printing of *Venus* probably began soon after Field's licensing of the copy (SR 18 April 1593).

9. The entry in Stonley's account book (Folger Shakespeare Library; SDL no. 93) is the first recorded purchase of a book by Shakespeare. On John Eliot (who is not included in *ODNB*) see John Lindsay, ed., *The Parlement of Prattlers* (1928); Lever 1953, 79–80; Nicholl 1984, 177–9. On Shakespeare's use of his language manual *Ortho-epia Gallica* (1593) see note 15 below.

10. On 'The Booke of Sir Thomas More' (BL Harley MS 7368) see W. W. Greg's introduction (1911) and Harold Jenkins's supplement (1961) to the Malone Society edn; T. H. Howard-Hill, *Shakespeare and 'Sir Thomas More'* (Cambridge, 1989); and SRI 109–16, with reproductions of the three pages attributed to Shakespeare (fols 8r–9r). Much of fol. 8 was damaged in a botched nineteenth-century restoration. The hands of Munday, Chettle and Dekker have also been identified in the MS. Various dates are proposed for the playscript, of which *c.* 1593 is the earliest. In the Shakespeare passage, 'spurn you like dogs' is close to *Merchant of Venice* (*c.* 1596), 1.3.113; and 'Friends, masters, countryman' to *Julius Caesar* (*c.* 1599), 3.2.78. But self-echoings are not necessarily close in time.

19. Shakespeare's aliens

11. Haughton 1598, A4v. A useful survey of Elizabethan and Jacobean theatrical representations of foreigners is in Hoenselaars 1992, 50–75, 108–43 (on Haughton's play: 54–8).

12. Nashe 1958, 1.365. Some forty foreign surgeons and physicians appear in Tudor denization lists, most of them French (Page 1893, l). Sisson relates Caius to Dr Peter Chamberlain, a French gynaecologist in London, but it is not certain he was in practice by 1597 (*Essays & Studies* 13 (1960), 10–11). French doctors were associated with the 'chymicall physick' of Paracelsus (Nashe's quack is a 'mettle-bruing Paracelsian'); there is no indication that Caius is a vehicle for satire on this, though I note elsewhere (Nicholl 1980, 76–80) that Falstaff's ordeal in the laundry basket (3.5.90–125) is comically expressed in terms of Paracelsian chemistry (he is 'stopt in like a strong distillation', etc).

13. Like Caius, Haughton's Delion is a 'clipper of the King's English, and . . . eternall enemie to all good language' (Haughton 1598, B2v). Dr Johnson comments, à propos Caius, on the limited comic appeal of 'language distorted and depraved by provincial or foreign pronunciations' (Johnson's *Shakespeare*, 1773 edn; Wimsatt 1969, 110–11). On broken English on the Elizabethan stage: Clough 1933.

14. *Henry V*, ed. J. Dover Wilson (1947), 152. The French in *Merry Wives* is also mangled in transmission, e.g. 'Il fait fort ehando' (1.4.46–7), where a compositor has mistranscribed *chaude*, 'hot'.

15. Shakespeare's use of *Ortho-epia* is elegantly demonstrated in Lever 1953. In *Henry V*, Pistol's French boy says: 'ce soldat icy est disposée tout asture de couppes vostre gorge' (4.4.35–6). The unusual contraction 'asture' (for *à cette heure*, 'immediately') is found in similar context in Eliot's dialogue, 'The Thief' (Eliot 1593, 104–7): 'Je vous couperay la gorge . . . Il est bien garrotté asteure.' Most interesting is the seepage of *Ortho-epia* into the Dauphin's praise of his horse (3.7.11–29). Perusing Eliot's dialogue, 'The Horseman' (pp. 87–9), Shakespeare's eye strayed to the top of page 87, which contains the last few lines of the previous dialogue, 'The Apothecary'. From this come the nutmeg, ginger, hares and flying horses which appear in the Dauphin's speech. See also Jean Fuzier, '"I quand sur le possession de Fraunce". A French Crux in *Henry V* Solved', *SQ* 32 (1981), 97–100; Timothy Billings, 'Two New Sources for Shakespeare's Bawdy French in *Henry V*', *NQ* 52 (2005), 202–4.

16. Shapiro 1995; Dominic Green, *The Double Life of Dr Lopez* (2003); Cecil Roth, *History of the Jews in England* (1941), 139–44.

17. William Rowley, *A Search for Money* (1609).

18. Shakespeare's more compassionate treatment of the outsider in the *Merchant* anticipates a comparable trend discerned by Hoenselaars in early Jacobean comedy, which moves away from hostile stereotyping of foreigners to a 'strategy of surprise' in which 'the foreigner who used to be the butt of comedy is converted into its agent to gull the English and expose their folly' (Hoenselaars 1992, 114; cf. Leinwand 1986, 46–8). Examples are in Dekker and Webster's *Westward Ho!* (1604), Edward Sharpham's *The Fleire* (1607) and Jonson's *Alchemist* (1610). But the (Jewish) playwright Arnold Wesker thinks the effect of the *Merchant* (whatever its intention) was 'irredeemably anti-Semitic'. The 'Hath not a Jew eyes' speech was 'so powerful a piece of special pleading that it dignified the anti-Semitism'; the audience came away with its prejudices 'confirmed but held with an easy conscience' (*The Birth of Shylock and the Death of Zero Mostel*, 1997, xv–xvi).

19. On racial issues in *Othello*, see Cowhig 1985, Bartels 1990, and (with reflection on the play's fortunes in Apartheid-era South Africa) Martin Orkin, 'Othello and the "Plain Face" of Racism', *SQ* 38 (1987), 166–88. For a panoramic background see Eldred Jones, *Othello's Countrymen: The African in English Renaissance Drama* (1965) and *The Elizabethan Image of Africa* (Charlottesville, 1971). 'Little black husband': Lytton Strachey, *Elizabeth and Essex* (1928), 279.

20. Forbes 1971, 3–4; Picard 2003, 123–4; Edward Scobie, *Black Britannia: A History of Blacks in Britain* (1972), 5–11.

21. Bartels 1990, 451: Iago attempts 'to demonize and disempower Othello' by luring him into a 'self-incriminating display of "alien" behaviour'.

20. Dark ladies

22. This cryptic lady has been variously identified. Mal Fitton was proposed by Frank Harris (*The Man Shakespeare*, 1909); Jacqueline Field by C. C. Stopes (*Shakespeare's Environment*, 1918); Jane Davenant by Arthur Acheson (*Shakespeare's Sonnet Story*, 1922); Lucy Morgan, a.k.a. 'Black Luce' or 'Lucy Negro' (G. B. Harrison, *Shakespeare under Elizabeth*, 1933; Leslie Hotson, *Mr W. H.*, 1964; Anthony Burgess, *Nothing like the Sun*, 1964); and Emilia Bassano by A. L. Rowse (Rowse 1973). I do not intend to add Marie Mountjoy to this list (the 'Dark Landlady'?), though her credentials are no worse than any of these.

23. *Astrophil and Stella* (1591), 8.9; *Lucrece* (1594), 420; *Venus and Adonis* (1593), 542. Other parallels are noted in Duncan-Jones 1997, 374. Eliot's *Ortho-epia* has a similar assemblage of sonneteering clichés: 'her eyes

twinkling stars . . . her mouth coral . . . her throat of snow' etc (Eliot 1593, 159).

24. *Love's Labour's Lost*, 4.3.56–69 (Jaggard no. 3) and 4.2.100–113 (Jaggard no. 5). The play was published in 1598 (according to the title-page not the first edition), but the Jaggard texts have variants that may come from an independent MS. There are also variants in his versions of Sonnets 138 and 144. According to F. T. Prince (*The Poems*, Arden edn, 1960, 153) they are 'of the kind that might be expected in an inaccurate report', but some critics argue that the 1609 texts represent Shakespeare's own revisions of the earlier versions. Jackson 1999, using statistical analysis of rhyme schemes, places the 'Dark Lady' sequence as 'mainly written in the 1590s'.

25. Another literary dark lady is Diamante, the Venetian courtesan in Nashe's novella *The Unfortunate Traveller* (1594): a 'pretty, round-faced wench . . . with black eye-brows' (Nashe 1958, 2.261). The book was dedicated to the Earl of Southampton, with whom both the Sonnets and *Love's Labours* are traditionally (though conjecturally) linked.

PART SIX: *SEX & THE CITY*

21. Enter George Wilkins

1. Wilkins was certainly in St Giles by late 1607, when his daughter was baptized there (parish register, GL MS 6419/2, 13 December 1607). He is first recorded as 'of Cow Cross' in a court case of April 1610 (Prior 1972, 144, 152). Fludd is described as of St Giles in his deposition of 1612, and in December 1616 'Humphrey son of Humphrey Flood, trumpeter' was baptized there. Thomas Floudd of St Giles, assessed at £20 in lands and fees in 1582 (PRO E179/251/16, fol. 286), may be a father or brother; the registers also have a Cadwallader Fludd, 'yeoman'.

2. See Part One, note 14.

3. There is no critical edition of Wilkins's works, but see Glenn Blayney's introduction to the Malone Society reprint of *The Miseries of Enforced Marriage* (1964) and other articles by Blayney listed in Sources/2. The nearest thing to a biography is Roger Prior's incisive sixteen-page 'Life' (Prior 1972), supplemented by Eccles 1975; Prior 1976; Anthony Parr, 'George Wilkins' (*ODNB* 2004).

4. The Wilkinses are sometimes claimed as the authors of two sonnets, signed 'G. W. Senior' and 'G. W. I[unior]', in Spenser's *Amoretti* (1595), but it is hard to imagine a teenaged Wilkins writing pastoral knick-knacks like this ('Ah! Colin, whether on the lowly plain / Piping to shepherds . . .',

etc). The sonneteers are more plausibly the emblem-writer Geoffrey Whitney and his father, also Geoffrey.

5. The Middlesex Sessions cases (first spotted by Mark Eccles) are described in Prior 1972, 144–9, and the Chancery suit of December 1614 in Prior 1976.

6. G. Warner, *Catalogue of the Manuscripts at Dulwich College* (1881), 134; Prior 1976, 33–4. She owed Henslowe £2.

7. Cf. John Day, *Law Tricks* (1608), to which Wilkins may have contributed: 'Ile ... give her a kicke a the lips, and a pipe of Tobacco be my witnesse, that's all the love I beare her' (431–6).

8. Cow Cross Street (still extant) ran west out of the top end of Smithfield market (Prockter and Taylor 1979, map 6). That Wilkins was of the parish of St Sepulchre's (as in the Belott–Mountjoy deposition) rather than St James, Clerkenwell, confirms that his tavern was at the western end of the street. Present-day Farringdon Station marks the approximate site of it. On Turnmill Street (named after a water-mill on the Fleet river), see also Ackroyd 2000, 463–4.

9. On the structure of the London sex-trade at this time see Griffiths 1993; Shugg 1977; Haynes 1997, 61–71 et passim. In cases studied by Griffiths, many brothel-owners took short-time 'rents' from independent prostitutes requiring a room. Anne Smith told the bench at Bridewell that she used 'Wattwood's, Marshall's, Jane Fuller's, Martyn's, Shaw's, and other naughty houses'; the last-mentioned, John Shaw, owned five houses and had recorded dealings with twenty-three prostitutes. A client might pay up to 10 shillings for a session in the relative comfort of a bawdy house; ambulant alley-girls charged as little as 6d.

10. Stephen Gosson, *Schoole of Abuse* (1579), ed. E. Arber (1869), 36.

11. Robert Greene, *Disputation*, in Salgãdo 1972, 274–5.

12. An anonymous 'biography', *The Life of Long Meg of Westminster*, was entered in SR in 1590, but the earliest known edn is 1620; it mainly concerns her alleged feats of strength. Her career as a prostitute or bawd is documented in Capp 1998. Marshall and Remnaunt: GL, Bridewell Hospital Court-books 1 (1559–62), fols 206–10; Capp 1998, 3.

22. The *Miseries*

13. J. Andreas Lowe, 'Walter Calverley' (*ODNB* 2004). Calverley refused to plead, and was pressed to death at York Castle on 5 August 1605.

14. The identities of Calverley's sweetheart ('Clare Hartop' in the play) and his guardian ('Lord Faulconbridge') remain uncertain (Blayney 1953;

Maxwell 1956, 157–69). His wife was daughter of Sir John Brooke and niece of Lord Cobham. For bibliographic evidence of revision see Blayney 1957. Among the remnants of an earlier version are two speech-prefixes, 'Hunsd' (324) and 'Huns' (453), which seem to suggest Wilkins first used the name of Shakespeare's former patron Lord Hunsdon for Calverley's guardian, before settling on the safely fictional 'Faulconbridge'. Such remnants strongly suggest *Miseries 1607* was printed from Wilkins's 'foul papers', though at least one garbling in the text seems the result of an aural misreporting (Matthew Steggle, '*Demoniceacleare* in *The Miseries of Inforst Mariage*', NQ 53 (2006), 514–15).

15. Chambers 1923, 4.339. The Act, issued 27 May 1606, threatened a fine of £10 for every offence. Its euphemizing effects are notoriously present in F1. The original text of *Othello* (as preserved in the 1622 Quarto) has over fifty oaths which are watered down in the Folio text (Wells 2006, 238).

16. On *The Yorkshire Tragedy*, see Malone Society reprint, ed. Sylvia Feldman (1973); Sturgess 1969, 30–38; Lisa Hopkins, '*A Yorkshire Tragedy* and Middleton's Tragic Aesthetic', *Early Modern Literary Studies* 8 (2003), 1–15. Wilkins's redrafting of the *Miseries* may be contiguous with Middleton's writing of *The Yorkshire Tragedy*.

17. In *1 Henry IV*, 2.4, a drawer who habitually calls 'Anon anon Sir' is baited by Hal and Poins; in *Merry Wives*, the Host often uses 'bully' as a form of address, as Ilford does earlier in this scene: 'A thousand good dayes, my noble bully' (1058).

23. Prostitutes and players

18. Rendle 1882, 70–77; Johnson 1969. Stow mentions various 'stewhouses' on the waterfront at Southwark, with signs painted 'on their frontes towardes the Thames' (Stow 1908, 2.55).

19. The pamphlet *Holland's Leaguer* by Nicholas Goodman, the play of the same name by Shakerley Marmion, and a ballad, 'Newes from Hollands Leaguer', all appeared in 1632, inspired by Bess Holland's defiance of official attempts to close her down; in December 1631 the house was briefly surrounded by armed officers. According to Goodman, the brothel had earlier been 'kept' by Margaret Barnes a.k.a. 'Long Meg' (see note 12 above). Other famous Southwark whorehouses were the Cardinal's Hat and the Castle: the latter was attached to the Hope Inn, on the site of the present-day Bankside pub, the Anchor (Ackroyd 2000, 689–91).

20. I follow the conventional emendation of F1's 'barne' to 'bars' (first proposed by Johnson) but 'barn' may be an authentic early plural, cf. 'eyne'

for 'eyes'. On Pickt-hatch see Sugden 1925, s.v. and commentators on *Merry Wives* 2.2.17 (Falstaff to Pistol: 'To your manor of Pickt-Hatch, go!').

21. Munday, *Retreat from Plays* (1580), ed. Hazlitt (1869), 139; Dekker and Wilkins 1607, 64; Prynne, *Histriomastix* (1633), 391. Reports (or polemical claims) of 'bawdy behaviour' in the playhouses are surveyed in Cook 1977.

22. Munday, *Retreat from Plays*, 126; John Lane, *Tom Tell-troths message* (1600), 133. For the pejorative use of 'housewife', see also 2 *Henry IV*, 3.2.311, 'over-scutched housewives'; and *Othello*, 4.1.94–5, where Bianca is described as 'a housewife that by selling her desires / Buys herself bread and clothes'.

23. Gosson, *Plays Confuted* (1583), sig. f1r. Cf. Dekker and Wilkins 1607, Jest 45: 'A wench having a good face, a good body, and good clothes on, but of bad conditions, sitting one day in the two-penny room of a playhouse, & a number of yong Gentlemen about her, against all whom she maintain'd talke'. The 'twopenny rooms' which feature often in these accounts of venery were partitioned sections of the upper galleries, the forerunner of the theatrical 'box'.

24. *Father Hubberds Tales* (1604); Middleton 1886, 8.79–80.

25. J. W. Lever, Arden edn (1965), xxxi–xxxv.

26. *The Blacke Booke* (1604); Middleton 1886, 8.16.

27. On prunes and brothels see Panek 2005.

28. According to John Jowett, *Measure* sometimes sounds like Middleton because it contains some later interpolations (*c.* 1621) by him (Jowett 2001).

29. Barbara Everett, 'A Dreame of Passion', *LRB* 25, 2 January 2003.

30. Jonson distinguishes different types of collaboration when he says he wrote *Volpone* 'without a co-adjutor, / Novice, journeyman or tutor' (Prologue, 17–8; cf. Wells 2006, 26–7). The play was performed by the King's Men in *c.* 1605–6, close in time to the Wilkins–Shakespeare collaboration. In terms of text contributed one could call Wilkins a full 'co-adjutor', though the skilled but subordinate 'journeyman' is perhaps a better summary of his role.

31. The perfunctory dialogue of 4.5, a very short scene where two unnamed 'gentlemen' quit the brothel unexpectedly converted ('I'll do anything now that is virtuous, but I am out of the road of rutting forever,' etc), sounds to me like Wilkins. The Arden edition's stage directions quibble unnecessarily in placing 4.2 'in front of' the brothel. Lines 50 ('Wife, take her in') and 122 ('Take her home') are cited to support this, but the first phrase would distinguish the reception area from the accommodation within; and the second is probably figurative for 'take proper control of her'. 4.6, where Marina is brought to a customer, is certainly set 'in' the brothel.

32. All information in this and the following paragraph is from St Giles parish register, GL MS 6419/2.

33. Wilkins 1953, 59; *Pericles*, 3.1.34. The phrase was first recognized as Shakespeare's by J. P. Collier. For other lights shed on *Pericles* 1609 by Wilkins's phrasing see Massai 1997.

34. The punchline of Jest 44 in the Wilkins–Dekker *Jests to Make you Merrie* (1607) sounds a note of bitter prophecy: 'Do but marry with a whore, or else have to do with players, and thou shalt quickly run mad.'

24. Customer satisfaction

35. *Father Hubberds Tales* (1604); Middleton 1886, 8.78-9.

36. Cf. Manningham's diary (October 1602, Sorlien 1976, 105): 'Mr Tanfeild, speaking of a knave and his queane, said he was a little to[o] inward with hir.'

37. Cf. *2 Henry IV*, 2.4.59, 'Can a weak empty vessel [Doll] bear such a huge full hogshead [Falstaff]?', and other examples in Partridge 1968, s.v. 'bear'.

38. Archer 2000, 186.

25. To Brainforde

39. On seventeenth-century Brentford see Turner 1922, 35-8, 128-35; Allison 1962; Edith Jackson, *Annals of Ealing* (1898). Within Ealing parish, Old Brentford was more populous than Ealing itself. In 1664 there were 116 households in Ealing and 259 in Old Brentford; in 1795 the figures were 200 and 500. A 'census' of Ealing village in 1599 lists 85 households, so we might guess (at the same sort of ratio) about 190 households in Old Brentford at the time of Mountjoy's leasehold there. I can find nothing to identify the particular house. A Southwark man, William Amery, inherited a house in Old Brentford on his father's death in 1597 (Allison 1962, 27, 32), and was taxed on it in 1598 (PRO E179/142/239); as he also inherited a house in Southwark, it is possible he let out the Brentford property. I also note that the wealthiest resident of Ealing parish, Edward Vaughan, assessed on £20 in lands in the 1598 subsidy (PRO E179/142/239), had his townhouse in St Giles, Cripplegate; in his will of 1612 he bequeathed money to the poor of St Giles, 'where I have long dwelt' (Allison 1962, 29). A servant listed at his Ealing household, Alice Eaton, was perhaps related to the Eatons of St Giles who include Stephen Belott's apprentice William Eaton

and Mary Byllett's husband Richard Eaton (see Chapter 23 above). But these are shots in the dark.

40. On the roads to Brentford see *MCR* 2.89–90. The summer fair was a particular magnet for urban revellers: it is described disapprovingly by Dr Dee, who lived across the river at Mortlake, as 'Bacchus feast at Brainford' (*Diaries*, ed. E. Fenton (1998), 248).

41. Martin Butler, 'John Lowin', *ODNB* 2004; John Downes, *Roscius Anglicanus* (1708), 21; Honan 1998, 300.

42. On the Three Pigeons, see Turner 1922, 129–31; anon, *Jests of George Peele* (1627 edn), 2. A visitor in 1847 (quoted but not identified by Turner) judged the interior not much changed from Jacobean days: 'twenty sitting or sleeping rooms; dark closets and passages and narrow staircases . . . The walls are in some places from seven to eight feet thick.' There was also an inn at New Brentford called the Three Doves, no doubt in emulation; its innkeeper was Roger Dove (*MCR* 1.146).

43. *MCR* 1.72 (Cornewall), 1.250 (Charche).

44. *MCR* 1.269 (Heyward), 2.4 (Anderton), 2.82 (Flood).

45. The Thomas Johnson who married at Ealing church on 16 February 1618 (Thomas Gurney, ed., *Middlesex Parish Registers: Marriages* (1910), 8.11) was possibly Joan's widower, but the name appears elsewhere in the marriage-registers. The church's baptism and burial records do not survive.

26. 'At his game'

46. Sorlien 1976, 208–9 (Diary, fol. 29v); cf. SDL doc. 115.

47. *Microcosmographie* (1628), no. 24.

48. Letter of Sir William Trumbull to Lord Hay, in R. F. Brinkley, *Nathan Field the Actor–Playwright* (1920), 42. Jonson and the Rutlands: Patterson 1923, 31. Jonson flattered the Countess that she 'was nothing inferior to her father, S[ir] P[hilip] Sidney, in poesie' (ibid., 20).

49. An anonymous 'Funeral Elegy' on Burbage (*c.* 1619) speaks of his 'stature small' (Sidney Lee, *DNB*, 1886). In Kyd's *Spanish Tragedy* Jeronimo is described as of 'short body', which is sometimes taken to refer to Burbage in the part; but there is no evidence he played it. Hamlet being 'fat and scant o' breath' is similarly interpreted, but Mary Edmond rejects this ('Richard Burbage', *ODNB* 2004). She notes Elizabethan use of 'fatty' to mean sweaty, dramatically appropriate during the duel with Laertes, and infinitely preferable to a 'portly prince lumbering about the small stage'.

50. Aubrey 1949, 85; Schoenbaum 1970, 101–2.

51. A detailed account of John and Jane Davenant is in Edmond 1987, 4–26. Her visit to Forman: Bod., Ashmole MS 226, fol. 287.

52. PRO SC6/JAS1/1646, fol. 28v. On Sheppard see Edmond 1987, 6–8, 16. His wife Ursula was another visitor to Forman in 1597–8 (Bod., Ashmole MS 226, fol. 153, etc).

53. A cynical coda to Emilia's speech is in *All's Well*, where Lavatch argues that an unfaithful wife suits the bored husband just fine: 'The knaves come to do that for me which I am aweary of. He that ears my land spares my team, and gives me leave to in the crop; if I be his cuckold, he's my drudge . . . Ergo he that kisses my wife is my friend' (1.3.40–48). All that Emilia says is ironically shadowed by the fact that her husband is Iago, whose secret life is so much darker and weirder than she imagines.

54. Cf. Samuel Rowlands, *Crew of Kind Gossips* (1609), where a housewife talks of certain 'kind gentlemen' that lodge with her: 'Two of them at my house in term-time lie, / And comfort me with jests and odd device / When as my husband's out a-nights at dice.' They 'will not see me want'. These 'odd devices' (the *s* is missing for the rhyme) sound flirtatious at the least. Real-life sexual encounters in a London lodging-house are examined in Capp 1995, from a case in the Bridewell court-books involving Shakespeare's friend Michael Drayton. In 1627 Elizabeth Hobcock, the maid-servant at a lodging-house in St Clement Dane's, deposed that she saw Mrs Mary Peters 'hold up her clothes unto her navel before Mr Michael Drayton, and that she clapt her hand on her privy part and said it was a sound and a good one, that the said Mr Drayton did then also lay his hand upon it and stroke it, and said that it was a good one'. The accusation turns out to be false; Capp uncovers a grubby saga of sexual intrigue and blackmail. Of course, the Mountjoy establishment was not a rooming-house of this kind.

55. Obviously this list is not exhaustive. Some, thinking of the 'Fair Youth' of the Sonnets and of the generally homoerotic overtone of the playhouse world, would add homosexual sex.

PART SEVEN: *MAKING SURE*

27. A handfasting

1. Heinrich Bullinger, *Hundred Sermons upon the Apocalypse*, trans. John Daus (1573), 23.

2. Frederick Pollock and F. W. Maitland, *History of English Law* (1923), 2.368.

3. *A Treatise of Spousals or Matrimonial Contracts* (1686), 13–15.

4. Giese 2006, 120.

5. On marriage contracts see also Cook 1977a and 1991, Hopkins 1998, and (on an earlier period) Ralph Houlbrooke, 'The Making of Marriage in Mid-Tudor England', *Journal of Family History* 10 (1985), 339–52.

6. Giese 2006, 117–19.

7. Ibid., 123, 129. The ceremony and its wordings were ancient: 'handfast' is found in a MS of *c.* 1200, 'troth-plight' in 1303, and a bridegroom at Ripon Cathedral in 1484 says, 'I take the Margaret to my handfest wif' (*OED*).

8. Museum of London, 62.121/10; Cooper 2006, no. 18. 'Gimmel' is from Latin *gemellus*, 'twin'. An attenuated version of the ring's motto is in Beaumont and Fletcher, *Wit at several Weapons* (*c.* 1616), 5.1: 'I knit this holy hand fast, and with this hand / The heart that owes this hand ever binding.' In Middleton's *Chaste Maid* (*c.* 1613) Moll's betrothal-ring from Touchwood reads, 'Love thats wise / Blinds parents eyes' (3.1). The other gifts listed are from Giese 2006, 133–44. Drinking, or pledging, to one another was also a common part of the troth-plight, as in the Honthorst betrothal scene (see Plate 32), and in Jonson's famous lyric, 'To Celia': 'Drink to me only with thine eyes / And I will pledge with mine' (*Complete Poems*, ed. G. Parfitt (1973), 106).

9. Cook 1991, 158; Bullinger, *The Christen State of Matrimonye*, trans. Miles Coverdale (1541), 49.

28. 'They have married me!'

10. 'Spousals *de praesenti* . . . [are] very matrimony, and therefore perpetually indissoluble except for adultery' (Swinburne, *Treatise of Spousals*, 15). Scarborrow's subsequent marriage would be technically adulterous, and the contract dissoluble.

11. Mendelson and Crawford 1998, 120. The Church's unease about the sexual implications of civil contracts was not unrealistic. In marital disputes before the Bishop's court in Chester, 'out of seventeen troth-plight cases, ten show us men trying to sneak out of their contracts when they have had their fill of pleasure with the woman' (F. J. Furnivall, *Child Marriages, Divorces and Ratifications in the Diocese of Chester* (1897), 43).

12. But note the opinion of Shakespeare's Princess Katherine (*Henry V*, 5.2.259–60): 'Les dames et les demoiselles pour être baissées devant leurs noces il n'est pas la coûtume de France' (For women and girls to be kissed before their wedding is not the custom in France). Henry dismisses this as a 'nice [fastidious] fashion', and kisses her anyway.

13. On marriage vows in *Measure* see Harding 1950, Schanzer 1960, Nagarajan 1963.

14. See Part 1, note 28.

15. The syntax of the subordinate clause (lines 180–81) is tightly knotted: the King apparently means that the wedding ('ceremony') will be best ('seem' = be seemly) performed swiftly ('expedient' = expeditious) on the authority which has just been given ('now-born brief') by the contract.

16. Shakespeare's references to troth-plights are not confined to the Silver Street plays. In *Henry V* (*c.* 1599), Nym is informed of Pistol's marriage: 'He is married to Nell Quickly, and certainly she did you wrong, for you were troth-plight to her' (2.1.21). As Quickly is a prostitute the term is used sardonically to mean he was a favoured customer. In *Twelfth Night* (1601), the offstage handfasting of Olivia and Cesare is described by the priest: 'A contract of eternal bond of love / Confirmed by mutual joinder of your hands, / Attested by the holy close of lips, / Strengthened by interchangement of your rings, / And all the ceremony of this compact / Sealed in my function, by my testimony' (5.1.154–9). One might call this a textbook troth-plight, except that both parties are female ('Cesare' is Viola in disguise). In *Troilus and Cressida* (*c.* 1602) Pandarus' efforts to get the eponymous couple in bed together include a kind of mock-handfasting: 'Go to, a bargain made. Seal it, seal it. I'll be the witness. Here I hold your hand, here my cousin's' (3.2.196–8). Pandarus is the prototypical 'pandar' or pimp ('Let all pitiful goers-between be called to the world's end after my name'), and what is 'sealed' by these actions is not a matrimonial contract but a sexual assignation involving his niece (here called 'cousin'). In *The Winter's Tale* (*c.* 1610) the shepherd attempts to handfast Perdita and Florizel, 'Take hands! A bargain! / And, friends unknown, you shall bear witness to't / ... Come your hand, / And daughter yours' (4.4.381–9), but the ceremony is halted by one of the witnesses, who is Florizel's father in disguise.

17. Johnson's 1765 edn of Shakespeare; Wimsatt 1969, 112.

18. Cf. John Earle's character-sketch of an actor: 'He is like our painting gentlewomen, seldom in his own face, seldomer in his clothes, and he pleases the better he counterfeits ... He does not only personate on the stage, but sometimes in the street, for he is masked still in the habit of a gentleman' (*Microcosmographie*, 1628, H3v).

29. Losing a daughter

19. The marriage of 'John Hall gentleman & Susanna Shaxspere' took place at Holy Trinity, Stratford, on 5 June 1607. Their only child, Elizabeth, was

born the following February. Susanna's dowry was 107 acres of Stratford land, purchased by Shakespeare in 1602 for £320 and doubtless rising in value (Honan 1998, 291–2; Maìri Macdonald, 'A New Discovery about Shakespeare's Estate', *SQ* 45 (1994), 87–9). This is somewhat bigger than Mary Mountjoy's alleged dowry of £260 (a 'marriage portion' of £60 and a legacy of £200), and considerably bigger than her actual dowry (£10 and some 'houshould stuffe').

20. Dr Hall himself seems to have been an 'honest fellow' tailor-made to Shakespeare's requirements. He was a gentleman from a well-off Bedford-shire family; a Cambridge graduate (Queens' College, MA 1597); and a respected physician (SDL 234–8; Harriet Joseph, *Shakespeare's Son-in-Law*, 1964). By tradition Susanna was spirited and intelligent ('witty above her sexe', as a contemporary epitaph complacently puts it). She signed her name in a clear, rounded hand (Honan 1998, plate 30). A year before her marriage she was fined for non-attendance at church, which may mean she had Catholic leanings; her husband, to judge from phrasings in his case-books, was staunchly Protestant.

Epilogue

1. Mary Edmond, 'Henry Condell' (*ODNB* 2004); cf. Hotson 1949, 184. Mountjoy's will (Appendix 4) has a further possible Shakespeare connec-tion. Another of its witnesses, Raphe or Ralph Merifield, may be a son-in-law of John Heminges, whose will includes a bequest to 'my daughter Merefeild' (PRO Prob 10/485, 9 October 1630; Honigmann and Brock 1993, 164–9). However Ralph Merifield was a professional scrivener, 'whose name appears frequently among the testamentary depositions of the Commissary Court'; the original will was probably in his hand (Whitebrook 1932, 94). This makes the connection with Heminges unnecessary but does not invalidate it. I have found nothing on the other two witnesses, 'Ed: Dendye' and Robert Walker.

2. The baptism dates are: Anne, 23 October 1608; Jane, 17 December 1609; Mary, 9 October 1614 (buried 1 May 1615); Hester, 30 November 1617 (died before 14 April 1620); Hester, 14 April 1620; Elizabeth, 21 September 1621. The date of Anne's marriage (apparently not at St Giles) is unknown. Jane married on 2 September 1633, aged twenty-three, and Hester on 29 June 1640, aged twenty. Jane's son, Francis Overing junior, baptized on 23 May 1636, is Stephen and Mary's first recorded grandchild, but he died at the age of fifteen months.

3. See Appendix 4; similar petitions can be found in *Journal of the House*

of Lords 3 (1620–28). On the gold-thread monopoly see W. R. Scott, *Joint Stock Companies* (1910–12), 1.174–7; Knights 1962, 77, 229; Sidney Lee and Sean Kelsey, 'Sir Giles Mompesson' (*ODNB* 2004). According to Thomas Wilson, the monopolists developed a 'new alchemistical way to make gold and silver lace with copper and other sophistical materials, to cozen and deceive the people; and so poisonous were the drugs that made up this deceitful composition that they rotted the hands and arms, and brought lameness upon those that wrought it' (*Life and Reign of James I*, c. 1625, 155).

4. Stow 1908, 2.28, 361; John Taylor, *Three Weeks from London to Hamburgh* (1617), 1.

5. Belott had probably died recently when his will (Appendix 4) was proved on 25 February 1647. The registers of St Sepulchre's parish, of which Long Lane was part, are not extant.

6. On the Blackfriars Gatehouse: see Part One, note 56. On Susanna and Ralph Smith (a Stratford hatter, and nephew of Shakespeare's friend Hamnet Sadler) see EKC 2.12–13; the consistory court found in favour of Susanna, 15 July 1613, and her slanderer, John Lane, was excommunicated. On the Welcombe enclosures: EKC 2.141–52, and cf. Part One, note 2.

7. On Thomas Quiney (son of Richard, with whom Shakespeare corresponded in 1598) see SDL 238–41. Judith died in 1662, and with the death eight years later of Shakespeare's childless granddaughter, Elizabeth Bernard *née* Hall, the direct line of descent from Shakespeare was extinguished.

8. Charles Severn, ed., *Diary of the Rev. John Ward, 1648–79* (1839), 183. The typhoid theory: Honan 1998, 406–7.

9. The speech is followed by an eighteen-line rhymed epilogue ('I would now ask ye how ye like the play', etc), but this is clearly by Fletcher.

Sources

1. COLLECTIONS

Acronyms in the Notes refer to the following sources:

Manuscripts

BL – British Library, London
Bod. – Bodleian Library, Oxford
GL – Guildhall Library, London
FPC – French Protestant Church, London
HLRO – House of Lords Record Office, Westminster
LMA – London Metropolitan Archives
PRO – Public Record Office, National Archives, Kew (citations given as
  PRO etc are an abbreviated form of the full citation, TNA PRO etc)

Shakespeare documents

EKC – E. K. Chambers, *William Shakespeare: Facts and Problems*, 2 vols
  (Oxford, 1930)
SDL – Samuel Schoenbaum, *William Shakespeare: A Documentary Life*
  (Oxford, 1975)
SRI – Samuel Schoenbaum, *William Shakespeare: Records and Images*
  (London, 1981)

Serials and other collections

CSP – Calendar of State Papers (printed abstracts)

DNB – *Dictionary of National Biography* (superseded by *ODNB* but still of use)

HMC – Historical Manuscripts Commission (printed abstracts)

HSL – Huguenot Society of London (Publications and Proceedings)

IGI – International Genealogical Index (http://www.familysearch.org)

LRB – *London Review of Books*

MCR – *Middlesex County Records*, ed. John C. Jeaffreson, 4 vols (1886–92)

MLR – *Modern Language Review*

NPG – National Portrait Gallery, London

NQ – *Notes & Queries*

ODNB – *Oxford Dictionary of National Biography*, 60 vols (Oxford, 2004)

OED – *Oxford English Dictionary*

RES – *Review of English Studies*

SQ – *Shakespeare Quarterly*

SR – Stationers' Register (SR plus a date refers to the licensing of a book, usually but not always prior to publication. SR entries can be consulted in the printed transcript: see Arber 1875–94 in Sources /2)

TLS – *Times Literary Supplement*

2. BOOKS AND ARTICLES

Unless otherwise stated, place of publication is London.

Ackroyd 2000. Peter Ackroyd, *London: The Biography*.

Allison 1962. K. J. Allison, 'An Elizabethan Census of Ealing'. *Ealing Local History Society Papers* 2.

Arber 1875–94. Edward Arber, *A Transcript of the Registers of the Company of Stationers of London*. 5 vols.

Archer 1991. Ian Archer, *The Pursuit of Stability: Social Relations in Elizabethan London*. Cambridge.

Archer 2000. Ian Archer, 'Material Londoners?' In Orlin 2000a, 174–92.

Arnold 1988. Janet Arnold, *Queen Elizabeth's Wardrobe Unlock'd*. Leeds.

Aubrey 1949. John Aubrey, *Brief Lives*. Ed. Oliver Lawson Dick.

Baddeley 1888. Sir John James Baddeley, *An Account of the Church and Parish of St Giles Without Cripplegate*.

Baddeley 1900. Sir John James Baddeley, *The Aldermen of Cripplegate Ward, 1276–1900*.

Baddeley 1921. Sir John James Baddeley, *Cripplegate*.

Baldwin 1944. T. W. Baldwin, *William Shakespere's Small Latine & Lesse Greeke*. 2 vols.

Bartels 1990. Emily Bartels, 'Making More of the Moor: Aaron, Othello and Renaissance Refashionings of Race'. *Shakespeare Quarterly* 41, 433–54.

Bate 1998. Jonathan Bate, *The Genius of Shakespeare*.

Beeman 1905. G. Beaumont Beeman, 'Notes on the Site and History of the French Churches in London'. *Proceedings of the Huguenot Society of London* 8.

Bentley 1971. G. E. Bentley, *The Profession of Dramatist in Shakespeare's Time*. Princeton, NJ.

Bentley 1984. G. E. Bentley, *The Profession of Player in Shakespeare's Time*. Princeton, NJ.

Blayney 1953. Glenn H. Blayney, 'George Wilkins and the Identity of Walter Calverley's Guardian'. *Notes & Queries* 198, 329–30.

Blayney 1957. Glenn H. Blayney, 'Wilkins's Revisions in *The Miseries of Inforst Marriage*'. *Journal of English and Germanic Philology* 56, 23–41.

Byrne 1925. Muriel St Clare Byrne, *Elizabethan Life in Town and Country*.

Byrne 1930. Muriel St Clare Byrne, *The Elizabethan Home*. Revised edn (1st edn 1925).

Capp 1995. Bernard Capp, 'The Poet and the Bawdy Court: Michael Drayton and the Lodging House World of Early Stuart London'. *Seventeenth Century* 10, 27–37.

Capp 1998. Bernard Capp, 'Long Meg of Westminster: A Mystery Solved'. *Notes & Queries* 45, 302–4.

Carson 1988. Neil Carson, *A Companion to Henslowe's Diary*. Cambridge.

Cerasano 1993. S. P. Cerasano, 'Henslowe, Forman and the Theatrical Community of the 1590s'. *Shakespeare Quarterly* 44, 145–58.

Cerasano 1994. S. P. Cerasano, '"Borrowed Robes", Costume Prices, and the Drawing of *Titus Andronicus*'. *Shakespeare Studies* 22, 45–57.

Chambers 1923. E. K. Chambers, *The Elizabethan Stage*. 4 vols. Oxford.

Chambers – see Sources/1.

Clough 1933. Wilson O. Clough, 'The Broken English of Foreign Characters on the Elizabethan Stage'. *Philological Quarterly* 12, 255–68.

Cook 1977a. Ann Jennalie Cook, 'The Mode of Marriage in Shakespeare's England'. *Southern Humanities Review* 11, 126–32.

Cook 1977b. Ann Jennalie Cook, '"Bargains of Incontinencie": Bawdy Behaviour in the Playhouses'. *Shakespeare Studies* 10, 271–90.

Cook 1991. Ann Jennalie Cook, *Making a Match: Courtship in Shakespeare and his Society*. Princeton, NJ.

Cooper 2006. Tarnya Cooper, *Searching for Shakespeare*. National Portrait Gallery.

Cotgrave 1611. Randle Cotgrave, *A Dictionarie of the French and English Tongues*.

Cottret 1985. Bernard Cottret, *Terre d'exil: l'Angleterre et les refugiés français et wallons, 1550–1700*. Paris.

Cowhig 1985. Ruth Cowhig, 'Blacks in English Renaissance Drama and the Role of Shakespeare's Othello'. In Dabydeen 1985, 1–25.

Cunnington 1955. C. Willett Cunnington and Phillis Cunnington, *Handbook of English Costume in the Seventeenth Century*.

Cunnington 1970. C. Willett Cunnington and Phillis Cunnington, *Handbook of English Costume in the Sixteenth Century*. (1st edn 1954.)

Dabydeen 1985. David Dabydeen, ed., *The Black Presence in English Literature*. Manchester.

Dasent 1890–97. J. R. Dasent, ed., *Acts of the Privy Council, 1542–1604*. 32 vols.

De Grazia et al. 1996. Margreta De Grazia, Maureen Quilligan and Peter Stallybrass, eds, *Subject and Object in Renaissance Culture*. Cambridge.

Dekker and Wilkins 1607. Thomas Dekker and George Wilkins, *Iests to Make You Merie*.

Donne 1912. John Donne, *Poems*. Ed. H. J. C. Grierson. 2 vols. Oxford.

Duncan-Jones 1997. Katherine Duncan-Jones, ed., *Shakspeare's Sonnets*. Arden Shakespeare.

Duncan-Jones 2001. Katherine Duncan-Jones, *Ungentle Shakespeare: Scenes from his Life*.

Eccles 1975. Mark Eccles, 'George Willkins'. *Notes and Queries* 220, 250–52.

Eccles 1982. Mark Eccles, 'Brief Lives: Tudor and Stuart Authors'. *Studies in Philology* 79, 1–135.

Eccles 1991–3. Mark Eccles, 'Elizabethan Actors'. *Notes & Queries* 236 (1991), 38–49 (Part 1, A–D), 454–61 (Part 2, E–K); *Notes & Queries* 237 (1992), 293–303 (Part 3, K–R); *Notes & Queries* 238 (1993), 165–76 (Part 4, S to end).

Edmond 1982. Mary Edmond, 'The Chandos Portrait: A Suggested Painter'. *Burlington Magazine* 124, 146–9.

Edmond 1987. Mary Edmond, *Rare Sir William Davenant*. Manchester.

Edmond 1991. Mary Edmond, 'It Was for Gentle Shakespeare Cut'. *Shakespeare Quarterly* 43, 339–44.

Eliot 1593. John Eliot, *Ortho-epia Gallica, or Eliot's Fruits for the French*. [Facsimile reprint, Scolar Press, Menston, Yorks, 1968].

Erondell 1605. Peter Erondell, *The French Garden for English Ladyes and Gentlewomen to Walke in.*

Feuillerat 1908. Albert Feuillerat, ed., *Documents relating to the Office of the Revels in the Time of Queen Elizabeth.*

Foakes 1977. R. A. Foakes, ed., *The Henslowe Papers.* 2 vols.

Foakes 2002. R. A. Foakes, ed., *Henslowe's Diary.* 2nd edn (1st edn, with R. T. Rickert, 1961). Cambridge.

Forbes 1971. Thomas Rogers Forbes, *Chronicle from Aldgate: Life and Death in Shakespeare's London.* London and Newhaven, Conn.

Foster 1887. Joseph Foster, *London Marriage Licenses 1521–1869.*

Foster 1891. Joseph Foster, *Alumni Oxonienses 1500–1714.* 4 vols. Oxford.

Giese 2006. Loreen L. Giese, *Courtships, Marriage Customs and Shakespeare's Comedies.* Athens, Ohio.

Giuseppi 1929. M. S. Giuseppi, 'The Exchequer Documents relative to Shakespeare's Residence in Southwark'. *Transactions of the London and Middlesex Archaeological Society* 5, 281–8.

Glover 1979. Elizabeth Glover, *The Gold and Silver Wyre-drawers.* Chichester.

Gollancz 1924. Sir Israel Gollancz, ed., *Studies in the First Folio.* Oxford.

Goodman 1970. Nicholas Goodman, *Hollands Leaguer* [1632]. Ed. Dean Stanton Barnard. The Hague.

Goose and Luu 2005. Nigel Goose and Lien Luu, eds, *Immigrants in Tudor and Early Stuart England.* Brighton.

Greenblatt 2004. Stephen Greenblatt, *Will in the World: How Shakespeare Became Shakespeare.*

Greg and Boswell 1930. W. W. Greg and E. Boswell, eds, *Records of the Court of the Stationers' Company, 1576–1602.*

Griffiths 1993. Paul Griffiths, 'The Structure of Prostitution in Elizabethan London'. *Continuity and Change* 8, 39–63.

Gurr 1987. Andrew Gurr, *Playgoing in Shakespeare's London.* Cambridge.

Haffenden 2001. John Haffenden, ed., *Berryman's Shakespeare.* 2nd edn (1st edn 1999).

Harding 1950. Davis P. Harding, 'Elizabethan Betrothals and *Measure for Measure*'. *Journal of English and German Philology* 49, 139–58.

Harington 1927. Sir John Harington, *The Metamorphosis of Ajax: A New Discourse of a Stale Subject* [1596]. Ed. Peter Warlock and Jack Lindsay.

Harris and Korda 2002. Jonathan Gil Harris and Natasha Korda, eds, *Staged Properties in Early Modern Drama.* Cambridge.

Haughton 1598. William Haughton, *Englishmen for my Money, or a Woman will have her Will.*

Haynes 1997. Alan Haynes, *Sex in Elizabethan England*.

Hazlitt 1864. William Carew Hazlitt, ed., *Shakespeare Jest Books: Reprints of Early and Rare Jest Books supposed to have been used by Shakespeare*. 3 vols.

Hearn 1995. Karen Hearn, *Dynasties: Painting in Tudor and Jacobean England, 1530–1630*. Tate Gallery.

Hoenselaars 1992. A. Hoenselaars, *Images of Englishmen and Foreigners in the Drama of Shakespeare and his Contemporaries*. Toronto and London.

Honan 1998. Park Honan, *Shakespeare: A Life*. Oxford.

Honigmann 1985. E. A. J. Honigmann, 'Shakespeare and London's Immigrant Community'. In Van der Motten 1985, 143–53.

Honigmann 1987. E. A. J. Honigmann, *John Weever: A Biography of a Literary Associate of Shakespeare and Jonson*. Manchester.

Honigmann and Brock 1993. E. A. J. Honigmann and Susan Brock, eds, *Playhouse Wills, 1558–1642: An Edition of Wills by Shakespeare and his Contemporaries in the London Theatre*. Manchester.

Hopkins 1998. Lisa Hopkins, *The Shakespearean Marriage: Merry Wives and Heavy Husbands*.

Hotson 1931. Leslie Hotson, *Shakespeare* versus *Shallow*.

Hotson 1937. Leslie Hotson, *I, William Shakespeare do Appoint Thomas Russell, Esquire . . .*

Hotson 1949. Leslie Hotson, *Shakespeare's Sonnets Dated and Other Essays*.

Howe and Lakin 2004. Elizabeth Howe and David Lakin, *Roman and Medieval Cripplegate: Archaeological Excavations 1992–8*. Museum of London Archaeology Service Monographs 21.

Jackson 1999. MacDonald P. Jackson, 'Rhymes in Shakespeare's Sonnets: Evidence of Date of Composition'. *Notes & Queries* 46, 213–19.

Jackson 2001. MacDonald P. Jackson, *Defining Shakespeare: Pericles as Test-case*. Oxford.

Jardine 1983. Lisa Jardine, *Still Harping on Daughters: Women and Drama in the Age of Shakespeare*. Brighton.

Jeayes 1906. Isaac Jeayes, ed., *The Letters of Philip Gawdy, 1576–1616*. Roxburghe Club.

Johnson 1969. David Johnson, *Southwark and the City*. Oxford.

Jonson 1925–51. *Ben Jonson*, ed. C. H. Herford and Percy and Evelyn Simpson. 11 vols. Oxford.

Jowett 2001. John Jowett, 'The Audacity of *Measure for Measure* in 1621'. *Ben Jonson Journal* 8, 229–48.

Judges 1930. A. V. Judges, ed., *The Elizabethan Underworld*.

Kassell 2005. Lauren Kassell, *Medicine and Magic in Elizabethan London: Simon Forman, Astrologer, Alchemist and Physician*. Oxford.

Kermode 2000. Frant Kermode, *Shakespeare's Language*.

Kirk 1910. R. E. G. and E. F. Kirk, *Lists of Aliens Dwelling in the City and Suburbs of London, Henry VIII to James I*. 4 vols. Publications of the Huguenot Society of London 10/1–4.

Kirwood 1931. A. E. M. Kirwood, 'Richard Field, Printer'. *The Library* (4th series) 12, 1–39.

Klarwill 1928. Victor von Klarwill, *Queen Elizabeth and Some Foreigners*. Trans. T. H. Nash.

Knights 1962. L. C. Knights, *Drama and Society in the Age of Jonson*. Revised edn (1st edn 1937).

Korda 2002. Natasha Korda, 'Women's Theatrical Properties', in Harris and Korda 2002.

Kozuka and Mulryne 2006. Takashi Kozuka and J. R. Mulryne, *Shakespeare, Marlowe, Jonson: New Directions in Biography*. Aldershot.

Lambley 1920. Kathleen Lambley, *The Teaching and Cultivation of the French Language in England during Tudor and Stuart Times*.

Lang 1993. R. G. Lang, ed., *Two Tudor Subsidy Rolls for the City of London, 1541 and 1582*. London Record Society.

Leinwand 1986. Theodore Leinwand, *The City Staged: Jacobean Comedy 1603–13*. Madison, Wisc.

Leishman 1949. J. B. Leishman, ed., *The Three Parnassus Plays*.

Lever 1953. John Lever, 'Shakespeare's French Fruits'. *Shakespeare Survey* 6, 79–89.

Lindeboom 1950. J. Linbloom, *Austin Friars: History of the Dutch Reformed Church in London*.

Lindley 1984. D. Lindley, ed., *The Court Masque*.

Linthicum 1936. M. Channing Linthicum, *Costume in the Drama of Shakespeare and his Contemporaries*. Oxford.

Luu 2005. Lien Bich Luu, *Immigrants and the Industries of London, 1500–1700*. Aldershot.

McManaway 1958. Mary R. McManaway, 'Poets in the Parish of St Giles, Cripplegate'. *Shakespeare Quarterly* 9, 561–2.

Maes-Jelinek 1988. H. Maes-Jelinek, Pierre Michel and Paulette Michel-Michot, eds, *Multiple Worlds. Multiple Words. Essays in Honour of Irène Simon*. Liège.

Massai 1997. Sonia Massai, 'On Behalf of a Bad Quarto: An "Unstrung Jewel" in 1609 *Pericles*'. *Notes & Queries* 44, 512–14.

Maxwell 1956. Baldwin Maxwell, *Studies in the Shakespeare Apocrypha*.

Melton 1620. John Melton, *Astrologaster, or the Figure-caster*.

Mendelson and Crawford 1998. Sara Mendelson and Patricia Crawford, *Women in Early Modern England, 1550–1720*. Oxford.

Middleton 1886. Thomas Middleton, *Works*. Ed. A. H. Bullen. 8 vols.

Milne and Cohen 2001. Gustav Milne and Nathalie Cohen, *Excavations at Medieval Cripplegate, London*. English Heritage Archaeological Reports.

Moens 1896. William Moens, ed., *Registers of the French Church, London, 1600–36*. Publications of the Huguenot Society of London 9.

Montaigne 1603. Michel de Montaigne, *The Essayes*. Trans. John Florio.

Murphy 1984. John Murphy, *Darkness and Devils: Exorcism and* King Lear. Athens, Ohio.

Nagarajan 1963. S. Nagarajan, '*Measure for Measure* and Elizabethan Betrothals'. *Shakespeare Quarterly* 14, 115–19.

Nashe 1958. Thomas Nashe, *Works*. Ed. R. B. McKerrow. Revised edn, with supplementary notes by F. P. Wilson. 5 vols. Oxford.

Nelson 2006. Alan Nelson, 'Calling All (Shakespeare) Biographers!' In Kozuka and Mulryne 2006, 55–68.

Newton 1975. Stella Mary Newton, *Renaissance Theatre Costume*.

Nicholl 1980. Charles Nicholl, *The Chemical Theatre*.

Nicholl 1984. Charles Nicholl, *A Cup of News: The Life of Thomas Nashe*.

Nicholl 2002. Charles Nicholl, *The Reckoning: The Murder of Christopher Marlowe*. Revised edn (1st edn 1992).

Nichols 1823. John Nichols, *The Progresses and Public Processions of Queen Elizabeth*. 3 vols.

Norris 1938. Herbert Norris, *Costume and Fashion: The Tudors*. 2 vols.

Orgel and Strong 1973. Stephen Orgel and Roy Strong, *Inigo Jones*. 2 vols.

Orlin 2000a. Lena Cowen Orlin, ed., *Material London, ca. 1600*. Philadelphia.

Orlin 2000b. Lena Cowen Orlin, 'Boundary Disputes in Early Modern London'. In Orlin 2000a, 345–76.

Page 1893. William Page, ed., *Letters of Denization and Acts of Naturalization for Aliens in England, 1509–1603*. Publications of the Huguenot Society of London 8.

Panek 2005. Jennifer Panek, 'Why were There Stewed Prunes in Shakespearean Brothels?' *English Language Notes* 42, 18–20.

Partridge 1968. Eric Partridge, *Shakespeare's Bawdy*. Revised edn (1st edn 1947).

Patterson 1923. R. F. Patterson, ed., *Ben Jonson's Conversations with Drummond of Hawthornden*. Glasgow.

Peacock 1984. J. Peacock, 'The French Element in Inigo Jones's Masque Designs'. In Lindley 1984.

Petti 1959. Anthony Petti, ed., *The Letters and Dispatches of Richard Verstegan*. Catholic Record Society 52.

Picard 2003. Liza Picard, *Elizabethan London*.

Piper 1964. David Piper, '*O Sweet Mr Shakespeare I'll have his Picture*'. National Portrait Gallery.

Platter 1937. Thomas Platter, *Travels in England*. Ed. and trans. Clare Williams.

Prior 1972. Roger Prior, 'The Life of George Wilkins'. *Shakespeare Survey* 25, 137–52.

Prior 1976. Roger Prior, 'George Wilkins and the Young Heir'. *Shakespeare Survey* 29, 33–9.

Prockter and Taylor 1979. Adrian Prockter and Robert Taylor, *The A–Z of Elizabethan London*. London Topographical Society 122.

Rendle 1882. William Rendle, 'The Stews on Bankside'. *Antiquarian Magazine*, August 1882, 70–77.

Richardson 2006. Catherine Richardson, 'The Material Culture of Stranger Life'. *Proceedings of the Huguenot Society of London* 28, 495–508.

Riggs 1989. David Riggs, *Ben Jonson: A Life*. Cambridge, Mass.

Rossiter 1961. A. P. Rossiter, *Angel with Horns: Fifteen Lectures on Shakespeare*. Ed. Graham Storey.

Rowse 1973. A. L. Rowse, *Shakespeare the Man*.

Rowse 1976. A. L. Rowse, *The Case Books of Simon Forman*. Revised edn (1st edn 1974).

Salgādo 1972. Gāmini Salgādo, ed., *Coney Catchers and Bawdy Baskets*. Harmondsworth.

Salgādo 1977. Gāmini Salgādo, *The Elizabethan Underworld*.

Sams 1995. Eric Sams, *The Real Shakespeare: Retrieving the Early Years, 1564–94*.

Scarisbrick 1995. Diana Scarisbrick, *Tudor and Jacobean Jewellery*. Tate Gallery.

Schanzer 1960. Ernest Schanzer, 'The Marriage Contracts in *Measure for Measure*'. *Shakespeare Survey* 13, 81–9.

Schoenbaum 1970. Samuel Schoenbaum, *Shakespeare's Lives*.

Schoenbaum – see Sources/1

Schofield 1987. John Schofield, ed., *The London Surveys of Ralph Treswell*. London Topographical Society 135.

Schofield 2000. John Schofield, 'The Topography and Buildings of London, ca 1600'. In Orlin 2000a.

Schrickx 1988. Willem Schrickx, '*All's Well that Ends Well* and its Historical Relevance'. In Maes-Jelinek 1988, 257–74.

Schuckman 1991. Christian Schuckman, 'The Engraver of the First Folio Portrait of Shakespeare'. *Print Quarterly* 8, 40–43.

Scoloker 1604. An[thony?] Sc[oloker?], *Diaphantus, or The Passions of Love.*

Scouloudi 1985. Irene Scouloudi, *Returns of Strangers in the Metropolis 1593, 1627, 1635, 1639.* Publications of the Huguenot Society of London 57.

Scouloudi 1987. Irene Scouloudi, 'The Stranger Community in London, 1558–1640'. *Proceedings of the Huguenot Society of London* 24, 434–41.

Shapiro 1995. James Shapiro, *Shakespeare and the Jews.*

Shapiro 2005. James Shapiro, *1599: A Year in the Life of William Shakespeare.*

Shaw 1911. W. Shaw, ed., *Letters of Denization and Acts of Naturalization for Aliens in England and Ireland.* Publications of the Huguenot Society of London 18.

Sheavyn 1969. Phoebe Sheavyn, *The Literary Profession in the Elizabethan Age.* Revised edn, ed. J. W. Saunders (1st edn 1909).

Shugg 1977. Wallace Shugg, 'Prostitution in Shakespeare's London'. *Shakespeare Studies* 10, 291–313.

Sisson 1935. C. J. Sisson, 'The Mythical Sorrows of Shakespeare' (British Academy Shakespeare Lecture, 1934). *Proceedings of the British Academy* 20.

Smith 1972. Raymond Smith, *The Archives of the French Protestant Church of London: A Handlist.* Publications of the Huguenot Society of London 50.

Sorlien 1976. Robert Parker Sorlien, ed., *The Diary of John Manningham of the Middle Temple.* Hanover, NH.

Spielmann 1907. 'The Portraits of Shakespeare'. In A. H. Bullen (ed.), *Works of Shakespeare*, vol. 10. Stratford-upon-Avon.

Spielmann 1924. M. H. Spielmann, *The Title Page of the First Folio of Shakespeare's Plays: A Comparative Study of the Stratford Monument.* Oxford.

Stallybrass 1996. Peter Stallybrass, 'Worn Worlds: Clothes and Identity on the Renaissance Stage'. In De Grazia et al. 1996, 289–320.

Steggle 1998. Matthew Steggle, *Wars of the Theatres: The Poetics of Personation in the Age of Jonson.* Victoria, BC.

Stow 1908. John Stow, *The Survay of London* [1598]. Ed. C. L. Kingsford. Oxford.

Streitberger 1986. W. R. Streitberger, ed., *Jacobean and Caroline Revels Accounts, 1603–42.* Malone Society Collections 13.

Strong 1969. Roy Strong, *Tudor and Jacobean Portraits.* National Portrait Gallery.

Strong 1983. Roy Strong, *The English Renaissance Miniature*.

Strype 1824. John Strype, *Annals of the Reformation*. 4 vols. Oxford.

Stubbes 1879. Phillip Stubbes, *The Anatomie of Abuses* (1583). Ed. F. J. Furnivall.

Sturgess 1969. Keith Sturgess, ed., *Three Elizabethan Domestic Tragedies*. Harmondsworth.

Sugden 1925. Edward H. Sugden, *A Topographical Dictionary to the Works of Shakespeare*.

Symonds 1952. R. W. Symonds, 'Of Jakes and Close Stools: Their Place in English Social History'. *Connoisseur* 129, 86–91.

Sypher 1955. Wylie Sypher, *Four Stages of Renaissance Style: Transformations in Art and Literature, 1400–1700*. New York.

Tawney and Power 1924. R. H. Tawney and Eileen Power, eds., *Tudor Economic Documents*. 3 vols.

Taylor 1925. George Coffin Taylor, *Shakespeare's Debt to Montaigne*. Cambridge, Mass.

Thomas 1985. David Thomas, *Shakespeare in the Public Records*. HMSO.

Thompson 1916. Edward Maunde Thompson, *Shakespeare's Handwriting*. Oxford.

Tillyard 1965. E. M. W. Tillyard, *Shakespeare's Problem Plays*. Revised edn (1st edn 1950).

Tiramani 2005. Jenny Tiramani, 'The Sanders Portrait'. *Costume* 39, 43–52.

Traister 2000. Barbara Traister, *The Notorious Astrological Physician of London: Works and Days of Simon Forman*. Oxford.

Turner 1922. Fred Turner, *The History and Antiquities of Brentford*. Brentford.

Van der Motten 1985. J. P. Van der Motten, ed., *Elizabethan and Modern Studies Presented to Professor Willem Schrickx*. Ghent.

Vecellio 1598. Cesare Vecellio, *Habiti antichi et moderni di tutto il mondo*. Venice.

Venn 1922–7. John and J. A. Venn, *Alumni Cantabrigienses*. 4 vols. Cambridge.

Vickers 2002. Brian Vickers, *Shakespeare Co-author: A Historical Study of Five Collaborative Plays*.

Wallace 1910a. Charles William Wallace, 'New Shakespeare Discoveries'. *Harper's Monthly Magazine* 22, no. 718, 489–510.

Wallace 1910b. Charles William Wallace, 'Shakespeare and his London Associates as Revealed in Recently Discovered Documents'. *University of Nebraska Studies* 10, no. 4.

Webb 1995. Clifford Webb, ed., *St Alban Wood Street and United Benefices, Transcribed and Indexed*. 6 vols.

Webster 1979. C. Webster, ed., *Health, Medicine and Mortality in the Sixteenth Century.*

Wells 2006. Stanley Wells, *Shakespeare & Co.*

Wells and Taylor 1987. Stanley Wells and Gary Taylor, *A Textual Companion to Shakespeare.* Oxford.

Whitebrook 1932. J. C. Whitebrook, 'Some Fresh Shakespearean Facts'. *Notes & Queries* 162, 93–5.

Wilkins 1607. George Wilkins, *The Miseries of Inforst Mariage.*

Wilkins 1953. George Wilkins, *The Painfull Adventures of Pericles Prince of Tyre* [1608]. Ed. Kenneth Muir.

Wilkins – see also Dekker and Wilkins 1607.

Williams 1937. Franklin B. Williams, 'Robert Tofte'. *Review of English Studies* 13, 282–96, 405–24.

Wilson 1932. J. Dover Wilson, *The Essential Shakespeare.*

Wimsatt 1969. W. K. Wimsatt, ed., *Dr Johnson on Shakespeare.* Harmondsworth.

Wood 2003. Michael Wood, *In Search of Shakespeare.*

Young 1890. Sidney Young, *Annals of the Barber-Surgeons of London.*

Yungblut 1996. Laura Hunt Yungblut, *Strangers Settled Here Amongst Us: Policies, Perceptions and the Presence of Aliens in Elizabethan England.*

Index